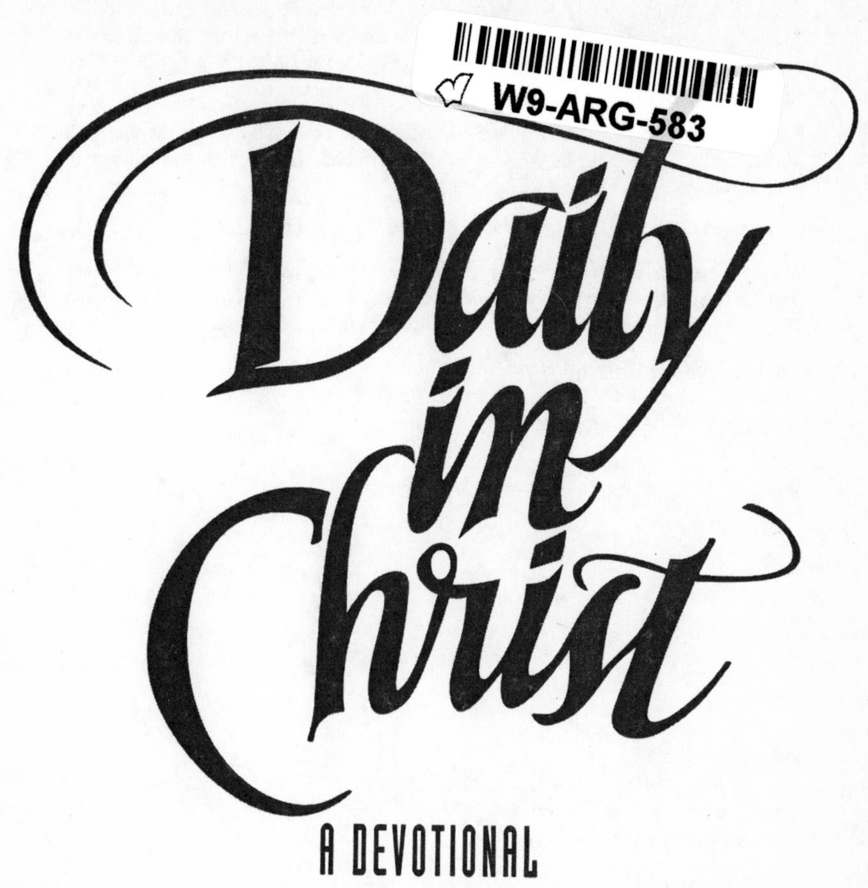

A DEVOTIONAL

NEIL ANDERSON
WITH JOANNE ANDERSON

Unless otherwise indicated, all Scripture quotations are taken from the New American Standard Bible®, © 1960, 1962, 1963, 1968, 1971, 1972, 1973, 1975, 1977, 1995 by The Lockman Foundation. Used by permission. (www.Lockman.org)

Scripture quotations marked NIV are taken from the Holy Bible, New International Version®, NIV®. Copyright © 1973, 1978, 1984 by Biblica, Inc.™ Used by permission of Zondervan. All rights reserved worldwide.

Verses marked KJV are taken from the King James Version of the Bible.

Daily in Christ is adapted and used by permission from *Victory Over Darkness* (Regal Books); *The Bondage Breaker* (Harvest House Publishers, Inc.); *Walking in the Light* (Thomas Nelson Publishers); *The Seduction of Our Children* (Harvest House Publishers, Inc.).

Cover by Left Coast Design, Portland, Oregon

DAILY IN CHRIST

Eugene, Oregon 97402
www.harvesthousepublishers.com

Library of Congress Cataloging-in-Publication Data
Anderson, Neil T., 1942—
Daily in Christ / Neil and Joanne Anderson.
p. cm.
ISBN 978-1-56507-098-1 (Hardcover)
ISBN 978-0-7369-0151-2 (Soft cover)
1. Devotional Calendars. I. Anderson, Joanne, 1941—. II. Title.
BV4811.A535 1993
242.'2—dc20
93-18858

Printed in the United States of America

10 11 12 13 14 15 16 17 18 / RDM / 18 17 16 15 14 13 12 11 10

Our Pilgrimage

Joanne and I have been on a pilgrimage for 50-plus years. More than 25 of those years have been in the covenant relationship of marriage. We were fortunate to have a solid, although rather stoic, Scandinavian family heritage. Our parents both celebrated their fiftieth wedding anniversaries. Religion has occupied center stage for most of our pilgrimage. Church was always a part of our life.

In our first years of marriage, the Lord arranged for our religious practices to be confronted, and we were torn from the colorless conformity of past traditions to the living dynamic of a personal relationship with God. I was the first to respond, happily throwing off the past and looking forward to a grand and challenging adventure. Then Joanne, struggling to let go of the comfort of her culture and roots, decided to trust Jesus.

The Lord called me from a successful career in engineering to seminary and then ministry. Once I started in seminary, higher education became a continuous part of our life. The result was five earned degrees and ten years of teaching at Talbot School of Theology. I never considered education, however, to be an end in itself. Ministry was always the focus. Connecting people to God was the desired result.

Joanne married an engineer, but dutifully followed me into ministry. She was the devotional and introspective one. I was the one who wanted to get it done. Joanne was content to raise Heidi and Karl, and to focus on her personal relationship with God. I wanted to reach the world for Christ. Consequently, Joanne sometimes saw ministry as a hindrance to our relationship. I didn't always see how the ministry could possibly be an interference in our marriage. A major life-threatening and life-changing event took place that brought me to the end of my resources and Joanne to the end of her past. I discovered the resources of God and deepened my commitment to the priority of relationships. Joanne surrendered to the care and protection of God. Jesus became the center of our relationship and ministry. The Freedom in Christ ministry was born, and now extends around the world.

Joanne and I have become partners in ministry. The Lord brought us to the end of ourselves. If we had known before we began this pilgrimage what we were going to go through, we probably wouldn't have chosen to come this way. Looking back, however, we're glad we came. Together we can say from experience and with confidence that God makes everything right in the end. The will of God *is* good, acceptable, and perfect (Romans 12:2). We have learned to never doubt in darkness what God has clearly shown in the light, and to be content in all of life's circumstances.

I never had a desire to write a book, but God graciously had just that in mind. In a period of two years, four bestselling books emerged: *Victory Over the Darkness*, *The Bondage Breaker*, *Walking in the Light* (originally titled *Walking Through the Darkness*), and *The Seduction of Our Children*. They serve as the basis for this devotional.

We know who we are. We are children of God, as are all true believers. We believe that Jesus came to give us life, and that eternal life is not something we get when we die. We are alive in Christ right now. We also believe that Jesus came to undo the works of Satan (1 John 3:8). In our journey, we have discovered the reality of God's presence in our lives, and also the reality of Satan's presence in this world. Learning to live as a child of God and standing against the powers of darkness are the foundations of this book. There is, however, only one book that should serve as the foundation for your faith and your daily walk. That is the Bible. If this book can enhance that process and keep you daily in Christ, we will be thrilled.

For every daily devotion, we tried to give a practical thought to help you in your own pilgrimage. Joanne concludes each devotion with a suggested prayer, capturing the heart of each message and offering direction for further prayer with your heavenly Father.

And we couldn't have done it alone. We want to thank Ed Stewart, who pulled much of this material out of my books and organized it. We also want to thank all the wonderful staff at Harvest House.

Finally, and close to our heart, we dedicate this book to our son, Karl. Our pilgrimage has been yours, but yours is just getting started. May your journey through life be one that is always drawing you near to Him, whom we call our Father.

NEIL AND JOANNE ANDERSON

For all who are being led by the Spirit of God, these are sons of God (Romans 8:14).

A young pilot had just passed the point of no return when the weather changed for the worse. Visibility dropped to a matter of feet as fog descended to the earth. Putting total trust in the cockpit instruments was a new experience to him, for the ink was still wet on the certificate verifying that he was qualified for instrument flying.

The landing worried him the most. His destination was a crowded metropolitan airport he wasn't familiar with. In a few minutes he would be in radio contact with the tower. Until then, he was alone with his thoughts. His instructor had practically forced him to memorize the rule book. He didn't care for it at the time, but now he was thankful.

Finally he heard the voice of the air traffic controller. "I'm going to put you on a holding pattern," the controller radioed. *Great!* thought the pilot. However, he knew that his safe landing was in the hands of this person. He had to draw upon his previous instructions and training, and trust the voice of an air traffic controller he couldn't see. Aware that this was no time for pride, he informed the controller, "This is not a seasoned pro up here. I would appreciate any help you could give me."

"You've got it!" he heard back.

For the next 45 minutes, the controller gently guided the pilot through the blinding fog. As course and altitude corrections came periodically, the young pilot realized the controller was guiding him around obstacles and away from potential collisions. With the words of the rule book firmly placed in his mind, and with the gentle voice of the controller, he landed safely at last.

The Holy Spirit guides us through the maze of life much like that air traffic controller. The controller assumed that the young pilot understood the instructions of the flight manual. His guidance was based on that. Such is the case with the Holy Spirit: He can guide us if we have a knowledge of God's Word and His will established in our minds.

Lord, as this new year begins, I choose to be sensitive to Your voice and resolutely committed to doing Your will.

Therefore do not be anxious for tomorrow; for tomorrow will care for itself (Matthew 6:34).

Trusting God for tomorrow is a question of our worth. Jesus said, "Look at the birds of the air, that they do not sow, neither do they reap, nor gather into barns, and yet your heavenly Father feeds them. Are you not worth much more than they?" (Matthew 6:26). Birds are not created in the image of God. We are! Birds will not inherit the kingdom of God, but we shall. Birds are mortal; mankind is immortal. If God takes care of the birds, so much more will He take care of us. That's why the apostle Paul could write, "My God shall supply all your needs according to His riches in glory in Christ Jesus" (Philippians 4:19).

Matthew 6:30,31 states: "If God so arrays the grass of the field, which is alive today and tomorrow is thrown into the furnace, will He not much more do so for you, O men of little faith? Do not be anxious then." God lays His own reputation on the line. If we trust and obey, He will provide. This is a question of God's integrity. "For your heavenly Father knows that you need all these things....Therefore do not be anxious for tomorrow; for tomorrow will care for itself. Each day has enough trouble of its own" (Matthew 6:32,34).

God's will is that we live responsibly today and trust Him for tomorrow. Are we people of little faith, or do we really believe that the fruit of the Spirit will satisfy us more than earthly possessions? Do we really believe that if we hunger and thirst after righteousness, we shall be satisfied? Do we really believe that if we seek to establish God's kingdom, God will supply all our needs according to His riches in glory? If we do, then we will seek first His kingdom and His righteousness, and all these things shall be added to us (Matthew 6:33).

Thank You, Lord, for so faithfully caring for me. I gladly cast all of my cares about today on You.

Has [God] said, and will He not do it? Or has He spoken, and will He not make it good? (Numbers 23:19).

One key to successful living is learning to distinguish a godly *goal* from a godly *desire*.

A godly *goal* is any specific orientation reflecting God's purpose for your life that does not depend on people or circumstances beyond your ability or right to control. Who do you have the ability and right to control? Virtually no one but yourself. The only person who can block a godly goal or render it uncertain or impossible is you.

By contrast, a godly *desire* is any specific orientation that depends on the cooperation of other people or the success of events or favorable circumstances you cannot control. You cannot base your self-worth or your personal success on your desires, no matter how godly they may be, because you cannot control all the people or circumstances that affect fulfillment.

When people or circumstances block our goals, we get angry. If our mentally perceived goal is uncertain, we feel anxious. If the goal appears impossible, we get depressed. But what God-given goal can be blocked, uncertain, or impossible? With God all things are possible, and I can do all things through Christ who strengthens me. No one can keep us from being what God wants us to be except us.

Notice how God distinguishes between goals and desires. John wrote, "My little children, I am writing these things to you that you may not sin" (1 John 2:1). Certainly God desires that we don't sin, but His status as God and His purposes cannot be blocked by anyone who exercises his will against repentance. But it is God's *desire* that everyone repent even though not everyone will.

God accomplished His goal when Jesus said, "It is finished." What God has determined to do, He will do, so we can be all that He created us to be.

Lord, show me Your purposes for my life and help me make them my goals.

BLOCKED GOALS

The fruit of the light consists in all goodness and righteousness and truth (Ephesians 5:9).

One morning I rose early, had my devotions, and started making a special breakfast for my family. I was stirring the muffin mix, singing and feeling great, when my sleepy-eyed son, Karl, wandered into the kitchen. He grabbed a box of cereal and an empty bowl and headed for the table.

"Hey, Karl, just a second. We're not having cereal this morning. We're going to sit around the table together and have a big breakfast with muffins."

"I don't like muffins, Dad," he mumbled, opening the cereal box.

"Wait, Karl," I insisted, starting to get annoyed. "We're going to sit around the table together and have a big breakfast with muffins."

"But I don't like muffins, Dad," he repeated.

I lost it. "*Karl, we're going to sit around the table together and have a big breakfast with muffins!*" I barked. Karl closed the cereal box, threw it in the cupboard, and stomped back to his room. My great idea had suddenly turned to shambles. I had to spend the next several minutes apologizing to Karl for my outburst.

Like me, I'm sure you have suffered your share of blocked goals. You had this great plan to do something wonderful for God, your church, your family, or a friend. Then your plan was thrown into disarray by hectic daily events over which you had no control. You didn't get your way at the board meeting. Your child decided to be the lead guitarist in a rock band instead of becoming a doctor like you planned.

When you base your life on the success of plans that are subject to people and circumstances, your life will be one long, emotional roller coaster ride. And the only way to get off the roller coaster is to walk by faith according to the truth of God's Word. Who you are must not be dependent on the cooperation of others or favorable circumstances. Decide to become the spouse, parent, leader, or worker God wants you to be. No one can block that goal except you.

Heavenly Father, show me today where I have allowed people or circumstances, instead of You, to determine what You want me to be.

We are to grow up in all aspects into Him (Ephesians 4:15). It was for freedom that Christ set us free (Galatians 5:1).

There are two concepts which determine the victory and fruitfulness of a Christian. The first concept is *maturity*. Paul wrote: "We are to grow up in all aspects into Him, who is the head, even Christ....to a mature man, to the measure of the stature which belongs to the fulness of Christ" (Ephesians 4:15,13). God has given us everything we need to grow to maturity in Christ (2 Peter 1:3). But Satan is opposed to our maturity and will do anything he can to keep us from realizing who we are and what we have in Christ. We must experience victory over the dark side before we can fully mature.

The second concept of the successful Christian life is *freedom*. Paul declared: "It was for freedom that Christ set us free; therefore keep standing firm and do not be subject again to a yoke of slavery" (Galatians 5:1). This verse not only assures us that God wants us free, but also warns us that we can lose our freedom by returning to the law.

Before we received Christ, we were slaves to sin. But because of Christ's work on the cross, sin's power over us has been broken. Satan has no right of ownership or authority over us. He is a defeated foe, but he is committed to keeping us from realizing that. He knows he can block your effectiveness as a Christian if he can deceive you into believing that you are nothing but a product of your past, subject to sin, prone to failure, and controlled by your habits. As long as he can confuse you and blind you with his dark lies, you won't be able to see that the chains which once bound you are broken. You are free in Christ, but if the devil can deceive you into believing you're not, you won't experience the freedom which is your inheritance. I don't believe in instant maturity, but I do believe in instant freedom, and I have seen thousands of people set free by the truth. Once a person is free, you would be amazed at how quickly he or she matures!

Lord, I rejoice that it was for my freedom that You came to set me free. Remind me today to walk in Your freedom.

January 6 AN INDISPENSABLE PREREQUISITE

Now this is eternal life: that they may know you, the only true God, and Jesus Christ, whom you have sent (John 17:3 NIV).

The focus of my ministry, both as a pastor and a seminary professor, has been the interrelated ministries of discipling and Christian counseling. I have been a discipler and a counselor of countless individuals. I have also taught discipleship and pastoral counseling at the seminary level and in churches and leadership conferences across the country. Much of my interaction with people has been to expose the insidious reality of Satan's relentless assault of deception on the Christian's mind. He knows that if he can keep you from understanding who you are in Christ, he can keep you from experiencing the maturity and freedom which is your inheritance as a child of God.

I am intrigued by the overlap of the ministries of discipling and counseling. Christian discipleship focuses on truth and tends to be future-oriented, provoking spiritual growth and maturity. Christian counseling considers the past to correct problems and address areas of weakness. Your past has shaped your present belief system and will determine your future unless it is dealt with. Biblically, discipleship and counseling are not separate ministries. Both are intensely personal ministries which are necessary to apply the truth to set people free from their past and establish them complete in Christ.

Furthermore, it is my conviction that discipleship and counseling must both start where the Bible starts: with a knowledge of God and our identity in Christ. If we really knew God, our behavior would change radically and instantly. That's what happened in Scripture. Whenever heaven opened to reveal the glory of God, individual witnesses were immediately and profoundly changed. I believe that the greatest determinant of mental and spiritual health and freedom is a true understanding of God and a right relationship with Him. A good theology is an indispensable prerequisite to a good psychology.

Father, I am eternally grateful to You that in Christ I am a saint dwelling in the heavenlies instead of a sinner wallowing in the mud.

For all who are being led by the Spirit of God, these are sons of God (Romans 8:14).

I enjoy asking people, "Who are you?" It sounds like a simple question requiring a simple answer, but it really isn't. For example, if someone asked me, "Who are you?" I might answer, "Neil Anderson."

"No, that's your name. Who are you?"

"I'm an American."

"No, that's where you live."

I could also say that I'm five feet nine inches tall and a little over 150 pounds—actually *quite* a little over 150 pounds! But my physical dimensions and appearance aren't me either. If you chopped off my arms and legs would I still be me? If you transplanted my heart, kidneys, or liver would I still be me? Of course! Now if you keep chopping you'll get to me eventually because I'm in here somewhere. But who I am is far more than what you see on the outside.

We may say with the apostle Paul that we "recognize no man according to the flesh." But we tend to identify ourselves and each other primarily by physical appearance (tall, short, stocky, slender) or what we do (plumber, carpenter, nurse, engineer, clerk). Furthermore, when asked to identify ourselves in relation to our faith, we usually talk about our doctrinal position (Protestant, evangelical, Calvinist, charismatic), our denominational preference (Baptist, Presbyterian, Methodist, Independent), or our role in the church (Sunday school teacher, choir member, deacon, usher).

But is who you are determined by what you do, or is what you do determined by who you are? That's an important question, especially as it relates to Christian maturity. I subscribe to the latter. I believe wholeheartedly that your hope for growth, meaning, and fulfillment as a Christian is based on understanding who you are—specifically your identity in Christ as a child of God. Your understanding of who you are in Christ will greatly determine how you live your life.

Lord Jesus, I know I am complete in You. Don't allow me to fall back into fleshly attributes today in an attempt to impress others or You.

Therefore if any man is in Christ, he is a new creature; the old things passed away; behold, new things have come (2 Corinthians 5:17).

Dan and Cindy were a fine young Christian couple who were preparing for ministry on the mission field. Then tragedy struck: Cindy was raped. As hard as she tried to get back to normal life, Cindy couldn't shake the horrible memories and feelings from her experience.

Six months after the tragedy, Dan and Cindy attended a church conference where I was speaking. During the conference Cindy called me in tears. "Neil, I know God can turn everything into good, but how is He going to do that?"

"Wait a minute, Cindy," I said. "God will work everything out for good, but He doesn't make a bad thing good. What happened to you was evil. God's good thing is to show you how you can walk through your crisis and come out of it a better person."

"But I just can't separate myself from my experience," she sobbed. "I've been raped, Neil, and I'll be a victim of that all my life."

"No, Cindy," I insisted. "The rape happened to you, but it hasn't changed who you are, nor does it have to control you. You were the victim of a terrible, ugly tragedy. But if you only see yourself as a rape victim for the rest of your life, you will never be free. You're a child of God. You can't fix the past, but you can be free from it."

All of us have a number of hurtful, traumatic experiences in our past which have scarred us emotionally. You may have grown up with a physically, emotionally, or sexually abusive parent. Any number of traumatic, emotional events can clutter your soul with emotional baggage which seems to limit your maturity and block your freedom in Christ. You must renounce the experiences and lies that have controlled you and forgive those who have offended you.

As a Christian, you are primarily the product of the work of Christ on the cross. You are literally a new creature in Christ. The old you is gone; the new you is here.

Father, thank You for working all things for good in my life, even the effects of evil attacks meant for my harm and destruction.

...the surpassing greatness of His power toward us who believe. These are in accordance with the working of the strength of His might... (Ephesians 1:19).

In Ephesians 1:19-21 Paul gives us a peek at the dynamic source of our authority in Christ. He explains that the authority at our disposal flows from the reservoir of power which raised Jesus Christ from the dead and seated Him at the Father's right hand. That power source is so dynamic that Paul used four different Greek words in verse 19 to describe it: *power* (*dunameos*), *working* (*energeian*), *strength* (*kratous*), and *might* (*ischuos*). Behind the resurrection of the Lord Jesus Christ lies the mightiest work of power recorded in the Word of God. And the same power which raised Christ from the dead and defeated Satan is the power available to us to overcome the works of Satan in our daily lives.

Paul opens our eyes to the expansive scope of Christ's authority, which is "far above all rule and authority and power and dominion, and every name that is named, not only in this age, but also in the one to come" (Ephesians 1:21). Think about the most powerful and influential political or military leaders in the world. Imagine the most feared terrorists, crime kingpins, and drug barons. Think about the notorious figures of the past and present who have blighted society with their diabolical misdeeds. Think about Satan and all the powers of darkness marshaled under his command. Jesus' authority is not only above all these human and spiritual authorities past, present, and future, but He is *far* above them. We share the same position because we are seated with Christ in the heavenlies, which enables us to live in freedom and victory over demonic intrusion and influence.

Don't be deceived. You are not under Satan's power or subject to his authority. You are in Christ above all demonic rule, authority, and power.

Reigning with You, Lord—what a liberating thought! I praise You today for the power You share with me.

IDENTIFYING A CHRISTIAN LEADER

There will also be false teachers among you, who will secretly introduce destructive heresies, even denying the Master who bought them, bringing swift destruction upon themselves (2 Peter 2:1).

What comes to mind when you hear the terms *false prophets* and *false teachers*? Many people tend to think of Eastern mystics and gurus, the spokespersons for nonbiblical religions, or dynamic cult leaders—people who are recognizably outside the boundaries of the Christian church. But the apostle Peter devoted an entire chapter in one of his letters (2 Peter 2) to false prophets and teachers who operate *within* the church. False teachers may operate in our churches disguised as workers of righteousness.

Notice that the lure of false teachers is not primarily their doctrine: "And many will follow their sensuality, and because of them the way of the truth will be maligned" (verse 2). What does Peter mean by "follow their sensuality"? He is talking about Christians who evaluate a ministry based on the outward appearance and charm of its leaders. We say, "He's such a nice guy"; "She's a very charismatic person"; "He's a real dynamic speaker"; "She's so sweet and sounds so sincere." But is physical attractiveness or a syrupy personality a biblical criterion for validating a ministry or a teacher? Of course not! The issue is always *truth and righteousness*. A Christian leader should be identified by his commitment to the truth, his righteous life, and his servant's heart.

Dear God, keep me from playing to the grandstand; I want only to live for You. Keep me accountable as a person of truth, righteousness, and love, ever fearful of discrediting Your name.

January 11 **SPRING-LOADED TOWARD THE SPIRIT**

Walk by the Spirit, and you will not carry out the desire of the flesh (Galatians 5:16).

When we first became Christians, we were like one-third horsepower lawn mower engines. We could accomplish something, but not very much because we weren't very mature. Our ambition as Christians is to become engines that can power earth-moving machinery—real powerhouses for the Lord. But neither a lawn mower nor a bulldozer can accomplish anything without gas. And neither can we accomplish anything apart from Christ (John 15:5). No matter how mature you are, you can never be productive unless you are walking in the Spirit.

When it comes to the choice between walking according to the flesh and walking according to the Spirit, our will is like a toggle switch. The new Christian's will seems to be spring-loaded toward fleshly behavior. He is still the unwitting victim of a thoroughly trained flesh which only knows how to operate independently of God. The mature Christian's will is spring-loaded toward the Spirit. He makes occasional poor choices, but he is learning to crucify the flesh and walk in the Spirit on a daily basis.

If you are hoping for a magic formula or a list of foolproof steps for walking in the Spirit, you will be disappointed. The moment you reduce the Spirit-filled walk to a formula or an intellectual exercise, you probably won't be Spirit-filled anymore.

The Holy Spirit is a "He," not an "it." Our walk with God is a personal experience, not a mechanical or legalistic formula. We see the immorality of fleshly indulgence everywhere, but simply preaching against it and telling people to shape up is not God's answer. The law is powerless to give life (Galatians 3:21). Reintroducing the law to believers won't work. But if we learn to walk by the Spirit, we won't carry out the desires of the flesh. Let's encourage others to do the same.

Lord, I desire to be patient with others in their walk of faith as You are patient with me. Help me have a gracious response and a gentle answer to others today.

With all prayer and petition, pray at all times in the Spirit, and with this in view, be on the alert with all perseverance and petition for all the saints (Ephesians 6:18).

The mother of one of my seminary students was a psychic. She said to him once, "Jim, have you been praying for me?"

"Of course I have, Mother."

"Well, don't," she insisted, "because you're disturbing my aura."

I say pray on! We never know completely the effects of our prayers, but we do know that God includes prayer as part of His strategy for establishing His kingdom and ensuring our spiritual victory.

One of the most dramatic deliverances I have observed happened in a man who was a high priest in the upper echelons of Satanism. Six months after he was set free he gave his testimony in our church. At the close of his testimony I asked him, "Based on your experience on 'the other side,' what is the Christian's greatest strategy against demonic influence?"

"Prayer," he answered forcefully. "And when you pray, mean it. Fervent prayer thwarts Satan's activity like nothing else."

What is prayer? It is communication with God by which we express our dependence on Him. God knows what we need in our battle with the powers of darkness, and He is more ready to meet our needs than we are to ask. But until we express our dependence on Him in prayer, God may not act. In prayer we say, "You are the Lord, not I. You know what's best; I don't. I'm not telling You what to do; I'm asking." Prayer is a means by which God guides and protects His children.

Praying in the Spirit is God's way of helping us pray when we don't know how: "The Spirit also helps our weakness; for we do not know how to pray as we should, but the Spirit Himself intercedes for us" (Romans 8:26). *Helps* (*sunantilambano*) depicts the Holy Spirit's role of coming alongside us in our condition of human frailty and spiritual vulnerability and bearing us to the other side of spiritual protection and victory.

Thank You, Lord, that prayer is such a powerful weapon in my arsenal against the powers of darkness.

Without faith it is impossible to please Him, for he who comes to God must believe that He is, and that He is a rewarder of those who seek Him (Hebrews 11:6).

The life of Wilma Rudolph, the great Olympic sprinter, is a remarkable story of faith. Wilma was born with health problems that left her crippled. "Will I ever be able to run and play like the other children?" Wilma asked her parents.

"Honey, you have to believe in God and never give up hope," they responded. "If you believe, God will make it happen." Taking her parents' counsel, she painfully struggled to walk. By the time she was 12, to the delight and surprise of many, Wilma no longer needed her braces. She went on to play basketball on her championship high school team and win three gold medals in the 1960 Olympics.

When you hear inspiring stories of faith like Wilma Rudolph's, do you sometimes wonder, "What could I accomplish if I took God at His Word?" Faith is the foundational principle of the Christian life. Believing who God is, what He says, what He has done, and what He will do defines the kingdom of God.

Furthermore, faith is the essence of the Christian's day-to-day activity. Paul wrote: "As you therefore have received Christ Jesus the Lord, so walk in Him" (Colossians 2:6). How did you receive Christ? By faith. How then are you to walk in Him? By faith. In Scripture, walking refers to the way you conduct your everyday life. Victorious Christian living and spiritual maturity are determined by our belief in God.

We tend to think of faith as some kind of mystical quality which belongs only in the realm of the spiritual. But everybody walks by faith. It is the most basic operating principle of life. The question is, in what or in whom do you believe? We are challenged to believe in God and take His Word seriously.

Thank You, Lord, that Your Word stands forever in heaven. I can trust in You and Your Word despite my changing feelings and circumstances.

A pupil is not above his teacher; but everyone, after he has been fully trained, will be like his teacher (Luke 6:40).

Your children need to see how you handle failure even more than how you handle success. If you make a mistake, you need to own up to it and ask forgiveness if the situation calls for it. If you don't model how to deal with your own fleshly responses, how are they going to learn how to own up to their mistakes and resolve them biblically?

One Sunday morning my daughter wasn't ready when I wanted to leave for church. I fumed about it until I exploded with anger. After the service I was about to say grace before a meal when I felt the convicting hand of God weighing heavily upon me. I stopped and asked my family to forgive me for my outburst of anger. I didn't confess my daughter's tardiness because it wasn't my responsibility. Nor did I ask their forgiveness in hopes that my daughter would own up to her tardiness. I asked their forgiveness because my outburst of anger was a deed of the flesh. I had to ask forgiveness to be right with God myself.

You never lose esteem in your child's eyes when you do what God requires you to do. You gain esteem because you are an honest person, and in the process you are modeling what they need to do when they blow it. Children need models, not critics. Modeling is what establishes our credibility to "bring them up in the discipline and instruction of the Lord" (Ephesians 6:4).

Lord, help me model a life of obedience and honesty before my children and others who look to me as an example. And when I fail, give me grace to admit my mistakes and resolve my conflicts.

Then God said, "Let Us make man in Our image, according to Our likeness" (Genesis 1:26).

Adam was created physically and spiritually alive. He possessed eternal life from his first breath and enjoyed God's abiding presence in the garden of Eden.

Furthermore, unlike the animal kingdom that operated by divine instinct, Adam was created in the likeness of God with a mind, emotions, and will, giving him the ability to think, feel, and choose. No other created being can make that claim.

After creating Adam, God said, "It is not good for the man to be alone" (Genesis 2:18). So He created a suitable helper for him: Eve. They both enjoyed a sense of belonging to God and each other. Not only that, God gave them a purpose: to "rule over the fish of the sea and over the birds of the sky and over the cattle and over all the earth" (Genesis 1:26). Adam and Eve didn't have to search for significance; they had it in their relationship with God. And because God was present with them, they lived in perpetual safety and security.

Eternal life, identity, purpose, significance, security, and a sense of belonging are all attributes of mankind created in the image of God. Adam and Eve experienced these attributes in full measure, and we were destined to enjoy them too. But when Adam sinned, he died spiritually and forfeited everything God had provided. Being separated from God, Adam's glowing attributes became glaring needs.

As children of Adam born separated from God, we come into the world with these same glaring needs. We wander through life striving to make a name for ourselves, looking for security in temporal things, and searching for significance apart from God. Is it a hopeless quest? No! We are able to fulfill these needs by establishing a personal relationship with God through faith in Jesus Christ. Everything Adam enjoyed in the garden before he sinned is now at our disposal.

Loving heavenly Father, thank You for sending Jesus to die for my sin so I may have eternal life. And thank You that in Christ my need for identity, significance, security, and a sense of belonging can be met.

Then the LORD *God formed man of dust from the ground and breathed into his nostrils the breath of life; and man became a living being* (Genesis 2:7).

Biblically, life means to *unite* and death means to *separate.* When Adam became a living being, his soul was in union with his body. When he died, his soul separated from his body.

As long as you are alive, your soul is united with your body. When you die physically, your soul separates from your body. But when that separation occurs, you do not cease to exist. Paul said that to be absent from the body is to be present with the Lord (2 Corinthians 5:8). Your primary identity is not found in your physical existence. Paul said, "From now on we recognize no man according to the flesh" (2 Corinthians 5:16).

Even though your principal identity is more than physical, in this temporal life you cannot function without your physical body. Your immaterial self needs your material self, and vice versa. You need your physical brain to control your movements and responses, and you need your immaterial mind to reason and make value judgments. Your brain is like a computer and your mind is the programmer. The finest human brain can't accomplish anything in a corpse which lacks a mind. And the most brilliant mind cannot function in a brain damaged by Alzheimer's disease.

In 2 Corinthians 5:1-4 Paul referred to the believer's body as a tent, the temporary dwelling place of the soul. Using his illustration, I must confess that my tent pegs are coming up, my poles are sagging, and my seams are becoming frayed! At my age I'm just glad that there's more to me than the disposable earth suit I walk around in.

You don't exist for your body; it exists for you. That's why Paul said, "I beat my body and make it my slave" (1 Corinthians 9:27 NIV). In order to fulfill your purpose for being here, you need to manage your body well through exercise, balanced diet, and adequate rest.

Lord, help me to not overemphasize or underemphasize the significance of my physical life but stay in step with Your view.

And this is the testimony: God has given us eternal life, and this life is in his Son. He who has the Son has life; he who does not have the Son of God does not have life (1 John 5:11,12 NIV*).*

When God breathed life into Adam, he was both physically and spiritually alive. Adam was spiritually alive because his soul was in union with God. We were never designed to be separated from God or to live independently of Him. We were born to be spiritually alive.

For the Christian, to be spiritually alive is to be in union with God. This concept is repeatedly presented in Scripture by the prepositional phrase *in Christ*. Being in Christ is the theme of the New Testament. Like Adam, we were created to be in union with God. But Adam sinned and his union with God, and ours as well, was severed. It is God's eternal plan to bring human creation back to Himself and restore the union He enjoyed with Adam at creation. That restored union with God, which we find in Christ, is the essence of our identity.

When you were born again, your soul was united with God and you came alive spiritually, as alive as Adam was in the garden before he sinned. As the New Testament repeatedly declares, you are now *in Christ*, and Christ is in you. Since Christ who is in you is eternal, the spiritual life you have received from Him is eternal. You don't have to wait until you die to get eternal life; you possess it right now!

The apostle John wrote, "He who has the Son has the life" (1 John 5:12). He probably remembered Jesus' statement to Martha: "I am the resurrection and the life; he who believes in Me shall live even if he dies, and everyone who lives and believes in Me shall never die" (John 11:25,26). After Jesus said this to Martha, He added, "Do you believe this?" (verse 26).

The Word of God is clear: Because of Jesus, we will continue to live spiritually even after we die physically. Do *you* believe this?

Dear Father, I declare my wholehearted belief that my spiritual life—eternal life—is in You. Help me live today with eternity's values in view.

Therefore, just as through one man sin entered into the world, and death through sin, and so death spread to all men, because all sinned (Romans 5:12).

Unfortunately, the idyllic setting in the Garden of Eden was shattered. Genesis 3 tells the sad story of Adam and Eve's lost relationship with God through sin. The effects of man's fall were dramatic, immediate, and far-reaching, infecting every subsequent member of the human race.

What happened to Adam and Eve spiritually because of the Fall? They died. Their union with God was severed and they were separated from God. God had specifically said: "You must not eat from the tree of the knowledge of good and evil, for when you eat of it you will surely die" (Genesis 2:17 NIV). They ate and they died.

Did they die physically? No. The process of physical death was set in motion, but they were alive physically for several hundred more years. They died spiritually; their souls were separated from God. They were banished from God's presence. They were cast out of the Garden of Eden and guarding the entrance were cherubim waving a flaming sword (Genesis 3:23,24).

After Adam, everyone who comes into the world is born physically alive but spiritually dead, separated from God. Paul wrote, "As for you, you were dead in your transgressions and sins, in which you used to live" (Ephesians 2:1 NIV).

How did Jesus remedy this problem? In two dramatic, life-changing ways. First, He died on the cross to cure the disease that caused us to die: sin. Romans 6:23 begins, "The wages of sin is death." Then He rose from the dead to give us spiritual life. The verse continues, "But the free gift of God is eternal life in Christ Jesus our Lord." Jesus Himself said, "I came that they might have life" (John 10:10).

The bad news is that, as a child of Adam, you inherited spiritual death. But the eternally good news is that, as a child of God through faith in Christ, you will live forever because of the life He has provided for you.

Thank You, heavenly Father, for sending Jesus to die on the cross for my sins and then raising Him from the dead so I may have life.

January 19 — DEAD TO SIN

Even so consider yourselves to be dead to sin, but alive to God in Christ Jesus. Therefore do not let sin reign in your mortal body that you should obey its lusts (Romans 6:11,12).

Sin is the condition into which all descendants of fallen Adam are born (Romans 5:12). Sin is living our lives independently of God. It's the result of being deceived by Satan to believe that meaning and purpose in life may be achieved apart from a personal relationship with, and obedience to, the Creator of life (Deuteronomy 30:19,20; 1 John 5:12). In the non-Christian, sin permeates the old nature, dominates the old self, and perpetuates the deeds of the flesh. Satan is at the heart of all sin (1 John 3:8). He deceives people into believing a lie and counsels them to rebel against God.

When you received Christ you died to sin and its power to dominate you was broken. Satan and sin have not died; they are still strong and appealing. But you no longer have to sin because you are dead to sin and alive to God in Christ (Romans 6:11). You are not dead to sin because you consider it so; you consider it so because it *is* so. In Christ you have already died to sin.

Paul goes on to say that we are not to use our bodies as instruments of unrighteousness (verse 13). If we do, we allow sin to rule in our mortal bodies. For example, it is virtually impossible for someone to commit a sexual sin and not use his body as an instrument of unrighteousness, allowing sin to rule. Ask the Lord to reveal to your mind how you have wrongly used your body, especially sexually. Renounce that wrong use and then submit your body to God as a living sacrifice. It is your responsibility not to let "sin reign in your mortal body that you should obey its lusts" (Romans 6:12).

Loving Lord, I know that sin's power over me has been broken. Help me live today in the light of that truth by renouncing sin and submitting my body to You.

If any man is willing to do His will, he shall know of the teaching, whether it is of God, or whether I speak from Myself (John 7:17).

Knowing the will of God is not just a twentieth-century problem. People were struggling at the time of Christ. Some people were saying of Him, "He's a good man." Others were saying, "He leads the multitude astray" (see John 7:12). How could these people know whether He was leading them into truth?

Seizing the opportunity, Jesus set forth standards of divine guidance. His first admonition was, "My teaching is not Mine, but His who sent Me. If any man is willing to do His will, he shall know of the teaching, whether it is of God, or whether I speak from Myself" (John 7:16,17). The essential prerequisite to know the will of God, according to Jesus, is a willingness to do it.

What is the will of God? God's will for those who believe in Him is to be alive in Christ for the purpose of establishing His kingdom by overcoming the evil one and becoming fully the people He has called us to be. Notice the opening words of the Lord's Prayer: "Our Father who art in heaven, hallowed be Thy name. Thy kingdom come. Thy will be done, on earth as it is in heaven" (Matthew 6:9,10). When praying this prayer, we are asking for God's will to be accomplished on earth as it presently is in heaven. Apparently God's will is being perfectly executed in heaven but not on earth.

Are you totally committed to do God's will without knowing for sure what it is? Do you hold any reservations about turning your will over to God? Do you really believe that God's will for you is good, acceptable, and perfect (Romans 12:2)? If God is God and you call Him Lord, doesn't He have the right to exercise His will in your life?

Father, may Your will be accomplished in my thoughts, words, and deeds today as it is being accomplished in heaven.

A Higher Priority

For all who are being led by the Spirit of God, these are sons of God (Romans 8:14).

Two significant events in my life brought into clear focus the priority of relationship over achievement. Before being called into the ministry I worked as an aerospace engineer on the Apollo program. I will never forget the day the lunar lander touched down on the moon. This bold headline dominated the front page of the *Minneapolis Star*: "Neil Armstrong Lands on the Moon." It was an achievement I was proud to be part of.

But the really big news came months earlier on page 7 in the third section: "Heidi Jo Anderson, born to Mr. and Mrs. Neil Anderson, Northwestern Hospital, March 12, 1969." That may not sound like big news to you, but it was to her mother and me. Heidi totally took over my den and captured an entire shelf in the refrigerator. She altered our sleeping pattern and restricted our social calendar. But she was ours to hold, to hug, and to care for.

What does God care about moon-shots? They are deeds to be outdone. Somebody will always come along and do it better, faster, and higher. What God cares about is little people like Heidi Jo Anderson, because they will be with Him forever.

The second significant event in my life was receiving my first doctoral degree. But it turned out to be one of the most anticlimactic days of my life. I heard no applause from heaven, and I don't believe my achievement added so much as an asterisk to my name in the Lamb's Book of Life. I was a child of God before that day, and I was still a child of God afterward.

But what happens in heaven when one sinner repents? Applause! Why? Because a relationship with God is eternal, while earthly achievements last only for time. Have you sacrificed the eternal to gain the temporal? Have you ignored personal and spiritual relationships in your pursuit of human achievements? Relationships must always have a higher priority than temporal achievements.

Lord, amidst the busyness of my schedule and clutter of my possessions, help me cherish and nurture my relationships today.

My heart says of you, "Seek his face!" Your face, LORD, I will seek (Psalm 27:8 NIV).

"If the sun is shining in the morning, I'll do it."

"If he's there when I open the door, I'll know he's the one."

"If I pass the class on world missions, I'll be a missionary. If not, I'll be a local pastor."

We all know better than this, but it's amazing how often scenarios just like these pop into our minds. Such propositions are referred to as "laying a fleece" before the Lord or "seeking a sign."

The term *fleece* comes from the account of Gideon. In Judges 6, Gideon is called by God to deliver Israel from the Midianites. Gideon questions whether God is even for Israel (verse 13), and he doubts his own ability (verse 15). So he asks God for a sign (verse 17). God gives him one, then tells him to tear down the altar of Baal. Gideon is afraid to go during the day, so he goes at night.

Then he questions again whether God will deliver Israel. This time he puts a lamb's fleece on the ground. If God will deliver Israel, then the lamb's fleece will be wet in the morning and the ground around it will be dry. The next morning it is so. That ought to satisfy him, right? Wrong! Wanting to be sure, and hoping that God won't get too mad, Gideon asks Him to do it again, but this time with the opposite results (i.e., the fleece dry and the ground wet). Not exactly the stuff heroes are made of. But God answers Gideon's request and then He reduces Gideon's army down to 300 men!

The whole point of the passage is that God, not man, is the deliverer. God chose a man desperately seeking assurance and reduced an army down to nothing so that the victory would clearly be His. The fleece wasn't a means of demonstrating faith; it was just the opposite. And it certainly wasn't used to determine God's will. God had already told Gideon what to do. Gideon was questioning the integrity of God, just as we do if we ask for a fleece when God has already shown us His will. "An evil and adulterous generation craves for a sign" (Matthew 12:39). As God's people, let's seek the face of God.

Lord, forgive me for the times I have looked for signs instead of seeking Your face. I commit myself today to walk only in the faith revealed in Your Word.

The Spirit explicitly says that in later times some will fall away from the faith, paying attention to deceitful spirits and doctrines of demons (1 Timothy 4:1).

A few years ago I was speaking in a Southern California church on the subject of the New Age Movement. My text was 1 Timothy 4:1. After my message I was surrounded at the front of the sanctuary by people wanting to hear more about freedom from spiritual conflicts caused by demonic influences.

Sitting about halfway back in the sanctuary was a 22-year-old woman who had been weeping uncontrollably since the service ended. As I approached the young woman I could hear her sobbing, "He understands! He understands!"

Later Nancy described to me her horrible childhood, which included an abusive father and a grandmother who identified herself as a black witch. "When I was three years old I received my guardians—spirit guides," she continued. "They were my companions, telling me how to live and what to say. I never questioned if having spirit guides was anything but normal until my mother took me to Sunday school."

"Would you like to get rid of your spirit guides?" I asked.

There was a long pause. "Will they really leave, or will I go home and be thrashed by them again?"

"You will be free," I assured her. An hour later Nancy *was* free.

Nancy's experience is not an obscure, erratic blip in the contemporary Christian community. In fact, in more than 20 years of ministry as a pastor, counselor, seminary professor, and conference speaker, I have met and ministered to more Christians in bondage to the dark side of the spiritual world than you may believe. Christians are woefully unprepared to deal with the dark world of Satan's kingdom or to minister to those who are in bondage to it.

Yes, as Timothy warned, "deceitful spirits and doctrines of demons" are real. But as you daily embrace Christ and His truth, you will be able to recognize Satan's lies and choose the truth.

Thank You, Jesus, for being the way, the truth, and the life. I know You are my weapon for overcoming the evil one.

If therefore the Son shall make you free, you shall be free indeed (John 8:36).

The contrast between bondage and freedom in a believer's life is beautifully illustrated in the following letter from a successful professional man.

> Dear Neil,
>
> My emotional troubles were probably rooted in my childhood experiences with horror movies, Ouija boards, etc. I clearly remember fearing a visit from devilish forces after I saw the movie titled *The Blood of Dracula.*
>
> My father had a pretty hot temper and was given to emotional outbursts. My survival response was to sulk and blame myself for upsetting him. Bottling my emotions inside became a way of life. As I grew into adulthood I continued to blame myself for any and all personal shortcomings and misfortunes.
>
> Then I accepted Christ as my personal Lord and Savior. I grew spiritually over the next several years, but I never enjoyed complete peace. There was always a lingering doubt about my relationship with God, whom I saw as distant and stern. I had difficulty praying, reading the Bible, and paying attention to the pastor's sermons. I seriously questioned the purpose of life. I experienced horrible nightmares which woke me up screaming.
>
> It was during my time of prayer with you that I finally found freedom in Christ. Now when I read God's Word I understand it like never before. I have developed a more positive attitude, and my entire relationship with my Lord has completely changed. Since our meeting I haven't had one nightmare.

I'm not saying that every spiritual problem is the result of direct demonic activity. But you may be in bondage because you have overlooked or denied the reality of demonic powers at work in the world. Your inheritance in Christ is the basis for your complete freedom promised in Scripture.

Help me not to be a spiritual ostrich today, but to be alert to my enemy's tactics and to Your truth.

Submit therefore to God. Resist the devil and he will flee from you (James 4:7).

Daisy was one of the first persons I dealt with who was caught in spiritual conflicts and suffered from demonic influences. She was a Christian and a university graduate, but she had severe mental and emotional problems which developed after her father divorced her mother. Within a period of five years Daisy had been institutionalized three times as a paranoid schizophrenic. After about three weeks of counseling with me, Daisy finally found the nerve to bring up the nighttime visitation of snakes.

"What about the snakes?" I asked.

"They crawl on me at night when I'm in bed," she confessed.

"What do you do when the snakes come?"

"I run in to my mother. But they always come back when I'm alone."

"Why don't you try something different," I continued. "When you're in bed and the snakes come, say out loud, 'In the name of Christ I command you to leave me.' "

"I couldn't do that," Daisy protested. "I'm not mature enough or strong enough."

"It's not a matter of your maturity; it's a matter of your position in Christ. You have as much right to resist Satan as I do."

Daisy squirmed at the prospect. "Well, I guess I could do that," Daisy sighed, sounding like she had just agreed to take castor oil.

The next week when Daisy walked in she said, "The snakes are gone!" If her problem had been strictly a neurological or chemical imbalance, taking authority over the snakes in Jesus' name wouldn't have worked. But in Daisy's case the problem was spiritual.

James wrote: "Resist the devil and he will flee from you" (James 4:7). But if you don't resist him, he doesn't have to go. Or if you just pull the covers over your head in fear and say, "O God, do something about these demonic influences," the evil spirits don't have to leave. Resisting the devil is your responsibility based on the authority you possess in Christ.

Dear Father, thank You for providing me with such wonderful power. Help me not to be afraid to use it for my sake and others.

Show me your ways, O LORD, teach me your paths (Psalm 25:4 NIV).

In today's and tomorrow's devotionals, I would like to share with you 10 questions you'll want to ask yourself and pray about when you're faced with a decision. The first five are generic. They represent moral issues and godly wisdom that are normative for all times.

1. *Have you prayed about it?* Prayer was never intended to be a fourth-down punting situation in which we ask God to bail us out of our hasty decisions. It was intended to be a first-down huddle. We aren't supposed to ask God to bless our plans; we're supposed to ask God for His plans.

2. *Is it consistent with the Word of God?* In our culture, ignorance of God's Word is no excuse since resources abound. I believe that every home should have at least a concordance, a Bible dictionary, a topical Bible, a good commentary, and a study Bible with notes. Most pastors would love to share what God has to say about a given matter. If they wouldn't, you have called the wrong pastor!

3. *Can I do it and be a positive Christian witness?* A seminary student stopped by my office and told me about a job he had been offered. It would take care of his financial needs, but he had some reservations concerning the sales pitch he was required to use. I asked him if he could use the sales technique and be a positive witness for Christ. He didn't take the job.

4. *Will the Lord be glorified?* Can I do this and give glory to God? In doing it, would I be glorifying God in my body? Am I seeking the glory of man or the glory of God? Am I doing this to be noticed by man or am I seeking to please the Lord?

5. *Am I acting responsibly?* God doesn't bail us out of our irresponsibility. He will let us suffer the consequences of our sins and irresponsible choices. But when we are faithful in little things, He will put us in charge of greater things. Don't get ahead of God's timing or you will be over your head in responsibilities. Seek to develop your life and message, and God will expand your ministry.

Dear Lord, help me take a good, hard look at these questions and then avoid at all costs any compromise with Your will in my life today.

Guide me in your truth and teach me, for you are God my Savior, and my hope is in you all day long (Psalm 25:5 NIV*).*

The next five questions to ask yourself regarding God's will are to help you when facing a change in direction.

6. *Is it reasonable?* God expects us to think. His guidance may transcend human reasoning, but it never excludes it. God doesn't bypass our mind; He operates through it: "Brethren, do not be children in your thinking; yet in evil be babes, but in your thinking be mature" (1 Corinthians 14:20). We are warned in Scripture not to put our mind in neutral. We are to think and practice what we know to be true (Philippians 4:8,9).

7. *Does a realistic opportunity exist?* Closed doors are not meant to be knocked down. If you have a hopeless scheme, let it go. If it isn't God's timing, wait. If a realistic opportunity exists, and all the other factors are in agreement, then take the plunge. God may open a window of opportunity, but it will close if not taken advantage of. The faithless man asks, "What do I stand to lose if I do?" The faithful man asks, "What do I risk losing if I don't?"

8. *Are unbiased, spiritually sensitive associates in agreement?* Be careful not to consult only those who will agree with you. Give your advisors permission to ask hard questions. Don't be afraid of "no" answers. If it isn't God's will, don't you want to know before you make the mistake of acting impulsively?

9. *Do I have a sanctified desire?* Don't think that being in the will of God must always be an unpleasant task. The joy of the Lord should be our strength. I find my greatest joy in serving God and being in His will. But don't get the idea that if everything is wonderful you must be in the will of God. Is this a desire to satisfy a lust of the flesh or a Spirit-filled desire to see God's kingdom established and people helped?

10. *Do I have a peace about it?* This is an inner peace. Is the peace of God guarding your heart and mind?

If you have been able to answer yes to all 10 of these deciding factors, what are you waiting for?

Thank You, Lord, that I can trust You with the details and direction of my life today.

Now you Pharisees clean the outside of the cup and of the platter; but inside of you, you are full of robbery and wickedness (Luke 11:39).

The *Talmud*, a collection of ancient rabbinic writings, relates the story of Rabbi Akiba, who was imprisoned. Rabbi Joshua brought him some water, but the guard spilled half of the container. There was too little water to both wash and drink, and Rabbi Akiba faced the possibility of death for lack of water if he chose to use the water for ceremonial washing. He reasoned, "He who eats with unwashed hands perpetuates a crime that ought to be punished by death. Better for me to die of thirst than to transgress the traditions of my ancestors!"

Jesus responded harshly to such reasoning: "You blind guides, who strain out a gnat and swallow a camel!" (Matthew 23:24). The Lord cautions that the weightier matters of the law (such as justice and mercy) are overlooked when attention focuses on strict observances of religious practices. This leads to a corresponding negligence of the eternal laws of God. Jesus told people to pay more attention to cleansing their hearts and not be like their leaders who cleanse only their hands.

The laws of God are liberating and protective. They are restrictive only when they protect us from the evil one. The rules of any institution should ensure the freedom of each individual to reach his or her God-given potential. They should serve as a guide so we don't stray from our purpose, and they should protect us from those who abuse the system.

The principle that Jesus modeled could be stated as follows: If people are commanded to follow a traditional practice that makes life more difficult and no longer contributes to the purpose of the organization, then we must not participate as a matter of religious conscience. Jesus simply didn't observe such traditions, and He defended His disciples for not observing them as well.

Thank You for reminding me, Lord, that the law kills but the Spirit gives life. Help me walk in that freedom today.

I do not want you to become sharers in demons
(1 Corinthians 10:20).

While Christians have been questioning the reality of demonic influence in the church, the world has charged into the spiritual realm with reckless abandon. The Western world is experiencing a massive paradigm shift in its worldview, as best seen in the rise of the New Age Movement, the acceptance of parapsychology as a science, the growing popularity of the supernatural, and the increasing visibility of Satanism in our culture. New Age mysticism, which gathered its greatest strength with the influx of Eastern religions in the 1960s, has been popularized by a host of celebrities in the 1980s. It's commonplace to hear channelers (mediums) on radio and TV talk shows boasting about their spirit guides (demons).

But the New Age Movement is not just a celebrity issue. New Age philosophy is making significant inroads into business, education, and even religion across our nation. Recently I challenged two of my students to attend, for the sake of research, a New Age conference being held two blocks from our school. When they arrived at the door and discovered the cost to be $65 each, they started to walk away. But two strangers approached them saying, "We were told to give you these tickets." My wide-eyed students took the tickets and walked in.

They reported to me that one of the speakers led conference participants in a meditation exercise. He challenged everyone to imagine a spirit guide coming alongside. The speaker concluded the exercise by saying, "Now invite your spirit guide to come in." I could hardly believe it. The devil is giving altar calls just two blocks from Biola University!

Does the spread of New Age and the occult worry you or frighten you? It need not. In Christ you have every resource to defuse and dispel any threat of darkness in your life or family. Stand on the truth of His Word and walk in the light of your identity in Christ.

Keep me alert today, Lord, to inroads the devil is attempting in my world that I may tear down his strongholds with the weapons of the Spirit.

The Definition of Discipleship

Encourage one another, and build up one another, just as you also are doing (1 Thessalonians 5:11).

Jesus' primary call to His disciples is seen in His words "Come to Me" (Matthew 11:28) and "Follow Me" (Matthew 4:19). Mark records: "He appointed twelve, that they might be with Him, and that He might send them out to preach, and to have authority to cast out the demons" (Mark 3:14,15). Notice that Jesus' relationship with His disciples preceded His assignment to them. Discipleship is the intensely personal activity of two or more persons helping each other experience a growing relationship with God. Discipleship is being before doing, maturity before ministry, character before career.

Every Christian, including you, is both a disciple and a discipler in the context of his Christian relationships. You have the awesome privilege and responsibility both to be a teacher and a learner of what it means to be in Christ, walk in the Spirit, and live by faith. You may have a role in your family, church, or Christian community which gives you specific responsibility for discipling others, such as husband/father, pastor, Sunday school teacher, discipleship group leader, etc. But even as an appointed discipler you are never not a disciple who is learning and growing in Christ through your relationships. Conversely, you may not have an "official" responsibility to disciple anyone, but you are never not a discipler. You have the opportunity to help your children, your friends, and other believers grow in Christ through your caring and committed relationship with them.

Similarly, every Christian is both a counselor and counselee in the context of his Christian relationships. A good counselor should be a good discipler, and a good discipler should be a good counselor. Biblically, they are the same role. Your level of maturity may dictate that you do a lot of Christian counseling. But there will still be times when you need to seek or receive the counsel of other Christians. There will never be a day when we don't need each other.

Father, help me remember that I will never be so mature that I need not receive godly counsel from my brothers and sisters in Christ.

MODELING GROWTH

Prove yourselves doers of the word, and not merely hearers who delude themselves (James 1:22).

I am learning about pastors and missionaries across the country who are preaching against the very sins they are committing themselves. Nationally known Christian personalities who vehemently condemn immorality have themselves been found to be hiding an immoral lifestyle. Those of us who are called to preach or teach God's Word must put it on first. We must get on our knees before God as we prepare the message and say, "God, is this Scripture true in my life?" If not, we had better be honest enough to say to those who hear us, "I wish I were a better example of this passage than I am, but I'm still growing in this area." To proclaim the Word of God as if it were true in your life when it's not is a lie.

Those of us who receive the Word are also vulnerable to self-deception if we fail to put it into practice. We hear a sermon or a lesson and say, "Wow! What a great truth!" and hurry off to share it with someone else without processing it ourselves and applying it to our own lives. James said that hearers of the Word who are not also doers of the Word deceive themselves.

Why are we afraid to admit it when our lives don't completely match up to Scripture? I believe it's because many of us have a perfection complex. We think we have to model perfection and not admit to something less. But we can't model perfection, because we're not perfect; we can only model *growth.* The people around us need to know that we are real people in the process of maturing. They need to see how we handle failure as well as how we handle success. When we model this kind of honesty in the Christian community we greatly reduce the possibility of the deceiver gaining a foothold.

Lord, forgive me for the times I have placed the quest for earthly perfection ahead of growth in You and Your Word. Help me model growth in my life today.

February 1 — OUR TRANSFER

He delivered us from the domain of darkness, and transferred us to the kingdom of His beloved Son (Colossians 1:13).

Perhaps you have heard the illustration of the two dogs. Some people say that we have two natures within us vying for control of our lives. They claim that our old sin nature, which we inherited from disobedient Adam, is like a big black dog. Our new nature, which we inherited through Christ's redemptive work, is like a big white dog. These two dogs are bitter enemies, intent on destroying each other. Whenever you involve yourself in worldly thoughts or behavior, you are feeding the black dog. Whenever you focus your mind and activities on spiritual things, you are feeding the white dog. The dog you feed the most will eventually grow stronger and overpower the other.

This dramatic illustration may motivate Christians toward saintly behavior, but is it accurate based on who we really are in Christ? Since God "delivered us from the domain of darkness, and transferred us to the kingdom of His beloved Son" (Colossians 1:13), can we still be in both kingdoms? When God declares that we are "not in the flesh but in the Spirit" (Romans 8:9), can we be in the flesh and in the Spirit simultaneously? When God says that "you were formerly darkness, but now you are light in the Lord" (Ephesians 5:8), can you possibly be both light and darkness? When God states that "if any man is in Christ, he is a new creature; the old things passed away; behold, new things have come" (2 Corinthians 5:17), can we be partly new creature and partly old creature?

But be careful. Can a Christian sin? Of course! "If we say that we have no sin, we are deceiving ourselves, and the truth is not in us" (1 John 1:8). But *having* sin and *being* sin are two completely different issues. When we choose to walk by the flesh we will sin, but, as 1 John 2:1 reminds us, we don't have to: "My little children, I am writing these things to you that you may not sin."

We will spend the next few days exploring the scriptural bases for this truth.

How liberating to know today, Lord, that I am in the light, that I am a new creature, and that my new nature is firmly anchored in Your work of reconciliation.

February 2 A RADICAL, INNER TRANSFORMATION

By the grace of God I am what I am, and
His grace toward me did not prove vain
(1 Corinthians 15:10).

If you believe that you are part light and part darkness, part saint and part sinner, you will live in a very mediocre manner with little to distinguish you from the non-Christian. You may confess your proneness to sin and strive to do better, but you will live a continually defeated life because you perceive yourself to be only a sinner saved by grace who is hanging on until the rapture. Satan knows he can do nothing about who you really are, but if he can get you to believe you are no different from the natural person, then you will behave no differently from the natural person.

Why does this profile describe so many Christians? Because we are ignorant of our true identity in Christ. God's work of atonement in changing sinners to saints is His greatest accomplishment on earth. The inner change, justification, is effected at the moment of salvation. The outer change in the believer's daily walk, sanctification, continues throughout life. But the progressive work of sanctification is only fully effective when the radical, inner transformation of justification is realized and appropriated by faith.

"But didn't I read somewhere that Paul referred to himself as the chief of sinners?" you may wonder. Yes, but he was referring to his nature *before* his conversion to Christ (1 Timothy 1:12-16). He made a similar statement of self-depreciation in 1 Corinthians 15:9, but continued by saying: "But by the grace of God I am what I am, and His grace toward me did not prove vain" (verse 10). Paul knew that who he was before Christ and who he became in Christ were two separate identities.

If you claim to be just a sinner, what will you do? You will sin! You are professing that sin is at the core of your identity. That's not what the Bible teaches. Why don't we just believe God that Jesus is at the core of our being and then begin to live like it by His Spirit?

Thank You, Father, that I am complete in Your Son Jesus
and that my identity is rooted in Him and not in my sin.

SALVATION IS REGENERATION

He has granted to us His precious and magnificent promises, in order that by them you might become partakers of the divine nature (2 Peter 1:4).

What does the Bible specifically say about our nature? The Greek word for *nature* is used in this way only twice in the New Testament. Ephesians 2:1-3 describes the nature we all shared before we came to Christ: "And you were dead in your trespasses and sins...and were by nature children of wrath." What was your basic nature before you were born again spiritually? You and every other Christian "were by nature children of wrath," dead in sin, subject to Satan's power, living completely to fulfill sinful lusts and desires. This is the condition of every unbeliever today.

The second occurrence of the word is in 2 Peter 1:4 describing our nature after we came to Christ: "He has granted to us His precious and magnificent promises, in order that by them you might become partakers of the divine nature."

When you came into spiritual union with God through your new birth, you didn't *add* a new, divine nature to your old, sinful nature. You *exchanged* natures. Salvation isn't just a matter of God forgiving your sins and issuing you a pass to heaven when you die. Salvation is regeneration. God changed you from darkness to light, from sinner to saint. There is a newness about you that wasn't there before. If God hadn't changed your identity at salvation, you would be stuck with your old identity until you died. How could you expect to grow to maturity if you didn't start as a transformed child of God? Becoming a partaker of God's nature is fundamental to a Christian's identity and maturity.

We are no longer in Adam, we are in Christ. We can still choose to walk according to the flesh, but why should we want to? "You are not in the flesh but in the Spirit, if indeed the Spirit of God dwells in you. But if anyone does not have the Spirit of Christ, he does not belong to Him" (Romans 8:9).

Lord, may my understanding of who I am in Christ grow today so that I may walk in the victorious life You secured for me.

You were formerly darkness, but now you are light in the Lord; walk as children of light (Ephesians 5:8).

Ephesians 5:8 describes the essential change of nature which occurs at salvation. It doesn't say you were *in* darkness; it says you *were* darkness. Darkness was your nature, your very essence, as an unbeliever. Nor does it say you are now *in* the light; it says you *are* light. God changed your basic nature from darkness to light. The issue in this passage is not improving your nature. Your new nature is already determined. The issue is learning to walk in harmony with your new nature.

Why do you need the nature of Christ within you? So you can *be* like Christ, not just *act* like Him. God has not given us the power to imitate Him. He has made us partakers of His nature so that we can actually *be* like Him. You don't become a Christian by acting like one. We are not on a performance basis with God. He doesn't say, "Here are My standards, now you measure up." He knows you can't solve the problem of an old sinful self by simply improving your behavior. He must change your nature, give you an entirely new self—the life of Christ in you—which is the grace you need to measure up to His standards.

That was the point of His message in the Sermon on the Mount: "Unless your righteousness surpasses that of the scribes and Pharisees, you shall not enter the kingdom of heaven" (Matthew 5:20). The scribes and Pharisees were the religious perfectionists of their day. They had external behavior down to a science, but their hearts were like the insides of a tomb: reeking of death. Jesus is only interested in creating new persons from the inside out by infusing in them a brand-new nature and creating in them a new self. Only after He changes your identity and makes you a partaker of His nature will you be able to change your behavior.

Dear Jesus, thank You for rescuing me from the kingdom of darkness and transferring me into Your marvelous light. I choose to walk as a child of light today.

The Spirit Himself bears witness with our spirit that we are children of God, and if children, heirs also, heirs of God and fellow heirs with Christ (Romans 8:16,17).

Lydia is a middle-aged woman who was dealt a bad hand in life right from the beginning. Memories of ritual and sexual abuse that she suffered as a young child have haunted her continually throughout her Christian life. When she came to see me her damaged self-image seemed beyond repair. As she told me her story, Lydia displayed little emotion, but her words reflected total despair.

"Who are you, Lydia? How do you perceive yourself?" I asked with concern.

"I'm evil," she answered stoically. "I'm just no good for anybody. People tell me I'm evil, and all I do is bring trouble."

"You're not evil," I argued. "How can a child of God be evil? Is that how you perceive yourself?" Lydia nodded.

It is never pleasant to see the evil one express his ugly personality through a victim like Lydia. But realizing that she is primarily the product of the work of Christ on the cross instead of the victim of her past, she was able to throw off the chains of spiritual bondage and begin living according to her true identity as a child of God.

Nothing is more foundational to your freedom from Satan's bondage than understanding and affirming what God has done for you in Christ and who you are as a result. We all live in accordance with our perceived identity. In fact, we cannot consistently behave in a way that is inconsistent with how we perceive ourselves. Your attitudes, actions, responses, and reactions to life's circumstances are often determined by your conscious and subconscious self-perception. If you see yourself as the helpless victim of Satan and his schemes, you will live like his victim and be in bondage to his lies. But if you see yourself as the dearly loved and accepted child of God that you really are, you will more likely live like a child of God.

Thank You, Jesus, that You have made me more than a conqueror. Because of Your love and power, I can live as a victor instead of a victim today.

The Essence of Temptation

For we do not have a high priest who cannot sympathize with our weaknesses, but one who has been tempted in all things as we are, yet without sin (Hebrews 4:15).

I have found that many Christians struggle with the distinction between temptation and sin. Bombarded by tempting thoughts, they conclude that there must be something pretty sick about them. But even Jesus was "tempted in all things as we are." But finish the verse: "Yet without sin." As long as we are in the world we are exposed to temptation just like Jesus was. But He didn't sin, and we don't have to sin either (1 Corinthians 10:13).

The basis for temptation is legitimate human needs. We will either look to the world, the flesh, and the devil to have our needs met, or we will look to Christ who promises to meet our needs (Philippians 4:19). The essence of temptation is the invitation to live independently of God.

The power of temptation depends on the strength of the strongholds which have been developed in our minds as we learned to live independently of God. If you were raised in a Christian home where magazines and television programs of questionable moral value were not allowed, the power of sexual temptation in your life will not be as great as for someone who grew up exposed to pornographic materials. Why? Because your legitimate need to be loved and accepted was met by parents who also protected you from exposure to illegitimate means of meeting your needs. The person who grew up in an environment of immorality may experience a greater struggle with sexual temptation simply because that stronghold in the mind was well-established before he was born again.

Jesus was tempted to meet His own physical needs by using His divine attributes independently of the Father to turn a rock into bread. But instead He responded, "Man shall not live on bread alone, but on every word that proceeds out of the mouth of God" (Matthew 4:4). We also must respond to temptation by relying on God to meet our needs.

Dear Jesus, help me not to listen to the voice of the tempter today but to run to You as the source for meeting all my needs.

All things are lawful for me, but not all things are profitable. All things are lawful for me, but I will not be mastered by anything (1 Corinthians 6:12).

Most of us won't often be tempted to commit obvious sins such as armed robbery, murder, or rape. Satan's tack is to entice us to push something good beyond the boundary of the will of God until it becomes sin. He treats us like the proverbial frog in the pot of water: gradually turning up the heat of temptation, hoping we don't notice that we are approaching the boundary of God's will and jump out before something good becomes sin.

Everything is good and lawful for us because we are free from sin and no longer under the condemnation of the law. But the following statements reveal how we can wrongly take good things beyond the boundary of God's will:

- physical rest becomes laziness
- ability to profit becomes avarice and greed
- enjoyment of life becomes intemperance
- physical pleasure becomes sensuality
- interest in the possessions of others becomes covetousness
- enjoyment of food becomes gluttony
- self-care becomes selfishness
- self-respect becomes conceit
- communication becomes gossip
- cautiousness becomes unbelief
- anger becomes rage and bad temper
- lovingkindness becomes overprotection
- judgment becomes criticism
- same-sex friendship becomes homosexuality
- sexual freedom becomes immorality
- conscientiousness becomes perfectionism
- generosity becomes wastefulness
- self-protection becomes dishonesty
- carefulness becomes fear

Lord, I seek Your balance in my life today to do what is profitable without being mastered by anything, even good things.

New wine must be put into fresh wineskins (Luke 5:38).

Jesus taught that the forms of our Christian practice must change. In His parable of the garment and the wineskin in Luke 5:36-39, the garment and the wineskin are the external dress and the container, not the substance of our faith. They represent the religious customs, practices, and traditions which the substance of our faith is packaged in. Jesus is stating a fact—the garment needs mending and the old wineskin is old! What worked before isn't working anymore. Times change, cultures change, and what worked 20 years ago may not work today. But what doesn't change is the object of our faith.

"Time-honored faith" and "long-established practice" blend together and become indistinguishable to the status quo. When someone advocates another form of practice, it becomes apparent that the security of the old wineskins rests in the long-established practice instead of the time-honored faith.

The reasoning behind the resistance is logical: "I came to Christ singing that song," or "It worked for me. I don't see why it won't work for my children." We have to ask, "Is it relevant? Does it relate?"

The older generation is the stable force in our churches. They are faithful and mature, and they represent the financial stability that every church needs. They also make up the boards and committees that determine the style of ministry, but they have a tendency to perpetuate long-established practices that are meaningful to them.

This problem is more sociological than spiritual. Why is it that a good, Bible-believing church which faithfully carries out its ministry struggles to hold onto its young people, when down the street a contemporary ministry rents a store building and has four times more young people in a matter of months? Because the contemporary ministry relates to the young and their style of music. It caters to their desire for expression and participation.

If we fail to provide new wineskins, we will be ill-equipped to serve the "new wine"—the next generation of believers.

Lord, help me never to cling to the old ways just because they make me feel comfortable.

February 9 LIMITING ANXIOUS FEELINGS

Cast all your anxiety on [God] because he cares for you (1 Peter 5:7 NIV).

Let's assume you have sought God's will for a certain direction, and you believe that He has led you to make specific plans. The problem is, you are still worried about whether your plans will come about as you have hoped. When I'm facing such situations, I try to follow the six steps described below to limit my anxious feelings.

First, *state the problem*. A problem well stated is half solved. In anxious states of mind, people can't see the forest for the trees. Put the problem in perspective. Will it matter for eternity? The danger at this juncture is to seek ungodly counsel. The world is glutted with magicians and sorcerers who will promise incredible results. Their appearance may be striking. Their personality may be charming. But they are bankrupt of character. Avoid them (Psalm 1:1).

Second, *separate the facts from the assumptions*. Since we don't know what's going to happen tomorrow, we make assumptions, and we usually assume the worst. If the assumption is accepted as truth, it will drive your mind to its anxiety limits. Therefore you must separate assumptions from facts.

Third, *determine what you have the right or ability to control*. You are responsible for that which you can control, and you are not responsible for that which you can't. Don't try to cast your responsibility onto Christ; He will throw it back.

Fourth, *list everything you can do which is related to the situation that is under your responsibility*. When people don't assume their responsibility, they turn to temporary cures for their anxiety, like eating, TV, sex, or drugs.

Fifth, *once you are sure you have fulfilled your responsibility, see if there is any way you can help others*. Turning your attention away from your own self-absorption and onto helping people around you is not only the loving thing to do, but it also brings a special inner peace.

Sixth, *the rest is God's responsibility*, except for your prayer, according to Philippians 4:6-8. So assume your responsibility, but cast your anxiety on Christ.

Lord, help me recognize the difference between today's responsibilities and anxieties, then put them in their proper places.

If we ask anything according to His will, He hears us. And if we know that He hears us in whatever we ask, we know that we have the requests which we have asked from Him (1 John 5:14,15).

There are several specific needs which we should consider as targets for prayer in spiritual warfare. One need relates to the condition of blindness which Satan has inflicted on unbelievers (2 Corinthians 4:3,4). People cannot come to Christ unless their spiritual eyes are opened. Theodore Epp wrote, "If Satan has blinded and bound men and women, how can we ever see souls saved? This is where you and I enter the picture. Spoiling the goods of the strong man has to do with liberating those whom Satan has blinded and is keeping bound....This is where prayer comes in."[1]

Prayer is a primary weapon in combating spiritual blindness. The apostle John wrote: "If we ask anything according to His will, He hears us. And if we know that He hears us in whatever we ask, we know that we have the requests which we have asked from Him" (1 John 5:14,15). Then he immediately challenged believers to apply this principle by asking God to bring life to unbelievers (verse 16). Our evangelistic strategy must include authoritative prayer that God's light would penetrate satanic blindness.

We also need to pray, as Paul did in Ephesians 1:18,19, that the eyes of believers may be enlightened to understand the spiritual power, authority, and protection which is our inheritance in Christ. As long as Satan can keep us in the dark about our position and authority in Christ, he can keep us stunted in our growth and ineffectual in our witness and ministry. We need to pray for each other continually that Satan's smoke screen of lies will be blown away and that our vision into the spiritual realm will be crystal-clear.

Lord, remind me frequently to pray against the deception which the enemy uses to block my vision of Your will for my life.

Overpowering the Captors

How can anyone enter the strong man's house and carry off his property, unless he first binds the strong man? (Matthew 12:29).

A prime target for our authoritative prayer is the "strong man" mentioned in Matthew 12:29. Jesus was saying that you cannot rescue people from the bonds of spiritual blindness or demonic influence unless you first overpower their captors. Satan's power is already broken, but he will not let go of anything he thinks he can keep until we exercise the authority delegated to us by the Lord Jesus Christ.

When we pray we are not trying to persuade God to join us in *our* service for Him; prayer is the activity of joining God in *His* ministry. By faith we lay hold of the property in Satan's clutches which rightfully belongs to God, and we hold on until Satan turns loose. He will hold on to these people until we demand their release on the basis of our authority in Christ. Once Satan is bound through prayer, he must let go.

Understanding the spiritual nature of our world should have a profound effect on our evangelistic strategy. All too often we proclaim the virtues of Christianity to unbelievers like someone standing outside a prison compound proclaiming to the inmates the virtues of the outside world. But unless someone overpowers the prison guards and opens the gates, how can the prisoners experience the freedom we're telling them about? We must learn to bind the strong man before we will be able to rescue his prisoners.

In the name and authority of the Lord Jesus Christ, I command Satan to release those loved ones in my family who are blinded to the truth and whose thoughts are raised up against the knowledge of God and to return them from enemy territory.

February 12 THE ULTIMATE FAITH-OBJECT

Jesus Christ is the same yesterday and today, yes and forever (Hebrews 13:8).

The fact that you claim to believe is not the issue of faith. It's *what* you believe or *who* you believe in that will determine whether or not your faith will be rewarded. Everybody walks by faith every day. Every time you drive on the highway you do so by faith. Are the objects of your faith on the highway reliable? Most of the time they are because most drivers drive safely. But you may have been involved in an accident because you placed your faith in another driver who proved to be untrustworthy.

What happens when the object of your faith fails you? You give up on it—maybe not immediately, but how many failures would you tolerate before saying never again? Once faith is damaged or lost, it is very difficult to regain. Your belief isn't the problem; it's the object of your belief that either rewards or destroys your faith. If your marriage partner has been unfaithful to you, or a friend or relative has hurt you badly, your faith in that person is weak because he or she did not live up to your trust. When faith in a person is shattered, it may take months to rebuild it.

Some faith-objects, however, are solid. You set your watch, plan your calendar, and schedule your day believing that the earth will continue to revolve on its axis and rotate around the sun at its current speed. If the earth's orbit shifted just a few degrees our lives would be turned to chaos. But so far the laws governing the physical universe have been among the most trustworthy faith-objects we have.

The ultimate faith-object, of course, is not the sun, but the Son. It is His immutability—the fact that He never changes—that makes Him eminently trustworthy (Numbers 23:19; Malachi 3:6). He has never failed to be and do all that He said He would be and do. He is eternally faithful.

All I have needed Your hand has provided. Great is Your faithfulness, Lord, unto me.

YOUR JOURNEY TOWARD CHRIST

The thief comes only to steal, and kill, and destroy (John 10:10).

How do evil spirits interfere with our lives? Let me answer with a simple illustration. Imagine that you are standing at one end of a long, narrow street lined on both sides with two-story row houses. At the other end of the street stands Jesus Christ, and your Christian life is the process of walking down that long street of maturity toward Him. There is absolutely nothing in the street which can keep you from reaching Jesus. So, when you receive Christ, you fix your eyes on Him and start walking.

But since this world is still under the dominion of Satan, the row houses on either side of you are inhabited by beings who are committed to keeping you from reaching your goal. They have no power or authority to block your path or even slow your step, so they hang out of the windows and call to you, hoping to turn your attention away from your goal and disrupt your progress by tempting you, accusing you, and deceiving you.

What is the enemy's goal in having his demons jeer you, taunt you, lure you, and question you from the windows and doorways along your path? He wants you to slow down, stop, sit down, and if possible, give up your journey toward Christ. He wants to influence you to doubt your ability to believe and serve God. Remember: He has absolutely no power or authority to keep you from steadily progressing in your walk toward Christ. And he can never again own you, because you have been redeemed by Jesus Christ and you are forever in Him (1 Peter 1:18,19). But if he can get you to listen to the thoughts he plants in your mind, he can influence you. And if you allow him to influence you long enough through temptation, accusation, and deception, he can control you.

If I could influence you to believe a lie, could I control your life? Yes. Let's fix our eyes on Jesus, "the author and perfecter of faith" (Hebrews 12:2) and take "every thought captive to the obedience of Christ" (2 Corinthians 10:5).

Lord, I know this world is a crazy, unsafe place, full of obstacles and impediments. I trust You today to protect me from the enemy, to light my path, and to watch over me with Your sure presence.

An Everlasting Love

I have loved you with an everlasting love; therefore I have drawn you with lovingkindness (Jeremiah 31:3).

One night I came home from work and my wife Joanne met me at the door. "You better go talk to Karl," she said solemnly. "I think Karl threw his hamster, Johnny, this afternoon."

I went to Karl and asked him point-blank, "Did you throw Johnny this afternoon?" He denied it firmly. Unfortunately for poor Karl, there was an eyewitness that afternoon. Again I confronted Karl, this time with one of those oversized plastic whiffle bats which make a lot of noise on a child's behind without inflicting too much damage. "Karl, tell me the truth. Did you throw Johnny?"

"No." *Whack!* No matter how much I threatened, Karl wouldn't confess. I was frustrated. Finally I gave up.

A couple of days later Joanne met me at the door again. "You better go talk to Karl. Johnny died."

I found Karl in the backyard mourning over his little hamster. Karl and I talked about death and dying, then we buried Johnny. "Karl, I think you need to pray now," I said.

"No, Dad. You pray."

"Karl, Johnny was your hamster. I think you need to pray."

Finally he agreed. This was his prayer: "Dear Jesus, help me not to throw my new hamster." What I couldn't coax out of him with a plastic bat, God worked out in his heart.

Why did Karl lie to me? He thought if he admitted to throwing his pet, I wouldn't love him. He was willing to lie in order to hold onto my love and respect, which he feared he would lose if he admitted his misbehavior. I reached down and wrapped my arms around my little son. "Karl, I may not approve of everything you do, but I'm always going to love you."

What I expressed to Karl that day is a small reflection of the love that God has for you. He says to you, "No matter what you do in life, I'm always going to love you. I may not approve of everything you do, but I'm always going to love you."

Thank You, Father God, for Your unconditional love for me. You are such a wonderful parent.

THE ACCUSER OF THE BRETHREN

The accuser of our brethren...who accuses them before our God day and night (Revelation 12:10).

Next to temptation, perhaps the most frequent and insistent attack from Satan to which we are vulnerable is accusation. By faith we have entered into an eternal relationship with the Lord Jesus Christ. As a result, we are dead to sin and alive to God, and we now sit with Christ in the heavenlies. In Christ we *are* important, we *are* qualified, we *are* justified. Satan can do absolutely nothing to alter our position in Christ and our worth to God. But he can render us virtually inoperative if he can deceive us into listening to and believing his insidious lies accusing us of being of little value to God or other people.

Satan often uses temptation and accusation as a brutal one-two punch. He comes along and says, "Why don't you try it? Everybody does it. Besides, you can get away with it. Who's going to know?" Then as soon as we fall for his tempting line, he changes his tune to accusation: "What kind of a Christian are you to do such a thing? You're a pitiful excuse for a child of God. You'll never get away with it. You might as well give up because God has already given up on you."

We have all heard Satan's lying, hateful voice in our hearts and consciences. He never seems to let up on us. Many Christians are perpetually discouraged and defeated because they believe his persistent lies about them. And those who give in to his accusations end up being robbed of the freedom that God intends His people to enjoy.

The good news is that we don't have to listen to Satan's accusations and live in despair and defeat. Satan is not your judge; he is merely your *accuser*. When Satan's accusations of unworthiness attack you, don't pay attention to them. Instead respond, "I have put my trust in Christ, and I am a child of God in Him. I have been rescued by God from the fire of judgment, and He has declared me righteous. Satan cannot determine a verdict or pronounce a sentence. All he can do is accuse me—and I don't buy it."

Lord God, when Satan accuses me and reminds me of my past, help me resist him and remind him of his future.

If you then, being evil, know how to give good gifts to your children, how much more shall your Father who is in heaven give what is good to those who ask Him! (Matthew 7:11).

Most people in spiritual conflict have a distorted concept of God. Mentally they may have embraced correct theology, but emotionally they feel something different. True concepts of God are filtered through a grid of negative experiences to produce false concepts of God. These false concepts must be replaced by truth in order for freedom to be realized.

A pastor's wife who came to me for counseling told me about her rigidly moral home which was dominated by her demanding mother. The father was a wimp who knew better than to interrupt the mother's tirades against their daughter.

"You really love Jesus, don't you?" I asked the pastor's wife.

"Oh, yes," she responded.

"And you really love the Holy Spirit?"

"Yes, I do."

"But you don't even like God the Father, do you?"

She could only respond with tears. Her concept of the heavenly Father was distorted by the image of her earthly father. She perceived Jesus and the Holy Spirit as actively involved with her, but in her mind God the Father, like her earthly father, just sat around passive and uncaring while she went through torture in her life.

I often ask, "If you performed better, would God love you more?" Most people know the right answer: no. But when I ask if they feel loved by God, most express that they show more love and concern for their own children than they expect God to show for them (see Luke 11:9-13). This is all part of Satan's strategy to raise up thoughts against the knowledge of God (2 Corinthians 10:5). If the enemy can keep people from a true concept of God, he can destroy their hope in God.

Dear Father, I don't want any distorted concepts of You to come between us. Correct me where my concepts are wrong so I can know You in complete truth.

I am not practicing what I would like to do, but I am doing the very thing I hate (Romans 7:15).

Perhaps the most vivid description of the contest with sin which goes on in the life of the believer is found in Romans 7:15-25. In verses 15 and 16, Paul describes the problem: "For that which I am doing, I do not understand; for I am not practicing what I would like to do, but I am doing the very thing I hate. But if I do the very thing I do not wish to do, I agree with the Law, confessing that it is good."

Notice that there is only one player in these two verses—the "I," mentioned nine times. Notice also that this person has a good heart; he agrees with the law of God. But this good-hearted Christian has a behavior problem. He knows what he should be doing but, for some reason, he can't do it. He agrees with God but ends up doing the very things he hates.

Verses 17-21 uncover the reason for this behavior problem: "So now, no longer am I the one doing it, but sin which indwells me....If I am doing the very thing I do not wish, I am no longer the one doing it, but sin which dwells in me." How many players are involved now? Two: sin and me. But sin is clearly not me; it's only dwelling in me. Sin is preventing me from doing what I want to do.

Do these verses say that I am no good, that I am evil, or that I am sin? Absolutely not. They say that I have something dwelling in me which is no good, evil, and sinful, but it's not me. If I have a sliver in my finger, I could say that I have something in me which is no good. But it's not me who's no good. I'm not the sliver. The sliver which is stuck in my finger is no good. I am not sin and I am not a sinner. I am a saint struggling with sin which causes me to do what I don't want to do.

Romans 6:12 informs us that it is our responsibility not to allow sin to reign in our lives. Sin *will* reign if we use our bodies as instruments of unrighteousness (Romans 6:13). We must renounce every such use and submit our bodies to God as instruments of righteousness.

Thank You, Lord, that I don't have to sin. You made it possible for me to control sin's power over me. You delivered me from the wages of sin and blessed me with the gift of eternal life in Christ.

Thanks be to God through Jesus Christ our Lord!...There is therefore now no condemnation for those who are in Christ Jesus (Romans 7:25; 8:1).

Romans 7:22,23 pinpoints the battleground for the contest between me and sin: "For I joyfully concur with the law of God in the inner man, but I see a different law in the members of my body, waging war against the law of my mind, and making me a prisoner of the law of sin which is in my members."

Where does my desire to do what's right reside? Paul uses the phrase "the inner man," referring to my new self where my spirit and God's Spirit are in union. This is the eternal part of me. And where does sin wage its war to keep me from doing what I really want to do? In the physical members of my body (James 4:1). Sin operates through my flesh, that learned independence that continues to promote rebellion against God. This is the temporal part of me. Where then do these two opponents wage war (Galatians 5:17)? The battleground is my mind. That's why it is so important that we learn how to renew our minds (Romans 12:2) and to take every thought captive to the obedience of Christ (2 Corinthians 10:5).

Paul concluded his description of the contest between sin and the new self with the exclamation: "Wretched man that I am! Who will set me free from the body of this death?" (Romans 7:24). Notice that he didn't say, "Sinful man that I am!" *Wretched* means miserable, and there is no one more miserable than the person who has allowed sin to reign in his mortal body. If we use our bodies as instruments of unrighteousness, we give the devil an opportunity in our lives, and he brings only misery.

The good news is that Romans 7:24 is followed by Romans 7:25 and Romans 8:1: "Thanks be to God through Jesus Christ our Lord!...There is therefore now no condemnation for those who are in Christ Jesus." The battle for the mind is a winnable war.

Thank You, Jesus, for knowing me, understanding me, and providing for me a way of escape for every possible temptation.

Keeping an Honest Account

If we say that we have no sin, we are deceiving ourselves, and the truth is not in us (1 John 1:8).

We deceive ourselves when we say we have no sin. The Scripture doesn't say that we *are* sin; it says that it is possible for us to sin and for sin to reside in our mortal bodies (Romans 6:12). We are not sinless saints; we are saints who sin. It's important to keep honest account of our failures and pick up our cross daily. When we become aware of a discrepancy between our identity and our behavior, we must confess it and deal with it. The person who deceives himself by ignoring these sinful discrepancies and allowing them to build up is headed for a great fall.

Those of us who live in earthquake-prone Southern California keep hearing about "the big one," which is thought by many to be inevitable along the San Andreas fault. Whenever we experience minor earthquakes (up to about 4.0 on the Richter scale), we may be frightened by them a bit, but we also see them as a good sign. These little tremors mean that the plates in the earth's crust beneath us are shifting. As long as the crust is adjusting this way it's unlikely that "the big one" will hit. It's when we don't get any minor earthquakes for several months or years that the danger of a major, devastating quake increases.

Similarly, living in the light, holding ourselves accountable to God, and confessing and dealing with sin on a daily basis prevents the major spiritual crises from building up in our lives. If we keep saying, "I don't have any sin," or if we fail to acknowledge our shortcomings and settle our differences with people as God convicts us of them, we're in for "the big one." We will eventually lose our health, our family, our job, or our friendships. Unacknowledged sin is like a cancer which will grow to consume us.

Lord, I know Your guidance is for my benefit. I refuse to allow stubbornness and pride to render me insensitive to Your nudges and warnings in my life today.

I am with you always, even to the end of the age (Matthew 28:20).

In the early 1980s I counseled a Christian young woman who was languishing in deep spiritual, mental, and emotional torment. She wrote:

Dear God,

Where are You? How can You watch and not help me? I hurt so bad, and You don't even care. If You cared You'd make it stop or let me die. I love You, but You seem so far away. I can't hear You or feel You or see You, but I'm supposed to believe You're here. Lord, I feel them and hear them. They are here. I know You're real, God, but they are more real to me right now. Please make someone believe me, Lord. Why won't You make it stop? Please, Lord, please! If You love me You'll let me die.

A Lost Sheep

Many Christians I deal with are filled with such confusion that their daily walk with Christ is unfulfilling and unproductive. When they try to pray they begin thinking about a million things they should be doing. When they sit down to read the Bible they can't concentrate. When they have an opportunity to serve the Lord in some way they are brought up short by discouraging thoughts of self-doubt.

Having found freedom, "The Lost Sheep" penned a response to her own prayer based on her new understanding of God's provision in Christ.

My Dear Lost Sheep,

You ask Me where I am. My child, I am with you and I always will be. You are weak, but in Me you are strong. I am so close that I feel everything you feel. Be crucified with Me and I will live in you, and you shall live with Me. I will direct you in paths of righteousness. My child, I love you and I will never forsake you, for you are truly Mine.

Love, God

Loving Shepherd, thank You for tending me and feeding me daily, showing me that I am precious to You.

February 21 BE GOD-CENTERED

[Jesus] called the twelve together, and gave them power and authority over all the demons, and to heal diseases. And He sent them out to proclaim the kingdom of God, and to perform healing (Luke 9:1,2).

Notice how Jesus equipped His disciples for ministry. He knew that when they began preaching the kingdom of God and healing the sick, demonic powers would bring opposition. So He specifically gave them power and authority over demons.

Later Jesus sent out 70 of His followers on a similar mission, and they "returned with joy, saying, 'Lord, even the demons are subject to us in Your name'" (Luke 10:17). These missionaries were spiritually in tune enough to know that demons existed and that they were a force to be reckoned with in their ministry. Jesus' followers had been eyewitnesses as the evil spirits opposed the Master, and they probably anticipated the same treatment. Perhaps they even started out on their mission with pangs of fear and doubt about encountering demonic resistance. But they came back astonished at the victory they experienced over evil spirits.

But Jesus quickly brought the issue of spiritual conflicts into perspective: "Do not rejoice in this, that the spirits are subject to you, but rejoice that your names are recorded in heaven" (Luke 10:20). Jesus sent out the 70 to preach the gospel and to heal, but all they could talk about when they came back was how they sent the demons running. "Don't be demon-centered," Jesus replied. "Be kingdom-centered, be ministry-centered, be God-centered."

That's a good warning. As you learn to exercise authority over the kingdom of darkness in your life and in the lives of others, you may be tempted to see yourself as some kind of spiritual freedom fighter, looking for demons behind every door. But it's *truth* which sets you free, not the knowledge of error. You are not called to dispel the darkness; you are called to turn on the light. You would have no authority at all if it weren't for your identity as a child of God and your position in Christ.

Lord, Your light is strong enough to overcome the deepest darkness. Praise You!

February 22 **THE LIGHT TO OUR PATH**

Thy word is a lamp to my feet, and a light to my path (Psalm 119:105).

We live in a world where the flip of a switch instantly lightens or darkens a room. The lamps in biblical times, on the other hand, burned brightly but required proper tending. If not cared for, they would become a dwindling flame. God's Word uses the metaphor of a lamp to teach us about guidance for our lives. And it provides the opportunity for some graphic applications of this teaching.

Earnestly seeking the clear teaching of God's Word allows the lamp to burn brightly and us to stay on the path. When we fail to acknowledge our theological bias and limited perspective, the light lessens and our path becomes twisted. The lamp flickers when form replaces function and traditions push aside the commandments of God. The light dims when we stay away from God's Word and the fellowship of believers. It goes out when we serve another master.

Sometimes we overlook the obvious: God's will is expressed by His Word. As a child, I didn't struggle with knowing my earthly father's will. He clearly expressed it to me. I learned early on that we lived together peacefully if I was quick to obey. Being a farm boy, it made sense to help my father establish his kingdom (the family farm). Farmers know from nature that we reap what we sow. Not only that, I stood to inherit the family farm along with my brother and sisters as my father had with his sisters. Yet I wonder how many Christians realize that what they are presently sowing in the kingdom of God is what they will reap for all eternity.

God's will is revealed to us in His Word. There is no substitute for being "diligent to present yourself approved to God as a workman who does not need to be ashamed, handling accurately the word of truth" (2 Timothy 2:15). The Bible is a light to your path.

Father, don't let anything enter my life today that would dim Your glorious light. I choose to find my way by the light of Your Word.

RELATIONSHIP, NOT REGIMEN

The law of the Spirit of life in Christ Jesus has set you free from the law of sin and of death (Romans 8:2).

Walking according to the Spirit is more a relationship than a regimen. Think about your marriage as an illustration. You may have started out relying on some rules for effective communication, meeting each other's sexual needs, etc. But if after several years you can't even talk to each other or make love without following an outline or list of steps, your marriage is still in infancy. The goal of a marriage is to develop a relationship which supersedes rules.

Or think about prayer. Perhaps you learned to pray using the simple acrostic ACTS: adoration, confession, thanksgiving, supplication. But if you have been a Christian for a few years and your prayer life is no deeper than an acrostic, you've missed the point of prayer. Prayer is not a formula; it's the language of your relationship with God. Similarly, walking in the Spirit is essentially a relationship with the indwelling Spirit which defies quantification.

Even though Scripture doesn't give us a formula, it does help us see what the Spirit-filled walk *is* and what it *is not*. Helpful parameters are found in Galatians 5:16-18: "Walk by the Spirit, and you will not carry out the desire of the flesh. For the flesh sets its desire against the Spirit, and the Spirit against the flesh; for these are in opposition to one another, so that you may not do the things that you please. But if you are led by the Spirit, you are not under the Law."

So how do you walk by the Spirit? If I answered by giving you a rigid formula, I would be putting you back under the law. The Spirit is not an "it"; the Holy Spirit is a "He"—a person. Walking by the Spirit is a relational issue, not a legal issue or ritualistic exercise. It is a walk with God.

Over the next several days we will examine what the Spirit-walk is and what it is not.

Father, thank You that my life in You is a relationship, not a set of rules.

If you are led by the Spirit, you are not under the Law (Galatians 5:18).

Paul said that walking according to the Spirit is not license: an excessive or undisciplined freedom constituting an abuse of privilege. As a Christian you may see the phrase "You are not under the Law" in Galatians 5:18 and exclaim, "Wow, I'm free! Walking in the Spirit means I can do anything I want!" Not at all. In the previous verse Paul wrote, "You may not do the things that you please." Being led by the Spirit doesn't mean you are free to do anything you want to do. It means you are finally free to live a responsible, moral life—something you were incapable of doing when you were the prisoner of your flesh.

Once I was invited to speak to a religion class at a Catholic high school on the topic of Protestant Christianity. At the end of my talk, an athletic-looking, streetwise student raised his hand and asked, "Do you have a lot of don'ts in your church?"

Sensing that he had a deeper motive, I answered, "What you really want to ask me is if we have any freedom, right?" He nodded.

"Sure, I'm free to do whatever I want to do," I answered. "I'm free to rob a bank. But I'm mature enough to realize that I would be in bondage to that act for the rest of my life. I'd have to cover up my crime, go into hiding, or eventually pay for what I did. I'm also free to tell a lie. But if I do, I have to keep telling it, and I have to remember who I told it to and how I told it or I will get caught. I'm free to do drugs, abuse alcohol, and live a sexually immoral lifestyle. All of those 'freedoms' lead to bondage. I'm free to make those choices, but considering the consequences, would I really be free?"

What appears to be freedom to some people isn't really freedom, but a return to bondage (Galatians 5:1). God's laws, from which we seek to be free, are not restrictive, but protective. Your real freedom is your ability to choose to live responsibly within the context of the protective guidelines God has established for our lives.

Thank You, Lord, for the privilege I have to choose to live in freedom. Help me not to abuse that privilege today and find myself in bondage.

God...made us adequate as servants of a new covenant, not of the letter, but of the Spirit; for the letter kills, but the Spirit gives life (2 Corinthians 3:5,6).

Walking by the Spirit is not legalism, the opposite extreme from license. Paul said: "If you are led by the Spirit, you are not under the Law" (Galatians 5:18). Stringently striving to obey Christian rules and regulations doesn't enable the Spirit-filled walk; it often kills it (2 Corinthians 3:6). We're told in Galatians 3:13 that the law is really a curse, and in Galatians 3:21 that it is impotent, powerless to give life.

Laying down the law—telling someone that it is wrong to do this or that—does not give them the power to stop doing it. Christians have been notorious at trying to legislate spirituality with don'ts: Christians don't drink, don't smoke, don't dance, don't attend movies, don't play cards, don't wear makeup, etc. But legalism can't curb immorality. In fact, laying down the law merely serves to heighten the temptation. Paul said that the law actually stimulates the desire to do what it forbids (Romans 7:5)! When you tell your child not to cross a certain line, where does he immediately want to go? Forbidden fruit often seems to be the most desirable.

Neither will a Spirit-filled heart be produced by demanding that someone conform to a religious code of behavior. We often equate Christian disciplines such as Bible study, prayer, regular church attendance, and witnessing with spiritual maturity. All these activities are good and helpful for spiritual growth. But merely performing these admirable Christian exercises does not guarantee a Spirit-filled walk.

Does this mean that establishing rules is wrong? Of course not. God's law is a necessary protective moral standard and guideline. But the means by which we live a life of freedom is not the law but grace. Within the confines of God's law we are free to nurture a spirit-to-Spirit relationship with God, which is the essence of walking in the Spirit.

Lord, help me encourage other believers to freedom in their walk with You and not impose on them a religious code of behavior.

The Lord is the Spirit; and where the Spirit of the Lord is, there is liberty (2 Corinthians 3:17).

The Spirit-filled walk is neither characterized by license nor legalism, but liberty. Paul stated that we are "servants of a new covenant, not of the letter, but of the Spirit; for the letter kills, but the Spirit gives life....Now the Lord is the Spirit; and where the Spirit of the Lord is, there is liberty" (2 Corinthians 3:6,17).

I believe that our freedom in Christ is one of the most precious commodities we have received from our spiritual union with God. Because the Spirit of the Lord is in you, you are free to choose to live a responsible and moral life. You are no longer compelled to walk according to the flesh as you were before conversion. And now you are not even compelled to walk according to the Spirit. You are free to choose to walk according to the Spirit or to walk according to the flesh.

Walking according to the Spirit implies two things. First, it's not passive. We're talking about *walking* in the Spirit, not *sitting* in the Spirit. One of the most dangerous and harmful detriments to your spiritual growth is passivity—putting your mind in neutral and coasting. The Christian classic *War on the Saints*, by Jessie Penn-Lewis, was written to combat such passive thinking. Sitting back and waiting for God to do everything is not God's way to spiritual maturity.

Second, we're talking about *walking* in the Spirit, not *running* in the Spirit. The Spirit-filled life is not achieved through endless, exhausting activity. We mistakenly think that the harder we work for God, the more spiritual we will become. That's a subtle lie from the enemy. Satan knows that he may not be able to stop you from serving God by making you immoral, but he can probably impede your service by simply making you busy. Our service *for* God can become the greatest detriment of our devotion *to* God.

Lord, I desire to walk according to the Spirit today at Your pace, not sitting passively through inactivity or running myself ragged by becoming too busy.

But go and learn what this means, "I desire compassion, and not sacrifice" (Matthew 9:13).

I used to ask my seminary students two questions:

1. What attributes, strengths, and characteristics would you look for in a person with whom you could share your deepest personal problems?
2. Would you be willing to commit yourself to become that kind of person—someone others could confide in?

The essential prerequisite for a Christian counselor is to become the kind of person with whom others feel confident in sharing the problems of their present and past. Christian counseling doesn't require a college degree, although those who counsel professionally can be greatly helped by receiving Bible-based training. Whether you sit on the platform or in the pew, whether you sit at a desk in a counseling clinic or at a dining room table, God can use you to minister to people with problems if you are compassionate.

You can't really help a person unless you hear his whole story, and you won't hear it unless you are the kind of person he can trust. People don't care how much we know until they know how much we care. Compassion is not a question of learning a professional technique; it's a question of Christian character and love.

Counseling seeks to help people deal with the present by resolving conflicts from the past. Many of these conflicts relate to areas of bondage where Satan-induced strongholds have been erected in the mind. People cannot grow and mature because they are not free. The goal of Christian counseling—whether done by a pastor, a professional counselor, or a friend—is to help people experience freedom in Christ so they can move on to maturity and fruitfulness in their walk with Him.

Lord, increase my compassion so I can be an effective counselor of others. Keep me from jumping to self-righteous conclusions.

As you therefore have received Christ Jesus the Lord, so walk in Him, having been firmly rooted and now being built up in Him and established in your faith (Colossians 2:6,7).

Some Christians believe that walking by faith means being carried along by a mysterious, ethereal, indescribable inner sense called "faith." But the walk of faith is much more practical and definable than that. Walking by faith simply means that you function in daily life on the basis of what you believe. Your belief system determines your behavior. If your behavior is off in a certain area, you need to correct your belief in that area because your misbehavior is the result of your misbelief.

"But how can I know what I really believe?" you may ask. Take a few minutes to complete the following statements as concisely and truthfully as possible.

I would be more successful if…
I would be more significant if…
I would be more fulfilled if…
I would be more satisfied if…
I would be happier if…
I would have more fun if…
I would be more secure if…
I would have more peace if…

Whatever you believe is the answer to these statements constitutes your present belief system.

Assuming that your basic physiological needs (food, shelter, safety, etc.) are met, you will be motivated in life by what you believe will bring you success, significance, fulfillment, satisfaction, happiness, fun, security, and peace. If what you believe about these eight values does not line up with what God says about them, your walk of faith will be off to the same degree that your belief is off.

Father, enable me to grow in my understanding of Your Word today so my faith-walk will be strengthened.

Make my joy complete by being of the same mind, maintaining the same love, united in spirit, intent on one purpose (Philippians 2:2).

Most Christian parents would do the right thing if they were sure what the right thing was. But what does a good parent do? Should you try to control your children? Is loving them the same as controlling them? Is controlling them the same as disciplining them? What kind of parents produce the following?

1. Children who have a good self-image and are happy being who they are.
2. Children who conform to the authority of others and have the capacity to get along with their teachers and other authority figures.
3. Children who follow the religious beliefs of their parents, attend the church of their parents.

The two most powerful influences in parenting are control and support. Parental control is defined as the ability to manage a child's behavior. You can coerce your kids through intimidation, verbally batter them into submission, lay a guilt trip on them, or firmly establish boundaries and provide choices.

Parental support is defined as the ability to make a child feel loved. You need to do more than simply tell your child that you love him in order to help him feel loved. You must be physically and emotionally available in such a way that your child *knows* that you love him. Your love comes across in the way you communicate with and touch your child throughout the day.

The best children come from parents who can manage their behavior and communicate their unconditional love. The worst children come from homes where they are controlled but not loved. You may not be able to manage your child's behavior, but by the grace of God you can love him.

Dear Lord, I need Your wisdom today to help me love my children unconditionally and manage their behavior.

So then as through one transgression there resulted condemnation to all men, even so through one act of righteousness there resulted justification of life to all men (Romans 5:18).

The reason so many Christians are not enjoying the maturity and freedom which is their inheritance in Christ is because they hold wrong self-perceptions. They don't see themselves as they really are in Christ. They don't understand the dramatic change which occurred in them the moment they trusted in Him. They don't see themselves the way God sees them, and to that degree they suffer from a poor self-image. They don't grasp their true identity. They identify themselves with the wrong Adam.

Too many Christians identify only with the first Adam, whose sad story of failure is found in Genesis 1-4. Sure, you inherited physical life from Adam. But if you're a Christian, that's where the similarity ends. You are now identified with the last Adam, Jesus Christ. You are not in Adam; you are in Christ. You are seated with Christ in the heavenlies (Ephesians 2:6). The difference between the two Adams in your history is eternally profound. You need to be sure you're identifying with the right one.

The first thing we notice about Christ, the last Adam, is His complete dependence on God the Father. The first Adam was tempted to live independently of God and chose to believe the serpent's lie about the tree of the knowledge of good and evil. But Jesus was totally dependent on the Father (John 5:30; 6:57; 8:42; 14:10; 17:7).

A second vital difference between the two Adams relates to spiritual life. Adam was born physically and spiritually alive. But when Adam sinned, he died spiritually. Like the first Adam, Jesus was born spiritually alive as well as physically alive. But unlike the first Adam, Jesus did not forfeit His spiritual life at some point through sin. He kept His spiritual life all the way to the cross. There He died, taking the sins of the world upon Himself. Now in His resurrected, glorified body, Christ lives on today and for all eternity.

Are you identifying with Jesus Christ, the last Adam, today?

Thank You, Father, for the last Adam—Jesus Christ—through whom I am saved and sealed. I purpose by Your help to live in my true identity today.

Truly, truly, I say to you, unless one is born again, he cannot see the kingdom of God (John 3:3).

Being in Christ, and all that it means to Christian maturity and freedom, is the overwhelming theme of the New Testament. For example, in the six chapters of the book of Ephesians alone there are 40 references to being in Christ and having Christ in you. For every reference to Christ being in you there are 10 to you being in Christ. Being in Christ is the most critical element of our identity.

But we weren't born in Christ. We were born in sin, thanks to the first Adam. What is God's plan for transforming us from being in Adam to being in Christ? We must be born again (John 3:3). Physical birth only gains us physical life. Spiritual life, the eternal life Christ promises to those who come to Him, is only gained through spiritual birth (John 3:36).

What does it mean to be spiritually alive in Christ? The moment you were born again your soul came into union with God in the same way Adam was in union with God before the Fall. Your spiritual union with God is complete and eternal because it is provided by Christ, the last Adam. As long as Christ remains alive spiritually, you will remain alive spiritually —and that's for eternity.

Contrary to what many Christians believe, eternal life is not something you get when you die. You are spiritually alive in Christ right now. That's how you got to be in union with God, by being born again spiritually. You'll never be more spiritually alive than you are right now. The only thing that will change when you die physically is that you will exchange your old earthbound body for a new one. But your spiritual life in Christ, which began when you personally trusted Him, will merely continue on.

Salvation is not a future addition; it's a present transformation. And that transformation occurs at spiritual birth, not physical death. God's Word promises, "He who has the Son has the life; he who does not have the Son of God does not have the life" (1 John 5:12). Eternal life is something you possess right now because you're in Christ. Believe it. Rejoice in it.

Thank You, Lord, that my eternal salvation is a present-day reality. I rejoice in this wonderful security and assurance.

THE TRUE CHAIN OF COMMAND

Lord, even the demons are subject to us in Your name (Luke 10:17).

It was an eye-opening experience for the disciples to discover that the demons were subject to them in Jesus' name. *Subject* (*hupotasso*) is a military term meaning "to arrange under." It pictures a group of soldiers snapping to attention and following precisely the orders of their commanding officer.

Perhaps the disciples suffered under the same misconception which blinds many Christians today. We see God and His kingdom on one side and Satan and his kingdom on the other side. Both kingdoms seem to be very powerful, and here we are, stuck in the middle between the two, like the rope in a tug of war. On some days God seems to be winning, and on other days the devil appears to have the upper hand. And we don't seem to have anything to say about who wins the battle.

But the disciples came back from their mission with a new perspective, a true perspective. Spiritual authority is not a tug-of-war on a horizontal plane; it is a vertical chain of command. Jesus Christ has all authority in heaven and on earth (Matthew 28:18); He's at the top. He has given His authority and power to His servants to be exercised in His name (Luke 10:17); we're underneath Him. And Satan and his demons? They're at the bottom, subject to the authority Christ has invested in us.

Why, then, does the kingdom of darkness exert such negative influence in the world and in the lives of Christians? In a word, the lie. Satan is not an equal power with God; he is a vanquished foe. But if he can deceive you into believing that he has more power and authority than you do, you will live as if he does! You have been given authority over the kingdom of darkness, but if you don't believe it and exercise it, it's as if you didn't have it.

Authority is the right to rule based on position. You have the authority to do the will of God because of your position in Christ. It's an authority you could never have independent of God, so you need to remain dependent on Him to live victoriously.

I praise You, Lord, for the inexhaustible supply of power to defeat the enemy that You have provided me in Your Son, Jesus Christ.

Spiritual and Unspiritual Leaders

The Lord knows how...to keep the unrighteous under punishment for the day of judgment, and especially those who indulge the flesh in its corrupt desires and despise authority (2 Peter 2:9,10).

The apostle Peter reveals two ways by which we can identify false prophets and false teachers who operate within the church. First, they will be involved in immorality of some kind, indulging "the flesh in its corrupt desires." They may be discovered in illicit activities involving sex and/or money. They may be antinomian, claiming that God is all love and grace so we don't need to abide by any law. Their immorality may not be easy to spot, but it will eventually surface in their lives (2 Corinthians 11:15).

Second, false prophets and teachers "despise authority" and are "daring, self-willed." These people have an independent spirit. They do their own thing and won't answer to anybody. They either won't submit to the authority of a denomination or board, or they will pick their own board which will simply rubber-stamp anything they want to do.

There are historic leadership roles in Scripture: prophet (preaching and teaching), priest (pastoring and shepherding), and king (administration). Only Jesus in His perfection is capable of occupying all three roles simultaneously. I believe we need the checks and balances of a plurality of elders in the church, distributing the three critical roles to more than one person. No one can survive his own unchallenged authority. Every true, committed Christian in a leadership role needs to submit himself and his ideas to other mature believers who will hold him accountable.

We need spiritual leaders like those described by Peter: "Shepherd the flock of God among you, not under compulsion, but voluntarily, according to the will of God; and not for sordid gain, but with eagerness; nor yet as lording it over those allotted to your charge, but proving to be examples to the flock" (1 Peter 5:2,3). Are you praying for your spiritual leaders to be conformed to God's standard of leadership or yours?

Great Shepherd, protect me from irresponsible spiritual leaders, mere "hired hands" who run away in times of crisis instead of shepherds. Give my pastor a true shepherd's heart.

YIELDING CONTROL

For we are not ignorant of [Satan's] schemes
(2 Corinthians 2:11).

We generally agree that Christians are vulnerable to the enemy's temptation, accusation, and deception. But for some reason we hesitate to admit that Christians can lose their freedom and can surrender to demonic influences. However, the evidence of Scripture is abundant and clear that believers who repeatedly succumb to Satan can come under bondage.

Demonic *control* does not mean satanic *ownership*. You have been purchased by the blood of the Lamb, and not even the powers of hell can take your salvation away from you (1 Peter 1:17-19; Romans 8:35-39). Satan knows he can never own you again. But if he can deceive you into yielding control of your life to him in some way, he can neutralize your growth and your impact in the world for Christ.

Since we live in a world whose god is Satan, the possibility of being tempted, deceived, and accused is continuous. If you allow his schemes to influence you, you can lose control to the degree that you have been deceived. If he can persuade you to believe a lie, he can control your life.

The term *demon possessed* never occurs in the Bible after the cross. We lack theological precision as to what demon possession constitutes in the church age. But don't come to any conclusion that you can't be affected by Satan. We are more a target than we are immune to his strategies. However, we have all the sanctuary we need in Christ, and we have the armor of God to protect us.

Thank You, Lord, for the armor You have provided to protect me from Satan. Keep me aware of his schemes today and help me resist him in the power and authority You provide.

Grace and peace be multiplied to you in the knowledge of God and of Jesus our Lord; seeing that His divine power has granted to us everything pertaining to life and godliness, through the true knowledge of Him who called us by His own glory and excellence (2 Peter 1:2,3).

"If our identity in Christ is the key to wholeness," you may ask, "why do so many believers have difficulty with self-worth, spiritual growth, and maturity?" Because we have been deceived by the devil. Our true identity in Christ has been distorted by the great deceiver himself.

This deception was brought home to me a few years ago when I was counseling a Christian girl who was the victim of satanic oppression. I asked her, "Who are you?"

"I'm evil," she answered.

"You're not evil. How can a child of God be evil? Is that how you see yourself?" She nodded.

Now she may have done some evil things, but she wasn't evil. She was basing her identity on the wrong equation. She was letting Satan's accusations of her behavior influence her perception of identity instead of letting her identity—as a child of God in Christ—influence her behavior.

Sadly, a great number of Christians are trapped in the same pit. We fail, so we see ourselves as failures, which only causes us to fail more. We sin, so we see ourselves as sinners, which only causes us to sin more. We've been sucked into the devil's futile equation. We've been tricked into believing that what we do makes us what we are. And that false belief sends us into a tailspin of hopelessness and defeat.

Don't be deceived. You are not a product of what you do or don't do. You are a product of who you are in Christ and His work on the cross. You are not saved by how you behave but by how you believe. God's Word assures us, "Beloved, now we are children of God.... And everyone who has this hope fixed on Him purifies himself, just as He is pure" (1 John 3:2,3).

Dear Lord, I pray that my mind will be renewed by Your Word today so I may overcome the old, fleshly programming I have believed and lived by.

FREE OF SATAN'S BONDAGE

God is light, and in Him there is no darkness at all (1 John 1:5).

Nobody loses control to Satan overnight; it's a gradual process of deception and yielding to his subtle influence. It is my observation that no more than 15 percent of the evangelical Christian community is completely free of Satan's bondage. These people consistently live a Spirit-filled life and bear fruit. The other 85 percent are struggling along fruitlessly at one of at least three levels of spiritual conflict.

First, a believer may lead a fairly normal Christian life on the outside while wrestling with a steady barrage of sinful thoughts on the inside: lust, envy, greed, hatred, apathy, etc. These people have virtually no devotional life. Prayer is a frustrating experience for them, and they usually struggle with interpersonal relationships and a problem-filled thought life. Most Christians in this condition have no idea that they are in the middle of a spiritual conflict. Approximately 65 percent of all Christians live at this level of spiritual conflict.

The second level of conflict is characterized by those who are plagued by condemning evil thoughts and strange "voices" which seem to overpower them. They wonder if they are mentally ill. Yet the majority of Christians at this stage still fail to see their struggle as a spiritual conflict. Approximately 15 percent of all Christians fall into this category. Most of these people are depressed, anxious, paranoid, bitter, or angry, and they may have fallen victim to drinking, drugs, eating disorders, etc.

At the third level of conflict, the individual has lost control and hears voices inside his mind which tell him what to think, say, and do. These people stay at home, wander the streets talking to imaginary people, or occupy beds in mental institutions or rehab units. Sadly, about 5 percent of the Christian community falls victim to this level of deception and control.

I don't say these things to frighten you but to encourage you to walk daily in the light. As you walk in the light you need not fear the darkness at any level. Every child of God can and should be free in Christ.

Dear Lord, I choose to walk in the light today and set aside the sinful thoughts and deeds that so easily entangle me.

For this is the will of God, your sanctification (1 Thessalonians 4:3).

In a personal sense, God's will for our lives is that we conform to the image of God, something the apostle Paul makes clear in 1 Thessalonians 4:3: "For this is the will of God, your sanctification." In his letter to Roman Christians, Paul writes, "For whom He foreknew, He also predestined to become conformed to the image of His Son" (Romans 8:29) and adds in 1 Timothy 1:5, "The goal of our instruction is love from a pure heart and a good conscience and a sincere faith." Divine guidance will never come to those whose primary goal is not first and foremost conforming to the image of God.

There is no instruction in the Bible concerning career choice, where we live, or who we should marry. There is, however, an abundance of instruction on how we're to relate to our employer and behave on the job we already have (Colossians 3:22-25). And there is much about how to relate with one another (Colossians 3:10-14) and live with our families (Colossians 3:18-21).

The Bible overwhelmingly instructs that to do God's will means living in harmony with God and man: " 'You shall love the LORD your God with all your heart, and with all your soul, and with all your mind.' This is the great and foremost commandment. And a second is like it, 'You shall love your neighbor as yourself.' On these two commandments depend the whole Law and the Prophets" (Matthew 22:37-40).

The whole purpose of the Bible is to teach us how to have a relationship with God and live in harmony with one another. We do this by assuming our responsibilities for today and trusting God for tomorrow.

I'm not sure the Lord cares primarily whether you are a carpenter, teacher, or doctor. But He does care what kind of carpenter, teacher, or doctor you are. Determine to be the person He has called you to be. No one can prevent you from being God's person except you.

Lord, I want to be Your person today, to live in harmony with You and with those around me.

Accept one another, just as Christ also accepted us to the glory of God (Romans 15:7).

There are four concepts we deal with as parents in communicating with our children: authority, accountability, affirmation, and acceptance. We usually line them up this way:

- We exert our parental authority over them.
- We demand that they be accountable to us.
- When they respond to our authority and comply by being accountable, we affirm them.
- When they put together a positive track record of affirmative behaviors, we convey our love and acceptance.

The reason we have such difficulty communicating with our children is that we have it all backward. Look at God's approach to us as His children. At which end of the list does our heavenly Father start? He starts by expressing His love and acceptance (John 3:16; Romans 5:8). Our children won't care how much we know until they know how much we care. Paul instructs us to "accept one another, just as Christ also accepted us to the glory of God" (Romans 15:7).

When your child shares something personal with you, what is he looking for initially? Not a lecture, not a list of rules he must obey, but acceptance and affirmation. "Tell me I'm all right," he begs. "Give me some love and hope."

When you know that you are unconditionally loved and accepted by God and affirmed in your identity as His child, you voluntarily submit to His authority and hold yourself accountable to Him. Similarly, when your child knows that you love him and accept him regardless of his failures, he will feel safe sharing his problems with you and responding to the direction you give. Children who know they are loved are free to be themselves, free to grow, and free to be the people God wants them to be.

Lord, I know I can't be a perfect parent, but help me trust You day by day to be the affirming, accepting parent You want me to be.

The wind blows where it wishes and you hear the sound of it, but do not know where it comes from and where it is going; so is everyone who is born of the Spirit (John 3:8).

What does it take to be the selfless, loving Christian we desire to be? What is needed to move us beyond our inconsequential selfish, fleshly pursuits to deeds of loving service to God and others?

First, it requires a firm grasp on your identity in Christ. You can't love like Jesus loved until you accept the reality that, since you are in Christ, His divine nature is united with your spirit.

Second, you must begin to crucify daily the old sin-trained flesh and walk in accordance with who you are: a child of God whose spirit is filled with God's Spirit.

The fact that the Holy Spirit resides in us and that we can live according to His leading is an awesome but elusive concept to many. The problem is not new. Nicodemus was a learned man, but he couldn't comprehend life in the Spirit. So Jesus told him, "The wind blows where it wishes and you hear the sound of it, but do not know where it comes from and where it is going; so is everyone who is born of the Spirit" (John 3:8). Trying to reduce life in the Spirit to a formula is like trying to capture the wind.

Someone reflecting on the mysteries of walking by the Spirit said, "I think we need to pull in the oars and put up the sail!" I like that. When we walk by the Spirit, we stop striving. We are no longer driven; we are led. "For all who are being led by the Spirit of God, these are sons of God" (Romans 8:14). When we come to the end of our resources, we discover His.

Father, help me to quickly set aside human resources today so I may walk in the strength and adequacy of Your Spirit.

PLAN A VS. PLAN B

Trust in the LORD with all your heart, and do not lean on your own understanding. In all your ways acknowledge Him, and He will make your paths straight (Proverbs 3:5,6).

Untold numbers of Christians are spiritually unaware and defeated in their daily lives. They don't realize that there is a battle going on for their minds. When struggling believers perceive the nature of the conflict and realize that they can be transformed by the renewing of their minds, they will experience freedom.

Faith is God's way to live and reason is man's way, but faith and man's ability to rationalize are often in conflict. It's not that faith is unreasonable, nor am I suggesting that you ignore your responsibility to think. On the contrary, we are required by God to think and choose. God is a rational God and He does work through our ability to reason. The problem is that our ability to reason is limited. The Lord said: "As the heavens are higher than the earth, so are My ways higher than your ways, and My thoughts than your thoughts" (Isaiah 55:9). We are incapable of determining God's thoughts through human reasoning, therefore we are dependent on divine revelation.

So we can live God's way: operating by faith, which I like to call Plan A. Or we can live our way: operating by our limited ability to reason, which is Plan B. Plan B is based on our tendency to rationalize, "I don't see it God's way" or "I don't believe it," so we do it our way. Solomon urged us always to live God's way when he wrote: "Do not lean on your own understanding" (Plan B), but "in all your ways acknowledge Him" (Plan A) (Proverbs 3:5,6).

The strength of Plan A in your life is determined by your personal conviction that God's way is always right and by how committed you are to obey Him. The strength of Plan B is determined by the amount of time and energy you invest in entertaining thoughts which are contrary to God's Word. You may really know God's way is best. But the moment you begin to entertain thoughts or ideas which are contrary to God's Word, you have established Plan B as an escape route in case Plan A should fail. Is it rational to choose our way over God's way?

Lord, I want to be done with self-centered, mediocre planning. I choose to submit my will to Your perfect way and trust You for the outcome.

THE SOURCE OF PLAN B

Let not [the doubting] man expect that he will receive anything from the Lord, being a double-minded man, unstable in all his ways (James 1:7,8).

When you continue to vacillate between God's Plan A and your Plan B, your spiritual growth will be stunted, your maturity in Christ will be blocked, and your daily experience as a Christian will be marked by disillusionment, discouragement, and defeat. Where do Plan B thoughts come from? There are two primary sources.

First, your flesh still generates humanistic thoughts and ideas. Your flesh is that part of you which was trained to live independently of God before you became a Christian. At that time there was no Plan A in your life; you were separated from God, ignorant of His ways, and determined to succeed and survive by your own abilities.

When you were born again, God gave you a new nature and you became a new person, but nobody pressed the CLEAR button in your brain. You brought with you into your new faith all the old Plan B habits and thought patterns of the flesh. So while your new self desires to live dependently on God and follow Plan A, your flesh persists in suggesting Plan B ways to live independently of God.

Second, there is a person active in the world today who has opposed Plan A in God's human creation since the Garden of Eden. Satan and his demons are relentless in their attempts to establish negative, worldly patterns of thought in your mind which will in turn produce negative, worldly patterns of behavior.

The essence of the battle for the mind is the conflict between Plan A, living God's way by faith, and Plan B, living man's way by following the impulses of the world, the flesh, and the devil. You may feel like you are the helpless victim in this battle, being slapped back and forth like a puck in a match between rival hockey teams. But you are anything but helpless. In fact, you are the one who determines the winner in every skirmish between Plan A and Plan B.

Thank You, Lord, that I can live above the world, the flesh, and the devil as long as I choose Your plan for my life.

God's Feedback System

"For I know the plans that I have for you," declares the LORD, "plans for welfare and not for calamity to give you a future and a hope" (Jeremiah 29:11).

I believe that God desires all His children to be successful, significant, fulfilled, satisfied, joyful, secure, and to live in peace. From birth you have been developing in your mind a means for experiencing these values and reaching other goals in life. Consciously or subconsciously you continue to formulate and adjust your plans for achieving these goals.

But sometimes your well-intended plans and noble-sounding goals are not completely in harmony with God's plans and goals for you. "How can I know if what I believe is right?" you may be wondering. "Must I wait until I am 45 years old or until I experience some kind of mid-life crisis to discover that what I believed was wrong?" I don't think so. I believe that God has designed us in such a way that we can know on a regular basis if our belief system is properly aligned with God's truth. God has established a feedback system which is designed to grab your attention so you can examine the validity of your goal.

That system is your emotions. When an experience or relationship leaves you feeling angry, anxious, or depressed, those emotional signposts are there to alert you that you may be cherishing a faulty goal which is based on a wrong belief. If our goals are blocked, we become angry. If our goals are uncertain, we feel anxious. If we perceive our goals as impossible, we become depressed because the heart of depression is hopelessness.

Can any God-given goal be blocked, uncertain, or impossible? Put another way, if God wants something done, can it be done? Of course! The question is, do we have a biblical understanding of success, significance, fulfillment, satisfaction, joy, security, and peace? When we see and pursue these values from God's perspective, we will reach our goals because they are God's goals for us.

Lord, help me recognize when my goals today are not in line with Yours and make the proper adjustments in my belief system.

[God] Himself has said, "I will never desert you, nor will I ever forsake you" (Hebrews 13:5).

A devout Christian heard an urgent news report on his radio that a flash flood was within minutes of entering the peaceful valley where he lived. Immediately he went to his knees and prayed for safety. The words were still on his lips when he became aware that water was gushing under his door. He retreated to the second floor and finally onto the roof of his house.

While he sat on the roof, a helicopter flew by and the pilot asked over the loudspeaker if they could lift him off. "It's not necessary since I have the Lord's protection," he replied.

Moments later the house began to break up and he found himself clinging to a tree. A police boat, braving the waters, approached him for rescue, but he assured them that the Lord would save him. Finally, the tree gave way and the man went to his death.

Standing before the Lord, he asked, "Lord, I'm glad to be here, but why didn't You answer my prayer for safety?"

The Lord responded, "Son, I told you over the radio to get out of there. Then I sent you a helicopter and a motor boat!"

Nowhere in the Bible are we given the idea that God works only in the extraordinary. Much of the time He supernaturally works through His created order. Many people think God is present only when there is a miracle and that He leads only through signs and wonders.

There are people who *always* look for a sign. They walk by sight, not by faith. To them, God is only present in the miraculous. God was "really" at the church service if something unusual happened. Many desire and look for "visitations" from God.

But how does that square with God's omnipresence and the fact that He will never leave us or forsake us? Isn't God at every church service? Since God created the fixed order of the universe, would you expect Him to work primarily within that fixed order or outside of it? If God gave us a watch, would we be honoring Him more by asking Him what time it is or by simply consulting the watch?

Lord, forgive me for looking for signs when I only need to trust Your Word and live by Your promises.

Thine, O L*ORD, is the greatness and the power and the glory and the victory and the majesty (1 Chronicles 29:11).*

During a conference, I noticed a lady who wouldn't sing with the rest of the group and seemed quite agitated. She slipped me a note after a morning session: "Please don't leave town without helping me. I have been diagnosed as having multiple personalities and a dissociative disorder."

During our time together the Lord revealed that when she was seven years old a terrifying dark presence appeared in her room. It told her it would kill her unless she granted its request to share her body. The presence didn't leave until the day we met together. Later she wrote:

> I started hearing voices and having imaginary friends when I was seven years old. Bulimia began at age 10, promiscuity at age 12. I spent 10 years in a cult. When I came out of the cult I sought deliverance at the suggestion of a Catholic priest. But I beat up the priest and left bruised myself. It frightened me so badly I never did anything about it again.
>
> I am now of a sound mind; the voices are gone. I feel clean and fresh inside for the first time I can remember. I don't live in a tiny corner of my mind or outside my body. I live inside now with my Lord.

I wish that this woman's experience of childhood seduction was an exception. But I have counseled hundreds of adults who can trace their problems back to childhood. That's why it's critical that you teach your children the reality of the spiritual world and equip them to defeat Satan's attempts to seduce them with his lies.

Dear Father, help me teach my children that resisting an evil presence in their room is as important as avoiding strangers on the street.

I have been crucified with Christ; and it is no longer I who live, but Christ lives in me; and the life which I now live in the flesh I live by faith in the Son of God, who loved me, and delivered Himself up for me (Galatians 2:20).

All unbelievers have an old nature which is characterized by sin. Before you came to Christ you were one of those individuals. You were a sinner because it was your nature to sin. This "natural man" cannot accept or understand the things of the Spirit (1 Corinthians 2:14).

What happened to the old you at salvation? You died—not the physical you, of course, but that old inner self which was empowered by the old nature you inherited from Adam (Romans 6:2-6; Colossians 3:3). What was the method of execution? Crucifixion with Christ. Paul announced in Galatians 2:20: "I have been crucified with Christ." And in Galatians 6:14, Paul disclaimed any right to boast "except in the cross of our Lord Jesus Christ, through which the world has been crucified to me, and I to the world." At salvation you were placed into Christ, the one who died on the cross for your sin. Being in Christ, your old self died with Him there.

Notice the remarkable difference. In Adam you had an old self; in Christ you have a new self. In Adam you had a sin nature (Ephesians 2:1-3); in Christ you are a partaker of the divine nature (2 Peter 1:4). In Adam you were in the flesh (Romans 8:8); in Christ you are in the Spirit (Romans 8:9). In Adam you could only walk after the flesh; in Christ you may choose to walk after the Spirit or after the flesh.

Aren't you glad to be a new creature in Christ?

Thank You, Jesus, that You have set me free from my old sin nature and that I can choose to walk after the Spirit today.

No Longer Under Obligation

Our old self was crucified with Him, that our body of sin might be done away with, that we should no longer be slaves to sin (Romans 6:6).

Why did the old self need to die? The old self was independent and disobedient to God, so it had to die in order that "our body of sin might be done away with, that we should no longer be slaves to sin" (Romans 6:6). Death is the ending of a relationship, but not of existence. Sin hasn't died; it is still strong and appealing. But when your old self died with Christ on the cross, your relationship with sin ended forever. You are no longer "in the flesh" but "in Christ" (Romans 8:9). Your old self (the sinner) and your old nature (characterized by the sin which was inevitable since you were separated from God) are gone forever because you are no longer separated from God.

Does this mean that you are now sinless? By no means. The death of your old self formally ended your relationship with sin, but it did not end sin's existence. Sin and Satan are still around, and they are strong and appealing. But by virtue of the crucifixion of the old self, sin's power over you is broken (Romans 6:7,12,14). You are no longer under any obligation to serve sin, to obey sin, or to respond to sin.

You commit sin when you willfully allow yourself to act independently of God as the old self did as a matter of course. When you function in this manner you are violating your new nature and your new identity. Such actions must be confessed and forsaken.

Even though the old self, which you were in Adam, is dead, you still have to contend with the flesh. The way you learned to live your life before Christ is still programmed into your mind. Knowing that your old self was crucified with Christ makes it possible for you to choose not to sin. You no longer have to walk after the flesh; you may now walk after the Spirit. You are free.

Father, help me overcome the fleshly ways I followed before coming to You. I choose today to be tuned in to Your Spirit.

For you have died and your life is hidden with Christ in God (Colossians 3:3).

A pastor visited me a few years ago, and he was in real turmoil. "I've been struggling to live a victorious Christian life for 20 years. I know what my problem is. Colossians 3:3 says: 'For you have died and your life is hidden with Christ in God.' I've been struggling all these years because I haven't died like this verse says. How do I die, Neil?"

"Dying is not your problem," I said. "Read the verse again, just a little slower."

" 'For you have died and your life is hidden with Christ in God.' I know, Neil. That's my problem. I haven't died."

"Read it once again," I pressed, "just a little bit slower."

" 'For you have died—' " and suddenly a light switched on in his understanding. "Hey, that's past tense, isn't it?"

"Absolutely. Your problem isn't dying; you're already dead. You died at salvation. No wonder you've been struggling as a Christian. You've been trying to do something that's already been done, and that's impossible. The death Paul talks about in Colossians 3:3 isn't something God expects you to do; it's something He expects you to know, accept, and believe. You can't do anything to become what you already are."

Thanks to the incredible redemptive work of Christ in your life, your old self has been replaced by a new self, governed by a new nature, which was not there before (2 Corinthians 5:17). Your old self was destroyed in the death of Christ and your new self sprang to life in the resurrection of Christ (1 Corinthians 15:20-22). The new life which characterizes your new self is nothing less than the life of Jesus Christ implanted in you (Galatians 2:20; Colossians 3:4).

Lord, I'm so grateful that I don't have to work for new life. You have already paid the price, done the job, and handed me the prize.

THE SPIRIT'S CONVICTION

I now rejoice, not that you were made sorrowful, but that you were made sorrowful to the point of repentance; for you were made sorrowful according to the will of God *(2 Corinthians 7:9).*

I'm often asked, "How can I tell the difference between the devil's accusations and the Holy Spirit's conviction?" Every Christian is faced with the choice of walking by the Spirit or by the flesh on a daily basis. The moment you choose to walk according to the flesh, the Holy Spirit brings conviction because what you have just chosen to do is not compatible with who you really are. If you continue in the flesh you will feel the sorrow of conviction.

"How do I know which kind of sorrow I'm experiencing?" you may ask. "The devil's accusation and the Spirit's conviction both make me feel sorrowful." Determine whether your feelings reflect thoughts of truth or error, and you will identify their source. Do you feel guilty, worthless, stupid, or inept? That's a sorrow provoked by accusation because those feelings don't reflect truth. Judicially, you are no longer guilty; you have been justified through your faith in Christ, and there is no condemnation for those who are in Christ. You are not worthless; Jesus gave His life for you. You are not stupid or inept; you can do all things through Christ. When you find lies lurking beneath your feelings of sorrow—especially if your feelings persistently drive you into the ground—you are being falsely accused. To disarm the sorrow of accusation you must submit yourself to God and resist the devil and his lies.

But if you are sorrowful because your behavior doesn't reflect your true identity in Christ, that's the sorrow according to the will of God which is designed to produce repentance. It's the Holy Spirit calling you to admit on the basis of 1 John 1:9, "Dear Lord, I was wrong." As soon as you confess and repent, God says, "I'm glad you shared that with Me. You're cleansed; now get on with life." And you walk away from that confrontation free. The sorrow is gone, and you have a positive new resolve to obey God in the area of your failure.

Thank You, Lord, for the "tough love" of Your Holy Spirit in bringing me to repentance when I sin.

The sorrow that is according to the will of God produces a repentance without regret, leading to salvation; but the sorrow of the world produces death (2 Corinthians 7:10).

A graphic example of the contrast between accusation and conviction is found in the lives of Judas Iscariot and Simon Peter. Somehow Judas allowed Satan to deceive him into betraying Jesus for 30 pieces of silver (Luke 22:3-5). When Judas realized what he had done, he was so remorseful that he hung himself. Was his suicide the result of Satan's accusation or of God's conviction? It had to be accusation because it drove Judas to kill himself. Accusation leads to death; conviction leads to repentance and life.

Peter also failed Jesus by denying Him. It apparently began with pride as the disciples argued over who was the greatest among them (Luke 22:24-30). Jesus told Peter, "Simon, Simon, behold, Satan has demanded permission to sift you like wheat" (verse 31). That's right—Jesus allowed Satan to put Peter through the mill because Peter had given the enemy a foothold through pride. But Jesus also looked at Peter and said, "I have prayed for you, that your faith may not fail; and you, when once you have turned again, strengthen your brothers" (verse 32).

Peter vowed to die with Jesus, but Jesus told him that he would deny Him three times (verses 33,34), which he did. The remorse Peter felt was every bit as painful as that which Judas experienced. But Peter's sorrow was from conviction which led to his eventual repentance and restoration to Christ (John 21:15-17). When your feelings of remorse drive you from God, you are being accused by Satan. Resist it. But when your sorrow draws you to confront Christ and confess your wrong, you are being convicted by the Spirit. Yield to it through repentance.

According to Revelation 12:10, Satan's continuing work is to accuse the brethren. But the good news is that Christ's continuing work is to intercede for us as He did for Peter (Hebrews 7:25). We have a persistent adversary, but we have an even more persistent, eternal advocate who defends us before the Father on the basis of our faith in Him (1 John 2:1).

I rejoice, Lord, that You are constantly defending me against accusation before the Father.

The thoughts of the righteous are just, but the counsels of the wicked are deceitful (Proverbs 12:5).

False self-concepts are very common in people under demonic attack. Many will state that they are different, that the Christian life won't work for them as it does for others, and that they are not entitled to claim God's promises. Many of those in spiritual conflict fear a mental breakdown and are filled with anxiety. Almost all feel unloved, worthless, and rejected. They have tried everything they can think of to improve their self-image, but nothing works. Most of these suspect that their problem is spiritual in nature, but they have no one to turn to. The subject of demonic influence is not taught in their churches, and there is a terrible stigma attached to those who are afflicted by anything demonic. Even when they are helped, few people will stand up and testify of their newfound freedom.

Stephanie, one of our undergraduates at Biola University, had been deceived into such a bad self-concept that she developed anorexia. She was admitted to an eating-disorder clinic and underwent extensive counseling, but with little progress. One of my students suspected a spiritual problem and brought Stephanie to see me. After two counseling sessions she was free of the oppression. Stephanie returned to the clinic to tell her counselor about her freedom in Christ. The counselor told her she was only on a temporary high. If so, Stephanie is still on it, because today she enjoys her freedom in Christ while serving the Lord on the mission field!

Mental health is usually defined as being in touch with reality and living relatively free of anxiety. Anyone under spiritual oppression would fail on both counts and may consider themselves mentally ill. I have encountered hundreds who have feared mental illness only to discover that a spiritual battle was going on for their mind. The way to win this battle is to submit to God and resist the devil.

Lord, I'm thankful that I can overcome Satan in my life today by the blood of the Lamb and the word of my testimony. Thank You for these powerful instruments of freedom.

THE ONLY LIMIT TO FAITH

Faith comes from hearing, and hearing by the word of Christ (Romans 10:17).

When people struggle with their faith in God, it's not because their faith-object is insufficient. It's because people have unreal expectations of God. They expect Him to operate a certain way or answer prayer a certain way—their way, not His—and when He doesn't comply they say, "Forget You, God." But God doesn't change; He's the perfect faith-object. Faith in God only fails when people hold a faulty understanding of Him.

If you want your faith in God to increase you must increase your understanding of Him as the object of your faith. If you have little knowledge about God and His Word, you will have little faith. If you have great knowledge of God and His Word, you will have great faith. Faith cannot be pumped up by coaxing yourself, "If only I can believe! If only I can believe!" Any attempt to push yourself beyond what you know about God and His ways is to move from faith to presumption. You choose to believe God according to what you already know to be true from His Word. And the only way to increase your faith is to increase your knowledge of God, your faith-object (Romans 10:17).

"Well," you may say, "that means there's a limit to our faith." Yes, there's a limit. But God isn't controlling it; you are. As the object of your faith, He is infinite. The only limit to your faith is your knowledge and understanding of God, which grows every time you read your Bible, memorize a new Scripture verse, participate in a Bible study, or meditate on a scriptural truth. Can you see the practical, tangible potential for your faith to grow as you endeavor to know God through His Word? It's boundless!

Furthermore, it is important to know that God is under no obligation to us. There is no way you can cleverly word a prayer so that God must act on your behalf. If God declares something to be true, you simply believe Him and live according to what is true. If God didn't say it, no amount of faith in the world will make it so. Believing doesn't make God's Word true; His Word is true, therefore I believe it.

Dear Lord, increase the boundaries of my faith today as I increase my understanding of You through Your Word.

If anyone thinks he is something when he is nothing, he deceives himself (Galatians 6:3).

Satan promotes his lies in the world by encouraging us to self-deception. We deceive ourselves when we think we are something we are not. The Scriptures instruct us not to think of ourselves more highly than we ought to think. "But I know who I am," you say. "I'm a child of God, I'm seated with Christ in the heavenlies, I can do all things through Him. That makes me pretty special." Yes, you are very special in the eyes of God. But you are what you are by the grace of God (1 Corinthians 15:10). The life you live, the talents you possess, and the gifts you have received are not personal accomplishments; they are expressions of God's grace. Never take credit for what God has provided; rather, take delight in accomplishing worthwhile deeds which glorify the Lord.

Furthermore, we deceive ourselves when we think we are wise in this age (1 Corinthians 3:18,19). It is the height of intellectual arrogance to assume wisdom without the revelation of God. "Professing to be wise, they became fools" (Romans 1:22). Sometimes we are tempted to think we can match wits and intellect with the god of this world. But we are no match for him. Whenever we think we can outsmart Satan on our own, we are prime candidates to be led astray by his craftiness.

However, Satan is no match for God. It is important for us not to lean on our own understanding, but to employ the mind of Christ and acknowledge Him in all our ways (Proverbs 3:5,6; 1 Corinthians 2:16). We overcome the lies of Satan by divine revelation, not human research or reasoning. Satan is not impressed with our intellect; he is defeated by God's omniscience.

Lord, help me not to think more highly of myself than I ought, nor to demean myself, because I am created in Your image.

We are taking every thought captive to the obedience of Christ (2 Corinthians 10:5).

The nature of the battle for your mind is clearly presented in 2 Corinthians 10:3-5: "For though we walk in the flesh, we do not war according to the flesh, for the weapons of our warfare are not of the flesh, but divinely powerful for the destruction of fortresses. We are destroying speculations and every lofty thing raised up against the knowledge of God, and we are taking every thought captive to the obedience of Christ."

The first thing you need to know about the battle for your mind is that it is not fought on the plane of human ingenuity or ability. You can't outsmart or outmuscle the flesh or the devil on your own. Your weapons must be "divinely powerful" if you are going to win a spiritual conflict.

The main targets which must be destroyed are the "fortresses" in the mind. The King James Version uses the word *strongholds*. Strongholds are negative patterns of thought which are burned into our minds either through repetition over time or through one-time traumatic experiences.

Thoughts determine behavior, and thought patterns determine temperaments. Strongholds are revealed in un-Christlike temperaments and behavior patterns. A mind-set impregnated with hopelessness causes us to accept as unchangeable something known to be contrary to God.

How are these destructive strongholds established in our minds? Usually they are the result of a number of subtle steps which lead us away from God's plan for us and mire us in Plan B behavior. We will look at these steps and how we should respond to them over the next several days.

Lord, I determine to prepare my mind for action today and avoid passivity in my thinking, because Satan loves passivity.

See to it that no one takes you captive through philosophy and empty deception, according to the tradition of men...rather than according to Christ (Colossians 2:8).

The first step toward the formation of strongholds in our minds can be called "environmental stimulation." You were designed to live in fellowship with God and fulfill His purposes, but you were born physically alive and spiritually dead in a hostile world (Ephesians 2:1,2). Before you came to Christ, all your stimulation came from this environment. Every day you lived in this environment you were influenced by it and preconditioned to conform to it.

The worldly stimulation you were exposed to was both brief and prevailing. Brief stimulation includes individual events, situations, places, and personal encounters you experienced. You were influenced by books you read, movies you watched, music you listened to, and traumatic events you experienced or witnessed, such as a car accident or a death in the family. You learned a way (which may or may not have been God's way) to cope with these experiences and resolve the conflicts they produced.

Prevailing stimulation consists of long-term exposure to your environment, such as the influence of your family, your friends and peers, your neighborhood, your teachers, and your job. If you grew up separated from God, and were raised in a non-Christian environment, you developed a philosophy of how to survive, cope, and succeed in this world apart from God.

When you became a Christian your sins were washed away, but your predisposition to think and behave a certain way, which you developed as you adjusted to your environment, remained programmed in your mind. In fact, you can become a born-again believer and continue to live on the basis of the lifestyle you developed while living independently of God. That is why Paul insists that we be transformed by the renewing of our minds (Romans 12:2).

I know I was saved in a moment, Lord. But my character still needs daily transformation. Help me be as patient with others in their transformation as You are with me.

The grace of God has appeared...instructing us to deny ungodliness and worldly desires and to live sensibly, righteously and godly in the present age (Titus 2:11,12).

Yielding to temptation is another step toward a stronghold being established in your mind. Whenever you are stimulated to conform to Plan B instead of God's Plan A for your life, you are experiencing temptation. The essence of all temptation is the invitation to live independently of God and fulfill legitimate needs in the world, the flesh, or the devil instead of in Christ. That's the great contest. And Satan knows just which buttons to push to tempt you away from dependency on Christ.

The moment you are tempted to get your need met in the world instead of in Christ, you are at the threshold of a decision. If you don't immediately choose to take that thought "captive to the obedience of Christ" (2 Corinthians 10:5), you will begin to consider it as an option. And if you begin to mull it over in your mind, immediately your emotions will be affected and the likelihood of yielding to that temptation is increased.

The Scriptures teach us that God has provided a way of escape from every temptation (1 Corinthians 10:13). But the escape is right at the threshold of the temptation. If you don't control the temptation at the threshold, you run the risk of allowing the temptation to control you. Rare is the Christian who can turn around after directing his will toward Plan B.

For example, a man sees a pornographic picture and is tempted toward lust. He has the opportunity to respond by saying something like, "My relationship with sin has ended. I choose to take this thought captive to the obedience of Christ. I'm not going to look at it or think about it." And he separates himself from the picture immediately and escapes the lust.

But if he hesitates at the threshold, stares at the picture, and begins to fantasize about it, he will trigger an emotional landslide producing a physical response which will be difficult to stop. He must capture the tempting thought in the threshold or it will probably capture him.

Dear God, I want to be obedient to Your perfect plan for my life today. I don't want to give in to Plan B thinking. Strengthen my will to obey.

March 27 WHEN STRONGHOLDS BECOME ENTRENCHED

No soldier in active service entangles himself in the affairs of everyday life, so that he may please the one who enlisted him as a soldier (2 Timothy 2:4).

Once your consideration of a temptation has triggered an emotional response leading to a Plan B choice, you will act upon that choice and own that behavior. You may resent your actions or claim that you are not responsible for what you do. But you *are* responsible for your actions at this stage because you failed to take a tempting thought captive when it first appeared at the threshold of your mind.

People who study human behavior tell us that if you continue to repeat an act for six weeks, you will form a habit. And if you exercise that habit long enough, a stronghold will be established. Once a stronghold of thought and response is entrenched in your mind, choosing to act contrary to that pattern is extremely difficult.

Like environmental stimulation, a stronghold of the mind can be the result of a brief encounter or a prevailing atmosphere. For example, a woman goes into a deep depression every time she hears a siren sound. It turns out that she was raped 20 years earlier while a siren was wailing in the distance. In the weeks and months after the rape, the sound of a siren triggered traumatic memories. Instead of resolving that conflict, she relived the tragedy in her mind, deepening the emotional scars and locking herself into a thought pattern she cannot seem to break. That's a stronghold.

Other strongholds are the result of a prevailing pattern of thinking and responding. Imagine, for instance, a nine-year-old boy whose father is an alcoholic. When the father comes home drunk and belligerent every night, the boy is simply scared stiff of him. He scurries out of sight and hides. As the boy continues in his defensive reaction to his hostile alcoholic father, he forms a pattern of behavior. Ten years later, when he faces any kind of hostile behavior, how do you think he will respond? He will run away. His deeply ingrained pattern of thinking and responding has formed a stronghold in his mind.

Father, don't allow the enemy to deceive me into weak-willed actions that dilute my testimony and effectiveness as a believer.

I am afraid, lest as the serpent deceived Eve by his craftiness, your minds should be led astray from the simplicity and purity of devotion to Christ (2 Corinthians 11:3).

Hostility is a stronghold. Plan A from God develops the character and the knowledge to love your enemy, pray for him, and turn the other cheek. If you cannot help being pugnacious or argumentative in a threatening situation, it's because you have learned to cope that way and your Plan B response has become entrenched as a stronghold.

Inferiority is a stronghold. Plan A says that you are a child of God, a saint who is inferior to no mortal. If you are constantly shrinking back from people because of feelings of inferiority, it's because the world, the flesh, and the devil have carved a negative, Plan B groove in your mind over the years.

Manipulation is a stronghold. Do you feel like you must control the people and circumstances in your life? Is it nearly impossible for you to give a problem to God and not worry about it? Somewhere in your past you developed a pattern of control which now masters you. It's a stronghold.

Homosexuality is a stronghold. In God's eyes there is no such thing as a homosexual. He created us male and female. There is homosexual behavior, which can usually be traced to past negative experiences. Such experiences prompted these individuals to doubt their sexual adequacy and they began to believe a lie about their sexual identity.

Anorexia and bulimia are strongholds. A 99-pound woman stands in front of a mirror believing that she is fat. She is the victim of negative thought patterns about herself which have been burned into her mind and direct all her activities concerning her body and the proper use of food.

Somewhere in the past you may have consciously or unconsciously formed patterns of thinking and behaving which now control you. That's a stronghold. Satan works through strongholds to keep our minds from focusing on Christ. But, thank God, as we appropriate God's truth we are set free.

Father, reveal to me and help me deal with any strongholds in my life. I claim Your truth in my life over Satan's lies.

Do not be conformed to this world, but be transformed by the renewing of your mind (Romans 12:2).

If the strongholds in your mind are the result of conditioning, then you can be reconditioned by the renewing of your mind. Anything that has been learned can be unlearned. Certainly this is the major path of renewal in the New Testament. Through the preaching of God's Word, Bible study, and personal discipleship you stop being conformed to this world and experience the transformation of the renewing of your mind (Romans 12:2).

If your past experiences were spiritually or emotionally devastating, then counseling and Christ-centered support groups will help the transformation. Since some of these strongholds are thoughts raised up against the knowledge of God (2 Corinthians 10:5), learning to know God as a loving Father and yourself as His accepted child is your starting place.

But you're not just up against the world and the flesh. You're also up against the devil who is scheming to fill your mind with thoughts which are opposed to God's plan for you.

Notice how Paul uses the word for *thoughts* (*noema*) in 2 Corinthians in relation to Satan's activity. We've already seen it in 2 Corinthians 10:5: "We are taking every thought [*noema*] captive to the obedience to Christ." Why do these thoughts need to be taken captive? Because they may be the enemy's.

In 2 Corinthians 3:14 and 4:4, Paul reveals that Satan is responsible for our spiritual hardness and blindness when we were unbelievers: "But their minds [*noema*] were hardened....The god of this world has blinded the minds [*noema*] of the unbelieving." In 2 Corinthians 11:3 and 2:11, Paul states that Satan actively plots to defeat and divide believers: "I am afraid, lest as the serpent deceived Eve by his craftiness, your minds [*noema*] should be led astray from the simplicity and purity of devotion to Christ....We are not ignorant of his [Satan's] schemes [*noema*]."

If Satan can place his thought in your mind—and he can—it isn't much more of a trick for him to make you think it's your thought. That's the deception.

In the name of Jesus, I renounce and refuse any thoughts which are raised up against the knowledge of God.

As you therefore have received Christ Jesus the Lord, so walk in Him (Colossians 2:6).

There are three ways of responding to the demonic taunts and barbs being thrown at you during your daily walk with Christ, and two of these ways are wrong.

First, the most defeated people are those who consider demonic thoughts and believe them. A subtle thought is shot into your mind: "You don't pray, read your Bible, or witness like you should. How could God love you?" That's a bald-faced lie, because God's love is unconditional. But you start thinking about your failures and agreeing that you're probably not very lovable to God. Pretty soon you're sitting in the middle of the street going nowhere.

These Christians are totally defeated simply because they have been duped into believing that God doesn't love them, or that they will never be a victorious Christian, or that they are a helpless victim of the past. There is no reason why they can't get up immediately and start walking again, but they have believed a lie and the lie controls their life.

The second response is just as unproductive. You try to argue with the demons: "I am not ugly or stupid. I am a victorious Christian." You're proud that you don't believe what they say, but they're still controlling you and setting your agenda. You're standing in the middle of the street shouting at them when you should be marching forward.

We are not to believe evil spirits, nor are we to dialogue with them. Instead, we are to ignore them and choose the truth. You're equipped with the armor of God; they can't touch you unless you drop your guard. With every arrow of temptation, accusation, or deception they shoot at you, simply raise the shield of faith, deflect the attack, and walk on. Take every thought captive to the obedience of Christ. The way to defeat the lie is by choosing the truth.

In the face of the lies the enemy throws at me today, Lord, I choose and embrace Your truth.

The Operating Principle of Life

And Jesus answered saying to them, "Have faith in God" (Mark 11:22).

The sun is perhaps the most credible object of faith for the world. It appears to be immutable. It has always been there, 24 hours of every day, 365 days a year. Without the sun, people couldn't live. If the sun didn't rise tomorrow morning, what would happen to the world's faith? All of humanity would be thrown into confusion.

If we have such great faith in the sun, why don't we have even greater faith in the Son who made the sun and all the rest of the fixed order of the universe?

Our faith is in God. Genuine faith is born out of a knowledge of the will of God and exists only to fulfill that will. Faith is not a means of getting man's will done in heaven; it is the means of getting God's will done on earth.

After hearing me speak on spiritual conflicts, a young man came by to talk about his personal life. He said he'd had several experiences of not being able to speak the name of Jesus aloud. I asked him about his faith. He thought he had made a decision for Christ years earlier in an evangelistic meeting. He tried living with some American Indians to continue his spiritual journey, but that proved to be disastrous. He finally ended up living in a pastor's home where he was helped with the assurance of his salvation. The pastor encouraged him to just go live by faith.

The young man said to me, "I've been trying to live by faith for three years, and it has been one trial after another."

"Faith in what?" I asked.

He didn't know how to respond. This young man was trying to live by faith in faith. But faith itself is not a valid object. The only valid object for faith is God and the revelation we have of Him in His Word. Faith is the operating principle of life. The only difference between Christian and non-Christian faith is the object. God must be the object of our faith.

Lord God, I place my faith in You alone today. Help me not to allow anyone or anything to take Your place as the object of my faith.

Hope for Today and Tomorrow

Beloved, now we are children of God, and it has not appeared as yet what we shall be. We know that, when He appears, we shall be like Him, because we shall see Him just as He is. And everyone who has this hope fixed on Him purifies himself, just as He is pure (1 John 3:2,3).

As children of the sinful first Adam, we were obstinate and ornery, helpless and hopeless, with nothing in ourselves to commend us to God. But God's love overruled our unloveliness. Through Christ God provided a way for us into His family. As God's adopted child, you have been given a new identity and a new name. You're no longer a spiritual orphan; you're a son or daughter of God. Romans 8:16,17 tells us, "The Spirit Himself bears witness with our spirit that we are children of God, and if children, heirs also, heirs of God and fellow heirs with Christ."

If you're beginning to think you are someone special as a Christian, you're thinking right—you *are* special! Your specialness is not the result of anything you have done, of course. It's all God's doing. All you did was respond to God's invitation to be His child. But as a child of God, in union with God by being in Christ, you have every right to enjoy your special relationship with your new Father.

How important is it to know who you are in Christ? There are countless numbers of Christians who struggle with day-to-day behavior because they labor under a false perception of who they are. They see themselves as sinners who hope to make it into heaven by God's grace, but they can't seem to live above their sinful tendencies. Why can't they live the victorious Christian life? Because they have a misperception of who they are in Christ.

But look again at the hope-filled words of 1 John 3:2,3. What is the believer's hope? That he will someday be changed into Christ's image? That's part of it, but that's only a future hope. What is your hope for today and tomorrow? That you're a child of God *now*! You must see yourself as a child of God in order to live like a child of God. The blessed hope for the believer is "Christ in you, the hope of glory" (Colossians 1:27).

Thank You, Father, for the glorious hope of being Your child. I want to live in the security and blessing of that reality today.

A Blameless Conscience

I also do my best to maintain always a blameless conscience both before God and before men (Acts 24:16).

Folklore advises, "Let your conscience be your guide." This has serious limitations since our conscience is a function of our mind. Having been conformed to this world, the conscience can be programmed wrongly. It is always true to its own standard. Until we come to Christ, the standard is the world system we were raised in. Many people are falsely guided by a guilty conscience—not a true guilt, but a psychological guilt usually developed in early childhood. Satan works through this stronghold to accuse the brethren day and night (Revelation 12:10).

People like this are usually perfectionists who labor under condemnation, even though the Bible says there is no condemnation for those who are in Christ Jesus (Romans 8:1). They aren't led; they are driven. They constantly look for affirmation. They have a tendency to be man-pleasers. Paul said, "If I were still trying to please men, I would not be a bond-servant of Christ" (Galatians 1:10). If you are striving to please men, who are you a bond-servant of?

Since our minds were conformed to this world we need to renew them in such a way that what we believe is in accordance with truth. Chapter 14 of Romans deals with how we should walk in regard to nonmoral issues. Paul says, "The faith which you have, have as your own conviction before God. Happy is he who does not condemn himself in what he approves" (Romans 14:22).

However, we are to restrict our freedom if it causes a weaker brother to stumble. We never have the right to violate another person's conscience. Paul says, "I also do my best to maintain always a blameless conscience both before God and before men" (Acts 24:16). Be very cautious about going against your own conscience once you are committed to Christ. The Holy Spirit does work through our consciences as He seeks to renew our minds.

Thank You, Lord, that my mind and conscience can be renewed daily through the power of Your Word.

God...made us alive together with Christ (by grace you have been saved), and raised us up with Him, and seated us with Him in the heavenly places, in Christ Jesus (Ephesians 2:4-6).

The New Testament clearly reveals that Christ's power and authority over Satan and his kingdom have been conferred to those of us who are in Christ. In Ephesians 2:4-6 Paul explains that when Christ was raised from the dead, those of us who have believed in Him were also resurrected from our condition of spiritual death and made alive "together with Christ." It's only logical that the head (Christ) and the body (His church) should be raised together.

Furthermore, when God seated Christ at His right hand and conferred on Him all authority (Ephesians 1:20,21), He also seated us at His right hand and conferred on us through Christ all authority because we are "together with Christ." The moment you receive Christ, you take possession of what God did for you 2000 years ago. Your identity as a child of God and your authority over spiritual powers are not things you *are* receiving or *will* receive at some time in the future; you have them right now. You are a spiritually-alive child of God *right now*. You are seated in the heavenlies with Christ *right now*. You have power and authority over the kingdom of darkness *right now*. We have the authority because of our position in Christ, and we have the power when we are filled with the Holy Spirit.

Paul also related this life-changing truth in his letter to the Colossians: "In Him [Christ] you have been made complete, and He is the head over all rule and authority" (Colossians 2:10). Notice again that the action is past tense: We *have been* made complete. When? At the death, resurrection, and ascension of Jesus Christ. And since Christ is the God-appointed head over all rule and authority, and since we are seated with Him in the heavenlies, we have the authority and power to live responsible lives.

Father, help me want to live responsibly, to claim my position as Your child, and to grow to full stature in You.

We are from God; he who knows God listens to us; he who is not from God does not listen to us. By this we know the spirit of truth and the spirit of error (1 John 4:6).

People who know they are having spiritual problems usually have severe perceptual problems too. Satan seems to be more present, real, and powerful to them. These types of people usually hear opposing arguments in their head. They are constantly confronted with lies, told to get out of the counseling setting, or threatened with harm or embarrassment.

One dear lady I was ministering to suddenly bolted for the door. "Tell me what you're hearing," I said.

"You're going to hurt me," she answered fearfully.

"That's a lie," I assured her. Slowly she returned to her chair.

Some people experience internal interference when demonic powers are confronted by the truth. They may become dizzy or glassy-eyed. If you proceed without regard for their reaction they may lapse into catatonia.

The goal in helping people find freedom in Christ is to avoid all demonic activity which would short-circuit their ability to participate in the process. With this in mind, I usually begin the time of ministry with prayer, acknowledging God's presence, claiming His authority, and binding the enemy to silence.

I require one major point of cooperation from all those who want help: They must tell me what inner opposition they are experiencing. If they have a thought that is contrary to what we are doing, they are to share it with me. Some thoughts can be very hostile or threatening. Others will be very deceptive, such as "This isn't going to work." The power of Satan is in his lie. The moment the counselees bring the contrary thought to light, the power of it is broken. The power for the Christian is in the truth. That is why it is truth that sets us free.

Lord, I desire to be a committed student of Your Word. I know the truth of Your Word dispels the darkness in my life. Thank You for this powerful weapon.

What sort of people ought you to be in holy conduct and godliness (2 Peter 3:11).

I believe in setting goals and making plans. But a biblical vision for the future and godly goals for ministry or work have no value if they don't provide direction for our steps today. Goals for tomorrow that don't prioritize present activities are nothing more than wishful thinking. We make plans for tomorrow in order to establish meaningful activities for today. We need to ask the Lord each day if we are still on target, and give Him the right to order mid-course changes in direction.

Some people don't like to set goals because they feel goals only set them up for failure. But a goal should never be a god. It should be a target, not a whip. Other people become obsessed with goals for tomorrow. Biblically, the will of God is almost entirely directed at living responsibly today. Legitimate goal-setting should support that.

"Are you trying to tell us that we aren't to make any plans for the future or establish any goals for our ministry or work?" No, I'm trying to say that the primary focus of God's will is that we seek to establish His kingdom by becoming the person He wants us to be *today*.

Most people want to know what God has in store for them tomorrow. That's why prophecy has always been a popular subject. Most prophecy teachers know that the critical issue concerning the Lord's second coming is, "What sort of people ought you to be in holy conduct and godliness" (2 Peter 3:11). Jesus said, "But seek first His kingdom and His righteousness; and all these things shall be added to you. Therefore do not be anxious for tomorrow" (Matthew 6:33,34). Biblical prophecy is given to us as a hope (the present assurance of some future good) so we will have the courage to live righteously and confidently today.

Father, help me live in the present and not worry about tomorrow, accepting only Your will and guidance for my future.

Fathers, do not provoke your children to anger; but bring them up in the discipline and instruction of the Lord (Ephesians 6:4).

It's all too easy for children to find their identity wrapped up in external values like performance and appearance. Why? Largely because those are the values their parents and teachers glorify and reinforce. Children are applauded if they're cute, if they say funny things, or if they hit home runs. Thanks to the adults in their lives, it doesn't take long for children to internalize and begin to live by three pervasive principles:

1. If I am physically attractive and others admire me, I will be special.
2. If I perform well and accomplish great things, I will be accepted.
3. If I obtain social status and others recognize me, I will be significant.

But what about the child who isn't very cute or entertaining? What about the child who never wins a starring role in the school play or strikes out most of the time? Tragically, children like these are often compared, rejected, or ignored by the adults in their lives. They begin to question their identity and doubt their worth. Satan takes advantage of the false values our society promotes.

Children may struggle with identity and self-acceptance because their parents struggle with the same issues. Children who grow up with false principles for identity and acceptance don't automatically grow out of them when they reach adulthood. As adults they continue to base their identity on these external guidelines and tend to perpetuate them in their children. If you are going to help your child realize his identity and acceptance in Christ, you must lead the way by doing so in your own life.

Lord, give me wisdom to teach my children and grandchildren what it means to be a child of God and to be in Christ. Forgive me for the times I have promoted false values before them.

Let all bitterness and wrath and anger and clamor and slander be put away from you, along with all malice (Ephesians 4:31).

Feelings of anger should prompt us to reexamine what we believe and the mental goals we have formulated to accomplish those beliefs. My daughter Heidi helped me with this process one Sunday morning while I was trying to hustle my family out the door for church. I had been waiting in the car for several minutes before I stomped back into the house and shouted angrily, "We should have left for church 15 minutes ago!"

All was silent for a moment, then Heidi's soft voice floated around the corner from her bedroom: "What's the matter, Dad? Did somebody block your goal?" She was blocking my goal to get to church on time, but she wasn't blocking my goal to be the husband and father God wants me to be. The only one who can block that goal is me.

A wife and mother may say, "My goal in life is to have a loving, harmonious, happy family." Who can block that goal? Every person in her family can block her goal—not only *can*, they *will*! A homemaker clinging to the belief that her self-worth is dependent on her family will crash and burn every time her husband or children fail to live up to her image of family harmony. She will probably be a very angry woman, which could drive family members even farther away from her and each other. Her major goal in life should be to become the wife and mother God called her to be.

A pastor may say, "My goal in ministry is to reach this community for Christ." Good goal? It is a wonderful desire, but if his self-worth is dependent on that desire being fulfilled, he will experience tremendous emotional turmoil. Every person in the community can block his goal. Pastors who continue to believe that their success is dependent on others will end up fighting with their boards, praying their opposition out of the church, or quitting.

Make it your goal to be what God has called you to be. No one can keep you from reaching that goal but you.

Father, help me see Your long-range view of life so I can learn not to blow up at minor, short-term irritations.

SEALED IN HIM

Having also believed, you were sealed in Him with the Holy Spirit of promise (Ephesians 1:13).

After King Saul disobeyed God (1 Samuel 15), we're told that "the Spirit of the LORD departed from Saul, and an evil spirit from the LORD terrorized him" (1 Samuel 16:14). This is a difficult passage for two reasons. First, it seems to imply that a person can lose the Holy Spirit by an act of disobedience. But it must be understood that the presence of the Holy Spirit in the Old Testament was selective and temporary. The Spirit involved with Saul was probably the same Spirit involved with David in verse 13: a special equipping of the Spirit for ruling as God's anointed king. This unique equipping is not the same as the personal relationship in the Spirit that we enjoy with God as His children today.

Beginning after the cross, the church is identified by the indwelling presence of the Holy Spirit, who forever unites the children of God with their heavenly Father (Ephesians 1:13,14). Jesus promised that no one shall snatch us out of His hand (John 10:28), and Paul assured that nothing—not even disobedience—can separate us from the love of God (Romans 8:35-39). We are secure in Christ and indwelt by His Spirit through faith in the work of Christ on the cross.

The second problem concerns the bothersome idea that an evil spirit could come from the Lord. But we must remember that God is supreme, and He can use Satan and his emissaries as a means to discipline His people as He did with Saul. It is not inconsistent with the nature or plan of God to use anything to accomplish His will. Even the church is permitted to turn a grossly immoral member over to Satan "for the destruction of his flesh, that his spirit may be saved in the day of the Lord Jesus" (1 Corinthians 5:5). Why? Allowing people to experience the natural consequences of their actions has always been an effective means of discipline.

Do you want to do the devil's bidding? Go ahead, and maybe the painful consequences you suffer from your immorality will turn you back to God.

Thank You, Lord, for sealing me in Christ by Your Spirit. Help me live obediently today as an expression of thanks for what You have done.

The peace of God, which surpasses all comprehension, shall guard your hearts and your minds in Christ Jesus (Philippians 4:7).

Christians have frequently relied upon a sense of peace as evidence of the Holy Spirit's leading. It is common to hear people say, "I just don't have a peace about it." I think that is legitimate. I would be concerned about the person who proceeds when his spirit is disturbed. God doesn't lead through anxiety. We are to cast our anxiety upon Jesus, because He cares for us (1 Peter 5:7).

Still, a lot of money is spent on the temporary "cure" of anxiety. People consume alcohol, take illegal drugs, turn to the refrigerator, have sex, mindlessly repeat mantras, and escape to cabins, boats, and motor homes—all to reduce their anxiety. One lady said, "Whenever I feel anxious, I go on a shopping spree!" Prescription drugs are regularly dispensed for the ails brought on by anxiety.

The bartender, drug pusher, occult practitioner, and other peddlers of escapism all have one thing in common: They really don't care about the consumer. They are out to make a profit. Even worse, when the temporary "cure" wears off, we have to return to the same world with the added problem of hangovers and other negative consequences of fake healers.

Internally, we desperately need the peace of God: "Be anxious for nothing, but in everything by prayer and supplication with thanksgiving let your requests be made known to God. And the peace of God, which surpasses all comprehension, shall guard your hearts and your minds in Christ Jesus" (Philippians 4:6,7). The awareness of a troubled spirit should drive us to find the peace of God by turning to Him and assuming our responsibility to use our minds.

Thank You, Lord, for breaking through so many of my old anxieties and setting me free. I ask You to free me from those that remain.

For our struggle is not against flesh and blood, but against the rulers, against the powers, against the world forces of this darkness, against the spiritual forces of wickedness in the heavenly places (Ephesians 6:12).

One of the main reasons I fumbled and failed in my early days of ministering to people in bondage was because I labored under a number of misconceptions about the spiritual world. Perhaps you are struggling with some of these same faulty ideas which keep Christians in darkness. We'll consider these misconceptions over the next several days.

One common misconception is that *demons were active when Christ was on earth, but their activity has subsided today*. Christians who hold this extreme view in light of what God's Word says and what is transpiring in the world today are not facing reality. The New Testament clearly states that believers will wrestle against the powers of darkness (Ephesians 6:12). Paul goes on to itemize the pieces of spiritual armor that we are to put on in order to defend ourselves against "the flaming missiles of the evil one" (verses 13-17). In 2 Corinthians 10:3-5 Paul again specifies that believers are engaged in a spiritual battle against forces which oppose the knowledge of God. If dark spiritual powers are no longer attacking believers, why would Paul alert us to them and insist that we arm ourselves against them?

The powers and forces that Paul wrote about in the first century are still around at the dawn of the twenty-first century, evident in the popularity of the New Age Movement and the proliferation of Satanism and the occult.

God's people wrestling against dark spiritual forces is not a first-century phenomenon, nor is it an option for the Christian today; it's unavoidable. The kingdom of darkness is still present, and Satan is intent on making your life miserable and keeping you from enjoying and exercising your inheritance in Christ. Your only options in confronting spiritual opposition are how and to what extent you're going to wage the battle.

Thank You, Father, that I don't battle the forces of darkness alone. You have provided all the weapons I need to overcome and stand free.

THE REALITY OF THE SPIRITUAL WORLD

Your adversary, the devil, prowls about like a roaring lion, seeking someone to devour (1 Peter 5:8).

Here's another common misconception about the spiritual world that must be dispelled: *What the early church called demonic activity we now understand to be mental illness.* One counselor argued, "There is no way his problem can be demonic; he's a paranoid schizophrenic." Simply accepting secular psychology's definition of a human problem in no way establishes the actual cause of the problem. Terms such as schizophrenia, paranoia, psychosis, etc., are merely labels classifying symptoms.

But what or who is causing the symptoms? Is it a neurological or hormonal problem, or perhaps a chemical imbalance? Certainly these options must be explored. But what if no physical cause is found? Then it must be a psychological problem. But which school of psychology do you choose: biblical or secular? Why not explore the possibility that the problem may be spiritual?

We should not be surprised that secular psychologists, limited to a natural worldview, supply only natural explanations for mental problems. They offer their explanation from a viewpoint with no concept of God, much less the demonic. Even many Christians who vociferously reject the scientific community's explanation for the origin of the species naively accept the secular psychologist's explanation of mental illness. Research based on the scientific method of investigation of human spiritual problems is not wrong; it's just incomplete. It ignores the reality of the spiritual world because neither God nor the devil submit to our methods of investigation.

Hebrews 11:6 says, "Without faith it is impossible to please Him, for he who comes to God must believe that He is." Science is inadequate to explain matters of faith. We must trust God's Word to explain the reality of the spiritual world.

I praise You, Father, that I don't have to accept fallible man's knowledge as the last word on life. I know Your Word stands above all human reasoning and will remain forever in heaven.

How can anyone enter the strong man's house and carry off his property, unless he first binds the strong man? (Matthew 12:29).

Another common misconception of the spiritual world is that *some problems are psychological and some are spiritual.* This misconception implies a division between the human soul and spirit, which does not exist. There is no inner conflict which is not psychological, because there is never a time when your mind, emotions, and will are not involved. Similarly, there is no problem which is not spiritual. There is no time when God is not present or when it is safe for you to take off the armor of God. The tendency is to polarize into a deliverance ministry, ignoring the realities of the physical realm, or a psychotherapeutic ministry, ignoring the spiritual realm.

Dr. Paul Hiebert, a missions specialist, contends that, as long as believers accept a two-tier worldview with God confined to the supernatural and the natural world operating for all practical purposes according to autonomous scientific laws, Christianity will continue to be a secularizing force in the world. If your worldview does not recognize the activity of the god of this world in human problems, it is at best incomplete and at worst a distortion of reality.

Another misconception is that *Christians aren't subject to demon activity*. The prevailing belief among evangelicals today is that Christians cannot be severely oppressed by demons. Even the suggestion that demonic influence can be part of the problem often prompts the hasty disclaimer, "Impossible! I'm a Christian!"

Nothing has done greater damage to diagnosing spiritual problems than this untruth. If Satan can't touch the church, why are we instructed to put on the armor of God, to resist the devil, to stand firm, and to be alert? If we aren't susceptible to being wounded or trapped by Satan, why does Paul describe our relationship to the powers of darkness as a wrestling match? Those who deny the enemy's potential for destruction are the most vulnerable to it.

Father, I don't want to be ignorant in matters of the spiritual world. Remove all blinders from my eyes so I may see clearly and share the truth with others.

A Truth Encounter

Satan disguises himself as an angel of light. Therefore it is not surprising if his servants also disguise themselves as servants of righteousness (2 Corinthians 11:14,15).

Another common misconception of the spiritual world is that *demonic influence is only evident in extreme or violent behavior and gross sin.* Most Christians suffering from demonic activity lead relatively normal lives while experiencing serious personal and interpersonal problems for which no cause or solution has been found. Since they relegate satanic involvement only to mass murderers or violent sex criminals, these ordinary problem-plagued individuals wonder what's wrong with them and why they can't just "do better."

Satan's first and foremost strategy is deception. It is not the few raving demoniacs who are causing the church to be ineffective, but Satan's subtle deception and intrusion into the lives of "normal" believers. One Christian psychotherapist who attended my conference on spiritual conflicts and counseling said, "I discovered that two-thirds of my clients were having problems because they were being deceived by Satan—and so was I!"

A final misconception that must be dispelled is that *freedom from spiritual bondage is the result of a power encounter with demonic forces.* Freedom from spiritual conflicts and bondage is not a power encounter; it's a truth encounter. Satan is a deceiver, and he will work undercover at all costs. But the truth of God's Word exposes him and his lie. His demons are like cockroaches that scurry for the shadows when the light comes on. Satan's power is in the lie, and when his lie is exposed by the truth, his plans are foiled.

When God first disciplined the early church in Acts 5, He did so in a dramatic way. Peter confronted Ananias and Sapphira: "Why has Satan filled your heart to lie to the Holy Spirit?" (verse 3). God wanted the church to know that Satan the deceiver can ruin us if he can get us to believe and live a lie. If I could infiltrate a church, a committee, or a person undetected, and deceive them into believing a lie, I could control their lives! That's exactly what Satan is doing, and his lie is the focus of the battle.

Lord, enable me to stay alert to the enemy's wiles and arm myself with Your truth.

You shall know the truth, and the truth shall make you free (John 8:32).

When I was a boy on the farm, my dad, my brother, and I would visit our neighbor's farm to share produce and labor. The neighbor had a yappy little dog that scared the socks off me. When it came barking around the corner, my dad and brother stood their ground, but I ran. Guess who the dog chased! I escaped to the top of our pickup truck while the little dog yapped at me from the ground.

Everyone except me could see that the little dog had no power over me except what I gave it. Furthermore, it had no inherent power to throw me up on the pickup; it was my *belief* that put me up there. That dog controlled me by using my mind, my emotions, my will, and my muscles, all of which were motivated by fear. Finally I gathered up my courage, jumped off the pickup, and kicked a small rock at the mutt. Lo and behold, it ran!

Satan is like that yappy little dog: deceiving people into fearing him more than God. His power is in the lie. He is the father of lies (John 8:44) who deceives the whole world (Revelation 12:9), and consequently the whole world is under the influence of the evil one (1 John 5:19). He can do nothing about your position in Christ, but if he can deceive you into believing his lies about you and God, you will spend a lot of time on top of the pickup truck! You don't have to outshout him or outmuscle him to be free of his influence. You just have to *outtruth* him. Believe, declare, and act upon the truth of God's Word, and you will thwart Satan's strategy.

I have learned from the Scriptures and my experience that *truth* is the liberating agent. The power of Satan is in the lie, and the power of the believer is in knowing the truth. We are to pursue truth, not power.

Father God, when Satan is badgering and confusing me, remind me that Your Holy Spirit within me is greater than all the evil around me.

Beloved, do not believe every spirit, but test the spirits to see whether they are from God; because many false prophets have gone out into the world (1 John 4:1).

Paul warned us against the deception which comes through demonic influence (1 Timothy 4:1). John also cautioned us to test the spirits and to distinguish the spirit of truth from the spirit of error (1 John 4:1-6). Satan's demonic forces are at work attempting to pollute your mind with lies in order to keep you from walking in the truth. Hannah Whitall Smith wrote:

> There are the voices of evil and deceiving spirits, who lie in wait to entrap every traveler entering these higher regions of spiritual life....These spiritual enemies, whoever or whatever they may be, must necessarily communicate with us by means of our spiritual faculties, and their voices, as the voice of God, are an inward impression made upon our spirit. Therefore, just as the Holy Spirit may tell us by impressions what the will of God is concerning us, so also will these spiritual enemies tell us by impression what is their will concerning us, though not, of course, giving it their name.[1]

Due to the deceptive nature of his impressions, Satan's voice may not always be detected objectively. You need to pray in order to disassociate yourself from deceiving spirits.

Heavenly Father, I commit myself unreservedly to Your will. If I have been deceived in any way, I pray that You will open my eyes to the deception. I command in the name of the Lord Jesus Christ that all deceiving spirits depart from me, and I renounce and reject all counterfeit gifts (or any other spiritual phenomena). Lord, if it is from You, bless it and cause it to grow that Your body may be blessed and edified through it.

You have received a spirit of adoption as sons by which we cry out, "Abba! Father!" (Romans 8:15).

Claire attended a church college ministry I was involved in several years ago. On a physical, material level, Claire had absolutely nothing going for her. She had a dumpy figure and a bad complexion. Her father was a drunken bum who had deserted his family. Her mother worked two menial jobs just to make ends meet. Her older brother, a drug addict, was always in and out of the house.

When I first met Claire I was sure she was the ultimate wallflower. I didn't think there was any way she could compete for acceptance in a college-aged society which is attracted to physical beauty and material success. But to my delight, I learned that everybody in the group liked Claire and loved to be around her. She had lots of friends. And eventually she married the nicest guy in our college department.

What was her secret? Claire simply believed what she perceived herself to be: a child of God. She accepted herself for who God said she was in Christ, and she confidently committed herself to God's great goal for her life: to be conformed to His image and to love people. She wasn't a threat to anyone. Instead, she was so positive and caring toward others that everyone loved her.

Claire's experiences illustrate the importance of establishing our Christian lives on what we believe instead of how we behave. She knew that she couldn't compete with the world, so she gladly accepted her spiritual heritage, believed God, and lived accordingly. We need a firm grip on God's Word before we will experience much success at practical Christianity. We need to understand who we are as a result of who God is and what He has done. A productive Christian behavior system is the by-product of a solid Christian belief system, not the other way around.

Thank You for the Claires in my world, Lord, who reflect Your beauty. Forgive me for focusing on myself instead of looking to You and seeking Your eternal qualities.

The Seduction of Our Children

Bring [your children] up in the discipline and instruction of the Lord (Ephesians 6:4).

What are parents, Sunday school teachers, youth workers, and pastors to do in the face of Satan's assault on the minds of our children? Let's begin by stating what we can't do.

First, we can't bury our heads in the sand. This is not the time to respond in denial or claim that our Christian kids are immune to this kind of problem. Satan's seductive activities are aimed at destroying the church at its point of greatest vulnerability: the family. The enemy is after Christian families in general and the families of Christian leaders in particular. Half of all my counseling regarding demonic influence has been with Christian leaders and their families.

Second, we can't run in fear. Remember: Thanks to the death and resurrection of Jesus Christ, Satan is a defeated foe. The war against the seduction of our children is a winnable war. If we retreat instead of advance, we forfeit ground to the enemy that doesn't belong to him. We must exert our authority in Jesus Christ and claim His victory in the lives of our children.

How can we do that?

First, we must become aware of the spiritual nature of the world we live in. Our children are growing up in a seductive world. Many of the things that surround them are subtly influenced by the New Age Movement, the occult, and Satanism.

Second, we need to understand how parents and parenting styles can either assist or block the resolution of a child's spiritual conflicts. If a child comes from a dysfunctional home, it's rather pointless to deal with his problem only to send him back into the home that caused the problem in the first place.

Third, we need definite strategies for protecting our children from spiritual assault and helping them resolve their spiritual conflicts. This is a winnable war, and it is a war we must win for the sake of our kids and the cause of Christ.

Dear Father, keep me alert to spiritual opposition and bondage in my children, and equip me to assist them in appropriating Your freedom.

*Let them know that you, whose name is the LORD—
that you alone are the Most High over all the earth
(Psalm 83:18 NIV).*

The New Age Movement is very attractive to the natural man who has become disillusioned with organized religion and Western rationalism. He desires spiritual reality but doesn't want to give up materialism, deal with his moral problems, or come under authority.

I've discovered six unifying factors in New Age thinking. We will consider three of them today and three tomorrow.

The first is *monism*—the belief that all is one and one is all. It says we all swim in one great cosmic ocean. History is not the story of humanity's fall into sin and its restoration by God's saving grace. Rather, it is humanity's fall into ignorance and the gradual ascent into enlightenment.

Monism is a counterfeit to the unity Jesus prayed for in John 17:21. That unity is possible only when we are united together in Christian fellowship.

Second, *all is God*. If all is one, including God, then one must conclude that all is God—trees, snails, books, and people are all of one divine essence. A personal God is abandoned in favor of an impersonal energy force or consciousness, and if God is no longer personal, He doesn't have to be served.

New Agers say, "When I was a little child, I believed in God. When I began to mature, I stopped believing in God. Then I grew up and realized that I was God."

A third unifying factor refers to a *change in consciousness*. If we are God, we need to know we are God. We must become cosmically conscious, also called "at-one-ment" (a counterfeit of atonement), self-realization, god-realization, enlightenment, or attunement. Their faith has no object, neither does their meditation, so it becomes an inward journey. To us, the essential issue is not whether we believe or meditate, but who we believe in and what we meditate upon. We believe God and meditate upon His law day and night.

Lord, I affirm that I am nothing, can do nothing, and will amount to nothing apart from You. You are the object of my faith and life today.

There is one God, and one mediator also between God and men, the man Christ Jesus (1 Timothy 2:5).

The fourth unifying factor of the New Age Movement is *a cosmic evolutionary optimism*. There is a New Age coming. There will be a new world order with a one-world government. New Agers believe in a progressive unification of world consciousness eventually reaching the "omega point." This is a counterfeit kingdom and we know who its prince is.

Fifth, New Agers *create their own reality*. They believe they can determine reality by what they believe, so by changing what they believe, they can change reality. There are no moral absolutes because there is no distinction between good and evil.

Sixth, New Agers *make contact with the kingdom of darkness*. Calling a medium a "channeler" and a demon a "spirit guide" has not changed the reality of what they are. They are in contact with the god of this world instead of the God of Abraham, Isaac, and Jacob.

Recently I received a call from a lady who was concerned about the turn of events in a small group she was attending. It had started out as a group of supposedly Christian women. Then one woman began to function as a medium, and they thought they were hearing from God. They recorded six hours of videotape, and in that six hours, five different personalities can be identified in the medium. The group was convinced they were hearing from God, Jesus, the Holy Spirit, and two angels.

The lady functioning as a medium was later identified as not being a Christian. In the tape her eyes roll back in a trancelike state. At one point a voice says through her, "It's going to snow here tomorrow." I'm surprised that when it didn't snow the next day, they couldn't see the snow job being done on them!

How can a thinking person, professing to be a Christian, consider this as anything other than demonization? But it isn't just lonely homemakers who are being deceived. This deception is invading every area of society today.

Father, keep me alert to the deception of New Age thinking around me, and help me dismiss the darkness I encounter with the light of Your truth.

Your New Skipper

We are under obligation, not to the flesh, to live according to the flesh—for if you are living according to the flesh, you must die (Romans 8:12,13).

When I was in the Navy we called the captain of our ship "the Old Man." Our Old Man was tough and crusty, and nobody liked him. He used to go out drinking with all his chiefs while belittling and harassing his junior officers and making life miserable for the rest of us. He was not a good example of a naval officer. So when our Old Man got transferred to another ship, we all rejoiced. It was a great day for our ship.

Then we got a new skipper—a new Old Man. The old Old Man no longer had any authority over us; he was gone—completely out of the picture. But I was trained under that Old Man. So how do you think I related to the new Old Man? At first I responded to him just like I had been conditioned to respond to the old skipper. I tiptoed around him expecting him to bite my head off. That's how I had lived for two years around my first skipper.

But as I got to know the new skipper I realized that he wasn't a crusty old tyrant like my old Old Man. He wasn't out to harass his crew; he was a good guy, really concerned about us. But I had been programmed for two years to react a certain way when I saw a captain's braids. I didn't need to react that way any longer, but it took several months to recondition myself to the new skipper.

You also once served under a cruel, self-serving skipper: your old sinful self with its sinful nature. The admiral of that fleet is Satan himself, the prince of darkness. But by God's grace you have been transferred into Christ's kingdom (Colossians 1:13). You now have a new skipper: your new self which is infused with the divine nature of Jesus Christ, your new admiral. As a child of God, a saint, you are no longer under the authority of your old Old Man. He is dead, buried, gone forever.

So why do you still react as if your old skipper were still in control of your behavior? We'll answer that question tomorrow.

Praise You, Lord, that my relationship with my old skipper, that old sinful self, is gone. I choose to live today in the reality of my new nature in Christ.

Your Life Apart from God

If by the Spirit you are putting to death the deeds of the body, you will live. For all who are being led by the Spirit of God, these are sons of God (Romans 8:13,14).

Why do you still react as if your old skipper were still in control of your behavior? Because, while you served under it, your old self trained and conditioned your actions, reactions, emotional responses, thought patterns, memories, and habits in a part of your brain called "the flesh." The flesh is that tendency within each person to operate independently of God and to center his interests on himself. An unsaved person functions totally in the flesh (Romans 8:7,8), worshiping and serving the creature rather than the Creator (Romans 1:25). Such persons "live for themselves" (2 Corinthians 5:15), even though many of their activities may appear to be motivated by selflessness and concern for others.

When you were born again, your old self died and your new self came to life, and you were made a partaker of Christ's divine nature. But your flesh remains. You brought to your Christian commitment a fully conditioned mind-set and lifestyle developed apart from God and centered on yourself. Since you were born physically alive but spiritually dead, you had neither the presence of God nor the knowledge of God's ways. So you learned to live your life independently of God. It is this learned independence that makes the flesh hostile toward God.

During the years you spent separated from God, your worldly experiences thoroughly programmed your brain with thought patterns, memory traces, responses, and habits which are alien to God. So even though your old self is gone, your flesh remains in opposition to God as a preprogrammed propensity for sin, which is living independently of God.

Be aware that you no longer have to obey that preprogrammed bent to live independently of God. You are a child of God, and you are free to put to death those fleshly deeds and obey Christ.

Lord, I make a fresh declaration of dependence on You for today. I renounce all my old tendencies to live independently of You.

Walk by the Spirit, and you will not carry out the desire of the flesh (Galatians 5:16).

A careful distinction must be made concerning your relationship to the flesh as a Christian. There is a difference in Scripture between being *in* the flesh and walking *according* to the flesh. As a Christian, you are no longer in the flesh. That phrase describes people who are still spiritually dead (Romans 8:8), those who live independently of God. Everything they do, whether morally good or bad, is in the flesh.

You are not in the flesh; you are in Christ. You are no longer independent of God; you have declared your dependence upon Him by placing faith in Christ. But even though you are not *in* the flesh, you may still choose to walk *according* to the flesh (Romans 8:12,13). You may still act independently of God by responding to the mind-set, patterns, and habits ingrained in you by the world you lived in. Paul rebuked the immature Corinthian Christians as "fleshly" because of their expressions of jealousy, strife, division, and misplaced identity (1 Corinthians 3:1-3). He listed the evidences of fleshly living in Galatians 5:19-21. Unbelievers can't help but live according to the flesh because they are totally in the flesh. But your old skipper is gone. You are no longer in the flesh and you no longer need to live according to its desires.

Getting rid of the old self was God's responsibility, but rendering the flesh and its deeds inoperative is our responsibility (Romans 8:12). God has changed your nature, but it's your responsibility to change your behavior by "putting to death the deeds of the body" (Romans 8:13). You will gain victory over the flesh by learning to condition your behavior after your new skipper, your new self which is infused with the nature of Christ, and learning to transform your old pattern for thinking and responding to your sin-trained flesh by renewing your mind (Romans 12:2).

Lord, knowing that I am no longer controlled by sin is such a liberating concept. I can walk today in freedom from my old self, the world system, and the devil. Praise Your name!

I have written to you, fathers, because you know Him who has been from the beginning. I have written to you, young men, because you are strong, and the word of God abides in you, and you have overcome the evil one (1 John 2:14).

First John 2:12-14 describes three levels of Christian growth in relation to sin. The first level is compared to "little children" (verse 12). Little children in the faith are characterized by having their sins forgiven and possessing a knowledge of God. In other words, they are in the family of God and have overcome the penalty of sin, but they haven't grown to full maturity.

The second level is "young men" (verses 13,14), those who have overcome the evil one. These are aggressively growing believers who are strong because the Word of God abides in them. They know the truth and how to use it to resist Satan in the battle for their minds. They are no longer in bondage to uncontrollable habits, and they have resolved the personal and spiritual conflicts which keep many Christians from experiencing freedom in Christ. They are free, and they know how to stay free.

The third level is "fathers" (verses 13,14), those who have developed a deep personal knowledge of God. Their faith is securely founded on a close, intimate, loving relationship with God, which is the goal of our spiritual growth. What about your faith? Are you a "child," a "young man," or a "father"? Is it your daily goal to grow to maturity in your faith? Have you overcome the evil one?

Having challenged us to combat sin's power in our lives through a commitment to growth, John goes on to describe the avenues through which Satan tempts us: the lust of the flesh, the lust of the eyes, and the boastful pride of life. We will consider these avenues over the next few days.

Heavenly Father, please shake me good if I become stagnant, stale, or static in my spiritual growth. I want to grow into Your image of me.

Satan's Threefold Temptation

For all that is in the world, the lust of the flesh and the lust of the eyes and the boastful pride of life, is not from the Father, but is from the world (1 John 2:16).

You will be better prepared to resist temptation in your life when you realize that, according to the Scriptures, there are only three channels through which Satan will entice you to act independently of God. They are summarized in John's instructions to believers concerning our relationship to this world: "Do not love the world, nor the things in the world. If anyone loves the world, the love of the Father is not in him. For all that is in the world, the lust of the flesh and the lust of the eyes and the boastful pride of life, is not from the Father, but is from the world. And the world is passing away, and also its lusts; but the one who does the will of God abides forever" (1 John 2:15-17).

The three channels of temptation are the *lust of the flesh*, the *lust of the eyes*, and the *pride of life*. The lust of the flesh preys on our physical appetites and their gratifications in this world. The lust of the eyes appeals to self-interest and tests the Word of God. The pride of life stresses self-promotion and self-exaltation. Satan confronted both the first Adam and the last Adam through each of these three channels of temptation.

Notice how Satan used precisely those three channels to deceive Eve: "When the woman saw that the tree was good for food [lust of the flesh], and that it was a delight to the eyes [lust of the eyes], and that the tree was desirable to make one wise [pride of life], she took from its fruit and ate" (Genesis 3:6).

The first Adam failed miserably, and we still suffer the results of his failure. But the last Adam—Jesus Christ—met Satan's threefold temptation head-on and succeeded triumphantly. In Him we have the resources and the power to conquer every temptation Satan throws at us.

Dear God, please tear down any pride or self-deception I may have concerning Satan's strategies of temptation. I know I can never become complacent about spiritual warfare.

The Lust of the Flesh

The lust of the flesh...is not from the Father, but is from the world (1 John 2:16).

Satan first approached Eve through the channel of the lust of the flesh. He planted a doubt in her mind about the fruit of the tree when he said: "Has God said, 'You shall not eat from any tree of the garden'?" (Genesis 3:1). Eve answered, "God has said, 'You shall not eat from it or touch it' " (verse 3). But Satan had piqued her appetite for the forbidden fruit, and she "saw that the tree was good for food" (verse 6). Yielding to the lust of the flesh contributed to Adam and Eve's downfall.

Satan also challenged Jesus through the channel of the lust of the flesh. Our Lord had been fasting for 40 days when Satan tempted Him in the wilderness at the point of His apparent vulnerability: "If You are the Son of God, command that these stones become bread" (Matthew 4:3). Satan is not omniscient, but he's not blind either. He learned about Jesus' apparent vulnerability to physical temptation by watching Him go without food for 40 days. He's watching you too, looking for soft spots of vulnerability in your appetites for food, rest, comfort, and sex. Temptation is greatest when hunger, fatigue, and loneliness are acute.

The temptation of the lust of the flesh is designed to draw us away from the will of God to serve the flesh (Galatians 5:16,17). When Satan tempts you through the channel of the lust of the flesh, he will invite you to fulfill your needs in ways that are outside the boundary of God's will. Whenever you feel enticed to meet a legitimate need by acting independently of God, you are being tempted through the lust of the flesh.

When you resist the temptations of the lust of the flesh, you are declaring your dependence on God for your needs. As such you are remaining "in the vine," tapping into the resources Jesus referred to in John 15:5. But when you yield to temptation in this area your fruitfulness as a Christian will suffer, because apart from Christ you can do nothing.

You are a strong, fruitful vine, Lord, and I will not wither as long as I remain in You. Strengthen me today to resist the temptation to meet my needs apart from You.

The Lust of the Eyes

The lust of the eyes...is not from the Father, but is from the world (1 John 2:16).

The second channel of temptation through which Satan came to Adam and Eve related to his lie concerning the consequences of disobeying God. God had said that death would accompany disobedience, but Satan said, "You surely shall not die!" (Genesis 3:4). He was appealing to Eve's sense of self-preservation by falsely assuring her that God was wrong on the issue of sin's consequences. "Don't listen to Him; do what's right in your own eyes," he urged. The forbidden fruit was a delight to her eyes (verse 6), so she and Adam ignored God's command in order to do what appeared to serve their own best interests.

The lust of the eyes subtly draws us away from the Word of God and eats away at our confidence in God. We see what the world has to offer and desire it above our relationship with God. We begin to place more credence in our own perspective of life than in God's commands and promises. Fueled by the lust for what we see, ve grab for all we can get, believing that we need it and deceived that God wants us to have it. Wrongly assuming that God will withhold nothing good from us, we lustfully claim prosperity.

Instead of trusting God wholeheartedly, we adopt a "prove it to me" attitude. That was the essence of Satan's second temptation of Jesus: "If You are the Son of God, throw Yourself down [from the pinnacle of the temple]" (Matthew 4:6). But Jesus wasn't about to play Satan's "show me" game. He replied, "It is written, 'You shall not put the LORD your God to the test'" (verse 7).

God is under no obligation to us; He is under obligation only to Himself. There is no way you can cleverly word a prayer so that God must respond to it. That not only distorts the meaning of prayer but puts us in the position of God. The righteous shall live by faith in the written Word of God and not demand that God prove Himself in response to our whims or wishes, no matter how noble they may be. We are the ones being tested, not God.

Forgive me, Father, for the times I have listened to the enemy's lies and tried to meet my needs the way I saw fit. You are God, not me. I look to You to supply all my needs in Your own way.

The boastful pride of life is not from the Father, but is from the world (1 John 2:16).

The third channel of temptation is at the heart of the New Age Movement: the temptation to direct our own destiny, to rule our own world, to be our own god. Satan tantalized Eve concerning the forbidden fruit: "The day you eat from it your eyes will be opened, and you will be like God, knowing good and evil" (Genesis 3:5). Satan's offer was an exaggerated appeal to our God-instilled propensity to rule. "Don't be satisfied ruling *under* God," he seemed to say, "when you have the potential to be *like* God." When Eve was convinced that "the tree was desirable to make one wise" (verse 6), she and Adam ate.

Satan's promise that the couple would become like God was nothing more than a lie. When Adam and Eve yielded to his temptation, they didn't become the gods of this world as he claimed they would. Instead, they fell from their position of rulership with God, and Satan became the god of this world by default—exactly as he had planned.

Satan tried the same ploy with Jesus: "All [the kingdoms of the world and their glory] will I give You, if You fall down and worship me" (Matthew 4:9). When you think about it, Satan's offer was pretty ridiculous. Why would Jesus be tempted to worship Satan in exchange for the world when He already owned the universe? So He replied, "Begone, Satan! For it is written, 'You shall worship the LORD your God, and serve Him only' " (verse 10).

The temptation of the pride of life is intended to steer us away from the worship of God and destroy our obedience to God by urging us to become our own god. Whenever you feel that you don't need God's help or direction, that you can handle your life without consulting Him, that you don't need to bow the knee to anyone, beware: That's the pride of life. Whenever you stop worshiping and serving God you are in reality worshiping and serving Satan—which is what he wants more than anything else. Instead, your life should be characterized by worshipful humility and obedience to God (1 Peter 5:5-11; John 15:8-10).

Father, help me resist the temptation to be more than You have called me to be when I wrongfully assume Your role as captain of my soul.

Active Faith

You have faith, and I have works; show me your faith without the works, and I will show you my faith by my works (James 2:18).

When my son Karl was just a toddler, I would stand him up on the table and call for him to jump from the table into my arms. Did Karl believe I would catch him? Yes. How did I know he believed? Because he jumped. Suppose he wouldn't jump. "Do you believe I will catch you, Karl?" I might coax, and he may nod yes. But if he never jumps, does he really believe I will catch him? No. Faith is active, not passive. Faith takes a stand. Faith makes a move. Faith speaks up.

There are a lot of Christians who claim to have great faith in God but are spiritually lethargic and don't do anything. Faith without action is not faith; it's dead, meaningless (James 2:17,18)! If it isn't expressed, it isn't faith. In order to believe God and His Word, we must do what He says. If you don't do what He says, you don't really believe Him. Faith and action are inseparable.

Sadly, one of the common pictures of the church today is of a group of people with an assumed faith but little action. We're thankful that our sins are forgiven and that Jesus is preparing a place in heaven for us, but we're basically cowering in fear and defeat in the world, just hanging on until the rapture. We treat the church as if it's a hospital. We get together to compare wounds and hold each other's hands, yearning for Jesus to come take us away.

The church is not a hospital; it's a military outpost under orders to storm the gates of hell. Every believer is on active duty, called to take part in fulfilling the Great Commission (Matthew 28:19,20). Thankfully the church has an infirmary where we can minister to the weak and wounded, and that ministry is necessary. But our real purpose is to be change agents in the world, taking a stand, living by faith, and accomplishing something for God. You can say you believe God and His Word. But if you are not actively involved in His plan, are you really a mature believer?

Lord, if I'm not moving forward by faith and taking ground today, I'm only treading water or slipping backward. Nudge me forward today, Lord.

The Choice of Forgiveness

Be kind to one another, tender-hearted, forgiving each other, just as God in Christ has also forgiven you (Ephesians 4:32).

Most of the ground that Satan gains in the lives of Christians is due to unforgiveness. We are warned to forgive others so that Satan cannot take advantage of us (2 Corinthians 2:10,11). God requires us to forgive others from our hearts or He will turn us over to the tormentors (Matthew 18:34,35). Why is forgiveness so critical to our freedom? Because of the cross. God didn't give us what we *deserve*; He gave us what we *needed* according to His mercy. We are to be merciful just as our heavenly Father is merciful (Luke 6:36). We are to forgive as we have been forgiven (Ephesians 4:31,32).

Forgiveness is not forgetting. People who try to forget find that they cannot. God says He will "remember no more" our sins (Hebrews 10:17), but God, being omniscient, cannot forget. "Remember no more" means that God will never use the past against us (Psalm 103:12). Forgetting may be a result of forgiveness, but it is never the means of forgiveness. When we bring up the past and use it against others, we haven't forgiven them.

Forgiveness is a choice, a crisis of the will. We choose to face and acknowledge the hurt and the hate in order to forgive from the heart. Since God requires us to forgive, it is something we can do. (He would never require us to do something we cannot do.) But forgiveness is difficult for us because it pulls against our concept of justice. We want revenge for offenses suffered. But we are told never to take our own revenge (Romans 12:19). "Why should I let them off the hook?" we protest. You let them off *your* hook, but they are never off God's hook. He will deal with them fairly—something we cannot do.

If you don't let offenders off your hook, you are hooked to them and the past, and that just means continued pain for you. Stop the pain; let it go. You don't forgive someone merely for their sake; you do it for *your* sake so you can be free. Your need to forgive isn't an issue between you and the offender; it's between you and God.

Lord, I stand amazed at the example of Your forgiveness. I desire to grow in my willingness to forgive those who have hurt me.

Forgive your brother from your heart (Matthew 18:35 NIV).

Forgiveness is agreeing to live with the consequences of another person's sin. Forgiveness is costly; we pay the price of the evil we forgive. Yet you're going to live with those consequences whether you want to or not; your only choice is whether you will do so in the bondage of bitterness or the freedom of forgiveness. That's how Jesus forgave you—He took the consequences of your sin upon Himself. All true forgiveness is substitutional, because no one really forgives without bearing the penalty of the other person's sin.

Why then do we forgive? Because Christ forgave us. God the Father "made Him who knew no sin to be sin on our behalf, that we might become the righteousness of God in Him" (2 Corinthians 5:21). Where is the justice? The cross makes forgiveness legally and morally right: "For the death that He died, He died to sin, once for all" (Romans 6:10).

How do you forgive from the heart? First, you acknowledge the hurt and the hate. If your forgiveness doesn't visit the emotional core of your past, it will be incomplete. This is the great evangelical cover-up. Christians feel the pain of interpersonal offenses, but we won't acknowledge it. Let God bring the pain to the surface so He can deal with it. This is where the healing takes place.

Ask God to bring to your mind those you need to forgive. Make a list of all those who have offended you. Since God has forgiven them by His grace, you can forgive them too. For each person on your list, say: "Lord, I forgive (name) for (offenses)." Keep praying about each individual until you are sure that all the remembered pain has been dealt with. Don't try to rationalize or explain the offender's behavior. Forgiveness deals with your pain, not another's behavior. Remember: Positive feelings will follow in time; freeing yourself from the past is the critical issue.

Lord, I desire to be free from the hurt and the hate of offenses in my past. Today I move beyond desiring to forgive and asking Your help to forgive. Lord, I forgive ________ for ________.

To those who have been sanctified in Christ Jesus, saints by calling, with all who in every place call upon the name of our Lord Jesus Christ, their Lord and ours (1 Corinthians 1:2).

Have you noticed that one of the most frequently used words of identity for Christians in the New Testament is *saint*? A saint is literally a holy person. Yet Paul and the other writers of the Epistles used the word generously to describe common, ordinary, everyday Christians like you and me. For example, Paul's salutation in 1 Corinthians 1:2 reads: "To the church of God which is at Corinth, to those who have been sanctified in Christ Jesus, saints by calling, with all who in every place call upon the name of our Lord Jesus Christ, their Lord and ours."

Notice that Paul didn't say that we are saints by hard work. He clearly states that we are saints by calling. Some of us have bought into the mentality that saints are people who have earned their lofty title by living a magnificent life or achieving a certain level of maturity. No way. The Bible says you are a saint because God called you to be a saint. You were "sanctified in Christ"—made a saint by participating in the life of the only true holy one, Jesus Christ.

Many Christians refer to themselves as sinners saved by grace. But are you really a sinner? Is that your scriptural identity? Not at all. God doesn't call you a sinner; He calls you a saint—a holy one. If you think of yourself as a sinner, guess what you will do: You'll live like a sinner; you'll sin. Why not identify yourself for who you really are: a saint who sins. Remember: What you do doesn't determine who you are; who you are determines what you do.

Since you are a saint in Christ by God's calling, you share in Christ's inheritance. That which is true of Christ is now true of you, because you are *in* Christ. It's part of your identity. You are not the great "I AM," but with Paul you can say, "By the grace of God I am what I am" (1 Corinthians 15:10).

Your grace and Your calling in my life are totally undeserved, but it is my privilege to claim my inheritance. Thank You, Father. Thank You, Jesus.

How to Treat People

Be devoted to one another in brotherly love; give preference to one another in honor (Romans 12:10).

A pastor came to see me one day asking, "How can I get out of my church?"

"Why do you want out?" I asked him. "What's wrong with your church?"

"I've got a bunch of losers in my church."

"Losers? I wonder if they are really losers or if they just see themselves as losers because that's how you see them."

He agreed that it was probably the latter. And he was right, because there are no losers in the kingdom of God—none whatsoever. How can a child of God be called a loser? As important as it is for you to believe in your true identity as a child of God, it is equally important that you perceive other Christians for who they are and treat them accordingly.

I believe that the greatest determinant of how we treat people is how we perceive them. If we see people as losers we will begin to believe that they are losers. And if we believe they are losers we will treat them like losers and they will mirror our behavior and act like losers. But if we perceive our brothers and sisters in Christ as redeemed, righteous saints, we will treat them as saints and they will be greatly helped in behaving as saints.

When Paul led Onesimus, a runaway slave, to Christ, he sent him back to his master and told Philemon to accept him as a beloved brother (Philemon 16). We need to perceive and treat all believers, regardless of their socioeconomic strata, as beloved brothers. Peter instructed husbands to treat their wives as fellow heirs of the grace of life (1 Peter 3:7). Your spouse, regardless of his or her faults, is your spiritual equal and must be treated accordingly.

The New Testament clearly states that we are saints who sin. Any child of God who says he doesn't sin is called a liar (1 John 1:8). But we are not to focus on one another's sins. Instead we are called to perceive the Christlike nature in each other, believe in each other as saints, and build each other up.

Thank You, Lord, that love covers a multitude of sins. Help me to be loving and accepting of others today instead of critical.

Let no unwholesome word proceed from your mouth, but only such a word as is good for edification according to the need of the moment, that it may give grace to those who hear (Ephesians 4:29).

How do we express our perceptions of people? Primarily by what we say to them. Studies have shown that, in the average home, for every positive statement, a child receives 10 negative statements. The school environment is only slightly better; students hear seven negative statements from their teachers for every one positive statement. No wonder so many children are growing up feeling that they are losers. Parents and teachers are conveying that perception every day in how they talk to their children.

These studies go on to point out that it takes four positive statements to negate the effect of one negative statement. You probably verify that finding every time you wear a new suit or dress. A number of your friends may say, "Oh, what a good-looking outfit." But it only takes one comment like "It's really not you" to send you scurrying back to the store for a refund. We affect others significantly by what we say about them, and what we say is significantly determined by how we perceive them.

If we could memorize just one verse from the New Testament, put it into practice and never violate it, I believe we would resolve half to three-fourths of the problems in our homes and churches. The verse is Ephesians 4:29. Isn't it amazing that you and I have the power to give grace to others through the proper use of our words? If we said nothing to put others down, and only built up others as Ephesians 4:29 commands, we would be part of God's construction crew in the church instead of members of Satan's wrecking crew.

Father, I know my tongue is capable of blessing or cursing others. Guard my words today so I may edify others through what I say.

For God has not given us a spirit of timidity, but of power and love and discipline (2 Timothy 1:7).

Once I counseled a former high priest of Satanism who desperately wanted to be free of the demonic powers who had ruled his life. But Satan was not about to let go of him without a fight. As I tried to talk to him, Harry ranted and raved and rolled around the office like a crazy man. The demons who controlled Harry were using his mind, his will, his muscles, and his emotions in a noisy display of resistance.

But I just sat still. I learned a long time ago that Satan's show of power is just another facet of his deception designed to provoke fear. He knows that if he can deceive us into being afraid of him, fear will control our lives instead of faith. Satan "prowls about like a roaring lion, seeking someone to devour" (1 Peter 5:8). Why does a lion roar? To paralyze its prey with fear. Once its victim is immobilized by fear, the lion can easily subdue it and kill it.

But because of our position, authority, and protection in Christ, Satan can't touch us. If you cower in fear at Satan's show of power, then he has you on the defensive. But Peter instructed, "Resist him, firm in your faith" (1 Peter 5:9). Satan is defeated; believe it and stand up to him. When you do, he has no choice but to eventually back down.

As the devil roared at me through Harry, I began to read Scripture aloud and pray in a normal, controlled voice that the enemy would be bound in silence. After I had spent several minutes taking authority in Christ through prayer and reading Scripture, Harry fell flat on his stomach in front of me. "Lord Jesus, I need You!" he cried out. I led him in a prayer of commitment to Christ. And when Harry finally stood up he was free. He embraced me with a childlike joy he had never experienced before.

The devil's bark is much bigger than his bite. Stand firm in the faith and resist him, and he will flee.

Lord, help me be bold and not fearful in the face of Satan's attacks. I want to walk in freedom and help others find freedom as well.

Bloom Where You Are Planted

It is required of stewards that one be found trustworthy (1 Corinthians 4:2).

An important concept about the will of God that my students hear at seminary is, "Bloom where you are planted." Be the best you can be at your present assignment, and stay there until God calls you elsewhere.

Oftentimes my students will say, "There are no openings to serve at my church!" My response, "Oh, yes there are. They're probably begging for someone to teach third-grade boys." The momentary silence reveals this thought: "But anyone can teach third-grade boys. I had something bigger in mind." Like maybe an opening in the Trinity!

Take the opportunity before you and teach those third-grade boys. Decide to be the best teacher they've ever had. You may start with only three little boys, but at the end of that year you've got 12 boys excited about God, Sunday school, and church. Next year, when the personnel committee needs to fill leadership positions, they say, "We need some new life on the Christian education committee." Somebody aware of the fruit you are bearing says, "There's this guy doing a bang-up job with our third graders. Let's ask him to be on the committee."

Now that you are on the Christian education committee, decide to be the best committee member you can be. It won't be long before they recognize your initiative and say, "We could use this person on the board." Determine to become the best possible board member you can. Then an opening develops for an intern and guess who the people suggest! People hearing of your faithfulness and aware of the fruit you are bearing ask you to consider a full-time pastoral position. So you become the best youth pastor, small group pastor, or college minister you can possibly be. Before long you'll be bearing so much fruit that other churches will be inquiring about your availability.

God guides those who bloom where they are planted.

I want to be faithful in the small things, Lord, so You will advance me to greater responsibilities in Your timing and according to Your will.

Do not quench the Spirit; do not despise prophetic utterances. But examine everything carefully; hold fast to that which is good (1 Thessalonians 5:19-21).

If you accept prophetic utterances as valid for today, I would encourage you to test them in the following ways.

First, is the person giving the prophetic utterance living a balanced and righteous lifestyle? You must carefully evaluate the person announcing, "Thus saith the Lord." Also, be on guard for the person who wants to bring a "new thing." If it is true, it's not new. If it is new, it's not true.

Second, is the person committed to building God's kingdom or his own? Is Christ being lifted up or is he?

Third, does the prophetic utterance establish confidence in the Word of God, and is it consistent with a balanced presentation of it? Are people going to have a greater dependency on God's revelation or man's inspiration? Are prophetic utterances a substitute for the serious, personal study of God's Word?

Fourth, does the use of the spiritual gift bring unity to the church and build up the body? Be careful in this test, because those who hold to a form of godliness but deny its power are not in balance either. They will quench the Spirit through censorship and very little will be accomplished in the church. They can cause disunity as well.

Last, do the spiritual manifestations bypass the mind? God operates through our mind; Satan bypasses it. If a person takes on a medium-like trance, be assured it is occultic. God renews our mind and brings back to our mind all that He has taught us. We are to think so as to have sound judgment.

All of us receive input from a myriad of sources today. With Satan still using false prophets in his battle for your mind, determine to discern the truth God wants you to know to set you free and keep you free.

Lord, I want to be so in tune with Your Word that I can discern error and darkness even when it appears as truth and light.

What God Wants Done

Be anxious for nothing, but in everything by prayer and supplication with thanksgiving let your requests be made known to God (Philippians 4:6).

When you feel anxious in a task or a relationship, your anxiety may be signaling the uncertainty of a goal you have chosen. You are hoping something will happen, but you have no guarantee that it will. You can control some of the factors, but not all of them.

For example, a teenager may believe that her happiness at school depends on her parents allowing her to attend a school dance. Not knowing how they will respond, she is anxious. If they say no, she will be angry because her goal is blocked. But if she knows all along that there is no possible chance of them saying yes, she will be depressed because her goal will not be achieved.

When you base your future success on something that can never happen, you have an impossible, hopeless goal. Your depression is a signal that your goal, no matter how spiritual or noble, may never be reached. Some forms of depression can be caused by chemical imbalances. But if there is no physical cause for the depression, then that depression is the expression of hopelessness.

No God-given goal can be blocked, uncertain, or impossible. With God all things are possible. If God issued a command that could not be obeyed, it would undermine His authority. If God wants it done, it can be done.

The real question is: What does God want done? The answer? He wants us to be what He has called us to be. And if that's what God wants done, no situations or circumstances of life can keep you from being the engineer, homemaker, parent, or leader God has called you to be.

Lord, help me keep my eyes on what You want done in my life, not on the seemingly impossible hindrances that keep me from growing in You.

SOWING AND REAPING

Do not be deceived, God is not mocked; for whatever a man sows, this he will also reap (Galatians 6:7).

The Scriptures are full of warnings about self-deception. James 1:26 reminds us that we deceive ourselves when we think we are religious but do not bridle our tongue. There is nothing that grieves God more than when we bad-mouth people instead of building them up with our speech. We are never to use our tongues to put others down. Instead we are to edify one another in what we say and thereby give grace to those who hear us. If your tongue is out of control, you're fooling yourself to believe that you have your spiritual life together.

We also deceive ourselves when we think we will not reap what we sow (Galatians 6:7). As Christians we sometimes think we are exempt from this principle, but we are not. Even though our sins are forgiven, we will have to live with the results and consequences of our thoughts, words, and actions, whether good or bad.

Since I was privileged to be raised on a farm, I witnessed every year the law of cause and effect. If we didn't sow good seed in the spring, we didn't reap a good crop in the fall. If we didn't feed the sheep, they died. Our young people have difficulty grasping this simple sow-and-reap truth. Living from weekend to weekend or party to party, they fail to prepare themselves for the future.

Your life may be measured by what you reap, but it is determined by what you sow. For example, if you want a friend, be a friend. What you get out of life is what you put into it.

Lord, guard me from the self-deception of thinking You will always cover for me or pull me out of the jams I get myself into. Help me learn to sow what I hope to reap.

Enter His gates with thanksgiving, and His courts with praise. Give thanks to Him; bless His name (Psalm 100:4).

Praise and thanksgiving are part of every level of prayer. They are continuous as we walk in the light. To come before God with thanksgiving is no different than coming before our earthly parents with an attitude of gratitude. Nothing disturbs a parent more than a child who is always demanding, forever complaining, and never satisfied. How would you feel if you've given as much as you can as a parent and your child still wants more, more, more? On the other hand, how would you feel toward the child who snuggles up and says, "Thanks for being who you are. I just love you and I know you're doing the best you can for me." What a great parent-child relationship.

Can you imagine approaching God and demanding, "I want more!"

And He responds, "I gave you My only begotten Son."

"But I want more!"

We ought to start every day by saying, "Thank You, heavenly Father. I deserved eternal damnation, but You gave me eternal life. How may I serve You today?"

Praising God is acknowledging His attributes. I try to be aware when I pray that God is the ever-present, all-powerful, all-knowing, loving heavenly Father. I don't praise Him because He needs me to tell Him who He is. He knows who He is. I am the one who needs to keep His divine attributes constantly in my mind. I try to keep the knowledge of God's presence foremost in my thoughts. No matter where I go, He is with me.

I'm always disturbed when I hear people asking God to "be there." It's like we are questioning His omnipresence. The same goes for asking God to be with our missionaries. We have the assurance of Scripture that He will be with them unto the ends of the earth. We can confidently acknowledge that He will neither leave us nor forsake us. We ought to thank God for His presence and ask Him to bring to our minds anything that may be keeping us from having perfect fellowship with Him.

Father God, teach me to practice the awareness of Your presence and accept the sufficiency of Your attributes.

A house divided against itself falls (Luke 11:17).

Satan's strategy is to use a problem situation to put you and your spouse at odds with each other. Jesus said, "A house divided against itself falls" (Luke 11:17). Many times I have said to parents, "Don't let this pull you apart." Inevitably they glance at each other, because that's precisely what's been going on.

"If you would have been more firm with our child, this wouldn't have happened," one blames.

"It's because you didn't set the standards by having family devotions every night," the other retorts.

Or if they did have devotions, "You just read to the children, you never communicate with them!"

"If you were home more often, I'd have more time to communicate with them!"

There may be a grain of truth in every statement above. But it's history, and tearing each other down will only make the problem worse. You must be united in order to survive the crisis. Character-bashing is from the pit.

Many parents are intimidated by a child's threats or find it easier to give in to a temper tantrum than not to. But you cannot let a rebellious child rule the home. It takes an iron will and the grace of God to stand your ground and not let your child control you. Sad are the children whose parents let them rule the roost. Even sadder are the children whose parents rule without love. If you manage to control through loveless intimidation and force, your child will be emotionally crippled. Rules without a relationship lead to rebellion.

Any crisis in the home can make or break you. You can choose to grow through the crisis and become a better person than you were before. Romans 5:3,4 encourages, "We also exult in our tribulations, knowing that tribulation brings about perseverance; and perseverance, proven character; and proven character, hope."

Lord, I refuse Satan's strategy to divide our home by quenching our love or overemphasizing rules. Help me do my part to keep our home united in You.

BELIEVING IN CHRIST'S AUTHORITY

Truly I say to you, if you have faith as a mustard seed, you shall say to this mountain, "Move from here to there," and it shall move; and nothing shall be impossible to you (Matthew 17:20).

What does it take to effectively exercise Christ's authority over spiritual powers? Can any Christian do so regardless of his level of spiritual maturity? If so, why aren't we more consistent in demonstrating our authority over Satan's kingdom?

I believe there are at least four qualifications for demonstrating authority over rulers and authorities in the spiritual realm. We'll consider them over the next few days.

The first qualification is *belief*. In the spiritual realm, if you don't believe you have authority, you're not going to exercise it. If your belief is weak, your expression of it will also be weak and ineffective. But if you grasp with confidence the authority that Christ has conferred upon you, you will exercise it with confidence.

Imagine a rookie traffic cop approaching a busy intersection to direct traffic for the first time. They told him at the academy that all he had to do was step into the street and hold up his hand and the cars would stop, but he's not so sure. He stands on the curb, tweets his whistle weakly, and sort of waves at an oncoming car, which roars by him. His authority is diminished by his lack of confidence.

Now imagine a seasoned officer coming on the scene. He sizes up the situation, steps into the street carefully but confidently, gives a blast on his whistle, and stretches out his hand—and the cars stop. There's no doubt in his mind that he's in control in that intersection because he has a settled belief in his authority.

You may consider yourself just a "rookie" at stopping the devil's traffic in your life. But Jesus Christ is a seasoned veteran, and you're in Him. Build your faith in your authority by studying how Jesus operated against the powers of darkness in the Gospels and how we are commanded to do so in the Epistles.

Lord, enlarge my belief that I have been given authority over principalities and powers in Christ, and help me act on that belief.

Humble yourselves in the presence of the Lord, and He will exalt you (James 4:10).

The second qualification for demonstrating authority over rulers and authorities in the spiritual realm is *humility*. Humility doesn't mean that you're always looking for a rock to crawl under because you feel unworthy to do anything. In exercising our authority, humility is placing confidence in Christ, the source of our authority, instead of in ourselves. Jesus didn't shrink back from exercising His authority, but He showed tremendous humility because He did everything according to what His Father told Him to do.

Pride says, "I resisted the devil all by myself." False humility says, "God resisted the devil; I did nothing." True humility says, "I resisted the devil by the grace of God." Apart from Christ we can do *nothing* (John 15:5), but that doesn't mean we're not supposed to do *something*. We exercise authority humbly in His strength and in His name.

Seeing humility as self-abasement is similar to seeing meekness as weakness. The Lord was meek, but He wasn't weak. Meekness is great strength under great control. Humility is confidence properly placed. We are to "glory in Christ Jesus and put no confidence in the flesh" (Philippians 3:3).

Pride is a killer. Pride says, "I can do it." No you can't. We absolutely need God and each other.

Father, I know You can remove Your blessing from me if I move out from under Your protection and authority. I acknowledge today that You are in charge of my life.

Be strong and courageous! Do not tremble or be dismayed, for the LORD your God is with you wherever you go (Joshua 1:9).

The third qualification for demonstrating authority over rulers and authorities in the spiritual realm is *boldness*. A Spirit-filled Christian is characterized by a true, godly sense of courage and boldness in spiritual warfare. On the eve of taking authority over the Promised Land, Joshua was challenged four times to be strong and courageous (Joshua 1:6,7,9,18). When the early church prayed about their mission of sharing the gospel in Jerusalem, "the place where they had gathered together was shaken, and they were all filled with the Holy Spirit, and began to speak the word of God with boldness" (Acts 4:31). Spirit-inspired boldness is behind every successful advance in the church today.

The opposite of boldness is cowardice, fear, and unbelief. Notice what God thinks about these characteristics:

> I am the Alpha and Omega, the beginning and the end. I will give to the one who thirsts from the spring of the water of life without cost. He who overcomes shall inherit these things, and I will be his God and he will be My son. But for the cowardly and unbelieving and abominable and murderers and immoral persons and sorcerers and idolaters and all liars, their part will be in the lake that burns with fire and brimstone, which is the second death (Revelation 21:6-8).

That's pretty serious—cowards lined up at the lake of fire alongside murderers, sorcerers, and idolaters! It should serve to motivate us to exercise authority with boldness (2 Timothy 1:7).

A lot of Christians I meet fear the dark side of the spiritual world. It's true that a little knowledge can be a dangerous and frightful thing, but a growing knowledge of the truth is liberating. Seminary students have told me, "I used to be afraid of that stuff, but now I know who I am in Christ, and I'm not afraid anymore." That's exactly the perception we should have.

Lord, increase my courage to light candles of truth and dispel the darkness in Your name. I will fear only You today, not the enemy.

I am the vine, you are the branches; he who abides in Me, and I in him, he bears much fruit; for apart from Me you can do nothing (John 15:5).

The fourth qualification for demonstrating authority over rulers and authorities in the spiritual realm is *dependence*. A Spirit-filled life is dependent on God the Father. Even Jesus and the Holy Spirit modeled this dependency. Jesus said: "I can do nothing on My own initiative" (John 5:30); "Now they know that everything you have given me comes from you" (John 17:7 NIV); "But when He, the Spirit of truth, comes, He will guide you into all the truth; for He will not speak on His own initiative, but whatever He hears, He will speak" (John 16:13).

Spiritual authority is not an independent authority. We don't charge out on our own initiative like some kind of evangelical ghostbusters to hunt down the devil and engage him in combat. God's primary call is for each of us to focus on the ministry of the kingdom: loving, caring, preaching, teaching, praying, etc. However, when demonic powers challenge us in the course of pursuing this ministry, we deal with them on the basis of our authority in Christ and our dependence on Him. Then we carry on with our primary task.

Nor is the spiritual authority of the believer an authority to be exercised over other believers. We are to be "subject to one another in the fear of Christ" (Ephesians 5:21). There is a God-established authority on earth which governs the social structures of government, work, home, and church (Romans 13:1-7). It is critically important that we submit to these governing authorities unless they operate outside the scope of their authority, command us to do something against God's will, or restrict us from doing what God has commanded. Then we must obey God rather than men.

Lord, it's a great relief to know I can depend on You. You are the Rock, the Almighty, unchanging, full of glory. I praise You.

An Intact Belief System

In pointing out these things to the brethren, you will be a good servant of Jesus Christ, constantly nourished on the words of the faith and of the sound doctrine which you have been following (1 Timothy 4:6).

One problem with Christian maturity is trying to base spiritual growth on practical sections of the Scriptures and spending too little time internalizing the doctrinal sections. Each of Paul's letters tends to fall into two major parts. The first part is generally doctrinal, such as Romans 1-8, Ephesians 1-3, Colossians 1-2, etc. These sections reveal what we need to *know* about God, ourselves, sin, and salvation. The second half of each letter is the practical section: Romans 12-15, Ephesians 4-6, Colossians 3-4, etc. These passages describe what we need to *do* to live out our faith in daily experience.

In our zeal to correct the problems in our lives—doubt, temptation, satanic attack, conflict in families, friendships, and churches which are falling apart—we jump to the practical instructions of God's Word. We want a quick fix, a rule or instruction which we can apply like a Band-Aid to make things better.

Perhaps you have already discovered that a Band-Aid approach to daily living doesn't work. Why not? Because when you don't understand the truth pertaining to your position in Christ, you have no ground for success in the practical arena. How can you rejoice in hope and persevere in tribulation (Romans 12:12) without the confidence of knowing you have been justified by faith and have peace with God through the Lord Jesus Christ (Romans 5:1)?

When your basic belief system about God and yourself is shaky, your day-to-day behavior system will be shaky. But when your belief system is intact and your relationship with God is based on truth, you'll have very little trouble working out the practical aspects of daily Christianity. Show me someone who knows who they are in Christ and who is filled with the Holy Spirit, as is taught in the first half of the Epistles, and I will show you someone who will instinctively live according to the second half of the Epistles. It will be the "natural" thing to do.

Loving Father, I desire to know what I need to know about You so I can live the way You desire for me to live.

OUR CHILDREN, SATAN'S TARGETS

These words, which I am commanding you today, shall be on your heart; and you shall teach them diligently to your sons (Deuteronomy 6:6,7).

Christian children and teenagers populating our schools, attending our churches, and living in our homes are the targets of Satan's strategy. Many Christian young people hear voices as if a subconscious self is talking to them. Satan seeks to destroy our families and churches by seducing our children away from their parents and from God (1 Timothy 4:1).

Is every evil thought in our mind the "voice" of Satan or a demon? No, the flesh—that part of our brain that urges us to operate independently of God and to center our interests on ourselves—also introduces sinful thoughts and suggests evil deeds. Furthermore, input from worldly movies, music, books, TV, etc. also introduces evil ideas into our minds. As we grow in Christ we learn to say no to the deeds of the flesh and walk in the Spirit.

But the world and the flesh are not the only culprits, even though we tend to place most of the blame on them. The devil and "spiritual forces of wickedness" (Ephesians 6:12) are shrewdly at work introducing evil suggestions as thoughts or inner voices. Just as we learn to deal with worldly and fleshly influences, so we must learn to distinguish Satan's subtle, personal influence and resist him, and we must teach our children to do the same. Whether your child's evil thoughts are coming from the world, the flesh, or the devil, you need to help him bring "every thought captive to the obedience of Christ" (2 Corinthians 10:5).

Our children aren't saying much about Satan's seduction in their lives because most of them don't know that he's at the heart of it. Satan is the great deceiver. He doesn't march into their lives accompanied by a brass band. He slyly worms his way in through the opportunities they and we give him. And since kids haven't been taught what the Bible says about Satan's strategies, they blame themselves, and their sense of guilt and fear of punishment further contributes to their silence.

Father God, raise up a standard of truth to defeat the enemy in my children's lives, and help me teach them to resist the enemy themselves.

The Responsibility of Leadership

Shepherd the flock of God among you…not under compulsion, but voluntarily, according to the will of God (1 Peter 5:2).

Our ability to speak with authority stems from the same source as was true of Jesus Himself. The authority Jesus possessed was not based on any earthly position, but in the quality, conduct, and character of His life.

The true shepherd exercises spiritual leadership with the heart of a servant. As servants, we are subject to the needs of those we are called to lead. That's why Jesus said we will know His disciples by their love. The requirements to be a spiritual leader in 1 Timothy 3 and Titus 1 are all character requirements. All of this is made possible by the indwelling presence of God the Holy Spirit. Peter writes, "Shepherd the flock of God among you, exercising oversight not under compulsion, but voluntarily, according to the will of God; and not for sordid gain, but with eagerness; nor yet as lording it over those allotted to your charge, but proving to be examples to the flock" (1 Peter 5:2,3).

You never hear Jesus say, "You do this because I'm God." What happens to a marriage relationship when a husband authoritatively demands obedience because he is the head of the home? Nothing good, let me assure you. The spiritual head of a home, church, Sunday school class, Bible study group, etc. assumes his responsibility by meeting the needs of those under his care. Being a leader is an awesome responsibility, not a right to be demanded. A wise leader listens carefully to the counsel of his charges and depends on the Holy Spirit. With the Holy Spirit's enablement, he can live a righteous life out of which he can lead with loving authority.

As spiritual leaders, we must be like Christ and base our leadership in the quality, conduct, and character of our life. We may speak with authority if what we say is true according to God's Word and when our character is Christlike.

Lord, I desire greater humility so I can properly lead and teach in areas where You have given me responsibility.

One Fear-Object

It is the LORD of hosts whom you should regard as holy. And He shall be your fear, and He shall be your dread (Isaiah 8:13).

A severe storm hit the East Coast, and the Coast Guard was summoned to respond to a ship in crisis. A young sailor, new on board, was terrorized by the prospect and proclaimed, "We can't go out. We'll never come back!" The seasoned captain responded, "We must go out. We don't have to come back." Duty called and responsibility overcame fear.

If we're going to walk by faith, there can be only one fear-object in our life, and that's God. We are responsible to Him. He is the ultimate fear-object because He is omnipotent and omnipresent. The fear of the Lord is healthy because it is the one fear that expels all other fears (Isaiah 8:11-14). All other fear-objects pale in comparison to our holy God. We need to be like David who proclaimed before Goliath, "Who is this uncircumcised Philistine, that he should taunt the armies of the living God?" (1 Samuel 17:26). The Hebrew army saw Goliath in relation to themselves and cowered in defeat. David saw Goliath in relation to God and conquered in His strength.

When the 12 spies checked out the Promised Land, 10 of them came back and responded, "We are not able to go up against the people, for they are too strong for us" (Numbers 13:31). They didn't see God in the land, they saw giants (verse 33). With that perspective, "all the congregation lifted up their voices and cried, and the people wept that night" (Numbers 14:1).

Joshua and Caleb responded, "Do not rebel against the LORD; and do not fear the people of the land, for they shall be our prey. Their protection has been removed from them, and the LORD is with us; do not fear them" (Numbers 14:9). The people *did* rebel. They accepted the majority report instead of listening to Caleb and Joshua. By accepting the Canaanites' will over God's will, they elevated the power and eminence of the Canaanites over the omnipotence and omnipresence of God. To honor God as the ultimate fear-object is to worship Him. To be controlled by any other fear-object is to allow it to usurp God's place in our lives.

Lord, I want to be a God-pleaser in all I do today, not a man-pleaser or a coward.

Appearance, Performance, and Status

Just as a father has compassion on his children, so the LORD has compassion on those who fear Him (Psalm 103:13).

If you seek your identity or sense of worth in the temporal values of this world instead of in Christ, your family can become a threat to your pursuits in the following three ways.

Appearance. What image is more appealing to a woman: a youthful, athletic figure or the sometimes sagging frame of a responsible mother? Say goodbye to the bikini with those stretch marks! Mothers who are hooked on appearances may end up resenting their children for robbing them of their girlish figure.

Performance. If you as a husband/father get your identity from your work, your primary goal may be to climb the corporate ladder. That means working some evenings and weekends to get ahead. "I'd like to be at your Little League game, Son," you say, "but I can't. I'll make it up to you later." Only later may be too late in some cases. What about performing well as a husband/father or wife/mother? Granted, few outside your home will see that performance. But God will and your children will! And in 20 years the world will see the results of your performance in the lives of your godly, well-adjusted children.

Status. Getting married and having children used to offer a woman favorable social status. Now a wife/mother is "just" a housewife. A status-seeking woman will see her family as a bother or a hindrance. This is the driving force behind the abortion advocates. They want the "freedom" to have sex without the responsibility of having children. But what's wrong with being a responsible, caring mother? What can be more challenging and satisfying than raising godly children today? Perhaps it's too challenging for some; that's why they are opting out.

If your sense of worth comes through your identity in Christ and your godly character, then your family will serve as the essential foundation for your personal development, since God works primarily through committed relationships.

Lord, help me see my family as Your instrument to turn my focus to eternal values instead of temporal rewards

Satan's Primary Strategy

Why has Satan filled your heart to lie to the Holy Spirit? (Acts 5:3).

Satan's primary strategy is deception. He will introduce his thoughts and ideas into your mind and deceive you into believing that they are yours. It happened to King David. Satan "moved David to number Israel" (1 Chronicles 21:1), an act God had forbidden, and David acted on Satan's idea. Did Satan walk up to David one day and say, "I want you to number Israel"? I doubt it. David was a godly man and he wouldn't have obeyed Satan. But what if Satan slipped the idea into David's mind in first-person singular? What if the thought came to David as "I need to know how large my army is; I think I'll count the troops"?

If Satan can place a thought in your mind—and he can—it isn't much more of a trick for him to make you think it's your idea. If you knew it was Satan, you'd reject the thought, wouldn't you? But when he disguises his suggestion as your idea, you are more likely to accept it. That is his primary deception. If you knew where the thought came from, you wouldn't be deceived.

I don't think Judas realized that it was Satan's idea to betray Jesus (John 13:2). It probably came to him as a way to prompt Jesus to deliver Israel from the Romans. Ananias and Sapphira might have thought that it was their idea to withhold some of their offering while getting the strokes and attention from others who believed they had given everything. If they knew that it was Satan's idea, they probably wouldn't have done it (Acts 5:1-3). If Satan can get you to believe a lie, he can control your life. That's why it is truth that sets you free (John 8:32).

There is one common characteristic shared by everyone in bondage: They all lie. The alcoholic lies about his drinking. The anorexic lies about her eating. The first step to recovery is to get out of denial, stop lying, and start telling the truth.

Lord, I really want Your truth, and the freedom it brings, in my life at all times. Help me face up to the truth, receive it, and act on it today.

The devil...does not stand in the truth, because there is no truth in him. Whenever he speaks a lie, he speaks from his own nature; for he is a liar, and the father of lies (John 8:44).

Satan's power is in the lie. He has no power over you except what you give him when you believe his lies. You break his power when you expose the lie. Scripture says, "We know that we are of God, and the whole world lies in the power of the evil one" (1 John 5:19).

How much deception is actually going on in Christians today I can only speculate. In my ministry I encounter it in nearly every counseling session. Many Christians I talk to struggle with oppressive thoughts, but they are afraid to tell anyone for fear that others will think they have a mental problem. Seldom do they realize that these distractions reflect the battle which is going on for their minds, even though Paul warned us: "The Spirit explicitly says that in latter times some will fall away from the faith, paying attention to deceitful spirits and doctrines of demons" (1 Timothy 4:1).

Since Satan's primary weapon is the lie, your defense against him is the truth. Dealing with Satan is not a power encounter; it's a truth encounter. When you expose Satan's lie with God's truth, his power is broken. That's why Jesus said: "You shall know the truth, and the truth shall make you free" (John 8:32). That's why He prayed: "My prayer is not that you take them out of the world but that you protect them from the evil one....Sanctify them by the truth; your word is truth" (John 17:15,17 NIV). That's why the first piece of armor Paul mentions for standing against the schemes of the devil is the belt of truth (Ephesians 6:14). Satan's lie cannot withstand the truth any more than the darkness of night can withstand the light of the rising sun.

Lord, I seek Your boldness today to defeat the enemy's lies in my life and in the lives of those around me.

The one who practices righteousness is righteous, just as He is righteous; the one who practices sin is of the devil (1 John 3:7,8).

God's Word is the basis for righteous judgment. Is the person proclaiming the Word of God? Is it biblically true? Accepting the fact that God's Word is both foundational and central, however, is not the only criterion. Satan will quote Scripture. He even had the audacity to quote it to Jesus. Any organization can make up a doctrinal statement. I have even encountered hard-core Satanists who have infiltrated the church and occupied leadership positions in evangelical ministries.

Paul warned, "For such men are false apostles, deceitful workers, disguising themselves as apostles of Christ. And no wonder, for even Satan disguises himself as an angel of light. Therefore it is not surprising if his servants also disguise themselves as servants of righteousness; whose end shall be according to their deeds" (2 Corinthians 11:13-15).

I know of a false teacher who teaches the Bible. In fact, he teaches the Bible very well, but his moral life is decadent. Two of our seminary students were mesmerized by his intellectual brilliance. I personally wouldn't care to do intellectual battle with him, but I wouldn't want to battle Satan intellectually either. This man indulges the flesh in its corrupt desires and despises authority, which are traits identified in 2 Peter 2:10 as those of a false prophet.

I'm always amazed at how gullible some people are and how easily deceived. "He's such a wonderful speaker!" "What a charismatic person!" "I could feel the electricity in the air!" They're not judging righteously; they're judging by appearance (or worse, by how they feel). John wrote, "Do not judge according to appearance, but judge with righteous judgment" (John 7:24); and "Little children, let no one deceive you; the one who practices righteousness is righteous, just as He is righteous; the one who practices sin is of the devil" (1 John 3:7,8).

Dear Father, I desire the capacity for righteous judgment based on Your Word to deal effectively with the enemy's subtle schemes.

All things for which you pray and ask, believe that you have received them, and they shall be granted (Mark 11:24).

If God wants it done, can it be done? Yes! "All things are possible to him who believes" (Mark 9:23). If God wants me to do it, can I do it? Of course! "I can do all things through Him who strengthens me" (Philippians 4:13).

What are the "all things" mentioned in those verses? Is this "miracle-a-moment" living? Can we just name it and claim it? No. "All things" pertains to God's will. What God makes possible is the doing of His will; what He empowers us to do is what He desires done. Every miracle outside the will of God is made possible by the god of this world. Satan can work miracles, but he cannot please God (Matthew 7:20-23).

Jesus shocked His disciples when He cursed a fig tree which bore no fruit for Him. The next day Peter noticed the tree was withered from the roots up. When Peter pointed it out to Him, Jesus answered, "Whoever says to this mountain, 'Be taken up and cast into the sea,' and does not doubt in his heart, but believes that what he says is going to happen, it shall be granted him. Therefore I say to you, all things for which you pray and ask, believe that you have received them, and they shall be granted" (Mark 11:23,24).

Can such a miraculous thing happen by prayer and faith? Yes, if we understand what a God-wrought miracle is. A miracle from God is a supernatural intervention in the fixed order of the universe for the sole purpose of establishing His kingdom. A true miracle can only be accomplished by God and only to help fulfill His redemptive purpose.

Moving a mountain into the sea fulfills no redemptive purpose. Besides, given enough time and earth-moving equipment, we could accomplish that without God. The point Jesus is making is this: If God wants it done, it can be done. Nothing can keep us from doing the will of God, if we believe. Nobody can stop us from being the person God wants us to be. "Mountains" are often obstacles standing in the way of accomplishing God's will. Faith removes such barriers.

Lord, I ask that I will be so sensitive to Your Spirit and full of faith that my prayers will be in harmony with Your will.

Under the Same Yoke

Come to Me, all who are weary and heavy-laden, and I will give you rest. Take My yoke upon you, and learn from Me, for I am gentle and humble in heart; and you shall find rest for your souls. For My yoke is easy, and My load is light (Matthew 11:28-30).

Matthew 11:28-30 contains a beautiful description of the purpose and pace of the Spirit-filled walk. Jesus invites you to a restful walk in tandem with Him, just as two oxen walk together under the same yoke. "How can a yoke be restful?" you ask. Because Jesus' yoke is an easy yoke. As the lead ox, Jesus walks at a steady pace. If you pace yourself with Him, your burden will be easy. But if you take a passive approach to the relationship, you'll be painfully dragged along in the yoke because Jesus keeps walking. Or if you try to race ahead or turn off in another direction, the yoke will chafe your neck and your life will be uncomfortable. The key to a restful yoke-relationship with Jesus is to learn from Him and open yourself to His gentleness and humility.

The picture of walking in the Spirit in tandem with Jesus also helps us understand our service to God. How much will you get done without Jesus pulling on His side of the yoke? Nothing. And how much will be accomplished without you on your side? Nothing. A yoke can only work if both are pulling together.

Paul said, "I planted, Apollos watered, but God was causing the growth" (1 Corinthians 3:6). You and I have the privilege to plant and water, but if God isn't in it, nothing will grow. However, if we don't plant and water, nothing will grow. God has chosen to work through the church, in partnership with you to do His work in the world today. He's the lead ox. Let's learn from Him.

Dear Jesus, I want You to be my yoke-mate today. Keep me from going ahead or lagging behind. I want to walk step-by-step with You.

I rejoice that in everything I have confidence in you (2 Corinthians 7:16).

When I was 14 years old my family moved off the farm in Minnesota where I was born. But I never adjusted to our new home in Arizona. When I was only 15 my parents let me take a bus back to Minnesota to work on the farm for the summer. The following summer I drove an old car back to Minnesota by myself. The family I stayed with asked if I would like to live with them and finish high school in Minnesota. To my great joy my parents said it was okay.

What impact did my parents' trust have on me? I never wanted to do anything to lose their trust. Their trust in me was a great driving force in my life and the greatest gift they ever gave me. Next to the Holy Spirit in me, that trust has been the greatest deterrent to immorality. Even years later when I was in the military and thousands of miles from home, I didn't want to lose their trust.

When you effectively communicate your love, trust, and respect to your children, they will learn to value these qualities so much that they will never intentionally do anything to lose them. Then when they are introduced to Christ, they will also value His love, trust, and respect. "But my child isn't trustworthy," you say. Neither are you completely trustworthy. Yet God has entrusted you with the gospel. That gives you something to live up to. What can you possibly gain by communicating anything less than your trust in your child?

Paul wrote to the church at Corinth: "I rejoice that in everything I have confidence in you" (2 Corinthians 7:16). But Corinth was a messed up place. Is Paul's statement a bunch of psychological hype? No, I don't think so. Paul's confidence was in the Lord, and he knew that the work God had begun in the Corinthian believers would be completed. Under the inspiration of God he also knew that expressing belief and confidence in them was foundational for building them up.

Thank You, Lord, for the love and trust You have expressed to me which frees me to love and obey You. Help me encourage my children by communicating my love, trust, and respect to them.

You are mistaken, not understanding the Scriptures, or the power of God (Matthew 22:29).

Dee, a bright young woman and a pastor's daughter, developed physical symptoms which were later diagnosed as multiple sclerosis.

"When did you first become aware of the symptoms?" I asked.

"I started feeling the first tingling sensations right after a special time of devotions I had with the Lord," Dee replied.

"What was so special about your devotions that day?"

"My devotions were in 2 Corinthians 12, and I read the passage where Paul told about his thorn in the flesh. Paul said God's power was perfected in his weakness, and I wanted God's power in my life too. So I asked God to give me a thorn in the flesh."

"Do you know what Paul's thorn in the flesh was?" I asked, shocked.

"Some sort of physical problem, wasn't it?"

"Well, we're not told how it was manifested, but 2 Corinthians 12:7 clearly states that it was a 'messenger of Satan,' literally an angel of Satan—a demon! Paul never asked for it. In fact, he prayed three times that it be removed. Dee, I think Satan took advantage of your unscriptural prayer and afflicted you with these symptoms. I strongly recommend that you renounce your request for a thorn in the flesh and pray that any influence by Satan be removed from your life."

Dee received my counsel and we prayed together. She began to feel better. The symptoms disappeared and she resumed her normal activities.

By excluding the supernatural from their worldview, many Christians exclude God's power from their theology and practice, becoming subject to Satan's power. Furthermore, they also explain all human failure—even that which is induced by demonic influence, such as Dee's symptoms—as the result of psychological or natural causes. We typically exhaust every natural explanation first, then say, "Well, there's nothing left to do but pray." Why don't we first determine if there is a spiritual explanation? Spiritual conflicts are by far the easiest to resolve.

Lord, keep me sensitive to the spiritual nature of the battle, and protect me from the fiery darts the evil one hurls at me today.

Solid food is for the mature, who because of practice have their senses trained to discern good and evil (Hebrews 5:14).

A good systematic theology is the foundation upon which we build our lives. It is to our walk with God what our skeleton is to our body. It holds us together and keeps us in the right form. But right doctrine is never an end in itself. True doctrine governs our relationship with God and man. Many Christians have a relationship with God that is only theological, not personal. Those accustomed to the word of righteousness should be sensitive to the personal leading of the Holy Spirit.

Solomon started with a love for God. He "became greater than all the kings of the earth in riches and in wisdom. And all the earth was seeking the presence of Solomon, to hear his wisdom which God had put in his heart" (1 Kings 10:23,24). He had the ability to discern, but moral demise led to his downfall. His wives turned his heart away, and he was no longer accustomed to the words of righteousness. His heart was not wholly devoted to the Lord, and the kingdom of God was torn in two.

I'm not sure my senses would have been trained if God hadn't called me into the ministry of setting captives free. If we are going to minister in a world of deception, we had better learn to rely on God and not lean on our own understanding. We need more than intellectual discernment; we need spiritual discernment. All spiritual discernment is on the plane of good and evil. Because the Holy Spirit bears witness with our spirit, we should be able to sense when something is right or wrong.

The Holy Spirit is our first line of defense. Our personal relationship with God is made possible by the indwelling presence of the Holy Spirit who does not silently sit by in the face of danger, but prompts us to choose what is true and right.

Thank You, Lord, for the protection of Your indwelling Holy Spirit. Forgive me for the times I have failed to discern good from evil because I ignored or overlooked Your guidance.

Stand firm therefore, having girded your loins with truth (Ephesians 6:14).

Persons in bondage are not liberated by what I do as the pastor/counselor, but what they do with my help. It's not what *I* believe that breaks the bonds, it's what *they* believe, confess, renounce, and forgive. Notice the progressive logic of Scripture:

> You shall know the *truth*, and the *truth* shall make you free (John 8:32).
>
> I am the way, and the *truth*, and the life (John 14:6).
>
> But when He, the Spirit of *truth*, comes, He will guide you into all the *truth* (John 16:13).
>
> I do not ask Thee to take them out of the world, but to keep them from the evil one....Sanctify them in the *truth*; Thy word is *truth* (John 17:15,17).
>
> Stand firm therefore, having girded your loins with *truth* (Ephesians 6:14).
>
> Finally, brethren, whatever is *true*...let your mind dwell on these things (Philippians 4:8).

When Satan harasses you, you may be prone to languish in the shadows of your misery. You cry out for God to deliver you, like Jesus miraculously and instantaneously delivered the demonized people in the Gospels. But when you read through the Epistles it is obvious that your deliverance has already been accomplished in Christ's work on the cross and His resurrection. Since you are with Christ in the light, you never again need to live in the shadows.

You must choose the truth and assume your responsibility to exercise your authority and resist the devil. From your position in Christ, you must resist the devil, renounce participation in his schemes, confess sin, and forgive those who have offended you.

Lord, Your truth gives me life and leads me in the everlasting way. I embrace Your truth to direct my steps today.

When you enter the land which the LORD your God gives you, you shall not learn to imitate the detestable things of those nations (Deuteronomy 18:9).

The lure of the occult is almost always on the basis of acquiring knowledge or power. We desire the power that comes from unusual insight and a knowledge of the unknown. We want to experience a power that is spiritual and supernatural in origin. In a sense these are God-given desires, but they are intended to be fulfilled by the knowledge and power which comes from God. However, Satan is busy trying to pass off his counterfeits for God's knowledge and power as the real thing. If he can get you to accept his versions of knowledge and power, he has a foothold in your life.

The lure of satanic knowledge and power is nothing new. God's people have been warned against it from the earliest times. The command in Deuteronomy 18:9-12 is as viable for us today as it was for the Israelites under Moses' leadership. We live in a contemporary Canaan where it is socially acceptable to consult spiritists, mediums, palm-readers, psychic counselors, and horoscopes for supernatural insights and abilities.

This was clearly brought home to me while I was finishing my doctorate in a class I took on business forecasting. One of the men in the class presented a paper describing a scenario of the future he had researched. He excitedly explained that we were on the threshold of new frontiers in the mind: astral projection, telepathic images, levitation, etc. This public school principal was promoting New Age and the occult, and the other class members were eating it up.

After the class had enjoyed several minutes of lively discussion I asked, "In all your exploration of your subject, did you ever ask yourself if it is right for people to get involved in it?"

"Oh, I'm not interested in whether it's right or not," he replied. "I just know it works."

"I have no question that it works," I argued. "The question we need to answer is not whether or not it works, but whether or not it's right. What you are presenting is as old as Bible history."

Create in me a constant thirst for knowing You, Lord, and a readiness to recognize and reject Satan's counterfeits.

There shall not be found among you anyone who makes his son or his daughter pass through the fire, one who uses divination, one who practices witchcraft, or one who interprets omens, or a sorcerer, or one who casts a spell, or a medium, or a spiritist, or one who calls up the dead. For whoever does these things is detestable to the LORD (Deuteronomy 18:10-12).

The dark side of Satan's versions of spiritual knowledge and power mentioned by Moses—ritual sacrifice, witchcraft, sorcery—is also thriving in our culture, though not as openly as some of the more socially acceptable New Age practices. Our police departments are trying to tell parents today, "Wake up! Your kids are not just into drugs and illicit sex. They're into *Satanism.* We've seen the blood and the mutilated animals." It's getting so bad that one of the animal control agencies in our area will no longer release a black dog or cat at Halloween for fear that it will become the victim of satanic ritual abuse.

The man who heads up our campus security belongs to a group of security officers from campuses across Southern California which meets once a month. When it was our school's turn to host the meeting, he asked me to speak to the group about spiritual phenomena in our culture. "There aren't many Christians in the group," he said, "but they'll be on our campus, so I want you to speak to them." I agreed to do so.

It was a veteran crowd of former military men and police officers. When I started talking about the rise of Satanism and ritual abuse in our community, there wasn't a doubter or a scoffer in the bunch. Every one of them had a story to share about finding grisly evidence of Satanism being active on their respective campuses.

Every aberration of spiritual knowledge and power that Moses warned the Israelites to avoid in Canaan—from "harmless" horoscopes to unthinkable atrocities of animal and human sacrifice—is in place and operating in our culture today. We must wake up to the reality that "our struggle is not against flesh and blood, but against...spiritual forces of wickedness" (Ephesians 6:12).

Mighty Lord, equip me today not just to stand my ground against the enemy but to actively reclaim in Jesus' name territory he has stolen.

Do It Anyway

While we have opportunity, let us do good to all men, and especially to those who are of the household of the faith (Galatians 6:10).

After I had driven home the point that nobody or nothing can keep us from being what God wants us to be, one of my students gave me this nugget of truth.

People are illogical, unreasonable, and self-centered.
  Love them anyway.
If you do good, people will accuse you of selfish ulterior motives.
  Do good anyway.
If you are successful, you will win false friends and true enemies.
  Succeed anyway.
The good you do today will be forgotten tomorrow.
  Do good anyway.
Honesty and frankness make you vulnerable.
  Be honest and frank anyway.
The biggest men and women with the biggest ideas can be shot down by the smallest men and women with the smallest minds.
  Think big anyway.
People favor underdogs but follow only top dogs.
  Fight for a few underdogs anyway.
What you spend years building may be destroyed overnight.
  Build anyway.
People really need help but may attack you if you help them.
  Help people anyway.
Give the world the best you have and you'll get kicked in the teeth.
  Give the world the best you have anyway.[1]

Lord, I purpose today not to listen to my detractors or look to the left or the right, but to stay on the clear, sure path You have set before me.

Do not lay up for yourselves treasures upon earth, where moth and rust destroy, and where thieves break in and steal. But lay up for yourselves treasures in heaven (Matthew 6:19,20).

There are material goods which Jesus identifies as "treasures upon earth." And there are immaterial goods which Jesus calls "treasures in heaven." Treasures upon earth have two characteristics.

First, all natural things decay. What rust doesn't destroy, moths or termites will. Second, because of the value of earthly treasures, there is always a concern for security. It is hard to be anxiety-free if we are worried about our possessions. The more we possess, the more we cause others to covet, hence the reason why "thieves break in and steal."

On the other hand, treasures in heaven are beyond the reach of thieves and secure from the ravages of moths and rust. Paul puts it this way: "Discipline yourself for the purpose of godliness; for bodily discipline is only of little profit, but godliness is profitable for all things, since it holds promise for the present life and also for the life to come" (1 Timothy 4:7,8).

What do you treasure in your heart? What would you exchange for love, joy, peace, patience, kindness, goodness, faithfulness, gentleness, and self-control? Would you exchange these qualities for a new car, a cabin in the hills, a boat in the marina, exceptional status at the top of the corporate ladder?

Achievement is determined by who or what you serve. There is a moral healthiness and simple, unaffected goodness present in the single-minded person that is absent from the one serving many masters. Jesus said, "No one can serve two masters; for either he will hate the one and love the other, or he will hold to one and despise the other. You cannot serve God and mammon. For this reason I say to you, do not be anxious" (Matthew 6:24,25).

There will be no peace serving two masters. To whichever master we yield, by that master we shall be controlled.

Father, the treasures of this world call out to me temptingly. I trust You to give me what I need and not what I selfishly desire.

If any man's work...remains, he shall receive a reward (1 Corinthians 3:14).

Significance is a time issue. What is forgotten in time is of little significance. What is remembered for eternity is of great significance. Paul wrote to Timothy: "Discipline yourself for the purpose of godliness...since it holds promise for the present life and also for the life to come" (1 Timothy 4:7,8). If you want to increase your significance, focus your energies on significant activities: those which will remain for eternity.

Brian was a pastor of a small church who attended one of my classes at the seminary. He was in his mid-thirties and married when he found out he had cancer. The doctors gave him less than two years to live.

One day Brian came to talk to me. "Ten years ago somebody gave a prophecy about me in church," he began. "They said I was going to do a great work for God. I've led a few hundred people to Christ, but I haven't had a great work for God yet. Do you think God is going to heal me so the prophecy can be fulfilled?"

My mouth dropped open in shock. "You've led a few hundred people to Christ and don't think you have accomplished a great work for God? Brian, I know some big-name pastors in large churches who can't make that claim. I know some great theologians who have probably never led anyone to Christ. If a few hundred people are believers today because of you, and they have influenced who knows how many other people for Christ, I'd call that a great work for God." (Brian is now with the Lord, having completed his significant ministry of reaching hundreds for Christ.)

As children of God, we are in the significant business of collecting treasures for eternity. What we do and say for Christ, no matter how insignificant it seems in this world, will last forever. There are no insignificant children of God, because our life is eternal.

Lord, I desire to use wisely the time You have allotted to me. May my life count for gold, silver, and precious jewels, not wood, hay, and stubble.

Fences Around the Laws

You are not under law, but under grace
(Romans 6:14).

In His ministry, Jesus often violated the traditional instructions surrounding the observance of the Sabbath because they were a clear distortion of God's commandment. A common practice, born out of a desire to protect a known law or principle, is to establish additional rules to keep us from breaking the laws or violating the principles. We establish fences around the laws, but within a short time the fences become laws.

For instance, we are not to be unequally yoked (2 Corinthians 6:14,15). To ensure that this doesn't happen, we sometimes build a fence around the law by establishing additional rules such as, "You can't associate with or date a non-Christian." That may be advisable in some cases, but don't make it a law. Some have gone to the extreme by requiring that their children never associate with non-Christians. This makes the Great Commission a formidable task!

Here's another example. A common practice in many churches, left over from the Prohibition era, is to require total abstinence from alcohol. Again, that may be wise in many cases, but the Bible instructs against strong drink and drunkenness and teaches us to do all things in moderation. The major biblical concern is not the alcohol, but whether we're being a stumbling block to a weaker brother. Total abstinence may actually keep some from the medicine they need or it may be detrimental when relating to a weaker brother.

The point is, we can easily distort the true Word of God by adding our own traditional practices and making them equal with the original intent of God. We may need to stand against Pharisaic practices as the Lord did—before we find ourselves in bondage to man-made traditions.

Dear Father, make me sensitive to the spirit of Your law and nonjudgmental toward others no matter what their practices may be. Help me preserve the unity of the Spirit.

Faith is the assurance of things hoped for, the conviction of things not seen (Hebrews 11:1).

If You Believe You Can, You Can

If you think you are beaten—you are.
If you think you dare not—you don't.
If you want to win but think you can't,
It is almost a cinch you won't.
If you think you'll lose—you've lost.
For out in the world we find
That success begins with a fellow's will;
It's all in the state of mind.
Life's battles don't always go
To the stronger or faster man;
But sooner or later the man who wins
Is the one who thinks he can.

This poem, whose author is unknown to me, reflects the popular view of life known as the power of positive thinking. The Christian community has been somewhat reluctant to buy into this view, and for good reason. Thinking is a function of the mind which cannot exceed its input and attributes. Attempting to push the mind beyond its limitations will only result in moving from the world of reality to fantasy.

The Christian, however, has far greater potential for success in life in the power of positive believing. Belief incorporates the mind but is not limited by it. Faith actually transcends the limitations of the mind and incorporates the real but unseen world. The believer's faith is as valid as its object, which is the living (Christ) and written (Bible) Word of God. With the infinite God of the universe as the object of Christian faith, there is virtually no limit to the spiritual heights that positive believing can take you.

Lord, You have said that I can accomplish great things with faith the size of a tiny mustard seed. May my life today be marked by the power of positive believing.

Not Available in the Secular World

For as the heavens are higher than the earth, so are My ways higher than your ways, and My thoughts than your thoughts (Isaiah 55:9).

When we boldly and humbly exercise the authority that Christ has conferred upon us over the spiritual realm, we experience the freedom from bondage which Christ promised (John 8:32). It's a freedom that the secular world can't produce, as a friend of mine discovered.

Christy, a young woman, came to my friend Barry because of the horrible abuse she suffered growing up. Barry dealt with Christy on family and social issues, and Christy complied with his suggestions. But she didn't get any better. After working with Christy for nearly four years, Barry brought her to me.

"Tell me about your childhood friends, Christy," I probed.

"The only other girl on our block lived across the street from me, so we were friends."

"What was her family like?"

Christy lowered her eyes. "Her mother did strange things in their home," she almost whispered.

"Did these strange things involve candles and sacrifices, sometimes even killing animals?"

"Yeah."

Christy's neighbor finally moved away. But every night the witch appeared to Christy in her room and talked with her. I led her through the steps to freedom, and she exercised her authority in Christ and dismissed the evil influence from her life. It came back occasionally, and sometimes Christy failed to stand against it because she was "just tired of fighting the battle." But when she stood her ground on Christ's authority, she was free.

Satan can do nothing about your position in Christ. But if he can, he will cloud your perspective and thus diminish your faith and dull your effectiveness in the spiritual battle.

Father God, I don't want my effectiveness in spiritual battles to be hindered by a clouded understanding of my position in Christ. Help me take my stand against the enemy today with Your truth.

Give your servant a discerning heart to govern your people and to distinguish between right and wrong (1 Kings 3:9 NIV).

Discernment is an overlooked spiritual discipline in many churches. But in reality, spiritual discernment should be our first line of defense against deception. It's that "buzzer" inside, warning you that something is wrong. For example, you visit someone's home and everything appears in order. But you can cut the air with a knife. Even though nothing visible confirms it, your spirit detects that something is wrong in that home.

The first step to understanding discernment is to understand the motive which is essential for employing it. In 1 Kings 3:9, Israel's king Solomon cries out to God for help. God answers: "Because you have asked this thing and have not asked for yourself long life, nor have asked riches for yourself, nor have you asked for the life of your enemies, but have asked for yourself discernment to understand justice, behold, I have done according to your words. Behold, I have given you a wise and discerning heart" (verses 11,12). The motive for true discernment is never to promote self, to amass personal gain, or to secure an advantage over another person—even an enemy.

The Greek word for discernment—*diakrino*—simply means to make a judgment or a distinction. Discernment has one primary function: to distinguish right from wrong. In 1 Corinthians 12:10 discernment is the divinely enabled ability to distinguish a good spirit from a bad spirit.

Discernment is not a function of the mind; it's a function of the Holy Spirit which is in union with your soul/spirit. When the Spirit sounds a warning, your mind may not be able to perceive what's wrong. Have the courage to acknowledge that something is wrong when your spirit is troubled. Share what you are sensing with others, and ask the Lord for wisdom.

Thank You, Father, for the discernment Your Holy Spirit provides. Without You I couldn't avoid the land mines the enemy places in my path.

My food is to do the will of Him who sent Me, and to accomplish His work (John 4:34).

I'm sometimes impressed by how much people can accomplish when they believe in themselves. When I worked on the Apollo space program in the 1960s, we bid on a contract for the space shuttle. The technology to build the type of rocket it would take to boost that size payload into space had not yet been developed, but NASA believed that given enough time and resources, it could be done. Ten years later it was. Some who believe only in science exhibit greater faith than Christians. How much more should we be able to accomplish if the object of our faith is God?

Every commandment of God comes with a promise: "For as many as may be the promises of God, in Him they are yes" (2 Corinthians 1:20). God will never command us to do something that He will not empower us to do. It is never a question of whether God can, but if He wills. If He wills, then we can, if we believe. Those predisposed to do His will understand what it is (John 7:17), and by the grace of God will do it.

It is critical to realize that God is under no obligation to man. God is only under obligation to Himself and to the covenants He has made with us. We don't need God jumping around in heaven catering to our every whim! There will never be a day when we say something and God has to do it because we said it. We cannot box God in.

There was a woman in my pastorate who wouldn't let me pray for her dying husband if I concluded my prayer with, "Be it done according to Thy will." I will never apologize for bowing to a higher authority. We are told to pray, "Thy will be done." Any other way would put us in the position of the Lord. The independent use of God's Word and divine attributes is precisely how Satan tempted Jesus. Jesus withstood the temptation to act independently of God the Father and declared that His food was to do the will of His Father who sent Him. That is our food as well

Thank You, Lord, that You have all the power I need to accomplish Your will for my life today. I tap into Your vast power source by faith to accomplish great things for You

THE TOTAL REALM OF REALITY

Seek first His kingdom and His righteousness; and all these things shall be added to you (Matthew 6:33).

A common question I am asked by those who believe the Bible and accept the reality of the spiritual world is, "When is a problem spiritual and when is it psychological or neurological?" Our problems are never not psychological. Our mind, will, and emotions, along with developmental issues, always contribute something to the problem and are necessary for the resolution. At the same time, our problems are never not spiritual. God is always present. Furthermore, it is never safe to take off the armor of God. The possibility of being deceived, tempted, and accused by Satan is a continuous reality.

Our culture assumes that any problem related to the mind must be psychological or neurological. Why can it not be spiritual? We must take into account the total realm of reality: body, soul, and spirit. If we don't we will polarize into a psychotherapeutic ministry that ignores spiritual reality or some kind of deliverance ministry that ignores developmental issues or human responsibility. The diagnosis and resolution of our problems must take into account both the psychological and the spiritual. I have assured hundreds of people under spiritual attack that they are not going crazy but that there is a battle going on for their minds. The relief this insight brings to people is incredible.

I fully acknowledge that some problems are caused by chemical imbalances or glandular disorders. For these you had better see your family physician. But it seems that the last possibility to be considered is always the spiritual, and only after every other possible natural explanation has been exhausted. But since we are instructed to seek first the kingdom of God, why not check out the spiritual area first? Frankly, I approach every problem hoping it *is* spiritual in nature, because I know on the authority of the Word of God that the problem is resolvable. If the battle is for the mind, we can win that war.

Father God, keep me tuned to the reality of the spiritual world and mindful of the problems that come when I fail to seek a spiritual solution to my daily problems.

THE GOALS YOU SHOULDN'T SET

The joy of the LORD is your strength (Nehemiah 8:10).

I was speaking at a church conference when a woman who was attending invited me to her home for dinner with her family. The woman had been a Christian for 20 years, but her husband was not a Christian. After I arrived it didn't take me long to realize that the real reason she had invited me to dinner was to win her husband to Christ.

I discovered later that the woman had been severely depressed for many years. Her psychiatrist insisted that her depression was endogenous and she staunchly agreed. But I believe her depression stemmed from a wrong goal. For 20 years she had based her success as a Christian on winning her husband and children to Christ. She had prayed for them, witnessed to them, and invited guest preachers home to dinner. She had said everything she could say and done everything she could do, but to no avail. As the futility of her efforts loomed larger, her faith faltered, her hope dimmed, and her depression grew.

Her husband adequately provided for the physical needs of his family. He simply didn't see any need for God. I shared with him about my life and ministry during our visit, but I didn't force my faith on him. I trust that I was a positive witness. In the meantime, his wife's increasing depression was destroying her witness.

You should, of course, desire that your loved ones come to Christ, and pray and work to that end. Your goal is to be a positive witness by becoming the spouse or parent God has called you to be. Then you must leave the results to God. Assuming responsibility for the salvation of your loved ones is beyond your ability. Every loved one can choose not to respond to Christ. Depression often signals that you are desperately clinging to a goal you have little or no chance of achieving, and that's not a healthy goal.

Lord, help me discover the joy of letting You do Your work Your way.

Simon, Simon, behold, Satan has demanded permission to sift you like wheat; but I have prayed for you, that your faith may not fail (Luke 22:31,32).

It is critical that Christians understand their vulnerability to demonic influence. Those who say a demon cannot influence a believer's life have left us with only two possible culprits for the problems we face: ourselves or God. If we blame ourselves we feel hopeless because we can't do anything to stop what we're doing. If we blame God our confidence in Him as our benevolent Father is shattered. Either way, we have no chance to gain the victory which the Bible promises us. In reality we are in a winnable war against the defeated kingdom of darkness. But the lies of Satan can gain a measure of control if we believe them.

What right did Satan have to sift Simon (Peter) like wheat? The context reveals that Peter and the other disciples were arguing about who was going to be the greatest in the kingdom of God. In other words, they were exercising pride. Sinful pride affords Satan a huge opportunity. Peter protested that he was willing to die or go to prison for the sake of Christ. But Jesus told him that, before the day was over, Peter would deny Him three times, and he did.

There are many believers who profess their faith and commit themselves to behave appropriately but can't seem to follow through. Why? We dare not overlook the reality of Satan and the ground we give him through pride and disobedience. God intervened in the early church and struck down Ananias and Sapphira because they allowed Satan to fill their hearts to lie to the Holy Spirit. The word *filled* in Acts 5 is the same word found in Ephesians 5:18: "Be filled with the Spirit." God delivered a dramatic message early: To whichever source you yield, by that source you shall be filled or controlled.

Father, I ask forgiveness for any ways I have allowed Satan to control me. I want to be controlled wholly by You.

The LORD will continually guide you (Isaiah 58:11).

An important concept of God's will is that God can only guide a moving ship. He is the rudder, but if the ship isn't under way it can't be directed. Willingness to obey His will gets the ship moving.

In Acts 15:36, Paul had decided to revisit the churches he helped establish on his first missionary trip. The churches were being strengthened and increasing in number (Acts 16:5). Luke reports:

> And they passed through the Phrygian and Galatian region, having been forbidden by the Holy Spirit to speak the word in Asia; and when they had come to Mysia, they were trying to go into Bithynia, and the Spirit of Jesus did not permit them; and passing by Mysia, they came down to Troas. And a vision appeared to Paul in the night: a certain man of Macedonia was standing and appealing to him, and saying, "Come over to Macedonia and help us" (Acts 16:6-9).

Sometimes God's leading does not make sense. If God wanted Paul to go to Macedonia in the first place, why didn't He make it easier and faster by having Paul travel by land to Caesarea and sail to Macedonia? Because God starts us out on a life course to fulfill a certain purpose and then, only when we are ready, He gives us course corrections. Like a good river pilot, He steers us away from troubled waters, and like a good coach, He never puts us in the game until we are ready.

I believe in divine guidance as described in Isaiah 58:11. But the context reveals that there are prerequisites that have to be satisfied. We are sometimes like a person who seeks to be an athlete by simply suiting up for the race. That's not how the skills are gained. It's in the course of dedication, training, and the contest itself that one gains the skill of an athlete.

It's in the doing of God's work that His will becomes known.

Thank You, Father, that You oversee every turn in the road of my life. I want to faithfully heed Your guidance today.

FREE FROM THE FEAR OF DEATH

O death, where is your victory? O death, where is your sting? (1 Corinthians 15:55).

Most phobias can be reduced to a fear of man or death. Death looms over many as the ultimate fear-object. The fact that death is imminent is clearly established in Scripture: "It is appointed for men to die once and after this comes judgment" (Hebrews 9:27).

But Christians need not fear death. Jesus removed death as a legitimate fear-object by taking away its power when He died for our sins. Jesus Himself said, "I am the resurrection and the life; he who believes in Me shall live even if he dies, and everyone who lives and believes in Me shall never die" (John 11:25,26). Even though we will eventually die physically, we will continue to live spiritually.

Every child of God is spiritually alive, and even physical death cannot separate us from the love of God (Romans 8:38). Paul says, "For to me, to live is Christ, and to die is gain" (Philippians 1:21). Why? When we physically die, we will receive a resurrected body and be far better off than we are today. Try putting something else into Paul's formula, for instance, "For me to live is success." Then to die would be what? Loss! "For me to live is a good physical body." Again, to die would be loss.

I often ask people, "What is the worst thing that could happen to you?" "Well, I could die," they answer. To which I respond, "Then you have nothing to fear, since the Bible says death may be the *best* thing that could happen to you!" The ultimate value is not physical life but spiritual life. If our life is hidden in Christ, then we won't suffer loss when we physically die. We can only gain. We can say confidently with Paul, "O death, where is your sting?" The person who is free from the fear of death is free to live today.

Thank You, Lord, that You have freed me to live fully in the here and now. I leave the time of my departure in Your hands.

Already Accepted

If we walk in the light as He Himself is in the light, we have fellowship with one another, and the blood of Jesus His Son cleanses us from all sin (1 John 1:7).

Fellowship with God is not an abstract theological concept, but a living relationship. Living in continuous agreement with God is to walk in the light. Satan can't accuse me if I live in the light, but walking in the light is not moral perfection (1 John 1:8). We are not sinless, but the confession mentioned in 1 John 1:9 brings us into agreement with God about our present moral condition before Him.

What makes it possible to be this open with God about our condition is the fact that we are already His children. Our eternal state is not at stake, only our daily victory. We don't have to pretend with God in the hope that He will accept us. As His children we're already accepted, so we are free to be honest with Him. We have no relationship to lose, only fellowship to gain. Knowing that we're secure in Christ, we can express ourselves honestly to Him. He already knows the thoughts and intentions of our hearts (Hebrews 4:12).

Knowing that we are forgiven, let's come before His presence with thanksgiving. God is our Father, and like any parent He doesn't appreciate grumbling, complaining children, especially since this Father sacrificed His only begotten Son for us. He will not be very interested in our list of demands if we haven't been obedient to Him. I also don't think He is going to be very interested in helping us develop our own kingdoms when we are to work at establishing the only one that will last—His!

To sit in the presence of my Father who loves me, who has made an incredible sacrifice so I can be there, doesn't have to be a dismal, failing experience. He invites us into His presence just as we are, because in Christ our weakness and sin have been covered: "Let us draw near with a sincere heart in full assurance of faith, having our hearts sprinkled clean from an evil conscience" (Hebrews 10:22).

Thank You, God the Creator, that You have opened up the way for me to approach You and enjoy fellowship with You.

It is for discipline that you endure; God deals with you as with sons; for what son is there whom his father does not discipline? (Hebrews 12:7).

There is a major difference between discipline and punishment in child-raising. Punishment is past-oriented. Punishment is paying your child back for hurting you in some way. Punishment says, "You ruined my day, so I'm going to ruin yours." Its motive is revenge. We are clearly instructed not to take revenge (Romans 12:19). Only the Lord knows how much vengeance is dished out in the name of discipline.

A humbled mother told me about an incident of vengeance she had with her daughter. "Neil, Mandy destructively poked several small holes in my toothpaste tube, so I did the same to her tube of toothpaste. 'See how you like it,' I said to her. Then Mandy looked at me with a crushed expression on her face. 'You're not supposed to return evil for evil,' she said. I suddenly realized that my act of revenge benefited neither of us."

Discipline is future-oriented. In Hebrews we read: "All discipline for the moment seems not to be joyful, but sorrowful; yet to those who have been trained by it, afterwards it yields the peaceful fruit of righteousness" (12:11). We don't punish our children for doing something; we discipline them so they won't do it again. Discipline superintends future choices. Discipline is proof of our love, not license to even the score.

Our discipline of our children is modeled after God's discipline of us. We know we are God's dearly loved children, not unloved illegitimate children, by His discipline. God disciplines us so that we may share in His holiness. Scripture acknowledges that discipline is not joyful at the time it is administered, but what joy ever comes from an undisciplined life? The same is true in your child's life.

Father God, I desire to parent my children in the same way You parent me: with wisdom and love.

Rebellion is as the sin of divination, and insubordination is as iniquity and idolatry (1 Samuel 15:23).

We live in a rebellious generation. Many feel it is their right to sit in judgment of those in authority over them. Christians are no exception. We critique the choir and criticize the sermon. We would be far better off if we entered into the worship experience and let the Word of God sit in judgment of us.

Rebelling against God leads to nothing but trouble. As our commanding general, the Lord says, "Get into ranks and follow Me. I will not lead you into temptation, and I will deliver you from evil." But we sometimes say, "No, I don't want to follow today." So we fall out of ranks, do our own thing, and get shot. Then we blame God for not protecting us.

We are also tempted to rebel against human authority. We have two biblical responsibilities in regard to God-ordained authority figures: pray for them and submit to them. The only time God permits us to disobey earthly leaders is when they require us to do something morally wrong before God or if they attempt to operate outside the realm of their authority. Study the following passages of Scripture to further understand our response to authority: civil government (Romans 13:1-5; 1 Timothy 2:1-4; 1 Peter 2:13-16); parents (Ephesians 6:1-3); husband (1 Peter 3:1,2); employer (1 Peter 2:18-21); church leaders (Hebrews 13:17).

Being submissive to God-ordained authority demonstrates faith. As you submit to God's line of authority, you are choosing to believe that God will protect you and bless you, and that all will go well with you. Ask God to forgive you for those times you have not been submissive, and declare your trust in God to work through His established lines of authority.

Lord, forgive me for areas of my life where I tend to rebel against authority. Help me demonstrate my faith in You through submission.

And you were dead in your trespasses and sins, in which you formerly walked according to the course of this world, according to the prince of the power of the air, of the spirit that is now working in the sons of disobedience (Ephesians 2:1,2).

In 1 Corinthians 2:14–3:3, Paul distinguishes between three types of people in relation to life in the Spirit: natural persons, spiritual persons, and fleshly persons. In the next few days we will examine the critical differences pertaining to spiritual life which exist between these three kinds of individuals.

Ephesians 2:1-3 contains a concise description of the natural person Paul identified in 1 Corinthians 2:14. This person is spiritually dead, separated from God. Living independently from God, the natural person sins as a matter of course.

The natural person has a soul, in that he can think, feel, and choose. But his mind, and subsequently his emotions and his will, are directed by his flesh which acts completely apart from the God who created him. The natural person may think he is free to choose his behavior. But since he lives *in* the flesh, he invariably walks *according* to the flesh and his choices reflect the "deeds of the flesh" listed in Galatians 5:19-21. The natural person's actions, reactions, habits, memories, and responses are all governed by the natural world. The natural person will struggle with feelings of inferiority, insecurity, inadequacy, guilt, worry, and doubt.

The natural person lives independently of God and His purposes and does not respond to life in harmony with God's plan for him. Living in a stressful age with no spiritual base for coping with life or making positive choices, the natural person is even more subject to physical ailments, such as tension or migraine headaches, nervous stomach, hives, skin rashes, allergies, asthma, some arthritis, spastic colon, heart palpitations, respiratory ailments, etc. Doctors agree that many physical problems are psychosomatic. Possessing peace of mind and the calm assurance of God's presence in our lives positively affects our physical health, since the Spirit gives life to the body (Romans 8:11).

Lord, thank You for redeeming me from my former life governed by sin and Satan and giving me peace of mind and calm assurance.

The fruit of the Spirit is love, joy, peace, patience, kindness, goodness, faithfulness, gentleness, self-control; against such things there is no law (Galatians 5:22,23).

The spiritual person also has a body, soul, and spirit. Yet this individual has been remarkably transformed from the natural person he was before spiritual birth. At conversion, his spirit became united with God's Spirit. The spiritual life which resulted from this union is characterized by forgiveness of sin, acceptance in God's family, and the realization of personal worth.

The soul of the spiritual person also reflects a change generated by spiritual birth. He can now receive his impetus from the Spirit, not just from the flesh. His mind is being renewed and transformed. His emotions are characterized by peace and joy instead of turmoil. It is our responsibility to choose *not* to walk according to the flesh, but to walk according to the Spirit. As the spiritual person exercises his choice to live in the Spirit, his life bears the fruit of the Spirit (Galatians 5:22,23).

As a spiritual person, your body is the dwelling place of God. We should offer our bodies as a living sacrifice of worship and service to Him. The flesh, conditioned to live independently from God under the old self, is still present in the spiritual person. But he responsibly crucifies the flesh and its desires daily as he considers himself dead to sin.

"That all looks and sounds great," you may say. "But I'm a Christian and I still have some problems. I know I'm spiritually alive, but sometimes my mind dwells on the wrong kinds of thoughts. Sometimes I give in to the deeds of the flesh. Sometimes I entertain the desires of the flesh instead of crucifying them."

The description of the spiritual person is the ideal. It's the model of maturity toward which we are all growing. God has made every provision for you to experience personally the description of the spiritual person in His Word (2 Peter 1:3). You will grow as a spiritual person and glorify God in your body as you learn to crucify the flesh and be filled by the Spirit.

Loving Lord, it is liberating to know that Your Spirit actually dwells in me. I choose to walk as a spiritual person today.

The Fleshly Person

I gave you milk to drink, not solid food; for you were not yet able to receive it. Indeed, even now you are not yet able, for you are still fleshly (1 Corinthians 3:2,3).

The spirit of the fleshly person is identical to that of the spiritual person. The fleshly person is a Christian, spiritually alive in Christ and declared righteous by God. But that's where the similarity ends. Instead of being directed by the Spirit, this believer chooses to follow the impulses of his flesh. As a result, his mind is occupied by carnal thoughts and his emotions are plagued by negative feelings. And though he is free to choose to walk after the Spirit and produce the fruit of the Spirit, he continues to involve himself in sinful activity by willfully walking after the flesh.

His physical body is a temple of God, but he is using it as an instrument of unrighteousness. He has the same troubling physical symptoms experienced by the natural person because he is not operating in the manner God created him to operate. He is not presenting his body to God as a living sacrifice. Since he yields to the flesh instead of crucifying it, the fleshly man is also subject to feelings of inferiority, insecurity, inadequacy, guilt, worry, and doubt.

Several years ago I did some research to discover how many Christians are still the victims of their flesh. I asked the same question to 50 consecutive Christians who came to me to talk about problems in their lives: "How many of the following characteristics describe your life: inferiority, insecurity, inadequacy, guilt, worry, and doubt?" Every one of the 50 answered, "All six." Here were 50 born-again, righteous children of God who were so bogged down by the flesh that they struggled with the same problems of self-doubt which inundate unbelievers who only live in the flesh.

If I asked you the same question, how would you answer? I imagine that many of you would admit that some or all of these six traits describe you. It is evident to me that a staggering number of believers are still confused about their spiritual identity in Christ and its implications for their daily lives. We are struggling with the behavior aspect of our growth because we are still struggling with the belief aspect of our growth: who we are in Christ.

Father, help me live above my fleshly desires today by exercising my spiritual inheritance at every temptation.

Living Below Our Potential

The flesh sets its desire against the Spirit, and the Spirit against the flesh; for these are in opposition to one another, so that you may not do the things that you please (Galatians 5:17).

Are you stymied in your growth because of feelings of inferiority? To whom or to what are you inferior? You are a child of God seated with Christ in the heavenlies (Ephesians 2:6). Do you feel insecure? Your God will never leave you nor forsake you (Hebrews 13:5). Inadequate? You can do all things through Christ (Philippians 4:13). Guilty? There is no condemnation for those who are in Christ (Romans 8:1). Worried? God has offered to trade His peace for your anxiety (Philippians 4:6,7; 1 Peter 5:7; John 14:27). Doubt? God provides wisdom for the asking (James 1:5).

Why is there often such great disparity between these two kinds of Christians: spiritual and fleshly? Why are so many believers living so far below their potential in Christ? Why are so few of us enjoying the abundant, productive life we have already inherited?

Part of the answer is related to the process of growth and maturity as the individual believer appropriates and applies his spiritual identity to his day-to-day experience. And yet there are countless numbers of Christians who have been born again for years—even decades—and have yet to experience significant measures of victory over sin and the flesh, a victory which is their inheritance in Christ.

Another part of the answer is due to our ignorance of how the kingdom of darkness is impacting our progress toward maturity. We have a living, personal enemy—Satan—who actively attempts to block our attempts to grow into maturity as God's children. We must know how to stand against him Paul wrote about Satan: "We are not ignorant of his schemes" (2 Corinthians 2:11). Perhaps Paul and the Corinthians weren't ignorant, but a lot of Christians today surely are. We live as though Satan and his dark realm don't exist. And our naiveté in this area is exacting a crippling toll from our freedom in Christ.

Dear Lord, I stand against Satan's schemes to pollute my life with deeds of sin and the flesh. I embrace my inheritance as a child of God today.

The Spirit also helps our weakness; for we do not know how to pray as we should, but the Spirit Himself intercedes for us with groanings too deep for words....He intercedes for the saints according to the will of God (Romans 8:26,27).

We really don't know how to pray or what to pray for, but the Holy Spirit does, and He will help us in our weakness. *Help* is a fascinating word in Greek (*sunantilambano*), two prepositions placed in front of the word *take*. The Holy Spirit comes alongside, bears us up, and takes us to the other side. The Holy Spirit connects us with God. He intercedes for us on our behalf. The prayer that the Holy Spirit prompts us to pray is the prayer that God the Father will always answer.

How does the Holy Spirit help us in our weakness? I didn't know, but one evening while preparing a message on the topic of praying in the Spirit I tried something. I said, "Okay, Lord, I'm setting aside my list, and I'm going to assume that whatever comes to my mind during this time of prayer is from You or allowed by You. I'm going to let You set the agenda." Whatever came to my mind that evening was what I prayed about. If it was a tempting thought, I talked to God about that area of weakness. If the busyness of the day clamored for attention, I discussed my plans with God. I dealt with whatever came to my mind.

I wasn't passively letting thoughts control me, though. I was actively taking every thought captive to the obedience of Christ (2 Corinthians 10:5). Let me warn you that if you passively listen to your thoughts, you may end up paying attention to a deceiving spirit (1 Timothy 4:1).

If you try this kind of praying, you will find out how personal God really is. If God determined and prioritized our prayer list, He would begin with personal issues that affect our relationship with Him. "Come on," God says. "You keep telling others you have a personal relationship with Me. Let's get personal!"

Lord, teach me what it means to pray in the Spirit at the deep, personal levels of our relationship.

The fruit of the Spirit is...self-control (Galatians 5:22,23).

More times than not, the need to control our children comes from the false belief that our identity and worth derives from how well our children behave. Think it through: If your worth comes from something outside yourself, your tendency is to control the people and factors on which your worth is based. Look at sick dictators like Adolf Hitler and Saddam Hussein who control their subjects through ruthless force and intimidation. But there is no one more insecure than a controller, because he labors under the false belief that the external affairs of this world are determining who he is, not God and his response to Him. The fruit of the Spirit is self-control (Galatians 5:23), not child- or spouse-control.

If your identity is in Christ and your heart is set on being the person God wants you to be, nobody can block that goal but you. "But what if my child rebels?" you ask. Your child can't stop you from being the father or mother God wants you to be. Only you can do that. In reality, during a crisis of rebellion your child and your spouse need you to be the parent God wants you to be more than ever.

Massive research has shown that the best children come from parents who love their children and manage their behavior. The worst children come from loveless controllers. The second best children are raised by permissive parents who love unconditionally.

Here's the point: You may not always be able to control your child, but based on your position and character in Christ you can always love him. Loving your child is dependent only on you and your response to God. Controlling him is somewhat dependent on the cooperation of your child. Your identity and security in Christ do not depend on things you have no right or ability to control.

Lord, continue to mature me as a loving parent and keep me from trying to control my children from selfish motives.

THE TRUTH OF CHRIST'S VICTORY

When He had disarmed the rulers and authorities, He made a public display of them, having triumphed over them through Him (Colossians 2:15).

One of the common objections to the ministry of setting captives free performed by Jesus and the apostles is the apparent lack of instruction on the subject in the Epistles. Let me offer another perspective which may help clarify the issue and suggest how we should confront demonic influence in our own lives and minister to others in bondage.

Prior to the cross, divinely empowered agents—such as Jesus and His specifically appointed apostles—were necessary to take authority over demonic powers in the world. But something radical happened at the cross and in the resurrection that changed the nature of spiritual conflicts forever. First, Jesus' death and resurrection triumphed over and disarmed the rulers and authorities of the kingdom of darkness (Colossians 2:15). Prior to the cross, "all authority...in heaven and on earth" had not yet been given to Christ. But Matthew 28:18 assures us that the resurrected Christ is now the seat of all authority. Because of the cross Satan is a defeated foe, and he has no authority over those who are in Christ. Affirming the truth of Christ's victory and Satan's defeat is the primary step to successfully combating the enemy's attempts to intimidate you and hassle you.

Second, in Christ's death and resurrection every believer is made alive with Him and is now seated with Him in the heavenlies (Ephesians 2:5,6). You no longer need an outside agent to effect authority for you; you now reside in Jesus Christ, who has all authority. In order to resist the devil, you need to understand and appropriate your position and authority in Christ. Freedom is your inheritance as a Christian. It is your responsibility to put on the armor of God and resist the devil.

Thank You, Jesus, for making me a partaker with You in defeating the devil. Help me fulfill my responsibility to resist him today.

Using Your Unique Gifts and Abilities

Do the work of an evangelist, fulfill your ministry (2 Timothy 4:5).

For the Christian, true fulfillment in life can be summarized by the popular bumper sticker slogan, "Bloom where you're planted." Peter said it this way: "As each one has received a special gift, employ it in serving one another" (1 Peter 4:10). Your greatest fulfillment in life will come when you discover your unique gifts and abilities and use them to edify others and glorify the Lord.

God allowed me to understand this vital principle before entering the ministry, while I was still employed as an aerospace engineer. I knew God wanted me to be an ambassador for Him where I worked, so I started a breakfast Bible study in the bowling alley next door. My announcement about the Bible study had only been posted in our office about an hour before a Jewish fellow pulled it off the wall and brought it to me. "You can't bring Jesus in here," he objected.

"I can't do otherwise," I said. "Every day I walk in here Jesus comes in with me." He was not impressed with my response!

One of the men who found Christ in the Bible study took over when I left Honeywell to enter seminary. A few months later I went back to visit my friends in the Bible study. "Do you remember the Jewish fellow?" the leader asked.

"Sure, I remember him," I said, recalling his brash opposition to our Bible study.

"Well, he got sick and almost died. I went to the hospital and visited him every night. Finally I led him to Christ."

I was ecstatic at the realization that I had become a spiritual grandparent. The sense of fulfillment was exhilarating. And it all happened because I started a simple little Bible study where I worked in order to do what Paul said: "Do the work of an evangelist, fulfill your ministry" (2 Timothy 4:5).

Father, I want to bloom where I am planted and resist the defeating temptation to compare myself to others.

Blessed are they who hunger and thirst for righteousness, for they shall be satisfied (Matthew 5:6).

Food is the ultimate appetite, since it is necessary for survival. So we eat to live, but when we begin to live to eat, food no longer satisfies. Instead, it consumes us, and millions of people feel powerless to control their appetite for food. When your body is deprived of necessary nutrients, you naturally crave those foods which will keep you healthy and keep your immune system functioning. If you eat to satisfy those natural cravings you will stay healthy and free. But when you turn to food to relieve anxiety or satisfy a lust for sweets, salt, etc., you will lose control, and the results will negatively affect your health.

It is no coincidence that Paul mentioned misuse of food in conjunction with his sober warning that "in later times some will fall away from the faith, paying attention to deceitful spirits and doctrines of demons" (1 Timothy 4:1). One of the evidences of the last days will be those who "advocate abstaining from foods" (verse 3) which are intended to meet a legitimate need. Every eating disorder I have dealt with had a spiritual component, yet virtually no counselors treating anorexia and bulimia expose the spiritual problem. A pastor's wife wrote to me after a conference:

> Dear Neil,
>
> I was bulimic for 11 years. But now I can be in the house alone all day with a kitchen full of food and be in peace. When a temptation or lie from Satan pops into my mind, I fend it off quickly with the truth. I used to be in bondage to those lies for hours and hours each day, always fearing food. Now I'm rejoicing in the freedom which the truth brings.

Temptation's hook is the devil's guarantee that what we think we want and need outside God's will can satisfy us. Don't believe it. You can never satisfy the desires of the flesh. Only sustaining right relationships, living by the power of the Holy Spirit, and experiencing the fruit of the Spirit will satisfy you.

Father God, protect me from giving in to the world, the flesh, and the devil. Keep me abiding in You so I can bear the fruit of righteousness.

Being diligent to preserve the unity of the Spirit in the bond of peace (Ephesians 4:3).

I really don't mind taking a stand on biblical grounds and living with the conflict that comes from those who oppose the gospel. I think that is part of our calling. What grieves God is when our ministry and work is stopped because well-intentioned people resist the inevitable and needlessly fight change.

I tell my students that the greatest asset they will have in their early years of ministry is older, mature saints in the church. The greatest liability they will have is old saints who have stopped growing years ago. All these saints do is censor. They reflect no more love or kindness now than they did 20 years ago. They don't worship—they critique the worship service. They no longer sit under the judgment of Scripture—they sit in judgment of the pastor. They no longer bear fruit—they actually prevent it. They insist that they are right when what they need to be is holy.

Mature saints have learned to restrict their freedom for the sake of weaker believers. Their faith doesn't rest in traditions, so they gladly accept changes in style of ministry that will reach the younger generation.

Another problem arises when young Christian leaders act impulsively as change agents without giving thought to what the consequences will be to the fellowship. Any movement forward that results in the loss of fellowship is not an improvement. We must be diligent to preserve the unity of the Spirit. Such change agents seem to be unaware that patience is a fruit of the Spirit. The modern generation wants it now. They seem to have forgotten the fact that God does everything decently and in order. He is not the author of confusion.

Father, please don't allow me to sit, soak, and sour, but to remain open-minded, lighthearted, and nonjudgmental.

And your ears will hear a word behind you, "This is the way, walk in it," whenever you turn to the right or to the left (Isaiah 30:21).

In a telephone conversation a lady asked, "Dr. Anderson, my pastor says my favorite television evangelist is a false teacher. Is he right?"

At a ministerial retreat, a pastor stopped me and said, "Neil, I've been at this church three years, and here's the situation..." After finishing his description he asked, "Do you think God is calling me out of there?"

A seminary student stopped by my office and asked, "You've met with my girlfriend and me twice now. Do you think we should get married?"

Good questions. Important questions for those asking them. They all hinge on the answer to a much larger question: Does God communicate His will to us? If so, how?

Each of these fine Christians was looking for direction or confirmation of God's leading. Possibly they lacked the spiritual discernment to make the right decision. They were thinking that I, like the referee in a game, would make the right "call" for them. I can advise and share what I know Scripture teaches, but only God can give divine guidance.

You *can* know God's will for your life. Ephesians 5:17 instructs us, "Do not be foolish, but understand what the will of the Lord is." God doesn't instruct us to do something we cannot do. The will of God is knowable. In the first place, we have the Bible, God's Word, which the Holy Spirit will enlighten for us as we meditate on it, providing us with remarkably clear guidance in most areas of our life. Second, we usually can experience the direct guidance of the Holy Spirit in areas not specifically covered by God's Word—if we are spiritually free and desire to do His will.

I have come to deeply believe that God gently guides our steps as we choose to walk with Him. I believe in divine guidance. I believe that God wants to make His presence known in our lives and in our ministries.

Lord, keep me sensitive to Your leading by staying close to You and giving my will to You.

For all who are being led by the Spirit of God, these are sons of God (Romans 8:14).

I had the privilege of feeding and caring for the sheep on the farm where I was raised. I discovered that sheep aren't the smartest animals on the farm. Sheep need to be shepherded. Left to themselves in a lush pasture, they will keep eating until it kills them. They need a shepherd to make them "lie down in green pastures" (Psalm 23:2) so they don't eat themselves to death!

The Lord often pictured our relationship with Him in Scripture like that of a shepherd and his sheep. Those of us who live in the West don't have a correct picture of what it means to be led like sheep. Western shepherds drive their sheep from behind the flock, often using dogs to bark at their heels. Eastern shepherds, like those in Bible times, lead their sheep from in front. I watched a shepherd lead his flock on a hillside outside Bethlehem during a visit to the Holy Land. The shepherd sat on a rock while the sheep grazed. After a time he stood up, said a few words to the sheep, and walked away. The sheep looked up and followed him. It was fascinating! The words of Jesus in John 10:27 suddenly took on new meaning to me: "My sheep hear My voice, and I know them, and they follow Me."

Sheep without a shepherd become disoriented and scatter. Rams arise from the flock and butt heads to determine who will lead. The ones with the hardest heads win. Without a shepherd, we too are left to the mercy of hard-headed, driven people or we wander around directionless, eating ourselves to death.

The Spirit-walk is one of being led, not driven. God won't make you walk in the Spirit, and the devil *can't* make you walk in the flesh, although he will certainly try to draw you in that direction. You are free to choose to follow the leading of the Spirit or the desires of the flesh (Romans 8:14).

Gentle Shepherd, thank You for searching for me when I was lost and for comforting me when I am hurt. I long to follow You today.

No Middle Ground

He who is not with Me is against Me; and he who does not gather with Me, scatters (Luke 11:23).

The early church included in its public declaration of faith, "I renounce you, Satan, and all your works and ways." The Catholic Church, the Eastern Orthodox Church, and many other liturgical churches still require this renunciation as part of confirmation. For some reason it has disappeared from most evangelical churches. Consequently, we have mislaid a very important truth: We must not only choose the truth but recognize and renounce the counterfeit. There is no middle ground with truth. Jesus said, "He who is not with Me is against Me; and he who does not gather with Me, scatters" (Luke 11:23). There are not many paths to God; there is only one way (John 14:6). Christians are not being narrow-minded when they stand on what God has declared.

The literal meaning of repentance is a change of mind. This is not merely mental acknowledgment. The idea is, "I used to think, believe, and walk one way, but now I think, believe, and walk a new way." People who say, "I believe the Bible, but I also believe what I learned that is contrary to the Word of God," are deceived and living in bondage.

The first step to freedom in Christ is to renounce previous or current involvement with satanically inspired occultic practices or false religions. Any activity or group which denies Jesus Christ, offers guidance through any source other than the absolute authority of the written Word of God, or requires secret initiations must be forsaken. No Christian has any business being part of a group that is not completely open about all they do. God does everything in the light because in Him there is no darkness at all. We are to walk in the light.

Great Deliverer, bring to my mind deceptions from Satan I need to renounce and remove so I can walk completely in the light.

I write to you, young men, because you are strong, and the word of God lives in you, and you have overcome the evil onc (1 John 2:14 NIV).

According to John, new Christians are like little children whose sins are forgiven and who have entered into the knowledge of God. Mature saints are likened to old men who have a deep knowledge of God. In between are the young men, growing Christians whose chief characteristic is that they have overcome the evil one. No wonder we don't have very many mature saints in the Western world. We scarcely recognize that there is an evil one, let alone overcome him!

Until you have overcome the evil one, you may not have a lot of mental peace. If you are attempting to deal with deceiving thoughts by trying to rebuke them, you'll be like the person treading water in the middle of the ocean whose life's purpose is to keep 12 corks, which are bobbing close by, submerged with a little hammer! Acknowledge the presence of the corks, but ignore them and swim to shore! Don't pay attention to deceiving spirits.

The whole thrust of Scripture directs us to choose truth. We dispel the darkness by turning on the light. If you are plagued by tempting thoughts, bring the issue before God and seek to resolve that which is keeping you from having perfect fellowship with Him. The devil isn't the primary issue—he is only taking advantage of the fact that your fellowship with God has been broken. James 4:7 has the right priorities: "Submit therefore to God. Resist the devil and he will flee from you." The primary issue is to submit to God.

Satan knows that if he can keep our minds distracted, we won't have much of a prayer life with God. Prayer is the vital link for God's guidance. If we are going to walk with God through the darkness, we must have the peace of God which surpasses all comprehension and guards our hearts and minds in Christ Jesus (Philippians 4:7).

Lord, thank You that as I submit to You and resist the devil, Satan must flee and I will be free.

Open Dialogue with Your Child

Like apples of gold in settings of silver is a word spoken in right circumstances (Proverbs 25:11).

All discipline must be based on prior instruction. Make a clear statement of your expectations for a given situation and the consequences for disobedience. Ask your child to repeat what you say to make sure he understands. Then invite his questions and comments.

Honest and open dialogue after disobedience is a powerful means of discipline. Many children would rather face a paddle than verbal confrontation. Even parental silence communicates volumes. For many children, sitting emotionally exposed before an authority figure is much more threatening and shameful than a simple spanking.

What is the motivating deterrent behind a verbal confrontation? The fear of being called into accountability. We find that in our relationship with the Lord. We fear Him because we are going to stand before Him someday and give an account of our lives (2 Corinthians 5:10,11)—not to be punished but to be rewarded. Knowing that we are going to be personally accountable before the Lord is a great driving force in our lives. We want to hear Him say, "Well done, good and faithful servant."

Your child feels the same way about having to answer to you. He doesn't want to look bad in your eyes. That's why it's often difficult for him to confess his misdeeds in a confrontation. When you sit down with him it will be easy for him to say, "I'm sorry," a little harder for him to say, "Will you forgive me?" and hardest for him to say, "I did it."

Helping your child learn to speak the truth in love will take a lot of love and skill on your part, especially if your child is prone to lying. If you allow him to establish a pattern of deception as a means of avoiding confrontation, you are in for a lot of pain during his adolescence. You must work toward honest confession or any method of discipline will be ineffective.

Lord, help me develop honesty and openness with You so I can model and teach these qualities to my children.

Delight yourself in the LORD; and He will give you the desires of your heart (Psalm 37:4).

Jeremiah said, "The heart is more deceitful than all else and is desperately sick" (17:9). With that description, you can imagine what the heart is capable of desiring. Delighting in what the world offers will only temporarily satisfy those desires and will sicken your heart even more. But if you delight in the Lord, your desires will change. I believe this process unfolds as we seek to do God's will.

I had very little desire to read until I came to Christ. Now I read volumes. After I received Christ, I wanted to serve Him full-time. I had completed engineering school and was preparing to do anything God wanted—except go back to school. But within a year I could hardly wait to get to seminary. It was the best educational experience of my life, and the only one I enjoyed up to that point. Since then I have finished four more degrees. If we delight in the Lord, He changes our desires!

We struggle between the desires of the flesh and the desires of righteousness. Jesus told us, "Blessed are those who hunger and thirst for righteousness, for they shall be satisfied" (Matthew 5:6). Do you believe that? I guarantee that if you try to satisfy the desires of the flesh, you will never satisfy them. The more you feed them, the greater the hunger.

When we first come to Christ, nothing contests our will more than the lusts of the flesh: "For the flesh sets its desires against the Spirit, and Spirit against the flesh; for these are in opposition to one another" (Galatians 5:17). Our will is like a toggle switch, but it's initially spring-loaded to the flesh. As we delight in the Lord it becomes spring-loaded to the Spirit.

My heart's desire, Father, is to be totally responsive to You and to delight in whatever gives You glory.

A WHOLE-BRAIN GOD

And I, if I be lifted up from the earth, will draw all men to Myself (John 12:32).

Some researchers have suggested that our brains have two hemispheres. We are led to believe that each hemisphere functions slightly differently from the other as follows:

Left Brain	**Right Brain**
reason	intuition
cognitive	subjective
task-oriented	relationship-oriented
verbal	visual
facts	feelings
language	arts
math	music
linear	spatial

When God works through the church, He doesn't bypass our minds. And neither does He bypass one hemisphere for the sake of the other. We only have one brain and one mind. We have a whole-brain God. Without Christ, the cognitive people are "always learning and never able to come to the knowledge of the truth" (2 Timothy 3:7). Without Christ, the intuitive people are "led on by various impulses" (2 Timothy 3:6).

Neither the rationalist nor the mystic will ever come to Christ by reason or intuition. Jesus is the ultimate revelation of God. He is the truth. He draws both the rationalist and the mystic to Himself when neither leans on his own understanding.

Cognitive-oriented Christians strive to be right and search for wisdom and knowledge. Intuitive-oriented Christians are zealous for reality and power. We need the biblical balance: "We preach Christ crucified...the power of God and the wisdom of God" (1 Corinthians 1:23,24).

Lord, keep me from being too rigid or too flexible in my thinking and learning. May my mind be balanced by the truth.

We are ambassadors for Christ, as though God were entreating through us; we beg you on behalf of Christ, be reconciled to God (2 Corinthians 5:20).

God has a unique place of ministry for each of us. It is important to your sense of fulfillment that you realize exactly where that place is. The key is to discover the roles you occupy in which you cannot be replaced, and then decide to be what God wants you to be in those roles.

For example, of the five billion people in the world, you are the only one who occupies your unique role as husband, father, wife, mother, parent, or child in your home. God has specially planted you to serve Him by serving your family and the community where you live.

"I don't understand women who are looking for fulfillment in the world in some meaningless job," said a mother of five children. "What could be more challenging and meaningful than raising five godly children and managing a Christian home?" I agree. Assuming the responsibility of our primary roles is too challenging for some, but it is the only path of fulfillment. You will never be fulfilled trying to become something you're not.

You occupy a unique role as an ambassador for Christ where you work and live. These are your mission fields and you are the worker God has appointed for the harvest there. Your greatest fulfillment will come from accepting and occupying God's unique place for you to the best of your ability. Sadly, so many miss their calling in life by looking for fulfillment in the world. Find your fulfillment in the kingdom of God by deciding to be an ambassador for Christ in the world. Paul said, "Do the work of an evangelist, fulfill your ministry" (2 Timothy 4:5).

Lord, keep me sensitive to the ministry You have for me in the ordinary places of my daily life.

Maintaining Your Freedom

It was for freedom that Christ set us free; therefore keep standing firm and do not be subject again to a yoke of slavery (Galatians 5:1).

The Revolutionary War was a hard-fought battle, and many lives were lost in order to ensure the freedom of our country. There is always a price to pay for freedom, and the moment we take our freedom for granted, we run the risk of losing it.

Freedom in Christ from our sinful nature and the god of this world is the inheritance of every believer. Christ has set you free through His victory over sin and death on the cross. But if you have lost a measure of your freedom because you have failed to stand firm in the faith or you have disobeyed God, it is your responsibility to do whatever is necessary to maintain a right relationship with God. Your eternal destiny is not at stake; you are secure in Christ. But your daily victory in Him will be tenuous at best if you fail to assume your responsibility to maintain your freedom in Christ.

Remember: You are not the helpless victim of a tug-of-war between two nearly equal heavenly superpowers. Compared to Satan's limited attributes, God is immeasurable in His omnipotence, omnipresence, and omniscience—and you are united with Him! Sometimes the reality of sin and the presence of evil may seem more real than the reality and presence of God, but that's part of Satan's deception. He is a defeated foe, and we are in Christ the eternal Victor. That's why we worship God: to keep His divine attributes constantly before us in order to counter Satan's lies. A true knowledge of God and our identity in Christ is the greatest determinant of our mental health. A false concept of God and the misplaced deification of Satan are the greatest contributors to mental illness.

Are you walking in freedom today?

I praise You, Lord, for the awesome freedom I enjoy in Christ. Strengthen my will so I may choose to walk in freedom daily.

Our Greatest Motivation

The fear of the LORD is the beginning of knowledge; fools despise wisdom and instruction (Proverbs 1:7).

To worship God is to acknowledge His divine attributes. He doesn't need us to tell Him who He is. We need to keep our minds renewed to the reality of His presence. Notice how this is brought out in 2 Corinthians 5:9-11: "Therefore also we have as our ambition, whether at home or absent, to be pleasing to Him. For we must all appear before the judgment seat of Christ, that each one may be recompensed for his deeds in the body, according to what he has done, whether good or bad. Therefore knowing the fear of the Lord, we persuade men."

Realizing that God knows the thoughts and intentions of our hearts, we should be motivated to live our lives to please Him. Someday we're going to stand before Him and give an account. The judgment that Paul is talking about in this passage is not for punishment but for rewards. We don't fear God because of the possibility of punishment: "There is no fear in love; but perfect love casts out fear, because fear involves punishment, and the one who fears is not perfected in love" (1 John 4:18). We have already been judged as to *where* we will spend eternity. But *how* we spend eternity depends on how we respond to God in this lifetime.

I personally don't want to limp into heaven and have Him say, "Well, okay, come on in." I want to stand before God someday and hear Him say, "Well done, good and faithful servant. Enter into the joy of your Lord." That's the greatest motivation in my life. As a child I didn't fear the spanking of my father nearly as much as I feared being accountable to him and facing his disappointment.

I'm not disappointed with God, and I sure don't want Him disappointed with me.

Lord, may the reality of my eternal salvation motivate me to wholehearted, grateful obedience today.

Every Christian's Responsibility

Humble yourselves, therefore, under the mighty hand of God, that He may exalt you at the proper time, casting all your anxiety upon Him, because He cares for you (1 Peter 5:6,7).

Several weeks after one of my conferences, a friend shared with me the story of a dear Christian woman who had attended. She had lived in a deep depression for several years. She "survived" by leaning on her friends, three counseling sessions a week, and a variety of prescription drugs.

During the conference this woman realized that her support system included everybody and everything but God. She had not cast her anxiety on Christ and she was anything but dependent on Him. She took her conference syllabus home and began focusing on her identity in Christ and expressing confidence in Him to meet her daily needs. She radically threw off all her other supports (a practice I do not recommend) and decided to trust in Christ alone to relieve her depression. She began living by faith in God rather than men and renewing her mind according to Scripture. After only one month she was a completely different person. The support of a caring community can become a poor substitute for our own personal relationship with God.

Persons who want to move forward in Christian maturity can certainly benefit from the discipling of others. And those who seek freedom from their past can be helped through the counseling of others. But ultimately every Christian is responsible for his or her own maturity and freedom in Christ. Nobody can make you grow. That's your decision and daily responsibility. We absolutely need God, and we also need the support of one another. Thankfully, none of us walks through the disciplines of personal maturity and freedom alone. The indwelling Christ is eagerly willing to walk with us each step of the way.

Lord, I affirm my total dependence on You for daily growth, victory, and freedom.

Wholeness and Meaning in Life

You are all sons of God through faith in Christ Jesus (Galatians 3:26).

Several years ago a 17-year-old girl drove a great distance to talk with me. I have never met a girl who had so much going for her. She was cover-girl pretty with a wonderful figure. She was immaculately dressed. She had completed 12 years of school in 11 years, graduating with a very high grade point average. As a talented musician, she had received a music scholarship to a Christian university. And she drove a brand-new sports car her parents gave her for graduation. I was amazed that one person could have so much.

She talked with me for half an hour and I realized that what I saw on the outside wasn't matching what I was beginning to see on the inside. "Mary," I said finally, "have you ever cried yourself to sleep at night because you felt inadequate and wished you were somebody else?"

She began to cry. "How did you know?"

"Truthfully, Mary," I answered, "I've learned that people who *appear* to have it all together are often far from being together inside."

Often what we show on the outside is a false front designed to disguise who we really are and cover up the secret hurts we feel about our identity. Somehow we believe that if we appear attractive or perform well or enjoy a certain amount of status, then we will have it all together inside as well. But that's not necessarily true. External appearance, accomplishment, and recognition don't necessarily reflect—or produce—internal peace and maturity. All the stuff and status you can acquire don't add up to personal wholeness. Millions of people climb those ladders to success, only to discover when they reach the top that they are leaning against the wrong wall!

Wholeness and meaning in life are not the products of what you have or don't have, what you've done or haven't done. You are already a whole person and possess a life of infinite meaning and purpose because of who you are—a child of God. The only identity equation that works in God's kingdom is you plus Christ equals wholeness and meaning.

Father God, I wouldn't trade the wholeness and meaning You have brought to my life for anything the world can produce.

Your Best Defense

You are from God, little children, and have overcome [evil spirits]; because greater is He who is in you than he who is in the world (1 John 4:4).

When you came to life in Christ, Satan didn't curl up his tail and pull in his fangs. He is committed to foul up your life through his deception to "prove" that Christianity doesn't work, that God's Word isn't true, and that nothing really happened when you were born again.

You don't have to be a defenseless hockey puck at the mercy of Satan and his demons. God has already supplied the protection you need to ward off any and every attack in the spiritual realm. You just need to know what God has provided and to apply it to your own experience. Your best defense against the god of this world is to live a righteous life in Christ.

Some Christians are a little paranoid about evil powers, suspecting that demons lurk around every corner just waiting to possess them. That's an unfounded fear. Our relationship to demonic powers in the spiritual realm is a lot like our relationship to germs in the physical realm. We know that germs are all around us: in the air, in the water, in our food, in other people, even in us. But do you live in constant fear of catching some disease? No—unless you're a hypochondriac! You know enough about wellness to eat the right foods, get enough rest, and keep yourself and your possessions clean. If you live a balanced life, your immune system will protect you.

It's the same in the spiritual realm. Demons are like little invisible germs looking for someone to infect. We are never told in Scripture to be afraid of them. You just need to be aware of their reality and commit yourself to live a righteous life in spite of them. Should you come under attack, deal with it and go on with life. Remember: The only thing big about a demon is its mouth. Demons are habitual liars. In Jesus Christ the Truth, you are equipped with all the authority and protection you need to deal with anything they throw at you.

Lord, I know that living a righteous life is my pathway to experiencing freedom. I renounce Satan's lies and choose righteousness today.

THE SOURCE OF ALL HOPE

Hope in God, for I shall again praise Him, the help of my countenance, and my God (Psalm 43:5).

Sometimes the depression resulting from a seemingly impossible situation is related to a wrong concept of God. David wrote: "How long, O LORD? Will you forget me forever? How long will you hide your face from me?...How long will my enemy triumph over me?" (Psalm 13:1,2 NIV). Had God really forgotten David? Was He actually hiding from David? Of course not. David had a wrong concept of God, feeling that He had abandoned him to the enemy. David believed a lie about God, and consequently he lost his focus. His situation seemed hopeless, and hopelessness is the basis for all depression.

But the remarkable thing about David is that he didn't stay in the dumps. He evaluated his situation and realized, "Hey, I'm a child of God. I'm going to focus on what I know about Him, not on my negative feelings." From the pit of his depression he wrote: "I trust in your unfailing love; my heart rejoices in your salvation" (Psalm 13:5 NIV). Then he decided to make a positive expression of his will: "I will sing to the LORD, for he has been good to me" (verse 6). He willfully moved away from his wrong concept and its accompanying depression and returned to the source of his hope.

If Satan can destroy your belief in God, you will lose your source of hope. But with God all things are possible. He is the source of all hope. You need to learn to respond to hopeless-appearing situations as David did: "Why are you in despair, O my soul? And why are you disturbed within me? Hope in God, for I shall again praise Him, the help of my countenance, and my God" (Psalm 43:5).

If Satan can't destroy your concept of God, then he will seek to destroy your concept of who you are as a child of God. He can't do anything about your position in Christ, but if he can get you to believe it's not true, you will live as if it's not, even though it is. The two most important beliefs you possess are who God is and who you are as His child.

Above all, Father, help me focus continually on who You are and who I am in Christ, and to take every thought captive to the obedience of Christ.

Predisposed to Do His Will

No one, after putting his hand to the plow and looking back, is fit for the kingdom of God (Luke 9:62).

Imagine, if you would, a door in the path ahead of you. God's will is on the other side of that door. We crave to know what it is. Will God show us what's on the other side of that door? No. Why not? Because we have to resolve an issue on this side of the door first. If He is Lord, He has the right to determine what's on the other side of the door. If we don't afford Him that right, then we are not acknowledging Him as Lord.

Why do we want to know what's on the other side of that door? Isn't it because we want to reserve the right to determine whether or not we will go through it? Some boldly walk halfway through, but keep their foot in the door just in case they don't like what they see and want to go back. It's going to be awfully hard to continue walking with God if your foot is stuck in the door. Jesus said, "No one, after putting his hand to the plow and looking back, is fit for the kingdom of God" (Luke 9:62).

One man probably spoke for many when he said, "I'm so used to running my own life. I'm not sure I even can or want to trust someone else. Besides, God would probably haul me off to some mission field I can't stand." What we need to realize is that if we did give our heart to the Lord, and God did call us to that mission field, by the time we got there we wouldn't want to be anywhere else.

Do you believe that the will of God is good, acceptable, and perfect for you (Romans 12:2)? That's the heart of the issue. In the Lord's Prayer we are taught to approach God with the intent that His will be accomplished on earth. It makes no sense to petition God if we are not predisposed to do His will.

Your will be done on earth as it is in heaven, Lord.
I open my heart for You to enter and accomplish Your purposes in me today.

Be on the alert, stand firm in the faith
(1 Corinthians 16:13).

The school administration in a Christian high school found out that nearly every student in the school had played "Bloody Mary," a popular party game among some groups of children. A common version of the game requires a child to go into a completely darkened bathroom alone, spin around six times, face the mirror, and call upon Bloody Mary to show herself. In many cases these children saw something frightening in the mirror. There was no physical explanation for seeing anything in a totally dark room. These children had unwittingly opened themselves up to the god of this world.

Bloody Mary is only one of the more "innocent" ways our children are giving Satan a foothold in their lives. Games like the Ouija board and Dungeons and Dragons are other common means by which children are introduced to the occult. The music, movies, magazines, television programs, and substances our children are exposed to create gaping doors of opportunity for Satan to seduce them. At one public high school in Southern California, 133 students were referred to the school psychologist during the first six weeks of classes because of their involvement with Satanism and the occult. Most children don't even realize the spiritual bondage they are submitting to when participating in these activities. What's worse, most parents don't either.

Children are dabbling in all kinds of occultic experiences: astral projection, table lifting, fortune-telling, astrology, crystals or pyramids, automatic writing, tarot cards, palm reading, spirit guides, and blood pacts. In addition, the New Age Movement permeating our society and our public education system today is the source of many pitfalls. Much of the world's attempt to amuse and entertain our children leads them into darkness.

No matter how many dark doorways beckon to your children, Christ is the ultimate door to freedom. He is the truth and the light that dispels the lies of Satan and the darkness of the world. Teach yourself and your children to know and choose the truth.

Lord, help me equip my children to recognize and dispel the darkness in the worldly amusements and entertainment which surround them.

When they had prayed, the place where they had gathered together was shaken, and they were all filled with the Holy Spirit, and began to speak the word of God with boldness (Acts 4:31).

Fear is a powerful controller. It either compels us to do what is irresponsible or it impedes us from living responsibly. Recently a denominational executive spoke in our chapel, and his opening statement was, "As I travel among our pastors, I'm overwhelmed by the realization that the number one motivation in their lives is fear of failure."

After several years of teaching evangelism and overseeing evangelistic outreaches, I can tell you with confidence that the number one reason people don't share their faith is fear. Agoraphobia, fear of being in public, is one of the fastest growing psychological disorders. Fear of failure, fear of the devil, fear of man, fear of everything is plaguing our society.

Do you know that the most frequent command of Jesus in the Gospels is, "Fear not"? In anticipation of Israel's entrance into the Promised Land, God tells His people four times, "Be strong and courageous" (Joshua 1). The writer of Proverbs says, "The wicked flee when no one is pursuing, but the righteous are bold as a lion" (Proverbs 28:1).

The fact that God doesn't look favorably on cowards and unbelievers is made evident in Revelation 21:8: "But for the cowardly and unbelieving and abominable and murderers and immoral persons and sorcerers and idolaters and all liars, their part will be in the lake that burns with fire and brimstone, which is the second death." Does it surprise you that cowardly, unbelieving people are listed in a rogue's gallery with murderers and liars?

It is a characteristic of the Spirit-filled life to be bold (Acts 4:31). The early church didn't pray for "divine appointments"; they prayed for boldness. God's kingdom can only be established by faithful and courageous people.

Lord, I purpose to be strong and courageous in Your name, ready and trustworthy to accomplish Your will.

For He delivered us from the domain of darkness, and transferred us to the kingdom of His beloved Son (Colossians 1:13).

The Western world today sees reality in two tiers. The upper tier is the transcendent world where God and angels—as well as ghosts and ghouls—reside, a world which is understood through religion and mysticism. The lower tier is the empirical world, which is understood through science and the physical senses. In two-tier mentality, the spiritual world has no practical bearing on the natural world; we have excluded it from our understanding of reality. Most attempts at integrating theology and psychology include only God and humanity (fallen and redeemed) and exclude the activity of Satan and demons.

In stark contrast to the secularism of the West, two-thirds of the inhabitants of the world hold an Eastern worldview. They live and operate believing that spiritual forces are an everyday reality. These people appease their gods with peace offerings and perform religious rituals to ward off evil spirits. To the common people in Third World nations, religious practice or superstition has more practical relevance in daily life than science.

It is easy for those of us raised in the West to dismiss the Eastern worldview as inferior on the basis of the "success" of the Western world. But both are worldly systems and neither reflects biblical reality. The West tries to ignore the reality of the spiritual world, and the East tries to appease it or naively enter into it. The Bible clearly depicts the reality of the kingdom of darkness and the kingdom of light. God's Word tells us we can have victory over the former by being transferred into the latter.

Many Christians either exclude the supernatural from their worldview altogether or consign it to the transcendental tier where it will have no effect on their lives. By doing so they not only exclude God's power from their theology and practice but they also explain all human failure—even that which is induced by demonic influence—as the result of psychological or natural causes.

Lord, I accept the worldview presented in Your Word. Help me deal victoriously with the reality of demonic forces in my world.

Do Not Be Deceived

Do not be deceived: "Bad company corrupts good morals" (1 Corinthians 15:33).

Is it really possible for Christians to deceive themselves? Yes, it is very possible. We deceive ourselves when we think the unrighteous will inherit the kingdom of God. I heard about a young Christian woman who was living in a lesbian relationship and asserting, "My lifestyle doesn't make any difference. God loves me and I'm forgiven." But 1 Corinthians 6:9,10 states, "Do not be deceived; neither fornicators, nor idolaters, nor adulterers, nor effeminate, nor homosexuals...shall inherit the kingdom of God." Living a brazenly sinful life is strong evidence of an unrighteous standing before God. You are deceived if you believe that your lifestyle does not need to line up with your profession.

We also deceive ourselves when we think we can continually associate with bad company and not be corrupted (1 Corinthians 15:33). When I was a young Christian I used to listen to records by an evangelist in New Orleans who was called "the Bourbon Street preacher." This man lived in the red-light district and claimed to have a ministry to prostitutes and other questionable characters. But according to 1 Corinthians 15:33, anyone who stays in that environment too long will get into trouble. And that's just what happened to this evangelist. He became so entangled with the seedy side of Bourbon Street that he eventually lost his ministry.

Does this mean that we shouldn't minister to those with bad morals? No, we must share Christ with them. But if we immerse ourselves in their environment, our ministry will eventually diminish and our morality will be affected for the worse. John wrote, "Little children, let no one deceive you; the one who practices righteousness is righteous, just as He is righteous; the one who practices sin is of the devil; for the devil has sinned from the beginning" (1 John 3:7,8).

Stay anchored in God's Word, and don't be deceived.

Father, forgive me for little compromises I have made with the world. I desire to live in complete harmony with my profession of faith.

The world is passing away, and also its lusts;
but the one who does the will of God abides forever
(1 John 2:17).

Over the last three decades people in the West have begun to sense that there is more to life than science has revealed and their senses have experienced—and, of course, they're right. On the surface this new hunger may sound encouraging to those of us with a Christian worldview, but in fact the same people who are disillusioned with the materialistic world are also disillusioned with established religion. Instead of turning to Christ and His church, they are filling their spiritual void with old-fashioned occultism dressed in the modern garb of parapsychology, holistic health, Eastern mysticism, and numerous cults marching under the banner of the New Age Movement.

Attempting to meet spiritual needs apart from God is nothing new. Christ encountered a secularized form of Judaism during His earthly ministry which was bound to its traditions instead of to the God of Abraham, Isaac, and Jacob. The religious leaders of the day didn't recognize the Messiah as their spiritual deliverer. They perceived the oppressor to be Rome, not Satan, the god of this world. But Jesus came to undo the works of Satan (1 John 3:8), not Caesar.

Satan's ultimate lie is that you are capable of being the god of your own life, and his ultimate bondage is getting you to live as though his lie is true. Satan is out to usurp God's place in your life. And whenever you live independently of God, focusing on yourself instead of the cross, preferring material and temporal values to spiritual and eternal values, he has succeeded. The world's solution to this conflict of identity is to inflate the ego while denying God the opportunity to take His rightful place as Lord. Satan couldn't be more pleased—that was his plan from the beginning.

Mighty God, I renounce any inclination within me
that I am capable of being the god of my life.
You alone are Lord and King.

I do believe; help my unbelief (Mark 9:24).

Someone has said that success comes in cans and failure in cannots. The "Twenty Cans of Success," taken from God's Word, will expand your knowledge of our faith-object, the Almighty God. Building your faith by internalizing these truths over the next two days will help lift you from the miry clay of the cannots to the reality that in Christ you can do all things.

Twenty Cans of Success

1. Why should I say I can't when the Bible says I can do all things through Christ who gives me strength (Philippians 4:13)?
2. Why should I lack when I know that God shall supply all my needs according to His riches in glory in Christ Jesus (Philippians 4:19)?
3. Why should I fear when the Bible says God has not given me a spirit of fear, but of power, love, and a sound mind (2 Timothy 1:7)?
4. Why should I lack faith to fulfill my calling knowing that God has allotted to me a measure of faith (Romans 12:3)?
5. Why should I be weak when the Bible says that the Lord is the strength of my life and that I will display strength and take action because I know God (Psalm 27:1; Daniel 11:32)?
6. Why should I allow Satan supremacy over my life when He that is in me is greater than he that is in the world (1 John 4:4)?
7. Why should I accept defeat when the Bible says that God always leads me in triumph (2 Corinthians 2:14)?
8. Why should I lack wisdom when Christ became wisdom to me from God and God gives wisdom to me generously when I ask Him for it (1 Corinthians 1:30; James 1:5)?
9. Why should I be depressed when I can recall to mind God's lovingkindness, compassion, and faithfulness and have hope (Lamentations 3:21-23)?
10. Why should I worry and fret when I can cast all my anxiety on Christ who cares for me (1 Peter 5:7)?

Lord, thank You for Your loving care reflected in the incredible promises in Your Word.

The righteous man shall live by faith (Romans 1:17).

Believing that you can succeed at Christian growth and maturity takes no more effort than believing you cannot succeed. So why not believe that you *can* walk in faith and in the Spirit, that you *can* resist the temptations of the world, the flesh and the devil, and that you *can* grow to maturity as a Christian. Allow the "Twenty Cans of Success" you began yesterday to encourage you.

Twenty Cans of Success (continued)

11. Why should I ever be in bondage knowing that there is liberty where the Spirit of the Lord is (2 Corinthians 3:17)?
12. Why should I feel condemned when the Bible says I am not condemned because I am in Christ (Romans 8:1)?
13. Why should I feel alone when Jesus said He is with me always and He will never leave me nor forsake me (Matthew 28:20; Hebrews 13:5)?
14. Why should I feel accursed or that I am the victim of bad luck when the Bible says that Christ redeemed me from the curse of the law that I might receive His Spirit (Galatians 3:13,14)?
15. Why should I be discontented when I, like Paul, can learn to be content in all my circumstances (Philippians 4:11)?
16. Why should I feel worthless when Christ became sin on my behalf that I might become the righteousness of God in Him (2 Corinthians 5:21)?
17. Why should I have a persecution complex knowing that nobody can be against me when God is for me (Romans 8:31)?
18. Why should I be confused when God is the author of peace and He gives me knowledge through His indwelling Spirit (1 Corinthians 14:33; 2:12)?
19. Why should I feel like a failure when I am a conqueror in all things through Christ (Romans 8:37)?
20. Why should I let the pressures of life bother me when I can take courage knowing that Jesus has overcome the world and its tribulations (John 16:33)?

I rejoice in Your eternal promises, Lord. You are a Rock that never crumbles.

Demonstrating What We Believe

Even so faith, if it has no works, is dead, being by itself (James 2:17).

Faith is an action word. We cannot passively respond to God. You may have heard the story of the circus performer who strung a wire over a river and proceeded to ride across it on a unicycle. When he returned, everyone applauded. Then he asked, "Who believes I can do that with a man on my shoulders?" Everyone responded in affirmation. He said, "All right, who will hop on?" The person who hops on is the person who really believes. Faith is not just giving credence to something or someone. Faith is demonstrated reliance upon something or someone.

Faith has the same operating dynamic as *agape* love. When we refer to love as a noun, we're talking about character: patience, kindness, etc. (1 Corinthians 13:4-7). When we say that God is love, we are describing His character. Paul says the goal of our instruction is love (1 Timothy 1:5); therefore, the goal of Christian education is character transformation.

When love is used as a verb, it is expressed by action: "For God so loved the world, that He gave..." (John 3:16). If we say we love someone and do nothing on their behalf, it's only sentimentality and not *agape* love. True love is expressed by meeting the needs of others.

Faith has a similar dynamic. When using faith as a noun, we're talking about what we believe. But if we're talking about faith as a verb, then it is expressed in the way we live. James says it like this: "Even so faith, if it has no works, is dead, being by itself. But someone may well say, 'You have faith, and I have works; show me your faith without the works, and I will show you my faith by my works.' You believe that God is one. You do well; the demons also believe, and shudder" (James 2:17-19).

The devil believes in the existence of Jesus and knows that God's Word is true. But he doesn't seek to glorify Jesus or to obey Him. He seeks his own glory, being a rebel at heart (Romans 1:25).

We demonstrate what we believe by how we live our lives. If we believe it, we will do it. If we don't, then what we believe is just wishful thinking.

Lord, help me put feet to my faith every day and not rely on past accomplishments.

Confessing What We Believe

If you confess with your mouth Jesus as Lord, and believe in your heart that God raised Him from the dead, you shall be saved; for with the heart man believes, resulting in righteousness, and with the mouth he confesses, resulting in salvation (Romans 10:9,10).

One primary means by which we express our belief is confession—verbally expressing what we believe. In fact, God requires us to take our stand in this world. Jesus says, "For whoever is ashamed of Me and My words in this adulterous and sinful generation, the Son of Man will also be ashamed of him when He comes in the glory of His Father with the holy angels" (Mark 8:38).

In rebuking the Pharisees, Jesus said, "For by your words you shall be justified, and by your words you shall be condemned" (Matthew 12:37). And in Mark 11:23, He said, "Whoever says to this mountain, 'Be taken up and cast into the sea,' and does not doubt in his heart, but believes that what he says is going to happen, it shall be granted him." Notice that Jesus does not say we shall have whatever we believe, but we shall have whatever we believe and confess. Confession gives expression to what is believed. The confession of the mouth must accurately express the belief of the heart.

To defeat Satan, we must speak forth the Word of God, which is the sword of the Spirit (Ephesians 6:17). In our English translations, two different words are used for the "Word" of God. The most common is *logos* and it indicates the whole revealed Word of God (John 1:1). The other word is *rhema*. There is only one Word of God, but the emphasis of *rhema* is in its expression. We are to hide the whole Word (*logos*) in our hearts, and when Satan attacks, we stand against him by confessing God's Word (*rhema*).

Confessing what we believe gives proof to our faith. Confession doesn't create faith; faith makes possible true confession. Confession is agreeing with God. It is living in the light by letting our life and our mouth demonstrate what we believe in our heart.

Father, I desire that what my heart believes and what my mouth confesses today line up with the truth of Your Word.

Perceptions and Emotions

The LORD's lovingkindnesses indeed never cease, for His compassions never fail. They are new every morning; great is Thy faithfulness (Lamentations 3:22,23).

In a general sense, your emotions are a product of your thought life. If you are not thinking right, if your mind is not being renewed, if you are not perceiving God and His Word properly, it will be reflected in your emotional life.

One of the best scriptural illustrations of the relationship between perceptions and emotions is found in Lamentations 3. In verses 1-6, Jeremiah expresses despair as he wrongly perceives that God is against him and that He is the cause of his physical problems. In verses 7-11,18 he vents his feelings of entrapment and fear. If your hope was in God, and these words were a correct portrayal of God, you would probably feel bummed out too.

What was Jeremiah's problem? His perception of God was way off center. God wasn't the cause of his affliction. God isn't a wild beast waiting to chew people up. But Jeremiah wasn't thinking right, perceiving right, or interpreting his circumstances right, so he wasn't feeling right or responding right either.

Suddenly, Jeremiah's countenance changes: "This I recall to my mind, therefore I have hope. The LORD's lovingkindnesses indeed never cease, for His compassions never fail. They are new every morning; great is Thy faithfulness" (verses 21-23). What a turnaround! Did God change? Did Jeremiah's circumstances change? No. His perception of God changed and his emotions followed suit.

You are not shaped so much by your environment as you are by your perception of your environment. Life's events don't determine who you are; God determines who you are, and your interpretation of life's events determines how well you will handle the pressures of life. In reality we have very little control over our emotions, but we do have control over our thoughts, and our thoughts determine our feelings and our responses. That's why it is so important that you fill your mind with the knowledge of God and His Word. You need to see life from God's perspective and respond accordingly.

Lord, continually adjust my perception of my environment to match Your perspective found in Your Word.

The Word became flesh, and dwelt among us, and we beheld His glory, glory as of the only begotten from the Father, full of grace and truth (John 1:14).

What effect did the Fall produce in Adam's mind? He and Eve lost their true perception of reality. We read in Genesis 3:7,8 that they tried to hide from God. Doesn't that reveal a faulty understanding of who God is? How can you hide from God? After the Fall, Adam and Eve weren't thinking straight.

In essence, when Adam and Eve sinned, their minds were robbed of the true knowledge of God. In God's original design, knowledge was relational. Knowing someone implied an intimate personal relationship. You can see it in Genesis 4:1: "Adam knew Eve his wife; and she conceived" (KJV). Yet we don't generally equate a knowledge of someone with personal intimacy.

Before the Fall, Adam and Eve knew God, not sexually of course, but in the intimacy of a close, personal relationship which we associate with marriage. They knew God by being with God. When they sinned and were banished from the garden, Adam and Eve lost their relationship with God and the knowledge of God which was intrinsic to that relationship. And you and I inherited Adam and Eve's darkened mind. Before Christ, we knew something *about* God, but we didn't *know* God because we had no relationship with Him.

The necessity of being in relationship to God in order to know God comes into sharp focus in John's announcement: "The Word"— *logos* in the Greek—"became flesh" (John 1:14). The word *logos* represented the highest form of philosophical knowledge. For the Greeks, saying that the logos became flesh was the same as saying that ultimate knowledge became personal and relational. God was announcing to the world through John: The true knowledge of God, which can only be discovered in an intimate relationship with God, is now available to the world through God in the flesh—Jesus Christ. In Christ we are able to know God personally, not just know about Him.

Lord, I thirst for deeper intimacy in my relationship with You. I want to know You more personally today.

Behaving Your Way into Good Feelings

If you know these things, you are blessed if you do them (John 13:17).

What happened to mankind emotionally as a result of the Fall? For one thing, we became fearful and anxious. One of the first emotions expressed by fallen humanity was fear (Genesis 3:10). Today fear is crippling our relationships and activities. Fear is a result of the Fall. If fear is controlling your life, then faith is not.

Another emotional by-product of sin is shame and guilt. Before Adam and Eve disobeyed God they were naked and unashamed (Genesis 2:25). God created them as sexual beings. Their sex organs and sexual activity were holy. But when they sinned, they were ashamed to be naked and they had to cover up (Genesis 3:7). Many people mask their inner self in fear that others may see them for who they really are.

Mankind also became depressed and angry after the Fall. Cain brought his offering to God and, for some reason, God was displeased with it. As a result, "Cain became very angry and his countenance fell. Then the LORD said to Cain, 'Why are you angry? And why has your countenance fallen? If you do well, will not your countenance be lifted up?' " (Genesis 4:5-7).

I believe God established a principle here which echoes all through the Bible: You don't feel your way into good behavior, you behave your way into good feelings. There are tons of things you don't feel like doing, but you do them. I never feel like going to the convalescent hospital to minister. And the moment I step in the door, the smell alone does away with any positive feelings of wanting to continue on. But I always leave feeling great; I'm glad I went. Good feelings follow right behavior. Jesus said, "If you know these things, you are blessed if you do them" (John 13:17).

Lord, help me do what You want me to do even when it seems unpleasant. I seek Your blessing for obedience.

Choose for yourselves today whom you will serve....As for me and my house, we will serve the L*ORD (Joshua 24:15).*

Adam and Eve's sin also affected the area of their will. Do you realize that in the Garden of Eden they could only make one wrong choice? Everything they wanted to do was okay except eating from the tree of the knowledge of good and evil (Genesis 2:16,17). They had the possibility of making a myriad of good choices and only one bad choice—*only one!*

Eventually, however, they made that one bad choice. As a result, you and I are confronted every day with a myriad of good *and* bad choices. You can choose to pray or not pray, read your Bible or not read your Bible, go to church or not go to church. You can choose to walk according to the flesh or according to the Spirit. You and I face countless choices like that every day, and we eventually make some bad ones.

Other than the Holy Spirit in your life, the greatest power you possess is the power to choose. Someone has said that pure Christianity lies in the exercise of the will. The animal kingdom operates out of divine instinct. But we are created in the image of God, which means we have a self-operated, independent will. The essence of temptation is to function independently of God. The basis for temptation is legitimate needs.

Sinful behavior is often a wrong attempt at meeting your basic needs. The real issue here is are you going to get your needs met by the world, the flesh, and the devil, or are you going to allow God to meet all your needs "according to His riches in glory in Christ Jesus" (Philippians 4:19)? It's an issue of identity and maturity. The more you understand your identity in Christ, the more you will grow in maturity. And the more mature you become, the easier it will be for you to choose to live your life in dependence on your heavenly Father.

Lord, I determine to exercise my great power of choice to live in moment-by-moment dependence on You today.

My God shall supply all your needs according to His riches in glory in Christ Jesus (Philippians 4:19).

Adam and Eve were created spiritually alive. The attributes they experienced before the Fall became glaring needs after the Fall.

1. *Acceptance was replaced by rejection, therefore we have a need to belong.* Ever since Adam and Eve's sin alienated them from God and disrupted human relationships, we have experienced a deep need to belong. Even when people come to Christ and fill their need to belong to God, they still need the acceptance of people. You will never understand the power of peer pressure in our culture until you understand the legitimate need to belong and the fear of rejection we all share.

2. *Innocence was replaced by guilt and shame, therefore we have a need for a sense of worth.* Many psychologists agree that people today generally suffer from a poor sense of worth. The secular psychologist responds by trying to stroke the human ego and encourage us to improve our performance. Your worth as a person is not an issue of giftedness, talent, intelligence, or beauty. It's an identity issue. Your sense of personal worth comes from knowing who you are: a child of God.

3. *Authority to rule over creation was replaced by weakness and helplessness, therefore we have a need for strength and self-control.* There is no one more insecure than a controller. The fruit of the Spirit is self-control, not spouse- or child-control.

Only Christ can meet the most basic needs of humanity, such as life, identity, acceptance, security, and significance. These needs are eternal, unlike our physical needs. If we present Christ as meeting only our physical needs, we will have stiff competition from every humanistic organization.

Father God, I reject any counterfeit fulfillment Satan offers me. I will live by every word that proceeds from Your mouth.

Three Levels of Prayer

Rejoice always; pray without ceasing; in everything give thanks; for this is God's will for you in Christ Jesus (1 Thessalonians 5:16-18).

I have observed three approaches to prayer which progress from level to level. The first level is *petition.* We are encouraged to let our requests be made known to God (Philippians 4:6). If it helps us to keep a list of daily prayer reminders, we should do so. However, most people weary of this, and their devotional life disappears over time. Often they don't see immediate results from their prayers, so they conclude that more can be accomplished if they just get busy for the Lord.

We've progressed to the second level when prayer becomes *personal.* We have discovered a new dimension when we are comfortable in His presence and don't feel obligated to talk. It's much like a marriage relationship. A mature couple can ride together in the car for hours, enjoying each other's company, without having to say a word. I can just be with God and I'm learning to listen.

Realizing that I need not feel obligated to keep the conversation going when I'm with God has changed my prayer life dramatically. This kind of prayer makes my relationship with God a 24-hour-a-day experience. Setting aside special times for prayer is still important. But when we leave our quiet time, the sense of God's presence should remain with us throughout the day.

I call the third dimension of prayer *true intercession.* True intercessors hear from God. They know how to pray and what to pray for. In my observation there are very few true intercessory prayer warriors. The ones I know of are usually older than 50, and most are women. They pray privately in their homes and often at night. Every church has at least one or two of them. Share your family needs with them. When these people pray, things happen because they don't just talk to God, they listen to Him.

Father, I want to grow in all dimensions of prayer to the point that I sense Your presence and hear Your voice.

GIVE YOUR CHILD TO GOD

Commit your way to the LORD, trust also in Him, and He will do it (Psalm 37:5).

You can and should uphold Christian values and standards in your own home. But when your child leaves your home, he leaves with his own values, beliefs, and personal agenda. This is the first half of the prodigal son story (Luke 15:11-32). The prodigal son wanted to do his own thing, so his father let him. I don't think the father would have let the boy rule in his home, but he did let him go. We don't like to see our children fail or make mistakes like that. When they do, we are too quick to rescue them from the natural consequences of their actions.

The father in the story welcomed his son home after the boy came to his senses. His repentance was complete: "Father, I have sinned against heaven and in your sight; I am no longer worthy to be called your son" (verse 21). The critical insight we need is offered by the father: "This son of mine was dead, and has come to life again" (verse 24). When your child is out of your sight, only God can bring him to his senses, bring him home, and give him life.

You can't go everywhere your child goes, but God can. He is the child's heavenly Father, and He is fully capable of protecting him.

I know of a dear lady who has buried two sons and witnessed the miracle healing of her husband from a near-fatal car accident. But her hardest trial was discovering that her beloved third son was struggling with homosexuality. Months of dark depression were lifted in one day when she realized that her son belonged to God, so she gave her boy to Him. For 11 years she didn't hear from him. Then one day he called and said he had a Mother's Day present for her. He had come back to the Lord!

God is in control. When you pray you release Him to do what only He can do in your child's life. And when you pray, He can mold your parenting style so you can do what He has called you to do in raising your child.

Lord, I release my children to Your care and protection, and I relinquish my will for them in favor of Your will.

The LORD is for me; I will not fear; what can man do to me? The LORD is for me among those who help me; therefore I shall look with satisfaction on those who hate me. It is better to take refuge in the LORD than to trust in man (Psalm 118:6-8).

David's question in Psalm 118:6 introduces a common fear among Christians: the fear of man. The timid man is quick to respond to the question, "I'll tell you what man can do to me. He can abuse me, he can fire me from my job, he can even kill me."

True, but Jesus tells us to lay those fears aside: "Do not fear those who kill the body, but are unable to kill the soul; but rather fear Him who is able to destroy both soul and body in hell" (Matthew 10:28). If you fail to take God as your refuge, the fear of man will control your life.

God appointed Saul to be the first king of Israel and commanded him to utterly destroy Amalek along with all of his family, followers, and possessions. Unfortunately, Saul didn't completely obey. Samuel confronted Saul, and after Saul's excuses ran out, he confessed, "I have sinned...because I feared the people and listened to their voice" (1 Samuel 15:24). Then the Lord rejected Saul as king of Israel. More than one king has fallen for fearing man more than God.

Suppose you are intimidated by your boss. You work in fear of him from eight to five. What power does he have over you? He could fire you! How could you overcome that power? You could quit or be willing to quit. By not allowing your boss to hold the job over your head, you would free yourself from his intimidations. God's Word says, "Do not fear their intimidation, and do not be troubled, but sanctify Christ as Lord in your hearts" (1 Peter 3:14,15).

I'm not suggesting that you rebel against your boss or become irresponsible. Servants are to obey their masters, and we are to work heartily as for the Lord rather than men (Colossians 3:22,23). However, when you make God your sanctuary, you free yourself to live a responsible life. If you lose your job in the process, you have the assurance that God will meet all your needs.

Lord, I want to be a God-pleaser, not a people-pleaser. Give me strength to stand up for the truth no matter what the cost.

I have fought the good fight, I have finished the course, I have kept the faith (2 Timothy 4:7).

Satisfaction in life comes from living righteously and seeking to raise the level of quality in the relationships, services, and products you are involved with. Matthew 5:6 says, "Blessed are those who hunger and thirst for righteousness, for they shall be satisfied." Do you really believe that? If you did, what would you be doing? You would spend more time feeding your spirit than trying to satisfy your fleshly desires. Have you ever tried to satisfy the flesh? It can't be done. The more you feed it, the more it wants.

What causes you to become dissatisfied? It's usually because the quality of the relationship, service, or product has diminished. I often ask people when they became dissatisfied. Inevitably they identify the time when the quality of a relationship, the service rendered, or the product produced diminished.

Satisfaction is a quality issue, not a quantity issue. You will achieve greater satisfaction from doing a few things well than from doing many things in a haphazard or hasty manner. The key to personal satisfaction is not in broadening your involvements but in deepening them through a commitment to quality.

The same is true in relationships. If you are dissatisfied in your relationships, perhaps you have spread yourself too thin. Solomon wrote: "A man of many friends comes to ruin, but there is a friend who sticks closer than a brother" (Proverbs 18:24). It may be nice to know a lot of people on the surface, but you need a few good friends who are committed to a quality relationship with each other. We all need the satisfaction which quality relationships bring.

Paul accomplished what he was called to do. He left a lot undone, but he fought the good fight, finished his course, and kept the faith. Jesus also left a lot undone, but He did His Father's will and was able to say, "It is finished." You may not be able to do all you want to do for Christ in your lifetime, but you can live obediently and faithfully day by day.

Lord, I desire the satisfaction that comes from righteousness and quality in my relationships and activities.

Who is among you that fears the LORD, that obeys the voice of His servant, that walks in darkness and has no light? Let him trust in the name of the LORD and rely on his God (Isaiah 50:10).

The life led by the Spirit of God is marvelous. Sensing His presence, living victoriously, and knowing the truth are characteristics of a free person. But what if you couldn't sense His presence? What if God, for some reason, suspended His blessings? What would you do if you were faithfully following God and suddenly all external circumstances turned sour?

My family and I have been through two extremely dark periods in our life. There were days I wasn't sure if we were going to make it. If it wasn't for the message of Isaiah 50:10, I'm not sure we would have survived spiritually. Isaiah is asking if there is a believer, somebody who fears the Lord, walking in darkness. He is not referring to the darkness of sin, or even the darkness of this world. He is talking about the darkness of uncertainty—that blanket of heaviness that settles in as though a black cloud has drifted over our very being. God has suspended His conscious blessings.

What is a person to do during these times? Isaiah tells us that, no matter how dark it gets, we are to keep on walking. In the light we can see the next step. The path ahead is clear. We know a friend from an enemy, and we can see where the obstacles are. But when darkness settles in, every natural instinct says to drop out, sit down, stop! We become fearful of the next step.

Isaiah says don't stop; keep on walking. Keep walking in the light of previous revelation. If it was true six months ago, it is still true. I try never to make a major decision when I am down. Rather, I wait until the cloud lifts and everything is clear and in focus again.

If God's ministry of darkness should envelop you, understand that God has not left you; He has only suspended His conscious presence so that your faith will not rest on feelings or be established by unique experiences or blessings. Listen to Isaiah's advice: Keep on walking. Never doubt in the darkness what God has clearly shown you in the light.

Thank You, Lord, for guiding me through the darkness of my trials with the light of Your truth.

Creating Our Own Light

Behold, all you who kindle a fire, who encircle yourselves with firebrands, walk in the light of your fire and among the brands you have set ablaze. This you will have from My hand; and you will lie down in torment (Isaiah 50:11).

When your way suddenly gets dark, don't light your own fire. Our natural tendency when we don't see life God's way is to do it our way. Resist the urge to create your own light.

In Isaiah 50:11, God is not talking about the fire of judgment; He's talking about fire that creates light. When we try to find our way out of the darkness by our own devices instead of waiting for God's light, God will allow it, but misery will follow.

Let me illustrate. God called Abraham out of Ur into the Promised Land. In Genesis 12, a covenant was made in which God promised Abraham that his descendants would be more numerous than the sands of the sea or the stars in the sky. Abraham lived his life in the light of that promise, then God turned out the light.

So many years passed that his wife Sarah could no longer bear a child by natural means. God's guidance had been so clear before, but now it looked like Abraham would have to assist God in its fulfillment. Who could blame Abraham for creating his own light? Sarah supplied the match by offering her handmaiden to Abraham. Out of that union came the Arab nation which has been in conflict with the Jewish nation ever since. Abraham created his own light, God allowed it, and misery followed.

We may not have to wait as long as Abraham did, but our darkness may last for weeks, months, and possibly, for some exceptional people, even years. But God is in control, and He knows exactly how big a knothole He can pull us through. When your faith is stretched to its limit and you are about to break, He will pull you through to the other side, and you will never go back to the shape you were in before.

The dark times are difficult, Lord, but I thank You for how I have grown and matured as I have trusted You through them.

If any man is thirsty, let him come to Me and drink. He who believes in Me, as the Scripture said, "From his innermost being shall flow rivers of living water" (John 7:37,38).

The story is told of a prospector in the last century who had to make a four-day journey across a burning desert. He couldn't carry enough water to make the journey without dying of thirst, but he was assured there was a well halfway across the desert. So he set out, and sure enough there was a well right where the map indicated. But when he pumped the handle, the well only burped up sand. Then he saw this sign: "Buried two feet over and two feet down is a jug of water. Dig it up and use the water to prime the pump. Drink all the water you want, but when you are done, fill the jug again for the next person."

Sure enough, two feet over and two feet down was enough water for the prospector to prime the pump or to finish his journey. Should he pour the water down the well or should he drink it?

To tell you the truth, I'd drink the water that was buried! I don't know who wrote the sign on that rusty old pump. It could be a cruel joke. I'd pour that water down a worthless well, only to watch my life drain away for lack of water.

Faith always has an element of risk, but there is one factor in the above story that doesn't exist when it comes to God. I know who wrote the sign. When I pour myself into a life of faith, I know that out of my inner being shall flow rivers of living water. God said so, history verifies it, and I, for one, can testify that it is true. In the final analysis, God is not only true, He's right.

There is more than enough water in God's well for everyone, but the pump is only activated by faith. Remember: "Without faith it is impossible to please Him, for he who comes to God must believe that He is, and that He is a rewarder of those who seek Him" (Hebrews 11:6).

Heavenly Father, You have proven Yourself trustworthy. Your river of living water never dries up or becomes polluted.

His Accepted, Adopted Child

Beloved, now we are children of God (1 John 3:2).

Having a right relationship with God begins with settling once and for all the issue that God is your loving Father and you are His accepted, adopted child. That's the foundational truth of your spiritual heritage. You are a child of God, you are created in His image, you have been declared righteous by Him because you trust that what Christ accomplished in His death and resurrection is applicable to you. As long as you believe that and walk accordingly, your daily experience of practical Christianity will result in growth. But when you forget who you are, and try to produce in your daily experience the acceptance God has already extended to you, you'll struggle. We don't serve God to gain His acceptance; we are accepted, so we serve God. We don't follow Him in order to be loved; we are loved, so we follow Him.

That's why you are called to live by faith (Romans 1:16,17). The essence of the victorious Christian life is believing what is already true about you. Do you have a choice? Of course! Satan will try to convince you that you are an unworthy, unacceptable, sin-sick person who will never amount to anything in God's eyes. Is that who you are? No, you are not! You are a saint whom God has declared righteous. Believing Satan's lie will lock you into a defeated, fruitless life. But believing God's truth about your identity will set you free.

Your perception of your identity makes such a big difference in your success at dealing with the challenges and conflicts of your life. It is imperative to your growth and maturity that you believe God's truth about who you are.

The Bible says, "See how great a love the Father has bestowed upon us, that we should be called children of God; and such we are" (1 John 3:1). Tragically, many believers are desperately trying to become something they already are, while others are living like something they aren't. It's true: "Beloved, now we are children of God" (1 John 3:2).

Lord God, I affirm anew that I am Your blood-bought child. The evil one cannot touch me as long as I live according to my position in Christ.

[Jesus] called the twelve together, and gave them power and authority over all the demons (Luke 9:1).

Jesus gave His disciples both *authority* and *power* over demons. What's the difference? Authority is the *right* to rule; it's a positional issue. A policeman has the right to stop traffic at an intersection because of the position of authority represented by his badge. Similarly, Jesus gave His disciples His badge to carry. They had the right to rule over the demons because of their position as followers of the One to whom all authority in heaven and on earth has been given (Matthew 28:18).

In contrast, power is the *ability* to rule. A policeman may have the authority to stop traffic, but he doesn't have the physical ability to do so. If he tries to stop traffic by his own power, he will probably get run over. However, if you move a 20-foot-square cement block into the middle of the intersection, it may not have any authority to make cars stop, but it certainly has the ability to do so!

No good manager would delegate *responsibility* to his underlings without also delegating *authority* to them and equipping them with the ability to get the job done. Jesus charged His disciples with the *responsibility* to proclaim the kingdom of God. Had He not also given them *authority and power* in the spirit world, the demons would have just scoffed at their feeble attempts and sent them running for cover (as they did the seven sons of Sceva in Acts 19).

The truth is that, while in yourself you don't have the ability to resist Satan and his demons, *in Christ you do*. The Israelites looked at Goliath fearfully and said, "We can't fight him." But young David looked at Goliath and said, "Who is this uncircumcised Philistine, that he should taunt the armies of the living God?" (1 Samuel 17:26). The army saw Goliath in relation to themselves and trembled; David saw Goliath in relation to God and triumphed. When you encounter the spiritual enemies of your soul, remember: "Be strong in the Lord [your authority], and in the strength of His might [your power]" (Ephesians 6:10).

Thank You, Father, for Your authority and power. Help me view my circumstances in light of what You can do, not according to what I can't do.

Our Access to Christ's Authority

I pray that the eyes of your heart may be enlightened (Ephesians 1:18).

Do we enjoy the same claim to Christ's authority in the spiritual realm as those who were personally sent out by Him? Absolutely! In fact, because of the death, resurrection, and ascension of Christ, and the subsequent outpouring of the Holy Spirit, we have an even greater advantage in spiritual warfare than the first disciples did. They were *with* Christ (Mark 3:14,15), but we are *in* Christ. That was Paul's great news in the opening lines of his letter to the church at Ephesus. Ten times in the first 13 verses he reminded us that everything we have is the result of our intimate, personal relationship with the resurrected Christ and His indwelling Spirit.

Having firmly established the reality of our position in Christ, Paul expressed his heart's desire for Spirit-filled believers in this prayer:

> I pray that the eyes of your heart may be enlightened, so that you may know what is the hope of His calling, what are the riches of the glory of His inheritance in the saints, and what is the surpassing greatness of His power toward us who believe. These are in accordance with the working of the strength of His might which He brought about in Christ, when He raised Him from the dead, and seated Him at His right hand in heavenly places (Ephesians 1:18-20).

Our problem with identity and self-perception as Christians is not that we aren't in Christ; it's that we don't *see* it or *perceive* it; we're just not conscious of it. We are not supposed to pursue power, because we already have it in Christ. We are to pursue truth and pray that our eyes be opened to our rich inheritance in Christ.

As long as we fail to perceive our access to Christ's authority over the kingdom of darkness, we will fail to exercise that authority in our lives, and we may live in bondage.

Open my eyes, Lord; I want to see Jesus. Open my ears and help me listen, abide in You, and draw strength moment by moment.

*Shout joyfully to the LORD, all the earth.
Serve the LORD with gladness; come before Him
with joyful singing (Psalm 100:1,2).*

Have you ever planned a major fun event and then asked yourself, "Are we having fun yet?" Fun is uninhibited spontaneity. Chances are the last time you really had fun it was a spontaneous, spur-of-the-moment activity or event. Big events and expensive outings can be fun, but sometimes we plan and spend all the fun right out of them. I've often had a lot more fun in an impromptu pillow fight with my children.

The secret to enjoying uninhibited spontaneity as a Christian is in removing non-scriptural inhibitors. Chief among the inhibitors of Christian fun is our fleshly tendency to keep up appearances. We don't want to look out of place or be thought less of by others, so we stifle our spontaneity with a form of false decorum. That's people-pleasing, and Paul suggested that anybody who lives to please people isn't serving Christ (Galatians 1:10).

I really like the uninhibited joy I see in King David, who knew the joy of being in the presence of the Lord. He was so happy about returning the ark to Jerusalem that he leaped and danced before the Lord in celebration. He knew there was joy in the presence of God. But Michal, his party-pooping wife, thought his behavior was unbecoming to a king, and she told him so in no uncertain terms. David said, "Rain on you, lady. I'm dancing to please the Lord, not you or anybody else. And I'm going to keep dancing whether you like it or not" (my paraphrase of 2 Samuel 6:21). As it turned out, Michal was the person God judged in the incident, not David (2 Samuel 6:23). You'll find a lot more joy in pleasing the Lord than in trying to please people.

Frankly, I think it's fun being saved. Being free in Christ means that we are free to be ourselves. We're free from our past, free from trying to live up to other people's expectations, free from sin and the evil one. What a joyful, uninhibited, spontaneous life for those who are free in Christ!

Lord, thank You for the joy of serving You, joy that is not detrimental to body, soul, or spirit.

Unless you believe that I am He, you shall die in your sins (John 8:24).

In assessing counterfeits to Christianity, no criterion is more important than the Person of Jesus Christ. Paul wrote: "I am afraid that just as Eve was deceived by the serpent's cunning, your minds may somehow be led astray from your sincere and pure devotion to Christ. For if someone comes to you and preaches a Jesus other than the Jesus we preached, or if you receive a different spirit from the one you received, or a different gospel from the one you accepted, you put up with it easily enough" (2 Corinthians 11:3,4 NIV).

Other religions may talk about Jesus, but they present Him in another way than He is presented in Scripture. They may talk about the same historical Jesus, but not about the Son of God, the Alpha and Omega, and the great I AM. Jesus said, "Unless you believe that I am He, you shall die in your sins" (John 8:24). If you believe in Jesus in any other way than how He is presented in the Bible, you will receive an altogether different spirit instead of the Holy Spirit and an altogether different gospel instead of the gospel of grace.

The counterfeit spirits which are at work in the cults and the occult are nothing like the Holy Spirit. Jesus said, "But when He, the Spirit of truth, comes, He will guide you into all the truth; for He will not speak on His own initiative, but whatever He hears, He will speak; and He will disclose to you what is to come. He shall glorify Me; for He shall take of Mine, and shall disclose it to you" (John 16:13,14). The Holy Spirit always leads us back to Christ.

The counterfeit gospel is not a gospel of grace because the blood of bulls and goats will never take away sin, so you are left with a gospel of works. But the real Jesus died for our sins, the Spirit of truth has come, and we are marvelously saved by grace.

Lord, I want to be so filled with the knowledge of Your truth that I may quickly recognize and turn from all counterfeits of the gospel.

You have been bought with a price: therefore glorify God in your body (1 Corinthians 6:20).

If I were asked to determine the spiritual vitality of any religious group using only one criterion, I would evaluate its representative leaders. Are they a group of individuals vying for power, arming themselves with arguments to defend their position and exert their will? Or are they servant leaders knit together by the Holy Spirit who are collectively trying to discern God's will?

Similarly, if I wanted to determine the spiritual vitality of an individual using only one criterion, I would evaluate whether the person desires to live according to the will of God, or if he desires to do his own thing. The prayer of a vital, growing Christian is, "Make me know Thy ways, O LORD; teach me Thy paths" (Psalm 25:4).

Once our will is bent in the right direction, Jesus raises the additional question of motive: "He who speaks from himself seeks his own glory; but He who is seeking the glory of the one who sent Him, He is true, and there is no unrighteousness in Him" (John 7:18). The person who is true glorifies the one who sent him.

This is perfectly modeled in the Godhead. Notice first the example of Jesus: "For I proceeded forth and have come from God, for I have not even come on My own initiative, but He sent Me" (John 8:42). The Holy Spirit acts in the same way. In John 16:13,14 Jesus said, "[The Spirit] will not speak on His own initiative, but whatever He hears, He will speak....He shall glorify Me."

I can take this one step further. Are you ready for this? Jesus said in John 20:21, "As the Father has sent Me, I also send you." Granted, that was said to the apostles, but we are all under the Great Commission. Do you want to be true? Then glorify the one who sent you! People who know they are God-sent and are committed to live like that, glorify God. Self-sent people seek their own glory.

Today, Lord, I purpose to reflect my appointment as Your sent-one by glorifying You instead of myself.

Trying to Control Others

Trust in the LORD with all your heart, and do not lean on your own understanding (Proverbs 3:5).

When a person's self-worth or success hinges on the achievement of a goal which can be blocked or which is uncertain or impossible, how will he respond to those who frustrate his goals? Often he will attempt to control or manipulate the people or circumstances who stand between him and his success.

For example, a pastor's goal is to have the finest youth ministry in the community. But one of his board members blocks his goal by insisting that a music ministry is more important. Every attempt by the pastor to hire a youth pastor is vetoed by the influential board member who wants to hire a music director first. The pastor wrongly perceives that his sense of worth and success in ministry is on the line. So he shifts into a power mode to push the stumbling block out of the way. He looks for a way to change the opposition's mind or remove him from the board, because he believes that his success in ministry is dependent on reaching his goal of a great youth ministry.

A mother believes that her self-worth is dependent on her children behaving in a certain way. Her goal is to raise perfect little Christians who will become pastors or missionaries. But as the children reach their teen years and begin to express their independence, their behavior doesn't always match their mother's ideal. So instead of helping them grow through adolescence and release them into adulthood, she tries to control them.

It is not hard to understand why people try to control others. They believe that their worth is dependent on other people and circumstances. This is a false belief, as evidenced by the fact that the most insecure people you will ever meet are manipulators and controllers of others. But people who are secure in their identity in Christ don't need to control others. Their goal is to be the leader, spouse, parent, or employee that God wants them to be, because nothing can keep them from being what God wants them to be but themselves.

Lord, I affirm that my worth is based on my relationship with You and that I am free to become the person You want me to be.

The voice of the LORD is powerful, the voice of the LORD is majestic (Psalm 29:4).

The concept of hearing "voices" is openly espoused in the secular media. The main character in the popular movie *Field of Dreams* hears an inner voice while standing in his cornfield at night. It's loud, direct, and very spooky! At first he's a little freaked out by the voice, but he is intrigued enough to test the voice's advice. It leads to a grand adventure that culminates in meeting the ghost of his deceased father, reconciling with him, and saving the family farm from foreclosure. Was the movie just an entertaining fantasy, or is Satan subtly promoting "nice" little spirit guides that will resolve all our problems?

According to New Age brain-mind researcher Willis Harmon, many people hear voices, but few are willing to admit it to anyone but their closest friends. "It's just one of those things we don't talk about," said the president of the Institute of Noetic Sciences in Sausalito, California. "I've talked to businessmen, scientists, educators, well-educated professional people, and not only is it reasonably common, it's cherished. It's invited."[1]

New Age proponents like Harmon are trying to give credibility to a phenomenon that was once understood as mental illness. Psychiatrists prescribe antipsychotic drugs for schizophrenics and others who admit that they hear voices. A common bit of advice among recovering alcoholics is, "Don't pay attention to the committee in your head." People seldom share the mental struggle going on inside them for fear that people will think they are going crazy. But I have counseled hundreds of troubled people who were hearing voices, and every one of the voices was demonic. The only exceptions are legitimate cases of multiple personality disorder. You need to know that inner voices that don't line up with God's Word are the suggestions of a real devil that must be countered and dispelled by the truth (1 Timothy 4:1).

Lord, I reject all voices in my mind, real or imagined, and accept only the authority of Your Word and Your Spirit.

He who gives an answer before he hears, it is folly and shame to him (Proverbs 18:13).

"I can't get a handle on my problems, Neil," Ruth complained. "I know my children are struggling at school, but they won't share it with me. Why won't they talk to me?"

"Do you really want to know, Ruth?"

"Of course!"

"They probably don't feel they can trust you," I responded.

"What do you mean they can't trust me? I'm their mother!"

"Let me illustrate," I said. "Suppose your 15-year-old daughter came home one day and said that her best friend was taking drugs. What would you say to her?"

Ruth paused for a moment, then said, "I'd probably tell her to find another friend."

"Exactly! And that's why she doesn't share that kind of information with you."

Like a lot of parents, Ruth was in the habit of reacting to her kids before she knew what was really going on. Two or three reactions like this from you and your child is ready to clam up forever. Whenever your child tells you about "my friend's problem," there is a very good chance that he's the one with the problem. He will drop little hints about his "friend" to see your reaction. If you are hasty and judgmental, you can bet he won't share any more. You must listen without judgment and hold the advice until you are sure you know the whole story.

Clear, loving communication in your family is imperative if you are going to foil Satan's attempt to seduce your child. After all, if you don't listen when he tells you about his school problems, he may not bother to tell you about his evil thoughts. And if you criticize him when he admits his mistakes, he won't want you to know about the terrifying dark presence he experiences in his room at night. Faulty communication doesn't necessarily cause spiritual problems in your child, but it can certainly block or delay the resolution of those problems.

Lord, make me a parent my children can trust and be comfortable with, and deliver me from being harsh and critical.

YOUR ADVOCATE

[Christ] is the atoning sacrifice for our sins, and not only for ours but also for the sins of the whole world (1 John 2:2 NIV).

When Mandy came to see me, she appeared to have her life all together. She was a Christian who was very active in her church. She had led her alcoholic father to Christ on his deathbed. She was pretty, and she had a nice husband and two wonderful children. But she had attempted suicide at least three times.

"How can God love me?" Mandy sobbed. "I'm such a failure."

"Mandy, God loves you, not because you are lovable, but because it is His nature to love you."

"But I've tried to take my own life, Neil. How can God overlook that?"

"Just suppose, Mandy, that your son grew despondent and tried to take his own life. Would you love him any less? Would you kick him out of the family? Would you turn your back on him?"

"Of course not. I'd feel sorry for him and try to love him more."

"Are you telling me that a perfect God isn't as good a parent to you as you, an imperfect person, are to your children?"

Mandy got the point. She began to realize that God, as a loving parent, can overlook weaknesses and forgive sin.

God wants us to do good, of course. The apostle John wrote: "I write this to you so that you will not sin." But John continued by reminding us that God has already made provision for our failure so His love continues constant despite what we do: "But if anybody does sin, we have one who speaks to the Father in our defense—Jesus Christ, the Righteous One. He is the atoning sacrifice for our sins, and not only for ours but also for the sins of the whole world" (1 John 2:1,2 NIV).

One reason we doubt God's love is that we have an adversary who uses every little offense to accuse us of being good-for-nothings. But your advocate, Jesus Christ, is more powerful than your adversary. He has canceled the debt of your sins past, present, and future. No matter what you do or how you fail, God has no reason not to love you and accept you completely.

Father in heaven, thank You for being my perfect parent, my haven of security and trustworthiness, and the victor over my enemy.

Gird your minds for action, keep sober in spirit, fix your hope completely on the grace to be brought to you at the revelation of Jesus Christ (1 Peter 1:13).

Since we came into this world physically alive but spiritually dead, we had neither the presence of God in our lives nor the knowledge of His will. Our minds were programmed to live independently of Him. We were mentally conformed to this world.

When we became Christians, nobody pushed the CLEAR button in our preprogrammed minds. Even as Christians we can still allow our minds to be programmed by the world. So what must we do?

First, "Do not be conformed to this world, but be transformed by the renewing of your mind" (Romans 12:2). How do you renew your mind? By filling it with God's Word.

Second, Peter directs us to prepare our minds for action (1 Peter 1:13). Do away with fruitless fantasy. To imagine yourself doing things without ever doing anything is dangerous. But if you can mentally prepare yourself in advance to obey the truth, you can motivate yourself toward productive living—as long as you follow through by doing what you imagine.

Third, take every thought captive in obedience to Christ (2 Corinthians 10:5). Practice threshold thinking. Evaluate every thought by the truth, and don't let your mind entertain thoughts contrary to the will of God.

Fourth, turn to God. When your commitment to do the will of God is being challenged by thoughts from the world, the flesh, or the devil, bring it to God in prayer (Philippians 4:6). By doing so you are acknowledging God and exposing your thoughts to His truth. Your double-mindedness will dissolve "and the peace of God...shall guard your hearts and your minds in Christ Jesus" (Philippians 4:7).

Fifth, assume your responsibility to think. "Finally, brethren, whatever is true, whatever is honorable, whatever is right, whatever is pure, whatever is lovely, whatever is of good repute, if there is any excellence and if anything worthy of praise, let your mind dwell on these things" (Philippians 4:8).

Lord, I commit myself to practice these steps daily in order to bring my mind under Your control.

Living Above Life's Circumstances

I have learned to be content in whatever circumstances I am (Philippians 4:11).

Some of us tend to assume that it is God's will if the circumstances are favorable and it isn't God's will if the circumstances are unfavorable. Next to the Bible, I would guess that more Christians are "guided" by this means than any other. Yet of all the possible means of guidance, this is the least authoritative and trustworthy.

I had the privilege of pastoring a church that purchased new property and went through a building program. Through most of the process the circumstances didn't seem favorable. Twice I sat with the mayor, who was also a local real estate agent, and asked him if he thought our plans were feasible. He advised us not to make the land trade, and he didn't think the city would allow us to build. He knew the real estate and the political climate better than anyone in the city. But the land swap increased our assets by millions and the city planning commission voted 7-0 in favor of our building plans.

You may have to set sail by the tide, but you'd better be guided by the stars or you're going to end up on the wrong shore. Circumstances may have their effect on your plans, but you have a far greater accountability to God. Make sure you follow Him, not the tide of circumstance.

I heard a motivational speaker say, "I don't like to recruit Christians because when the going gets tough they quit, concluding that it must not be God's will." Generally speaking, I believe that Christians should live above life's circumstances and not be guided by them.

Also be careful about applying too much significance to unusual circumstances or coincidences. "It must be God's will. Why else would that book be lying there!" It could be God's will, but I would never take that kind of a sign on its own merit. I have helped many people in occultic bondage who have made bizarre associations or attached far too much significance to irrelevant events.

Lord, I determine to test all guidance by Your Word and not to be swayed away from Your will by circumstances or popular opinion.

A Liberating Friend

Surely you desire truth in the inner parts; you teach me wisdom in the inmost place (Psalm 51:6 NIV).

Absolute truth is the revelation of God's Word, and we must live that truth in the inner self. When David lived a lie he suffered greatly. When he finally found freedom by acknowledging the truth, he wrote, "How blessed is the man...in whose spirit there is no deceit" (Psalm 32:2). When David later reflected on the same incident, he wrote, "Surely you desire truth in the inner parts; you teach me wisdom in the inmost place" (Psalm 51:6 NIV).

We are to lay aside falsehood and speak the truth in love (Ephesians 4:15,25). A mentally healthy person is one who is in touch with reality and relatively free of anxiety. Both qualities should epitomize the Christian who renounces deception and embraces the truth.

Deception is the most subtle of all satanic strongholds. Have you ever noticed that all people with addictive behavior lie to themselves and others almost continuously? The alcoholic lies about his drinking, the anorexic lies about her eating, and the sex offender lies about his behavior. Lying is an evil defense prompted by the father of lies, Satan (John 8:44).

The first step in any recovery program is to get out of denial and face the truth. Truth is never an enemy; it is always a liberating friend. People in bondage to the lie grow weary of the darkness. They hate to sneak around, lie, and cover up. "God is light, and in Him there is no darkness at all" (1 John 1:5). We must "walk in the light as He Himself is in the light" (1 John 1:7). There is great freedom when truth dispels the anguish of living a lie.

Choosing the truth may be difficult for you if you have been living a lie for many years. You may need to seek professional help to weed out the defense mechanisms you have depended on all this time to survive. The Christian needs only one defense: Jesus. Knowing that you are forgiven and accepted as God's child sets you free to face reality and choose the truth.

Lord, I choose the truth, and I renounce all self-deception and rationalization of wrong behavior and attitudes.

I will remain in the world no longer, but they are still in the world, and I am coming to you. Holy Father, protect them by the power of your name (John 17:11 NIV).

The Christian worldview perceives life through the grid of Scripture, not through culture or experience. And Scripture clearly teaches that supernatural, spiritual forces are at work in the natural world. For example, approximately one-fourth of all the healings recorded in the Gospel of Mark were actually deliverances from demon activity. The woman whom Jesus healed in Luke 13:11,12 had been the victim of a "sickness caused by a spirit" for 18 years.

Many people I have counseled came with physical problems which disappeared shortly after the demonic influence was dealt with. The most common symptoms I have seen are headaches, dizziness, allergies, nausea, and general pain throughout the body. The most conservative estimate by medical doctors is that 50 percent of their patients are suffering psychosomatic illnesses. Biblically, it is reasonable to expect if a person's personal and spiritual problems are resolved, the physical body will be benefitted. Stress is a leading cause of heart disease and cancer. The peace of God alone will cure many diseases.

I'm not saying that everyone who is ill or in pain is being terrorized by a demon. But I am convinced that many Christians battle physical symptoms unsuccessfully through natural means when the essence of the problem and the solution is spiritual. "He who raised Christ Jesus from the dead, will also give life to your mortal bodies through His Spirit who indwells you" (Romans 8:11).

The fact that Jesus left us "in the world" (John 17:11) to wrestle against "spiritual forces of wickedness in the heavenly places" (Ephesians 6:12) is a present-day reality. Supernatural forces are at work on planet Earth. We live in the natural world, but we are involved in a spiritual war.

Dear God, keep me alert to the spiritual conflicts occurring around me and ready to respond in Your authority and power.

If you love those who love you, what credit is that to you? For even sinners love those who love them (Luke 6:32).

For many people, loving others is a nebulous concept. Fortunately, *agape* love is very clearly defined in the Scriptures. When love is used as a noun in Scripture, it is referring to character. For example: "God is love" (1 John 4:8); "Love is patient, love is kind," etc. (1 Corinthians 13:4-8). Love is the highest of character attainments: "The goal of our instruction is love from a pure heart and a good conscience and a sincere faith" (1 Timothy 1:5). Love is the fruit of the Spirit (Galatians 5:22), the means by which a true disciple of Christ is identified (John 13:35). The attention given to love in passages such as 1 Corinthians 13 and 1 John 4 reveals its importance to God in our interpersonal relationships, of which the family is primary.

Agape love is not dependent on the person being loved, but on the lover. You may like someone because of who he is; but you love him because of who *you* are. God loves us not because we are lovable but because God is love. If it was any other way, God's love would be conditional. If you performed better would God love you more? Of course not. God's love for us is not based on our performance but on His character.

Love is also used as a verb in Scripture. "For God so loved the world that He gave His only begotten Son" (John 3:16). Used this way, love is grace in action. It is giving unconditionally to meet the needs of another.

If you say you don't love someone, you have said more about yourself than about that person. Specifically, you're saying that you haven't attained the maturity to love him unconditionally (Luke 6:32). The grace of God enables you to love others in a way that people without Christ cannot. God doesn't command you to like your family, your neighbors, and your coworkers, because you can't order your emotions to respond. But He does instruct you to love them. You can always choose to do the loving thing and trust that your feelings will follow in time.

Thank You, Father, for bestowing on me the greatest love of all by sending Jesus. Teach me to love others as You have loved me.

[Christ]...disarmed the rulers and authorities [and] made a public display of them, having triumphed over them through Him (Colossians 2:15).

In Colossians 2:15 Paul identifies something very important that happened at the death, resurrection, and ascension of Christ. Not only were we made alive in Christ, but Satan was also disarmed and defeated. His defeat is not pending, nor is it future; it has already happened.

If Satan is already disarmed, why don't we experience more victory in our lives? In a word, the lie. Satan roams around like a hungry lion, looking and sounding ferocious. In reality his fangs have been removed and he has been declawed, but if he can deceive you into believing that he can chew you up and spit you out, he can control you, which is just what he wants to do. He is gumming Christians to death!

The very reason Christ conferred His authority on us was to demonstrate to the kingdom of darkness who is really in control in this world. In Ephesians Paul wrote that his call was "to bring to light what is the administration of the mystery which for ages has been hidden in God, who created all things; in order that the manifold wisdom of God might now be made known through the church to the rulers and authorities in the heavenly places. This was in accordance with the eternal purpose which He carried out in Christ Jesus our Lord" (Ephesians 3:9-11).

How are we doing at making Christ's victory known to "the rulers and authorities in heavenly places," which is God's eternal purpose? In many quarters, not very well. Some of us are still saying, "What rulers and authorities?" We're not sure that demons even exist. How are we ever going to get our job done in the world if we don't believe what God says about the kingdom of darkness? Others of us are cowering in the corner pleading, "O God, please help us! The devil is roaring at us!" And God responds, "I've done all I'm going to do. I defeated and disarmed Satan at the cross. I conferred all authority on you in Christ. Now open your eyes. Realize who you are and start demonstrating the authority you already possess."

In Your name, Lord, I will take an active stand against the devil and his demons, renouncing both apathy and fear.

As for the person who turns to mediums and to spiritists, to play the harlot after them, I will also set My face against that person and will cut him off from among his people (Leviticus 20:6).

The craving for esoteric, "extra" knowledge in our culture was starkly illustrated to me when two conferences, both open to the public, were recently held in Pasadena, California. One was a major world conference on international missions, and about 600 people attended. At the same time, a New Age conference was being conducted nearby, and more than 40,000 people showed up! That's our society today. People don't want to hear what God has to say. They want information and direction from someone else who "knows": a psychic, a channeler, a palm-reader, a card-reader, or the spirit of a dead friend or relative. All you have to do is change the wording from *medium* to *channeler* and *demon* to *spirit guide* and a gullible society accepts it!

The Scriptures are very clear on the subject of seeking knowledge and direction for our lives from anyone but God. We're about as far away from that stance on the purveyors of psychic and spiritual advice as we can be. We have people channeling on TV and radio programs, and they're considered celebrities. I read recently that more women in Los Angeles consult spiritists than professional counselors. You can attend a psychic fair in practically any city in our land and get a personal spiritual "reading." The reader is either a fake or a spiritual medium who enters a trance and seemingly receives instruction for you from the spiritual world. Far from being seen as a blight on society, these people are often revered as highly as doctors and ministers for their "expertise."

Don't allow yourself to be sucked in by these "experts" no matter how socially acceptable they may be. Nothing is condemned more by God in Scripture than false guidance. All the wisdom and knowledge you need is available in your relationship with God and His Word.

Father God, forgive me for seeking guidance from sources outside Your authority. I commit myself to renew my mind through Your Word.

Do not put out the Spirit's fire; do not treat prophecies with contempt. Test everything. Hold on to the good (1 Thessalonians 5:19-21 NIV).

Alvin was discouraged and defeated. For several years he believed he had a special gift of prophecy from God. But over a period of months his personal life began to fall apart. By the time he came to see me he had been unemployed for two years, he was being cared for by his father, and he was a slave to prescription drugs.

Alvin and I read 1 Thessalonians 5:19-21. I said, "Alvin, Satan can counterfeit spiritual gifts. That's why the Scriptures instruct us to put everything to the test."

Alvin admitted, "I think my problems began when I failed to test the 'gifts' of tongues and prophecy conferred on me by false teachers."

"Would you be willing to put your gift of tongues to the test?" I asked. Alvin really wanted to be free. "Yes," he answered.

I instructed Alvin to begin praying aloud in his "spiritual language." As he began to chant an unintelligible prayer, I said, "In the name of Christ and in obedience to God's Word, I command you, spirit, to identify yourself."

Alvin stopped in the middle of his chanting and said, "I am he."

"Are you the 'He' who was crucified under Pontius Pilate, buried, raised on the third day, and who now sits at the right hand of the Father?" I asked.

Alvin almost shouted the response: "No! Not He!" I led Alvin through a prayer renouncing Satan's activity in his life, and he was free from that deception.

I am not against spiritual gifts, even prophesy and tongues. I am committed to obeying Scripture, and 1 Corinthians 14:39 says, "Desire earnestly to prophesy, and do not forbid to speak in tongues." But Scripture also requires that all spiritual phenomena be tested. I believe that false prophets and teachers flourish today simply because Christians accept their ministry without testing the spirits behind it.

Heavenly Father, help me to stay alert to spiritual seduction and reject all phenomena that do not come from God.

No one tears a piece from a new garment and puts it on an old garment; otherwise he will both tear the new, and the piece from the new will not match the old (Luke 5:36).

Determining the purpose of a Christian practice, and whether it is appropriate, requires an answer to the question, "Why?" "We have always done it this way before" is unacceptable. Christian practices continue for years, often outliving their purpose, until someone asks, "Why do we do that?" Characteristically, the defenses come up as though you were challenging what they believe!

For instance, having three church services a week is generally practiced by evangelical Christians, but few know why. Originally, Sunday morning was for instruction and worship, Sunday evening was for evangelism, and the Wednesday service was for prayer. Today few churches have three services for those same purposes. In many churches, evangelism has switched to Sunday morning (if there is an evangelistic service). Sunday evenings range from body life gatherings to an informal repeat of the morning service. Wednesday stopped being a prayer meeting years ago in most churches.

Few people can say why they have an adult fellowship group and, consequently, most never fulfill the greatest purpose for which they exist. Without a clear purpose, planning dribbles down to who is going to be the teacher and what is the next monthly social! The purpose of fellowship groups is to provide a base for incorporating new people into the church, going after those who stray, and meeting the needs of one another. Routine activities that lack purpose produce mindless participation. How is God going to guide such a group?

The greatest avenue for productive change is to clarify the purpose of any existing ministry or group. I sat with the leaders of an adult group and helped them hammer out a purpose statement. Some major changes took place in their class. Within two years they had doubled. Asking "Why?" forced them to evaluate their purpose and ministry, and necessary changes came.

Lord, I purpose not to waste my time or effort on traditions that are no longer valid vehicles for ministry.

You shall keep the commandments of the LORD your God, to walk in His ways and to fear Him (Deuteronomy 8:6).

I believe in miracles, and I accept as fact every one recorded in the Bible. I believe that our entire Christian experience is a miracle. It simply cannot be explained by natural means. And God's power is seen in other miraculous ways today, but must He always prove Himself by stepping outside His created order? If God doesn't primarily guide us through His Word (which never changes) and take into account the fixed order of the universe, how can we ever have any stability? How can we make any plans if God doesn't reveal His ways and then stay consistent with them?

God is not capricious in His dealings with man. He has clearly established His ways and He is faithful to them. I believe God has revealed His ways and we are to walk in them. The question is, how does God work through human responsibility and the natural order of the universe to bring about His will? Somehow He works through a less-than-perfect church, orchestrating human affairs in such a way as to guarantee the outcome of the ages. What really impresses me is His timing, not His miraculous interventions.

Notice how Jesus responded to those who insisted on a sign: "An evil and adulterous generation craves for a sign; and yet no sign shall be given to it but the sign of Jonah the prophet" (Matthew 12:39). Satan wanted a sign too. He said, "If You are the Son of God throw Yourself down" (Matthew 4:6). To this Jesus responded, "Do not put the Lord your God to the test" (verse 7 NIV). Jesus was saying that the sign we need is the Word of God, and we are to use the Word to guard against Satan's temptations to force the Lord to prove Himself.

I think it is better to prove ourselves to God rather than demand He prove Himself to us. We are the ones being tested, not God. "Be diligent to present yourself approved to God as a workman who does not need to be ashamed, handling accurately the word of truth" (2 Timothy 2:15).

Lord, I want to be responsible to use the gifts You have given me and lay aside sin and fruitless activities.

I urge you therefore, brethren, by the mercies of God, to present your bodies a living and holy sacrifice (Romans 12:1).

An African pastor was overwhelmed by rebels who demanded that he renounce his faith. He refused. The night before they took his life, he wrote the following lines on a scrap of paper:

> I am part of the "Fellowship of the Unashamed." I have Holy Spirit power. The die has been cast. I've stepped over the line. The decision has been made. I am a disciple of His. I won't look back, let up, slow down, back away, or be still. My past is redeemed, my present makes sense, and my future is secure. I am finished and done with low living, sight walking, small planning, smooth knees, colorless dreams, tame visions, mundane talking, chintzy giving, and dwarfed goals!
>
> I no longer need preeminence, prosperity, position, promotions, plaudits, or popularity. I don't have to be right, first, tops, recognized, praised, regarded, or rewarded. I now live by presence, lean by faith, love by patience, lift by prayer, and labor by power.
>
> My face is set, my gait is fast, my goal is heaven, my road is narrow, my way is rough, my companions few, my guide reliable, my mission clear. I cannot be bought, compromised, detoured, lured away, turned back, diluted, or delayed. I will not flinch in the face of sacrifice, hesitate in the presence of adversity, negotiate at the table of the enemy, ponder at the pool of popularity, or meander in the maze of mediocrity.
>
> I won't give up, shut up, let up, or burn up till I've preached up, prayed up, paid up, stored up, and stayed up for the cause of Christ.
>
> I am a disciple of Jesus. I must go till He comes, give till I drop, preach till all know, and work till He stops.
>
> And when He comes to get His own, He'll have no problems recognizing me. My colors will be clear.

Lord, develop in me the perseverance and faithfulness to pursue Your goal for my life even in the face of rejection.

Let the word of Christ richly dwell within you, with all wisdom teaching and admonishing one another with psalms and hymns and spiritual songs, singing with thankfulness in your hearts to God (Colossians 3:16).

Music is second only to television in influencing and shaping the values of our children. How can you help your kids recognize the subtle seduction to evil in some contemporary music and encourage them to make wise choices about what they listen to? Here are some practical suggestions:

1. *Avoid the "do as I say, not as I do" syndrome.* Before you can help your child evaluate his music, you'd better evaluate your own (Matthew 7:4,5). The lyrics of some soft rock, easy listening, and country-western tunes are as suggestive and immoral as those performed by heavy metal groups. One of the best ways to teach your child to avoid harmful lyrics is by modeling the same behavior.

2. *Be willing to find middle ground.* Your personal taste in music should not be the determining factor for what you allow your children to listen to. Nor should your child's taste determine what you listen to. Try to find some middle ground with your child when it comes to the kinds of music you will allow in your home. The key is to teach your child to be moderate and discerning, just as you are.

3. *Stay informed and involved.* When was the last time you looked through your child's music collection or sat down with him to listen to and discuss the lyrics of his favorite songs? You won't be able to understand the impact of the music in his life unless you are aware of it and what he thinks about it.

Take time to listen to your children's emotional struggles and notice how the music they listen to influences their behavior. Be as encouraging about their good choices of music as you are corrective of the bad choices. Someday they will thank you for the harmony you helped bring to their lives.

Guide me, Father, as I train my children to choose music and entertainment that is positive and uplifting.

Reflecting Reality

For as he thinks within himself, so he is (Proverbs 23:7).

Telling someone that they shouldn't feel the way they do is a subtle form of rejection. They can do little about how they feel. The real problem is that they have a wrong perception of their situation which is making them feel the way they do. You can't change how you feel, but you can change what you think.

For example, suppose your dream of owning your own home was in the hands of a lending institution which was screening your application for financing. All your friends are praying for the loan to be approved. But you get home one evening to find a message on your phone machine that you didn't qualify. Where would you be emotionally in just a matter of seconds? At the bottom!

Now suppose you're getting ready to break the bad news to your spouse that your dream house is still only a dream. Then you listen to the next message on the machine which tells you that the first message was a mistake. You actually did qualify! Now where are you emotionally? The top! What you first believed didn't reflect truth, so what you felt didn't reflect reality.

Imagine the real estate agent, who knows that you qualified, stopping by to congratulate you before you heard the second message on the machine. He expects to find you overjoyed, but instead you're in despair. "Why are you depressed?" he asks. "You should be happy." But his encouragement is meaningless until he tells you the truth about your loan. If what you believe does not reflect truth, then what you feel does not reflect reality.

The order of Scripture is to know the truth, believe it, walk according to it, and let your emotions be a product of your obedience. When you believe what you feel instead of the truth, how will your walk be? As inconsistent as your feelings. But when you believe and act on the truth, your feelings will reflect reality. Jesus said, "If you know these things, you are blessed if you do them" (John 13:17).

Lord, I commit myself to follow Your Word and do right. I want to enjoy the positive emotions that come from obedience.

*If [the prophets] had stood in My council,
then they would have announced My words to My
people, and would have turned them back from
their evil way and from the evil of their deeds
(Jeremiah 23:22).*

Every true prophet of God in the Old Testament was an evangelist. His ministry drew people back to God and His Word. The call to righteousness was the standard which separated the genuine prophet from the imitation, as the prophet Jeremiah wrote. If you come across someone who claims to be a prophet, but who is not involved in calling people to a righteous walk with God, you may be dealing with a counterfeit.

In the New Testament, the gift of prophecy has one primary purpose: to reveal unrighteousness and bring conviction. Paul wrote that, as a result of prophecy, "The secrets of his heart are disclosed; and so he will fall on his face and worship God, declaring that God is certainly among you" (1 Corinthians 14:25).

The Lord revealed through Jeremiah another criterion for distinguishing a true prophet from a false prophet: "I have heard what the prophets have said who prophesy falsely in My name, saying, 'I had a dream, I had a dream!'...The prophet who has a dream may relate his dream, but let him who has My word speak My word in truth. What does straw have in common with grain?" (23:25,28). God is warning His people against prophets who value their dreams above His Word.

God is not saying that dreams are unimportant. Indeed, He often spoke to people in the Bible through dreams before the full revelation of Scripture was complete. But in comparison to the nutritious grain of His Word, dreams are mere straw. If you feed straw to cattle, they'll die. They will sleep on it, but they won't eat it because it has no nutrients. Similarly, dreams may be of some value, but they are never to be equated with God's Word as the basis for our faith or our walk.

---

*Thank You, Lord, for the power of Your Word,
which cuts through falsehood and brings to light
everything hidden in darkness.*

Solid food is for the mature, who because of practice have their senses trained to discern good and evil (Hebrews 5:14).

In many counseling cases I am able to sense in my spirit that something is wrong or that the real issue has not surfaced. Sometimes I seem to know what it is, but instead of blurting it out, I test it. For example, if I discern that the counselee may be in bondage to homosexuality, I don't say, "You're a homosexual, aren't you?" Rather, I test the impression at the appropriate time by asking something like, "Have you ever struggled with homosexual thoughts or tendencies?" If the Spirit's discernment in me is matched by His conviction in the counselee, usually the problem surfaces and we can deal with it.

Have you ever "known" that someone was a Christian before he or she even said anything about it? Have you ever sensed a compatible spirit with other believers? There is nothing magical about that; it's just the presence of the Holy Spirit bearing witness with your spirit. At other times the Holy Spirit warns you that the spirit controlling another person is not a compatible spirit.

If we would learn to be more spiritually aware in our churches and homes, God could keep us from plowing head-on into so many disasters. In the Western world our cognitive, left-brain orientation all but excludes discernment as our essential guide for navigating through the spiritual world. But the writer of Hebrews identified discernment as a mark of maturity: "Solid food is for the mature, who because of practice have their senses trained to discern good and evil" (5:14).

A good systematic theology is the essential foundation upon which we build our lives. It is like the skeleton of our body. But dead orthodoxy is just that: dead! It is the Holy Spirit who gives life to the body. The church is in desperate need of biblically orthodox people who have also learned to be spiritually discerning.

Increase my sensitivity to the spiritual world, Lord, and keep me from the dangers of viewing life only from a human perspective.

But resist [the devil], firm in your faith, knowing that the same experiences of suffering are being accomplished by your brethren who are in the world (1 Peter 5:9).

I cannot accept someone saying, "The devil made me do it." No, he didn't make you do it; *you* did it. Somewhere along the line you chose to give the devil a foothold. He merely took advantage of the opportunity you gave him. You have all the resources and protection you need to live a victorious life in Christ every day. If you're not living it, it's your choice. When you leave a door open for the devil by not resisting temptation, accusation, or deception, you are vulnerable. And if you continue to allow him access to your life, he can gain a measure of control over you. You won't lose your salvation, but you will lose your daily victory.

Many Christians today who cannot control their lives in some area wallow in self-blame instead of acting responsibly to solve the problem. They berate themselves and punish themselves for not having the willpower to break a bad habit, when instead they should be resisting Satan in an area where he has obviously robbed them of control. Anything bad which you seemingly cannot stop doing, or anything good which you cannot make yourself do, could be an area of demonic control.

God's protection from demonic attack is not something you can take for granted irrespective of how you behave. This protection is conditional on your willingness to respond to God's provision. We are told to put on Christ and make no provision for the flesh (Romans 13:14), to put on the armor of God and to stand firm (Ephesians 6:11), to submit to God and resist the devil (James 4:7). If we irresponsibly ignore God's resources by failing to obey these commands, how can we expect Him to protect us?

Thank You, Lord, for the clear direction and mighty weapons You have provided for victory in spiritual warfare.

The wicked flee when no one is pursuing, but the righteous are bold as a lion (Proverbs 28:1).

How do you respond to fear situations in your life? The following steps will help you identify and hopefully eliminate any irrational fears.

First, *analyze your fear*. Most people aren't aware of what is controlling their lives. If you are struggling with anxiety attacks, determine when they first occurred. What experience preceded the first attack? People struggling with agoraphobia can usually identify one precipitating event. It is often associated with some tragedy or failure in their lives, such as a marital affair or an abortion. Satan takes advantage of victimized people if they don't seek a scriptural solution to their crisis (Psalm 38:18).

Second, *determine where God's place in your life has been usurped*. In what way does any fear prevent you from responsible behavior or compel you toward irresponsible behavior? You may need to confess any situations where you've allowed your actions to be controlled by fear (Psalm 28:1). We will always live less than a responsible life if we fear anything other than God.

Third, *work out a plan of responsible behavior*. A college student shared with me that she was living in terror of her father. They hadn't spoken to each other in six months. Obviously there was irresponsible behavior on both their parts. I suggested that she take the initiative that evening and say, "Hi, Dad!" We reasoned that there were three possible responses he could give. First, he could get mad. Second, he could respond with a greeting. Third, he could remain silent. It was the possibility of the third response that created the most fear.

We then discussed the fourth point: *Determine in advance what your response will be to any fear-object*. The young woman and I talked about what her response would be in each of those three cases we had mentioned. I then asked her if she would be willing to carry out our plan. She agreed to do it. I got a call that evening from a happy daughter who exclaimed, "He said 'Hi' back!"

Do the thing you fear the most, and the death of fear is certain.

Lord, give me the courage to meet my fears head-on and the persistence to overcome them in Your strength.

The Value of Counsel

Where there is no guidance, the people fall,
but in abundance of counselors there is victory
(Proverbs 11:14).

No one person has complete knowledge, and everyone has a limited perspective on the truth. God has structured the church in such a way that we need each other. I have made some dumb decisions that would never have been made if I had consulted someone. However, some people will only consult those who agree with them. That's a sign of immaturity.

At the same time, the counsel of others does have to be weighed. There is a fascinating account in Acts 21 where the Holy Spirit seemed to be warning Paul not to go to Jerusalem. Disciples in Tyre "kept telling Paul through the Spirit not to set foot in Jerusalem" (21:4). Then a prophet named Agabus gave a visual demonstration by binding himself and saying, "This is what the Holy Spirit says: 'In this way the Jews at Jerusalem will bind the man who owns this belt [Paul] and deliver him into the hands of the Gentiles' " (21:11).

Everyone began begging him not to go. "Then Paul answered, '...I am ready not only to be bound, but even to die at Jerusalem for the name of the Lord Jesus.' And since he would not be persuaded, we fell silent, remarking, 'The will of the Lord be done!' " (21:13,14).

Was the Holy Spirit guiding the disciples and Agabus? The information was mostly true, but the conclusion of the disciples wasn't. The Holy Spirit wasn't trying to prevent Paul from going; He was preparing Paul for the coming persecution. Paul was right in not wanting to take the easy way out.

The missionary Hudson Taylor went against advice, and circumstances nearly destroyed him. But he, more than anyone, opened up China to the gospel. Sometimes people can tell you the truth, but they draw selfish conclusions. Sometimes we need to ascertain our own motives as well as those of the people we seek counsel from, for our motives can be in error as well. The value of counsel is to get an unbiased opinion from a spiritually sensitive person which you can add to the recipe of ingredients God is giving to guide you.

Lord, grant me the patience to gather information and seek godly counsel for my decisions.

SELF-CENTERED VS. GOD-CENTERED

You are not setting your mind on God's interests, but man's (Matthew 16:23).

The apostle Peter is a glaring example of the struggle between self- and Christ-centered living. Only moments after Peter confessed the fundamental truth that Jesus Christ is the Messiah, the Son of the living God (Matthew 16:13-16), he found himself in league with the powers of darkness. Having just blessed Peter for his noble confession, Jesus announced to him and the other disciples the suffering and death which awaited Him at Jerusalem. "And Peter took Him aside and began to rebuke Him, saying, 'God forbid it, Lord! This shall never happen to You' " (verse 22).

Jesus responded: "Get behind Me, Satan! You are a stumbling block to Me; for you are not setting your mind on God's interests, but man's" (verse 23).

Jesus' memorable rebuke seems mercilessly severe. But the fact that He identified Satan as the source of Peter's words describes precisely and appropriately the character of the advice Peter tried to give: "Save yourself at all costs. Sacrifice duty to self-interest, the cause of Christ to personal convenience." Peter's advice was satanic in principle, for Satan's primary aim is to promote self-interest as the chief end of man. Satan is called the "prince of this world" because self-interest rules the secular world. He is called the "accuser of the brethren" because he does not believe that even a child of God has a higher motive than self-service. You can almost hear him hissing, "All men are selfish at heart and have their price. Some may hold out longer than others, but in the end every man will prefer his own things to the things of God."

That's Satan's creed, and unfortunately the lives of all too many Christians validate his claims. Satan has deceived them into thinking they are serving themselves when in fact they are serving the world, the flesh, and the devil. But the Christian worldview has a different center. Jesus confronts our humanistic, self-serving grids and offers the view from the cross. Only from this center can you escape the bondage of the one whose sole intent is "to steal, and kill, and destroy" (John 10:10).

Loving Father, help me forsake self-centered attitudes and actions in order to take up my cross daily and serve You.

Expressing Your Needs

A gentle answer turns away wrath, but a harsh word stirs up anger (Proverbs 15:1).

If you have legitimate needs in a relationship, and they are not being met, should you risk expressing your needs? Yes, but express them in such a way that you don't impugn the other person's character or act as his conscience. For example, you may feel unloved in a relationship and say, "You don't love me anymore." Or you feel that your spouse doesn't value you and say, "You make me feel worthless." Or you feel a distance developing between you and your friend and say, "You never write or call." You have expressed your need, but you have played the role of the conscience in that person. You are usurping the role of the Holy Spirit. And by pushing off your need as his problem, he will probably respond by getting defensive, further straining the relationship.

What if you expressed your needs this way: "I don't feel loved anymore"; "I feel like a worthless, unimportant person"; "I miss it when we don't communicate regularly"? By changing the "you" accusation to an "I" message, you express your need without blaming anyone. Your nonjudgmental approach allows God to deal with the person's conscience. The other person is free to respond to your need instead of defend himself against your attack.

When we assume the responsibility of another person's conscience, we misdirect that person's battle with God to ourselves, and we are insufficient for the task. We are under the commandment of God to love one another. So when a legitimate need is made known, trust God to bring the conviction that will move that person to meet the need.

Lord, enable me to express my needs and seek Your supply without judging or criticizing others.

One Basis for Temptation

Let our people also learn to engage in good deeds to meet pressing needs, that they may not be unfruitful (Titus 3:14).

We all have basic human needs to feel loved, accepted, and worthwhile. When these needs go unmet, it's very important that we express them to our family members and fellow Christians in a positive way and allow others to minister to those needs. I believe that one basis for temptation is unmet legitimate needs. When you are too proud to say, "I don't feel loved," or when you push others away by saying, "You don't love me anymore," your need for love goes unmet. So Satan comes along with a tempting alternative: "Your wife doesn't love you like you deserve. But have you noticed the affectionate gleam in your secretary's eye?"

Other than Himself, God's primary resource for meeting your needs and keeping you pure is other believers. The problem is that many go to Sunday school, church, and Bible study wearing a sanctimonious mask. Wanting to appear strong and together, they rob themselves of the opportunity of having their needs met in the warmth and safety of the Christian community. In the process, they rob the community of the opportunity to minister to their needs. By denying the fellowship of believers the privilege of meeting your legitimate needs, you are acting independently of God. You are vulnerable to the temptation of thinking that you can have your needs met in the world, the flesh, and the devil.

Instead, follow the guidance of Hebrews 10:24,25: "Let us consider how to stimulate one another to love and good deeds, not forsaking our own assembling together, as is the habit of some, but encouraging one another; and all the more, as you see the day drawing near."

Lord, grant me the humility to confess my needs and hurts to my Christian family in order to allow You to meet my needs in Your way.

I am convinced that neither death, nor life, nor angels, nor principalities, nor things present, nor things to come, nor powers, nor height, nor depth, nor any other created thing, shall be able to separate us from the love of God, which is in Christ Jesus our Lord (Romans 8:38,39).

When I was born physically I had a father. As Marvin Anderson's son, is there anything that I could possibly do which would change my blood relationship to him? What if I ran away from home and changed my name? Would I still be his son? Of course! We're related by blood and nothing can change that. But is there anything I could do which would affect the harmony of our relationship as father and son? Yes, indeed! The harmony of our relationship was interrupted countless times by my behavior.

In the spiritual realm, when I was born again I became a member of God's family. God is my Father and I enjoy an eternal relationship with Him through the precious blood of Christ (1 Peter 1:18,19). I am a child of God, in spiritual union with Him by His grace which I received through faith. My relationship with God was forever settled when I was born into His family. But is there anything I can do which will interfere with the *harmony* of my relationship with God? Absolutely. Living in harmony with God is based on the same issue as harmony with my earthly father: obedience. When I don't obey God the harmony of our relationship is disturbed and my life is usually miserable as a result. I love my heavenly Father and I want to be in harmony with Him, so I strive to obey Him. But even when we are in disharmony because of my disobedience, my relationship with Him is not at stake because we are related by the blood of Jesus Christ.

Paul was convinced that nothing could separate him from the love of God (Romans 8:35-39). Jesus said, "My sheep listen to my voice; I know them, and they follow me. I give them eternal life, and they shall never perish; no one can snatch them out of my hand" (John 10:27,28 NIV). Focus on your obedience to God so you may live in harmony with Him.

Thank You, heavenly Father, for the eternal relationship I enjoy with You because of the precious blood of Jesus. Teach me to obey that I may live in harmony with You.

Our First Line of Defense

The wise heart will know the proper time and procedure. For there is a proper time and procedure for every matter (Ecclesiastes 8:5,6 NIV).

I had dear friends who were being used by the Lord in full-time ministry. Some difficulty developed in their marriage so they consulted a pastor/counselor. The wife's response after the initial meeting was negative, but they continued with this particular counselor because other people they respected said he was a good man.

Over the next year the ministry my friends were in as well as our relationship deteriorated. A short time later their pastor/counselor was exposed for having sex with a number of counselees. The damage he did to several women was incredible. He justified his behavior by explaining, "What we do in the flesh doesn't matter. Only what we do in the spirit counts!"

My friends were confronted with an ultimatum by their ministry group: "Choose your ministry or choose him." They chose to stay with him!

Why won't people judge righteously? "Little children, let no one deceive you; the one who practices righteousness is righteous, just as He is righteous; the one who practices sin is of the devil" (1 John 3:7,8). The authoritative, arrogant spirit of this man had some kind of hold on many, since half his church stayed with him. The initial discernment of my friends was correct, but they ignored the warning of the Holy Spirit.

I believe discernment is a critical part of our walk with God. This divine enablement is our first line of defense when our ability to reason is insufficient. Jesus demonstrated spiritual discernment throughout His earthly ministry. We need to learn how to develop our ability to discern good from evil, truth from lies.

Dear Father, I want to have a wise and discerning spirit. Teach me to be responsive to Your leading so I can have my senses trained to discern good and evil.

[An overseer] must be one who manages his own household well, keeping his children under control with all dignity (1 Timothy 3:4).

A pastor friend of mine came face-to-face with a parent's worst fear: His teenage daughter had become pregnant before marriage. Perry was struggling with prickly questions: Should he resign his pastorate? Should he encourage an abortion to cover his embarrassment and save face? Should he put her on the pill to avoid future problems?

I reminded him, "The primary goal for your life—to be the father and husband that God wants you to be—has not been blocked by this unfortunate event. If there was ever a time that your wife needed a godly, committed husband and your daughter a loving, supportive father, it's now."

"But, Neil, what about being the pastor that God wants me to be?" Perry argued. "Doesn't this disqualify me from being a pastor?"

I directed him to one of the requirements for an elder in 1 Timothy 3:4,5: managing his household well and keeping his children under control. I said, "Even the best managers in the world have problems; they just know how to manage them. You didn't instruct your daughter to sleep with her boyfriend. That was a sinful decision she made. How are you going to manage your home now for the good of the family? Instructing your daughter to get an abortion so you can save face is mismanagement. Kicking her out of the house is mismanagement. But standing by your daughter, comforting your wife, walking in the light, and speaking the truth in love is managing your household well."

Spiritual leaders face the same temptations and difficulties other Christians do, they just face them in a fishbowl and their struggles are more visible. It's not a lack of problems that determines the quality of our ministry, but how we handle the problems we have.

Lord, I want to walk in the light even in problem situations. Help me face the difficulties of my life and seek Your way of resolution.

...Who by faith conquered kingdoms, performed acts of righteousness, obtained promises, shut the mouths of lions, quenched the power of fire, escaped the edge of the sword, from weakness were made strong (Hebrews 11:33,34).

Is faith a risk? Of course. But failing to step out in faith is to risk missing real life. I have been challenged by the following thought from an unknown author.

Risk

To laugh is to risk appearing the fool.
To weep is to risk appearing sentimental.
To reach out for another is to risk involvement.
To place our ideas, our dreams, before a crowd is to risk their loss.
To love is to risk not being loved in return.
To live is to risk dying.
To hope is to risk despair.
To try is to risk failure.

Risks must be taken because the greatest hazard in life is to risk nothing. The person who risks nothing does nothing, has nothing, is nothing. He may avoid suffering and sorrow, but he simply cannot learn, feel, change, grow, love...live. Chained by his certitudes, he is a slave; he has forfeited freedom.

What a privilege for us to be able to walk by faith in God Himself, armed with all the promises of His Word. I suppose we all desire the security of the solid tree trunk, but the fruit is out on the limb. Nothing ventured, nothing gained. The timid soul asks, "What do I stand to lose if I do it?" The fruit-bearing Christian asks, "What do I stand to lose if I *don't* do it?" Real life is lived on the cutting edge.

Heavenly Father, help me stand up for what is right, to reach out and love others, and to dare to believe.

GOD'S INDICATORS

Watch over your heart with all diligence, for from it flow the springs of life (Proverbs 4:23).

I played sports as a young man and I have the scars on my knees to prove it. The incision of my first knee surgery cut across a nerve and I had no feeling around that area of my leg for several months. Sometimes I would sit down to watch TV and, without thinking, rest a cup of hot coffee on my numb knee. I couldn't feel anything, but before long I could sure smell something: my skin burning! For awhile I had a neat little brown ring on the top of my knee.

Your emotions are to your soul what your physical feelings are to your body. Nobody in their right mind enjoys pain. But if you didn't feel pain you would be in danger of serious injury and infection. And if you didn't feel anger, sorrow, joy, etc., your soul would be in trouble. Emotions are God's indicators to let you know what is going on inside. They are neither good nor bad; they're amoral, just part of your humanity. Just like you respond to the warnings of physical pain, so you need to learn to respond to your emotional indicators.

Someone has likened emotions to the red light on the dashboard of a car which indicates an engine problem. There are several ways you can respond to the red light's warning. You can cover it with a piece of duct tape. "I can't see the light now," you say, "so I don't have to think about the problem." You can smash out the light with a hammer. "That'll teach you for glaring in my face!" Or you can respond to the light as the manufacturers intended for you to respond by looking under the hood and fixing the problem.

You have the same three options in responding to your emotions. You can respond by covering over them, ignoring them, stifling them. That's called *suppression*. You can respond by thoughtlessly lashing out, giving someone a piece of your mind, flying off at the handle. I call that *indiscriminate expression*. Or you can peer inside to see what's going on. That's called *acknowledgment*.

For the next few days we will explore these responses and see why the first two are inappropriate.

Lord, thank You for my emotions. Give me the courage to be emotionally honest and the grace to face the truth.

When I kept silent, my bones wasted away through my groaning all day long (Psalm 32:3 NIV).

Suppression of emotions is a conscious denial of feelings (repression is an *un*conscious denial). Those who suppress their emotions ignore their feelings and choose not to deal with them. Suppression is an unhealthy response to your emotions.

King David had something to say about the negative impact of suppressing his feelings in his relationship with God: "When I kept silent, my bones wasted away through my groaning all day long....Let everyone who is godly pray to you while you may be found; surely when the mighty waters rise, they will not reach him" (Psalm 32:3,6 NIV). David is not saying that God takes Himself out of our reach. When extraneous circumstances loom larger to you than God, it will not take long for your emotions to overcome you. When suppressed emotions build up within you like "mighty waters," you won't turn to God. Your emotions will be in control. It's important to open up to God while you can, because if you bottle up your feelings too long, it will disrupt the harmony of your relationship with Him.

David also commented on the impact of suppression on relationships with people: "I said, 'I will guard my ways, that I may not sin with my tongue; I will guard my mouth as with a muzzle, while the wicked are in my presence.' I was dumb and silent, I refrained even from good; and my sorrow grew worse" (Psalm 39:1,2).

Don't cover over your emotions. Suppression isn't good for you, for others, or for your relationship with God. God knows the thoughts and intentions of our hearts, and others can sense that something is wrong, because more is communicated nonverbally than verbally. When the verbal doesn't match the nonverbal, people believe the nonverbal. If we don't accurately express what we believe, people will believe our nonverbal messages about what we believe. Don't leave room for guesswork. Instead, "Speak truth, each one of you, with his neighbor, for we are members of one another" (Ephesians 4:25).

Lord, I want to live in honest agreement with You and others. Give me the grace to speak the truth in love.

September 7 INDISCRIMINATE EXPRESSION OF EMOTIONS

Let everyone be quick to hear, slow to speak and slow to anger; for the anger of man does not achieve the righteousness of God (James 1:19,20).

Another unhealthy way to respond to emotions is to thoughtlessly let it all hang out, to tell anybody and everybody exactly how you feel. The apostle Peter is a great example of indiscriminate expression. Peter was the John Wayne of the New Testament—a real door slammer. He had no problem telling anyone what was on his mind or how he felt. I like to refer to him as the one-legged apostle because he always had one foot in his mouth.

Peter's impulsive nature got him into trouble more than once. In one setting, he was the spokesperson for God, and Jesus said to him, "Blessed are you Simon Barjona, because flesh and blood did not reveal this to you, but My Father who is in heaven" (Matthew 16:17). Then moments later he spoke for Satan, and Jesus had to rebuke him: "Get behind Me, Satan!" (verses 22,23).

It was Peter who missed the point on the Mount of Transfiguration by suggesting that they build three tabernacles to honor Moses, Elijah, and the Master. It was Peter who impulsively whacked off the ear of Caiaphas' servant during Jesus' arrest in Gethsemane. And it was Peter who promised to follow Jesus anywhere, even to the death, then swearing only hours later that he never knew Him. The fact that Peter became a leader in the New Testament church is evidence of the powerful transformation effected by the Holy Spirit.

Indiscriminate expression of emotions may be somewhat healthy for you, but it may be unhealthy for others. "There, I'm glad I got that off my chest," you may say after an outburst. But in the process you just destroyed your wife, husband, or children. Paul admonished: "Be angry, and yet do not sin" (Ephesians 4:26). If you wish to be angry and not sin, then be angry the way Christ was: Be angry at sin. He turned over the tables, not the money changers.

Heavenly Father, teach me to express myself in a gracious way so I don't hurt others as I seek emotional release.

Help me, O LORD my God....With my mouth I will give thanks abundantly to the LORD (Psalm 109:26,30).

Nancy was a college student with an inability to express the anger and resentment she felt. "My roommate gets to the point sometimes where she just explodes emotionally to let off steam. I have deep feelings too, but I'm not sure that a Christian is supposed to let off steam."

I opened my Bible to Psalm 109:1-13 and read David's angry words against an enemy. "What's that doing in the Bible?" Nancy gasped. "How could David pray all those evil things about his enemy? That's pure hatred."

"David's words didn't surprise God," I answered. "God already knew what he was thinking and feeling. David was simply expressing his pain and anger honestly to his God."

I encouraged Nancy that when she is able to dump her hurt and hatred before God she probably won't dump it on her roommate in a destructive way. I also reminded her that David was as honest about his need for God as he was about expressing his feelings. He closed the psalm by praying: "Help me, O LORD my God....With my mouth I will give thanks abundantly to the LORD" (verses 26,30).

I think the way David acknowledged his feelings is healthy. If you come to your prayer time feeling angry, depressed, or frustrated, and then mouth a bunch of pious platitudes as if God doesn't know how you feel, do you think He is pleased? Not unless He's changed His opinion about hypocrisy. In God's eyes, if you're not real, you're not right.

Acknowledging your emotions also involves being real in front of a few trusted friends. During his travels, Paul had Barnabas, Silas, or Timothy to lean on. In the Garden of Gethsemane, Jesus expressed His grief to His inner circle of Peter, James, and John. If you have two or three people like this in your life, you are truly blessed.

Thank You, Lord, that I can be real and honest with You. Help me develop a few trusted friends who will also welcome my emotional honesty.

Consider it all joy, my brethren, when you encounter various trials, knowing that the testing of your faith produces endurance (James 1:2,3).

There certainly are a lot of distractions, diversions, disappointments, trials, temptations, and traumas which come along to disrupt the process of becoming the person God wants you to be. Every day you struggle against the world, the flesh, and the devil, each of which are opposed to your success at being God's person.

But Paul reminds us that the tribulations we face are actually a means of achieving our supreme goal of maturity: "We also exult in our tribulations, knowing that tribulation brings about perseverance; and perseverance, proven character; and proven character, hope; and hope does not disappoint, because the love of God has been poured out within our hearts through the Holy Spirit who was given to us" (Romans 5:3-5). James offers similar encouragement: "Consider it all joy, my brethren, when you encounter various trials, knowing that the testing of your faith produces endurance. And let endurance have its perfect result, that you may be perfect and complete, lacking in nothing" (James 1:2-4).

Maybe you thought your goal as a Christian was to escape tribulations. But God's goal for you is maturity in Christ, becoming the person He designed you to be. And tribulation just happens to be one of the primary stepping-stones on the pathway. That's why Paul says we exult—meaning to express heightened joy—in our tribulations. Why? Because persevering tribulations is the doorway to proven character, which is God's goal for us.

Our hope lies in proven character, not in favorable circumstances nor in the manipulation of others. Neither circumstances nor people can keep you from being what God wants you to be. Trials and tribulations are the most common means for bringing about His goal for your life.

Lord, help me see my trials as stepping-stones, not obstacles. Give me grace to persevere and develop proven character.

Do not hold back discipline from the child (Proverbs 23:13).

Some children are effectively disciplined when they must experience the natural consequences of their disobedience. For example, if your child fools around and misses his bus at school, you may choose to let him walk home instead of picking him up yourself. If he procrastinates on a school project you have urged him to complete, let him receive a bad grade instead of bailing him out by doing the project yourself. For many children the pain of the natural consequence is enough to prompt a change in behavior the next time. Strong-willed children may respond best to this means of discipline. They often have to learn the hard way.

Use wisdom when employing this method. Some natural consequences may be too severe when other methods of discipline could be used. For example, making a child walk home from school alone may not be advisable in dangerous neighborhoods or bad weather.

Sometimes you may want to plan a negative consequence that is logically related to your child's misbehavior. Logical consequences are effective because they teach children to be responsible. For example, if your child carelessly spills his milk, a logical consequence is for him to clean up the mess.

Logical consequences help avoid power struggles between the child and parent. They can also greatly reduce nagging, corrections, and spankings. When your child completes the consequence, the incident is over, and hopefully he has learned to avoid the problem in the future.

Using natural consequences for discipline may require some extra work on your part. For example, you may need to teach your child how to use a sponge mop, operate the washing machine, etc. Don't look for the easiest method of discipline; look for the best. What may be convenient may not be correct. What works best for one child may not work well for another. Logical consequences teach cause and effect and can be used as a positive reinforcer.

Heavenly Father, grant me the wisdom to discipline my children for their future good as You discipline me for my good.

When He, the Spirit of truth, comes, He will guide you into all the truth (John 16:13).

It's not hard to know the truth if you are the truth, and speaking with authority would come quite naturally if you're God! Discernment is also easier if you know, as Jesus does, what's in the hearts of men (John 2:24,25). Though we don't possess those attributes, we do have the Holy Spirit. If we are going to continue the work of Jesus, we must yield to the Holy Spirit and allow Him to control and guide us. Then we can know the truth, speak with authority, and discern good and evil.

We have as our guide the Spirit of truth. When Jesus promised to send the Holy Spirit, He said, "When He, the Spirit of truth, comes, He will guide you into all the truth…He will disclose to you what is to come. He shall glorify Me; for He shall take of Mine, and shall disclose it to you" (John 16:13,14). This promise has primary reference to the apostles, but its application extends to all Spirit-filled believers (1 John 2:20-27). The Holy Spirit is first and foremost the Spirit of truth, and He will lead us into all truth.

When Jesus prayed, He requested, "I do not ask Thee to take them out of the world, but to keep them from the evil one….Sanctify them in the truth; Thy word is truth" (John 17:15,17). Truth is what keeps us from the evil one. John wrote, "The whole world lies in the power of the evil one" (1 John 5:19), because Satan "deceives the whole world" (Revelation 12:9). The only way to overcome the father of lies is by revelation, not research or reasoning. Many in higher education lean on their own understanding and believe only in what can be validated by research. Truth is God's will made known through His Word. The Holy Spirit's role is to enable us to understand the Word of God from God's perspective. Jesus says, "You shall know the truth, and the truth shall make you free" (John 8:32).

Father, forgive me for leaning on my own understanding. Fill me with Your Spirit and lead me into all truth today.

The serpent said..."You will be like God, knowing good and evil" (Genesis 3:4,5).

Adam was the first to be tempted by the notion that he could "be like God" (Genesis 3:5), which is the essence of the self-centered worldview that Satan promotes. Millions have been seduced by Satan into believing that they are God. The New Age Movement is promoting this lie on a grand and international scale.

However, the biblical account of creation clearly establishes that only God the Creator is truly God. Adam and his descendents are not gods; we are created beings which cannot exist apart from God. The diabolical idea that man is his own god is the primary link in the chain of spiritual bondage to the kingdom of darkness.

The problem with man's attempt at being his own god is that he was never designed to occupy that role. He lacks the necessary attributes to determine his own destiny. Even sinless, spiritually alive Adam in the garden of Eden before the Fall wasn't equipped to be his own god. Contrary to what the New Agers tell us, the potential to be a god never was in you, isn't in you now, and never will be in you. Being God is God's capacity alone.

If you desire to live in freedom from the bondage of the world, the flesh, and the devil, this primary link in the chain must be renounced. The self-centered worldview which Satan and his emissaries are promoting must be replaced by the perspective that Jesus introduced to His disciples in the wake of Peter's self-preserving rebuke in Matthew 16: "If anyone wishes to come after Me, let him deny himself, and take up his cross, and follow Me. For whoever wishes to save his life shall lose it; but whoever loses his life for My sake shall find it" (verses 24,25). In the next several days we will examine the view from the cross.

Father, forgive me for the occasions when I have usurped Your place in my life. You are my Lord and my God.

ROYAL PALM BEACH
Magic
Baden
MAGIC
dsc_5117.jpg

If anyone wishes to come after Me, let him deny himself (Matthew 16:24).

A primary reason why we struggle to fulfill Christ's Great Commission is because we are guilty of a great *omission*: We fail to deny ourselves.

Denying yourself is not the same as self-denial. Students, athletes, and cult members practice self-denial, restricting themselves from substances and activities which keep them from reaching their goals. But the ultimate purpose of self-denial is self-glorification. The ultimate purpose of denying self is to glorify God.

Jesus was talking about denying yourself in the essential battle of life: the scramble for the throne, the struggle over who is going to be God. Jesus doesn't enter into that battle; He's already won it. He occupies the throne and graciously offers to share it with us. But we want to be king in our lives by ourselves. Until we deny ourselves that which was never meant to be ours—the role of being God in our lives—we will never be at peace with ourselves or God, and we will never be free.

You were not designed to function independently of God, nor was your soul designed to function as master. You will either serve God and His kingdom or Satan and his kingdom. Self-seeking, self-serving, self-justifying, self-glorifying, self-centered, and self-confident living is in actuality living and serving the world, the flesh, and the devil. On the other hand, denying yourself is not self-mortification. God is not trying to annihilate you; He is trying to restore you.

When you deny yourself, you invite God to take the throne of your life, to occupy what is rightfully His, so that you may function as a person who is spiritually alive in Christ. Denying yourself is essential to spiritual freedom.

Lord, too many times I have tried to live independently of You. I deny myself today and yield the throne of my life to You.

If anyone wishes to come after Me, let him...take up his cross (Matthew 16:24).

The cross we are to pick up on a daily basis is not our *own* cross but *Christ's* cross. We are closely identified with His cross, however, because we have been crucified with Christ and no longer live; Christ lives in us (Galatians 2:20). His cross provided forgiveness from what we have done and deliverance from what we were. We are forgiven because He died in our place; we are delivered because we died with Him. We are both justified and sanctified as a result of the cross.

To pick up the cross daily means to acknowledge every day that we belong to God. We have been purchased by the blood of the Lord Jesus Christ (1 Peter 1:18,19). When we pick up the cross we affirm that our identity is not based in our physical existence but in our relationship with God. We are identified as children of God (1 John 3:1-3) and our life is in Christ, who is our life (Colossians 3:3,4).

As a result of this acknowledgment we stop trying to do our own thing in order to live daily to please our heavenly Father. We stop trying to become something we aren't, and we rest in the finished work of Christ, who made us something very special.

Jesus said, "Whoever wishes to save his [natural] life shall lose it; but whoever loses his life for My sake shall find it" (Matthew 16:25). Those who strive to establish their identity and seek to establish purpose and meaning in their natural life will someday lose it. We can't take it with us! We must take up our cross daily by acknowledging that life only finds meaning in Christ.

Thank You, Lord, that because of the cross, I can soar in the heavenlies with You. You are my life.

September 15

If anyone wishes to come after Me, let him...follow Me (Matthew 16:24).

Seeking to overcome self by self-effort is a hopeless struggle. Self will never cast out self, because an independent self motivated by the flesh still wants to be God. We must follow Christ by being led by the Holy Spirit down the path of death to self-rule. As Paul wrote: "We who live are constantly being delivered over to death for Jesus' sake, that the life of Jesus also may be manifested in our mortal flesh" (2 Corinthians 4:11).

This may sound like a dismal path to walk, but I assure you that it is not. It is a tremendous experience to be known by the Shepherd and to follow Him as obedient, dependent sheep (John 10:27). The fact that we are led by the Spirit of God, even when it results in the death to self-rule, is our assurance of sonship (Romans 8:14). We were not designed to function independently of God. Only when we are dependent on Him and intent on following Christ are we complete and free to prove that the will of God is good, acceptable, and perfect (Romans 12:2).

Self-rule is motivated by self-interest and supported only by self-centered resources. When we come to the end of our resources, we discover God's resources. God will let us do our thing and patiently wait until self-interest and self-rule leave us spiritually and emotionally bankrupt. We can turn to God any time we weary of trying to run our own lives independently of Him. He doesn't force Himself on us, He just simply says, "If anyone wishes to come after Me, let him...follow Me." Are you willing to forsake self-rule and follow Him?

Loving Shepherd, I desire Your will for my life, and I purpose today to follow You in obedience and dependence.

Whoever wishes to save his life shall lose it; but whoever loses his life for My sake shall find it. For what will a man be profited, if he gains the whole world, and forfeits his soul? (Matthew 16:25,26).

Three guidelines from these verses summarize the view from the cross, which we must adopt to counteract the self-centered worldview promoted by the god of this world.

First, we must sacrifice the lower life to gain the higher life. If you want to save your natural life (i.e., find your identity and sense of self-worth in positions, titles, accomplishments, and possessions, and seek only worldly well-being) you will lose it. At best you can only possess these temporal values for a lifetime, only to lose everything for eternity.

Furthermore, in all your efforts to possess these earthly treasures, you will fail to gain all that can be yours in Christ. Shoot for this world and that's all you'll get, and eventually you will lose even that. But shoot for the next world and God will throw in the benefits of knowing Him in this present life as well. Paul put it this way: "Discipline yourself for the purpose of godliness; for bodily discipline is only of little profit, but godliness is profitable for all things, since it holds promise for the present life and also for the life to come" (1 Timothy 4:7,8).

Second, sacrifice the pleasure of things to gain the pleasure of life. What would you accept in trade for the fruit of the Spirit in your life? What material possession, what amount of money, what position or title would you exchange for the love, joy, peace, and patience that you enjoy in Christ? "Nothing," we all probably agree. Victory over self comes as we learn to love people and use things instead of using people and loving things.

Third, sacrifice the temporal to gain the eternal. Possibly the greatest sign of spiritual maturity is the ability to postpone rewards. It is far better to know that we are the children of God than to gain anything that the world calls valuable. Even if following Christ results in hardships in this life, He will make it right in eternity.

Heavenly Father, You alone are God. Help me to choose the higher life today instead of seeking the pleasures of this world.

By this is My Father glorified, that you bear much fruit, and so prove to be My disciples (John 15:8).

How can you know if you're being led by the Spirit or the flesh? Very simple: Look at your behavior. If you respond to a given situation by exercising love, joy, peace, patience, kindness, goodness, faithfulness, gentleness, and self-control, you are following the Spirit's lead (Galatians 5:22,23). If your reactions and responses reflect the deeds of the flesh listed in Galatians 5:19-21, you are following the flesh.

What do you do when you discover you are not walking by the Spirit? Acknowledge it for what it is. You have consciously or unconsciously chosen to live independently of God by walking according to the flesh. Walking according to the Spirit is a moment-by-moment, day-by-day experience. Acknowledge your sin to God, seek the forgiveness of anyone you may have offended, receive forgiveness, and be filled with the Spirit.

Here are a couple of things to consider when you are faced with righting fleshly wrongs.

First, the scope of your confession should only be as broad as the scope of your offense. If you lashed out at a relative with angry words, you need only confess to God and that relative. If you entertain a secret, lustful thought or proud attitude without any overt, offensive behavior, you need only confess it to God. Confession literally means to agree with God. When you recognize an internal fleshly response, immediately acknowledge it in your mind. That's it; just agree with God and walk in the light.

Second, the process of restoring a relationship through confession and forgiveness is a step of spiritual growth. Your role as a spouse, parent, friend, coworker, or fellow-Christian is to model growth, not perfection. If you're trying to keep up a front of Christian perfection in order to encourage saints and win sinners, forget it; it will never happen. But when you openly admit and ask forgiveness for your fleshly choices, you model the kind of spiritual growth which will touch saints and sinners alike.

Lord, I sometimes walk according to the flesh.
Fill me with Your Holy Spirit so the fruit of the Spirit will be evident in my life today.

Train up a child in the way he should go, even when he is old he will not depart from it (Proverbs 22:6).

Your primary responsibility as a parent is to lead your child to Christ and help him establish his identity in Christ. When a child comes into the world he is completely dependent on his earthly parents to feed him, change his dirty diapers, and provide shelter. Childhood and adolescence is the process of moving from total dependence as a child to total independence as an adult. In the process of finding out who they are as individuals, children gradually move away from many of the people, thoughts, and ideas they have experienced through their parents and move toward the people, thoughts, and ideas which they have made their own.

A child is capable of understanding God's love and protection and receiving Jesus Christ as Savior at a very early age. But understanding his spiritual identity is a process that takes place over the years of his childhood. It is the process of shifting his dependence from parents to God.

Children wrestle with identity around age 12. Researchers of cognitive development say that most 12-year-olds can think as adults. They are capable of abstract thinking and understanding symbolism. This is significant when you remember that Jesus appeared out of obscurity at age 12. Furthermore, the Jewish bar mitzvah has been celebrated for centuries when a boy turns 12, the age at which Jews believe that a boy becomes a man. Many churches have confirmation for children at or near the age of 12.

I believe age 12 is the approximate time in a child's life when we should help him establish his spiritual identity. Evangelicals have tended to minimize junior high ministry and focus on high school. High school is too late for some kids to be challenged with their spiritual identity. Don't make that mistake with your children. You must begin early helping them understand who they are as children of God and what their identity means to them spiritually. Seeing themselves as God sees them is the most important perception your children will ever have. If your kids don't find their identity in Christ, they will find it in the world.

Help me guide my children into a relationship with You, dear Father, so they may establish their identity in Christ.

Therefore you are no longer a slave, but a son; and if a son, then an heir through God (Galatians 4:7).

As you consider the importance of your spiritual identity and the spiritual identity of your children, meditate on these passages:

- The Spirit Himself bears witness with our spirit that we are children of God (Romans 8:16).
- For you are all sons of God through faith in Christ Jesus. For all of you who were baptized into Christ have clothed yourselves with Christ (Galatians 3:26,27).
- And because you are sons, God has sent forth the Spirit of His Son into our hearts, crying, "Abba! Father!" Therefore you are no longer a slave, but a son; and if a son, then an heir through God (Galatians 4:6,7).
- But you are a chosen race, a royal priesthood, a holy nation, a people for God's own possession, that you may proclaim the excellencies of Him who has called you out of darkness into His marvelous light; for you once were not a people, but now you are the people of God; you had not received mercy, but now you have received mercy (1 Peter 2:9,10).
- See how great a love the Father has bestowed upon us, that we should be called children of God; and such we are....Beloved, now we are children of God, and it has not appeared as yet what we shall be. We know that, when He appears, we shall be like Him, because we shall see Him just as He is. And anyone who has this hope fixed on Him purifies himself, just as He is pure (1 John 3:1-3).

Mom and Dad, do you want your sons and daughters to purify themselves? Then find out who you are as a child of God, and help your children establish the same eternal relationship by discovering their identity in Him.

Lord, continue to show me who I am in Christ that I may encourage my children in their relationship with You.

The LORD is my rock and my fortress and my deliverer, my God, my rock, in whom I take refuge; my shield and the horn of my salvation, my stronghold (Psalm 18:2).

The key to experiencing security in your life is to depend on things that are eternal, not temporal. Christians often feel insecure because they are depending on temporal things they have no right or ability to control. For example, some people rely on their money for material security instead of relying on God's promise to supply all our needs. The safest place to keep money a few years ago was a savings and loan institution. But many have failed and the security people had placed in them was shattered. Only eternal investments are secure.

I believe God is shaking the foundations of the world. Natural disasters are on the increase, kingdoms are being toppled, political boundaries are being redrawn, and anarchy reigns in many poor countries. Scripture warns us that such conditions would precede the second coming of Christ (Matthew 24). This shouldn't alarm us; we should be excited. Christ's return will be the day of the church for those who have stored up treasures in heaven (Matthew 6:19-21).

Security only comes from relating to that which is anchored in eternity. Jesus said that we have eternal life and that no one can snatch us out of His hand (John 10:27-29). Paul declared that nothing can separate us from the love of God in Christ (Romans 8:35-39) and that we are sealed in Him by the Holy Spirit (Ephesians 1:13,14). How much more secure can you get than that? When your ultimate trust is in temporal values and relationships, you are always subject to insecurity because these things are subject to failure and can be lost. The greatest sense of security you can experience is the byproduct of taking a firm grip on values and relationships which will endure as long as God Himself.

Lord, my Rock, thank You for the peace and security that comes from trusting in You instead of temporal values.

A Change in Our Very Essence

You were formerly darkness, but now you are light in the Lord; walk as children of light (Ephesians 5:8).

Ephesians 2:1-3 describes our nature *before* we came to Christ: "You were dead in your trespasses and sins, in which you formerly walked according to the course of this world, according to the prince of the power of the air...and were by nature children of wrath." Before we became Christians our very nature was sin, and the result of our sin was death (separation from God). As such we served ourselves and Satan as a matter of course.

But at salvation God changed our very essence; we became "partakers of the divine nature, having escaped the corruption that is in the world by lust" (2 Peter 1:4). You are no longer in the flesh; you are in Christ. You had a sinful nature before your conversion, but now you are a partaker of Christ's divine nature. You are neither eternal nor divine, but you are eternally united with Christ's divinity. Paul said it this way: "You were formerly darkness, but now you are light in the Lord; walk as children of light" (Ephesians 5:8); "Therefore if any man is in Christ, he is a new creature" (2 Corinthians 5:17). In the face of Satan's accusations that we are no different, we must believe and live in harmony with the fact that we are eternally different in Christ.

The New Testament refers to the person you were before you received Christ as your old self (*old man* in the King James Version). At salvation your old self, which was motivated to live independently of God and was therefore characterized by sin, died (Romans 6:6), and your new self, motivated by your new identity in Christ and characterized by dependence on God, came to life (Galatians 2:20).

Your old self had to die in order to sever your relationship with sin which dominated it. Being a new person doesn't mean that you are sinless (1 John 1:8). But since your old self has been crucified and buried with Christ, you no longer *need* to sin (1 John 2:1). You sin when you choose to act independently of God.

Lord, thank You for the hope that comes from knowing that my old self is dead and that I am now a new creature in Christ.

Our struggle is not against flesh and blood, but against the rulers, against the powers, against the world forces of this darkness, against the spiritual forces of wickedness in the heavenly places (Ephesians 6:12).

Virtually all evangelical Christians and even many liberals agree that Satan is a living being who is an evil force in the world. Historically, Christian confessions of faith have always included statements about belief in a personal devil—not that every person has his own personal devil, but that the devil is an actual personage rather than merely an impersonal force. But when you talk about demons being alive and active in the world today, a lot of Christians bristle, "Hold on there. I believe in the devil, but I don't buy that stuff about demons."

My question to these people is: How do you think Satan carries on his worldwide ministry of evil and deception? He is a created being. He is not omnipresent, omniscient, or omnipotent. He can't be everywhere in the world tempting and deceiving millions of people at the same moment. He does so through an army of emissaries (demons, evil spirits, fallen angels, etc.) who propagate his plan of rebellion around the world. It is clear from the context of Ephesians 6:12 that the rulers, powers, and forces which oppose us are spiritual entities in the heavenlies (the spiritual world).

Disbelief in personal demonic activity (or an inordinate fear of demons) is further evidence of the static that Satan perpetrates in our minds to distort the truth. In the classic *Screwtape Letters*, C.S. Lewis wrote: "There are two equal and opposite errors into which our race can fall about the devils. One is to disbelieve their existence. The other is to believe and feel an unhealthy interest in them. They themselves are equally pleased by both errors and hail a materialist or a magician with the same delight."[1]

Father God, I announce that You are the only legitimate fear-object and sanctuary, and I renounce all demonic activity in my life.

When the unclean spirit goes out of a man, it passes through waterless places seeking rest, and not finding any, it says, "I will return to my house from which I came."...Then it goes and takes along seven other spirits more evil than itself (Luke 11:24,26).

The Bible does not attempt to prove the existence of demons any more than it attempts to prove the existence of God. It simply reports on their activities as if its first readers accepted their existence. Nor did the early church fathers have a problem with the reality and personality of demons. Origen wrote: "In regard to the devil and his angels and opposing powers, the ecclesiastical teaching maintains that the beings do indeed exist; but what they are or how they exist is not explained with sufficient clarity. This opinion, however, is held by most: that the devil was an angel; and having apostatized, he persuaded as many angels as possible to fall away with himself; and these, even to the present time, are called his angels."

Luke 11:24-26 gives us a helpful view into the personality and individuality of evil spirits. We can glean several points of information about evil spirits from this passage.

1. Demons can exist outside or inside humans.
2. They are able to travel.
3. They are able to communicate.
4. Each one has a separate identity.
5. They are able to remember and make plans.
6. They are able to evaluate and make decisions.
7. They are able to combine forces.
8. They vary in degrees of wickedness.

But you need not fear Satan and his demons as long as you cling to God's truth. Their only weapon is deception. Irenaeus wrote, "The devil...can only go to this length, as he did at the beginning, to deceive and lead astray the mind of man into disobeying the commandments of God, and gradually to darken the hearts." If you continue to walk in the light you don't need to be afraid of the darkness.

Lord, I accept the reality of the spiritual world and Your rule over it. I will walk in the light and not fear the darkness.

If Your Faith Is Off

We walk by faith, not by sight (2 Corinthians 5:7).

When my son Karl was about eight years old, I introduced him to the game of golf. I gave him a little starter set of clubs and took him out to the course with me. Karl would tee up his ball and whale away at it with his mightiest swing. Usually he sprayed the ball all over the place. But since he could only hit it 60 or 70 yards at best, his direction could be off by 20 degrees and his ball would still be in the fairway.

As he grew up and got a bigger set of clubs, Karl was able to drive the ball off the tee 150 yards and farther. But if his drive was still 20 degrees off target, his ball no longer stayed in the fairway; it usually went into the rough. Accuracy is even more important for golfers who can blast a golf ball 200 to 250 yards off the tee. The same 20-degree deviation which allowed little Karl's short drives to remain in the fairway will send a longer drive soaring out of bounds.

This simple illustration pictures an important aspect of the life of faith: Your Christian walk is the direct result of what you believe about God and yourself. If your faith is off, your walk will be off. If your walk is off, you can be sure it's because your faith is off. As a new Christian, you needed some time to learn how to "hit the ball straight" in your belief system. You could be off 20 degrees in what you believed and still be on the fairway because you were still growing and had a lot to learn. But the longer you persist in a faulty belief system, the less fulfilling and productive your daily walk of faith will be. As you grow older you will find yourself stumbling through the rough or out of bounds spiritually if the course you have set for your life doesn't agree with Scripture.

For many adults, a mid-life crisis is the result of basing their concept of success and fulfillment on the world instead of on the Word of God. Tragically, many of our children and teenagers are heading for the same fall because their beliefs are not founded on Scripture. As a result, their lives are often bankrupt before they leave high school.

Lord, Your Word is a lamp to my feet and a light to my path. Teach me Your truth today that I may walk in it.

Be careful to do according to all the law which Moses My servant commanded you.... Then you will have success (Joshua 1:7,8).

A helpful perspective of success in the Christian life is seen in Joshua's experience of leading Israel into the Promised Land. God said to him: "Be strong and very courageous; be careful to do according to all the law which Moses My servant commanded you; do not turn from it to the right or to the left, so that you may have success wherever you go. This book of the law shall not depart from your mouth, but you shall meditate on it day and night, so that you may be careful to do according to all that is written in it; for then you will make your way prosperous, and then you will have success" (Joshua 1:7,8).

Was Joshua's success dependent on other people or circumstances? Absolutely not. Success hinged entirely on his obedience. If Joshua believed what God said and did what God told him to do, he would succeed. Sounds simple enough, but God immediately put Joshua to the test by giving him a rather unorthodox battle plan for conquering Jericho. Marching around the city for seven days, then blowing a horn, wasn't exactly an approved military tactic in Joshua's day!

But Joshua's success was conditional on obeying God regardless of how foolish His plan seemed. As Joshua 6 records, Joshua's success had nothing to do with the circumstances of the battle and everything to do with obedience. That should be your pattern too. Accept God's goal for your life and follow it obediently.

Don't take this truth lightly. You can be successful if you commit yourself to being what God has called you to be and follow Him obediently. You can be successful in business and remain in God's will even when your competition conducts business under the table and cheats on taxes. You can run for public office and win with a campaign that doesn't compromise God's will. Remember: You can be a failure in the eyes of the world and a success in the eyes of God—and vice versa.

Lord, I want to be a success in Your eyes. Help me to be strong and courageous in doing Your will.

Consider yourselves to be dead to sin, but alive to God in Christ Jesus (Romans 6:11).

Even though you are dead to sin, sin's strong appeal may still cause you to struggle with feeling that you are more alive to sin than you are to Christ. But Romans 6:1-11 teaches us that what is true of the Lord Jesus Christ is true of us in terms of our relationship to sin and death. God the Father allowed His Son to "be sin" in order that all the sins of the world—past, present, and future—would fall on Him (2 Corinthians 5:21). When He died on the cross, our sins were on Him. But when He rose from the grave, there was no sin on Him. When He ascended to the Father, there was no sin on Him. And today, as He sits at the Father's right hand, there is no sin on Him. Since we are seated in the heavenlies in Christ, we too have died to sin.

Christ already died to sin, and because you are in Him, you have died to sin too. Sin is still strong and appealing, but your relationship with sin has ended. I've met many Christians who are still trying to die to sin, and their lives are miserable and fruitless as a result because they are struggling to do something that has already been done. "For the law of the Spirit of life in Christ Jesus has set you free from the law of sin and of death" (Romans 8:2).

Romans 6:11 summarizes what we are to believe about our relationship to sin because of our position in Christ. It doesn't matter whether you feel dead to sin or not; you are to *consider* it so because it *is* so. People wrongly wonder, "What experience must I have in order for this to be true?" The only necessary experience is that of Christ on the cross, which has already happened. When we choose to believe what is true about ourselves and sin, and walk on the basis of what we believe, our right relationship with sin will work out in our experience. But as long as we put our experience before our belief, we will never fully know the freedom that Christ purchased for us on the cross.

Lord, teach me not always to believe what I feel about my relationship to sin, but to believe the truth that I am dead to it.

YOUR CHOICE

Therefore do not let sin reign in your mortal body that you should obey its lusts, and do not go on presenting the members of your body to sin as instruments of unrighteousness; but present yourselves to God as those alive from the dead, and your members as instruments of righteousness to God (Romans 6:12,13).

In Romans 6:1-11 Paul uses the past tense to emphasize that we died to sin the moment we placed faith in Christ. For example: "We who *died* to sin" (verse 2); "Our old self *was crucified* with Him" (verse 6); "For he who *has died* is freed from sin" (verse 7). Since these verses are past tense, indicating what is already true about us, we can only believe them.

On the basis of what Romans 6:1-11 instructs us to believe, Romans 6:12,13 tells us how to relate to sin. Sin is a taskmaster which demands service from its subjects. You are dead to sin, but you still have the capacity to serve it by putting your body at sin's disposal. It's up to you to choose whether you're going to let your body be used for sin or for righteousness. Satan, who is at the root of all sin, will take advantage of anyone who uses their body as an instrument of unrighteousness. For example, it is impossible to commit a sexual sin and not use your body, and sin will reign in your mortal body.

To further illustrate, suppose your pastor asks to use your car to deliver food baskets to the needy, and a thief asks to use it to rob a bank. It's your car and you can choose to lend it however you want, for good or for evil. Which would you choose? There should be no question!

Your body is also yours to use to serve either God or sin and Satan, but the choice is up to you. That's why Paul wrote so insistently: "I urge you therefore, brethren, by the mercies of God, to present your bodies a living and holy sacrifice, acceptable to God, which is your spiritual service of worship" (Romans 12:1). Because of Christ's victory over sin, you are completely free to choose not to give yourself to obey sin as your master. It is your responsibility not to let sin reign in your mortal body.

Lord, I renounce every use of my body as an instrument of unrighteousness, and I yield it to You today as a living sacrifice.

Thanks be to God, who gives us the victory through our Lord Jesus Christ (1 Corinthians 15:57).

Here's a wonderful example of what can happen to a Christian when the strongholds of the mind are overthrown by God's truth.

Jeannie is a beautiful and talented woman in her mid-twenties. As an active Christian for 13 years, she sings in a professional singing group, writes music, leads worship at her church, and oversees a discipleship group.

Jeannie recently attended one of my conferences. As I saw her smiling at me from her seat at the conference, what I didn't know was that she was bulimic, having been in bondage to the strongholds of food and fear for 11 years. When she was home alone she would be captivated by Satan's lies about food, her appearance, and her self-worth for hours at a time. She had submitted to counseling without success. All the while she believed that the thoughts prompting her to induce vomiting were her own based on a traumatic experience from her childhood.

When I was talking during the conference about destroying strongholds, I happened to be looking at Jeannie—quite unintentionally—when I said, "Every person I know with an eating disorder has been the victim of a stronghold based on the lies of Satan."

"You have no idea how that statement impacted my life," she told me the next morning. "I have been battling myself all these years, and I suddenly understood that my enemy was not me but Satan. That was the most profound truth I have ever heard. It was like I had been blind for 11 years and could suddenly see. I cried all the way home. When the old thoughts came back last night, I simply rejected them for the truth. For the first night in years I was able to go to sleep without vomiting. The truth has set me free."

If you think Jeannie's experience of finding freedom in Christ is unique, you're wrong. Winning the battle for the mind is possible for everyone who is in Christ.

Heavenly Father, help me take every thought captive to the obedience of Christ today. I choose to think upon that which is true.

WHO'S RESPONSIBLE FOR CONVICTION

Let us not judge one another anymore, but rather determine this—not to put an obstacle or a stumbling block in a brother's way (Romans 14:13).

I grew up with a good, moral background, and I even went to church, but I wasn't a Christian. In those days I really enjoyed beer, especially on a hot day after mowing the lawn. When I received Christ as a young man I joined a church which preached total abstinence from alcoholic beverages. I wasn't a drunk, so I decided to scratch that rule and keep my beer.

My beer-drinking wasn't excessive, but two years later the Lord convicted me about it. With the conviction came the power to obey. So I gave it up. I'm so glad that no one laid a guilt trip on me or made an issue over my drinking an occasional beer.

Sometimes we are tempted to play the role of the Holy Spirit or the conscience in someone else's life on issues where the Scriptures are not crystal clear: "Christians don't drink or smoke"; "You should spend at least 30 minutes a day in prayer and Bible study"; "Buying lottery tickets is not good stewardship." I'm convinced that the Holy Spirit knows exactly when to bring conviction on issues of conscience. It's part of the process of sanctification which He superintends. When we attempt to play His role we often do little more than convey criticism and rejection. Our job is to accept people and let the Holy Spirit bring conviction in His time.

God has given us the ministry of reconciliation, not condemnation. Paul wrote, "God was in Christ reconciling the world to Himself, not counting their trespasses against them, and He has committed to us the word of reconciliation" (2 Corinthians 5:19). There is a time and place to confront Christians about immoral behavior. But when we do so, it is only because we care about their relationship with God and desire to protect others.

Lord, teach me to confront others in love when I must and to accept others in love as You have accepted me.

Brethren, even if a man is caught in any trespass, you who are spiritual, restore such a one in a spirit of gentleness (Galatians 6:1).

Are there any occasions when Christians should confront each other on matters of behavior? Yes. We are required by God to confront and restore those who have clearly violated the boundaries of Scripture (Matthew 18:15,16). But let me alert you to an important distinction in this area: Discipline is an issue of confronting observed behavior—that which you have personally witnessed (Galatians 6:1); judgment is an issue of character. We are instructed to confront others concerning sins we have observed, but we are not allowed to judge their character (Matthew 7:1; Romans 14:13). Disciplining is our responsibility; judging character is God's responsibility.

For example, imagine that you just caught your child telling a lie. "You're a liar," you say to him. That's judgment, an attack on his character. But if you say, "Son, you just told a lie," that's discipline. You're holding him accountable based on an observed behavior.

Or let's say that a Christian friend admits to you that he cheated on his income tax return. If you confront him as a thief you are judging his character, and that's not your responsibility. You can only confront him on the basis of what you see: "By cheating on your taxes you are stealing from the government, and that's wrong."

Much of what we call discipline is nothing less than character assassination. We say to our disobedient child: "You're a bad boy." We say to a failing Christian brother or sister: "You're not a good Christian." Such statements don't correct or edify; they tear down character and convey disapproval for the person as well as his problem. Your child is not a liar; he's a child of God who has told a lie. Your Christian friend is not a thief; he's a child of God who has taken something which doesn't belong to him. We must hold people accountable for their behavior, but we are never allowed to denigrate their character.

Forgive me, Father, for judging others. Enable me to discipline in love those I care about and for whom I am responsible.

[The devil] was a murderer from the beginning, and does not stand in the truth, because there is no truth in him. Whenever he speaks a lie, he speaks from his own nature; for he is a liar, and the father of lies (John 8:44).

Alyce was one of the most pathetic-looking young women I have ever met. She was so skinny that she literally had no more body fat to lose. She had lost her job three days earlier, and her vacant eyes conveyed that she had lost all hope for her life. She was a very talented girl and a committed Christian in many ways, but she was also a Darvon junkie who had even been arrested once for illegal possession of prescription drugs.

"I want you to tell me who you think you are," I said to Alyce.

"I'm just a no-good failure," she whimpered.

"You're not a failure," I responded. "You're a child of God." She continued to pour out the negative self-talk and evidences of demonic deception she had been living under, and I continued to counter her negativism with the good news of her identity in Christ. The more we talked the more aware I became of Christ's presence ministering to Alyce. We tested the spirit that was harassing her, and she knew firsthand that she had been deceived. Astonished, she said, "Do you mean to tell me that my whole problem has been deception, that I have been listening to a pack of lies?" Today she's free.

The prevailing theme of the New Testament is the position we enjoy in Christ through our faith in Him. That's the good news: Christ in you and you in Christ. If there is a prevailing negative theme in the New Testament which capsulizes the opposition we face in Satan, I believe it is deception. There are at least three avenues through which Satan will attempt to dissuade you from God's truth and deceive you into believing his lies: self-deception, false prophets/teachers, and deceiving spirits. We are vulnerable to Satan's deception in these areas if we fail to clothe ourselves daily with the spiritual armor of the belt of truth.

Lord, I put on the belt of the truth of Your Word today and stand against the deception of Satan.

For those who are according to the flesh set their minds on the things of the flesh, but those who are according to the Spirit, the things of the Spirit (Romans 8:5).

The center of all spiritual bondage is the mind. That's where the battle must be fought and won if you are to experience the freedom in Christ He purchased for you on the cross. Paul wrote: "For though we walk in the flesh, we do not war according to the flesh, for the weapons of our warfare are not of the flesh, but divinely powerful for the destruction of fortresses. We are destroying speculations and every lofty thing raised up against the knowledge of God, and we are taking every thought captive to the obedience of Christ" (2 Corinthians 10:3-5).

Before you came to Christ, bad habits and sinful thought patterns were established as you learned to live your life independently of God. Your non-Christian environment taught you to think about and respond to life in a non-Christian way, and those patterns and responses were ingrained in your mind as strongholds. When you became a Christian, your old fleshly habits and patterns weren't erased; they are still a part of your flesh which must be dealt with on a daily basis. Thankfully, however, you are not just a product of your past; you are a new creature in Christ (2 Corinthians 5:17), and now you are primarily the product of the work of Christ on the cross.

Old strongholds can be destroyed. Patterns of negative thinking and behavior are learned, and they can be unlearned through disciplined Bible study. Some strongholds are the result of demonic influences and spiritual conflicts from past and present mental assaults. If people believe Satan's lies, those lies will control their lives. These people need to be freed from the shackles of Satan's lies by God's truth. Jesus said: "You shall know the truth, and the truth shall make you free" (John 8:32).

Victory is truly available for those who are in Christ. There is a war raging for our minds, but we are on the winning side, for we are more than conquerors in Christ!

Today, Lord, I tear down all thoughts established in my mind against the knowledge of You. I choose to believe who You are and who I am in Christ.

Beyond the Boundary of God's Design

Every other sin that a man commits is outside his body, but the immoral man [fornicator] sins against his own body (1 Corinthians 6:18).

Sex glands are a God-given part of our autonomic nervous system. Normal sexual functioning is a regular, rhythmic cycle of life. But when Jesus said, "Everyone who looks on a woman to lust for her has committed adultery with her already in his heart" (Matthew 5:28), He was describing something beyond the boundary of God's design for sex. The word for lust is *epithumos*. The prefix *epi* means "to add to," signifying that something is being added to a normal drive. Jesus challenged us not to add onto the God-given sexual drive by polluting our minds with lustful thoughts. The only way to control your sexual drive is to control your thought life.

Sexual lust demands physical expression, and that's where Romans 6 comes into play. We are not to let sin reign in our mortal bodies (verse 12) by using our bodies as instruments of unrighteousness (verse 13). Whenever you use your body wrongly through a sexual offense you give Satan a foothold, and your sexual problem becomes a spiritual problem. A missionary shared with me at the end of a conference that he was finally free after 20 years of bondage to lust. He sought counseling for his problem during his preparation for missionary service and on every furlough, but he never gained lasting victory until he realized that it was a spiritual problem which needed a spiritual solution.

Scripture indicates that sexual sins are in a class by themselves because they require the use of the body. Virtually every person I have counseled regarding a spiritual conflict has confessed some kind of sexual aberration.

Lord, I yield my sexual life to You as an expression of loving worship. I choose today to assume responsibility for my thoughts.

Submit yourselves for the Lord's sake to every human institution (1 Peter 2:13).

The world system in which we were raised says that you are nothing, so compete, scheme, achieve, and strive to get ahead. The Bible teaches that you are something, so be submissive. Here's how Peter said it: "You are a chosen race, a royal priesthood, a holy nation, a people for God's own possession, that you may proclaim the excellencies of Him who has called you out of darkness into His marvelous light; for once you were not a people, but now you are the people of God; you had not received mercy, but now you have received mercy" (1 Peter 2:9,10).

Only after that affirmation of us being the people of God does Peter say, "Submit yourselves for the Lord's sake to every human institution" (verse 13), and "Servants, be submissive to your masters" (verse 18). He even relates it to the home: "In the same way, you wives, be submissive to your own husbands" (1 Peter 3:1).

Submission is not a dirty word; it is a liberating word. We are all under God's protective authority, and we can only be free if we seek it and submit to it. Coming under authority is your protection. Living free is your opportunity to be all that God created you to be.

There are two types of people who will never live up to their potential in Christ: those who can't do what they are told to do and those who won't do anything unless they are told. Don't wait to be told what you are already free to do. Step out in faith and live up to your potential in Christ. You can bring light into a dark world if you will allow Christ to shine through you. You don't need a greater position; bloom where you are planted. Stop waiting for the big opportunity and seize the one you have. Someone in your world of influence desperately needs what Christ can do through you.

Lord, forgive me for my rebellious spirit. Teach me to be submissive and respectful to those in authority over me.

THE PROPER USE OF PROPHECY

For all who are being led by the Spirit of God, these are the sons of God (Romans 8:14).

The Bible says there is only one intermediary between God and man, and that is Jesus. False prophets and teachers often function like intermediaries. When God sent the prophet Nathan to David, it was for the purpose of bringing conviction in order to establish righteousness. In the church age, bringing conviction is a primary ministry of the Holy Spirit.

The proper use of the gift of prophecy would reveal unrighteousness in order to establish people in Christ. Once people are living righteously with the Lord, the Holy Spirit will lead them. False gifts will not consistently promote holiness but often will specify decisions concerning direction in life. That function is the role of the Holy Spirit alone (Romans 8:14).

Some churches encourage their members, including the immature, to come into the fullness of the Spirit with manifestations. I ask, "Why not the fullness of the truth?" It's the fullness of the truth the Holy Spirit has promised to lead us into. I'm deeply concerned for young converts in ministries that push for them to seek total manifestations of the Spirit. Many have not had the time to understand the foundation laid by the apostles and prophets. The church at Corinth had similar problems. They were exhorted by Paul to get back to the basics of faith, hope, and love, and govern very closely the use of tongues and prophecies in public worship because God does everything decently and in order (1 Corinthians 14:40).

A pastor received a letter from a former staff member who was dismissed for moral reasons. The letter contained a prophecy for the pastor's church. I asked, "Why would God give a prophecy for your church through this man?" I suggested that they shouldn't even read it since it would function like a curse. Everything that happened in the church would be evaluated by the prophecy (either to substantiate it or invalidate it).

If a person or church is earnestly seeking the Lord, God will work through the lines of authority He has established in His Word.

Father, protect me from false teaching and guide me into all truth by Your Spirit.

October 6 LOOKING FOR THE GOOD IN YOUR CHILDREN

Let us pursue the things which make for peace and the building up of one another (Romans 14:19).

It is difficult to estimate the damage done by saying to a child:

- You'll never amount to anything.
- You can't do anything right, can you?
- Why can't you be like him?
- You're no son of mine!
- I'm not going to invest any more money in you.
- You're just like all the other kids.

Why not communicate your trust instead and give your child something to live up to? See the potential, not the problems. Looking for the good in your children will bring out the best in them and you.

Imagine how Peter felt when Jesus looked at him and said, "You are Simon the son of John; you shall be called Cephas (which translated means Peter [rock])" (John 1:42). Peter went on about his business of fishing. Sometime later Jesus called him to be a disciple. After Peter's great confession that Jesus was the Christ, Jesus said to him, "You are Peter, and upon this rock I will build My church" (Matthew 16:18). What confidence Jesus expressed in a smelly, uneducated fisherman who would later deny Him three times!

Would you have chosen Peter and expressed confidence in him? Would you have stuck with Peter after he betrayed you? Jesus did, and He is sticking with you, too. He has entrusted you with His message, gifted you to serve, and blessed you with children. Are you trustworthy? Not completely. But His trust sure gives you something to live up to, doesn't it? Your trust in your child can do the same for him.

Loving Father, help me not to focus on my children's limitations and weaknesses but to notice and affirm their potential.

Rejoice with those who rejoice, and weep with those who weep (Romans 12:15).

Early in my pastoral ministry I received one of those middle-of-the-night telephone calls that every pastor dreads: "Pastor, our son has been in an accident. They don't expect him to live. Could you please come to the hospital?"

I arrived at the hospital about one in the morning. I sat with the parents in the waiting room hoping and praying for the best but fearing the worst. About 4:00 A.M. the doctor came out to give us the worst: "We lost him."

We were devastated. I was so tired and emotionally depleted that instead of offering them words of comfort, I just sat there and cried with them. I couldn't think of anything to say. I went home feeling that I had failed the family in their darkest hour.

Soon after the accident the young man's parents moved away. But about five years later they stopped by the church for a visit and took me out to lunch. "Neil, we'll never forget what you did for us when our son died," they said. "We knew you loved us because you cried with us."

One of our challenges in the ministry is in learning how to respond to others when they honestly acknowledge their feelings. I find a very helpful principle in the conversations between Job and his friends. Job said: "The words of one in despair belong to the wind" (Job 6:26). What people say in an emotional crisis is irrelevant, other than to convey how deeply hurt they are. We have a tendency to fixate on words and ignore the hurt. When grief-stricken Mary and Martha greeted Jesus with the news of Lazarus' death, He wept (John 11:35). Paul's words crystallize it for us: "Rejoice with those who rejoice, and weep with those who weep" (Romans 12:15). We are not supposed to instruct those who weep; we are supposed to weep with those who weep.

Lord, teach me to love like You love. Give me the freedom to respond emotionally to those who are in pain.

BEING EMOTIONALLY HONEST

Speaking the truth in love, we are to grow up in all aspects into Him, who is the head, even Christ (Ephesians 4:15).

You can guard your intimate relationships by monitoring how you verbally express your emotions to them. For example, you're having a terrible day at the office, so you call home and say to your wife, "Honey, I'm having a bear of a day. I won't be home until about 6:00 P.M. and I have a meeting at church at 7:00. Could you have dinner ready when I get home?"

When you hit the front door you discover that your wife doesn't have dinner ready as you hoped. "For crying out loud," you blaze at her, "I wanted dinner ready at six o'clock! That's why I called you!" Is your wife really the cause of your emotional outburst? Not really. You had a terrible day and you're tired, hungry, and stressed out. It's not her fault. Anything could have set you off. You could have just as easily kicked the dog.

Rather than level your wife, why not be emotionally honest? When it comes to acknowledging emotions with your inner circle, honesty is the best policy. But be sure to speak the truth in love (Ephesians 4:15).

Another important guideline for acknowledging and expressing your emotions is to know your limitations. Be aware that if you're on the edge emotionally—angry, tense, anxious, depressed—it's not a good time to make decisions on important issues. Your emotions may push you to resolve what you're struggling with, but you may regret your resolution if you push too hard. You're going to say things you'll later regret. Somebody's going to get hurt. You're far better off to recognize your emotional limits and say, "If we keep talking I'm going to get angry. May we continue this discussion at another time?"

Being emotionally honest lets others off the hook. When you honestly convey how you feel, others know you are not primarily mad at them and that the problem is not their fault. They can also love you better by meeting the needs you express.

Heavenly Father, enable me to be an honest and real person today, speaking the truth in love in all my relationships.

Godliness with contentment is great gain
(1 Timothy 6:6 NIV).

The world's concept of happiness is getting what we want. All merchandising is based on this idea. To really be happy, we need a flashier car, a sexier cologne, or any number of items that are better, faster, or easier to use than what we already have. We watch the commercials, read the ads, and pursue all the latest fashions, fads, and fancy doodads. We buy into the lie that we're not really happy until we get what we want.

God's concept of happiness is summed up in the simple proverb: "Happy is the man who wants what he has." As long as you are focusing on what you don't have, you'll be unhappy. But when you begin to appreciate what you already have, you'll begin to experience the joys of life. Paul wrote to Timothy: "Godliness with contentment is great gain. For we brought nothing into the world, and we can take nothing out of it. But if we have food and clothing, we will be content with that" (1 Timothy 6:6-8 NIV).

Actually, you already have everything you need to live a joyful life. You have Christ. You have eternal life. You are loved by a heavenly Father who has promised to supply all your needs. No wonder the Bible repeatedly commands us to be thankful (1 Thessalonians 5:18). If you really want to be happy, learn to be thankful for what you have and not covet what you don't have.

Father, today I want to seek first Your kingdom and Your righteousness, knowing that You will add to my life all that I need.

God's Goal for You

Make every effort to add to your faith goodness; and to goodness, knowledge; and to knowledge, self-control; and to self-control, perseverance; and to perseverance, godliness; and to godliness, brotherly kindness; and to brotherly kindness, love
(2 Peter 1:5-7 NIV).

A good summary of God's goal for you is found in 2 Peter 1:3-10. Your primary role is to diligently adopt God's character goals—goodness, knowledge, self-control, perseverance, godliness, brotherly kindness, and love—and apply them to your life. Focusing on God's goals will lead to ultimate success: success in God's terms. Peter promises that, as these qualities increase in your life through practice, you will be useful and fruitful, and you will never stumble. That's success!

Notice also that there is no mention in this list of talents, intelligence, or gifts which are not equally distributed to all believers. Your worth isn't determined by those God-given traits. Your worth is based on your identity in Christ and your growth in character, both of which are equally applicable to every Christian. Those who are not committed to God's goals for character will never fulfill their primary purpose for being here. According to Peter, they have forgotten who they are. They are out of touch with their true identity and purpose in Christ.

God loves you and will never leave you. You are forgiven by God and are His child. You have established your identity in Christ and live today in union with God. You are becoming increasingly characterized by the fruit of the Spirit. If you really believed everything that is true about you, would you be successful? Would you feel good about yourself? Should you feel good about yourself? Of course! God has not called you to be a failure, so follow His scriptural formula and be the success He has called you to be.

Thank You, Lord, that I can do all things today through Your Son Jesus, who strengthens me.

Totally Alive

Therefore we do not lose heart, but though our outer man is decaying, yet our inner man is being renewed day by day (2 Corinthians 4:16).

You are comprised of at least two major parts: your material self and your immaterial self. The outer man is your physical body, and the inner man is your soul/spirit which includes the ability to think, to feel, to choose (mind, emotions, and will are often collectively identified as the soul), and to relate to God (spirit). Your body is in union with your soul/spirit, and that makes you physically alive. As a Christian, your soul/spirit is in union with God as a result of your conversion, and that makes you spiritually alive.

When God created Adam, he was totally alive—physically and spiritually. But because of Adam's sin and subsequent spiritual death, every person who comes into the world is born physically alive but spiritually dead. Being separated from God, you lacked the presence and wisdom of God in your life, so you learned to live independently of God, centering your interests on yourself. This learned independence from God is characteristic of the flesh or the old nature.

When you were born again, your soul/spirit was united with God and you came alive spiritually, as alive as Adam was in the garden before he sinned. As the epistle of Ephesians repeatedly declares, you are now in Christ, and Christ is in you. Since Christ who is in you is eternal, the spiritual life you have received from Him is eternal. You don't have to wait until you die to get eternal life; you possess it right now!

Our hope does not lie in the preservation of the outer man. It lies in the developing nature of the inner man. Our soul is in union with God and we are being renewed day by day. We will eventually lose our physical life, but not our spiritual life. Our emphasis should be on what is eternal, not on what is temporal.

Lord, I won't lose heart over the setbacks in my life today because my hope lies in my eternal union with You.

Finally, be strong in the Lord, and in the strength of His might (Ephesians 6:10).

The Christian's Magna Charta of protection from Satan and his evil power is Ephesians 6:10-18. The first thing you should see in this passage about receiving God's protection is that our role is not passive. God requires us to be active participants in the spiritual defense that He has provided for us. Notice how often we are commanded to take an active role (emphasis added):

> Finally, *be strong* in the Lord, and in the strength of His might. *Put on* the full armor of God, that you may *be able* to *stand firm* against the schemes of the devil. For our struggle is not against flesh and blood, but against the rulers, against the powers, against the world forces of this darkness, against the spiritual forces of wickedness in the heavenly places. Therefore, *take up* the full armor of God, that you may *be able* to *resist* in the evil day, and having done everything, to *stand firm* (verses 10-13).

You may be wondering, "If my position in Christ is secure and my protection is found in Him, why do I have to get actively involved? Can't I just rest in Him and let Him protect me?" That's like a soldier saying, "Our country is a major military power. We have the most advanced tanks, planes, missiles, and ships in the world. Why should I bother with wearing a helmet, standing guard, or learning how to shoot a gun? It's much more comfortable to stay in camp while the tanks and planes fight the war." When the enemy troops infiltrate, guess who will be one of the first soldiers to get picked off!

God, our "commanding officer," has provided everything we need to secure victory over the evil forces of darkness. But He says, "I've prepared a winning strategy and designed effective weapons. But if you don't do your part by staying on active duty, you're likely to become a casualty." You can't expect God to protect you from demonic influences if you don't take an active part in His prepared strategy.

Lord, I choose to be strong in You today and actively stand in the strength of Your might.

You were dead in your trespasses and sins, in which you formerly walked according to the course of this world, according to the prince of the power of the air (Ephesians 2:1,2).

We live in a world which is under the authority of an evil ruler. Originally God created Adam and his family to rule over creation. But Adam forfeited his position of authority through sin, and Satan became the rebel holder of authority to whom Jesus referred as "the ruler of this world" (John 12:31; 14:30; 16:11). During Jesus' temptation, the devil offered Him "all the kingdoms of the world, and their glory" (Matthew 4:8) in exchange for His worship. Satan's claim that the earth "has been handed over to me, and I give it to whomever I wish" (Luke 4:6) was no lie. He took authority when Adam abdicated the throne of rulership over God's creation at the fall. Satan ruled from Adam until the cross. The death, resurrection, and ascension of Christ secured forever the final authority for Jesus Himself (Matthew 28:18). That authority was extended to all believers in the Great Commission so that we may continue His work of destroying the works of the devil (1 John 3:8).

All of us were born spiritually dead and subject to the ruler that Paul called "the prince of the power of the air" (Ephesians 2:2). But when we received Christ, God "delivered us from the domain of darkness, and transferred us to the kingdom of His beloved Son" (Colossians 1:13). Our citizenship was changed from earth to heaven (Philippians 3:20). Satan is the ruler of this world, but he is no longer *our* ruler, for Christ is our ruler.

But as long as we live on the earth, we are still on Satan's turf. He will try to rule our lives by deceiving us into believing that we still belong to him. As aliens in a foreign, hostile kingdom, we need protection from this evil, deceptive, hurtful tyrant. Christ has not only provided protection from and authority over Satan, but He has equipped us with the Spirit of truth, the indwelling Holy Spirit, to guide us into all truth and help us discern the evil one's schemes (John 16:13).

Heavenly Father, I affirm that You are my Lord today. I choose to be a bond servant to Christ and to no other.

Believing Truth Is a Choice

Without faith it is impossible to please Him, for he who comes to God must believe that He is, and that He is a rewarder of those who seek Him (Hebrews 11:6).

Faith is the biblical response to the truth, and believing truth is a choice. Faith is something you *decide to do*, not something you *feel like doing*. Believing the truth doesn't make it true; it's true, so we believe it. The New Age Movement and the "name it and claim it" adherents are distorting the truth by saying that we create reality through what we believe. We can't *create* reality; we can only *respond to* reality.

Faith must have an object. It's not the idea that you merely "believe" that counts; it's what or who you *believe in* that counts. Everybody believes in something, and everybody walks by faith according to what he or she believes. But if what you believe isn't true, then how you live won't be right. Thus, "Faith comes from hearing, and hearing by the Word of Christ" (Romans 10:17).

Your faith is only as great as your knowledge of the object of your faith. If you have little knowledge of God and His Word, you will have little faith. That's why faith can't be pumped up. Any attempt to live by faith beyond what you absolutely know to be true is presumption. If you only believe what you feel, you will be led through life by one emotional impulse after another. The path of truth begins with the truth of God's Word. Believe the truth and walk by faith according to what you believe, and then your feelings will line up with what you think and how you behave.

We can't decide for ourselves what we would like to believe and then believe it, expecting God to respond to our faith. God is under no obligation to man. There is no way we can cleverly word a prayer in such a way that God must answer it. He is under obligation only to Himself. He will always stay true to Himself and keep His Word and His covenants with mankind. It is not our place to determine what is true or try to persuade God to capitulate to our will. He is the truth. We are to ask according to His will and desire His will above all else.

Lord, I believe in You and Your Word. Help my faith grow as I enlarge my knowledge of You as my faith-object.

When you are praying, do not use meaningless repetition, as the Gentiles do, for they suppose that they will be heard for their many words (Matthew 6:7).

Jesus taught that Christian practices should be consistent with the inward condition of the heart. Holding to external practices which no longer correlate with the heart is repugnant to God. Jesus railed against praying in vain repetitions and putting on a gloomy face while fasting. Consistency cries for an affirmative answer to the question, "Is it real?" The Christian community searches for truth while the world searches for reality. These are large, overlapping circles, but I'm convinced that we must be real in order to be right. Change is most needed when Christians sit stoically week after week reciting endless creeds in utter hypocrisy.

Tragically, those who are coming to a church simply to fulfill a religious obligation are the most resistant to change. They have resisted the need to change under the instruction of the Word and are in a state of carnality. They are not coming to the changeless Christ and saying, "Change me so I may be like You." Time-honored faith and long-established practices often become intertwined in their thinking. When you advocate a different practice, they think you are tinkering with their faith!

Paradoxically, the ones who have a real Christian experience are the ones who are free to change their Christian practices. They are committed to the substance of their faith, not the form. Form always follows function, but people have a tendency to fixate on the form.

Organizational renewal will not bring spiritual renewal. When the spiritual tide is out, every little tadpole wants his own little tide pool to swim in. When the spiritual tide is in, the fish swim in one big ocean where someone is synchronizing every move. When the Holy Spirit is leading, almost any organization will work. But when He isn't, it doesn't matter how good the program and organization is, it won't work.

Lord, I will not rest my faith on my Christian practice, but I will base my faith and practice on the truth of Your Word.

Wives, be subject to your husbands....Husbands, love your wives....Fathers, do not exasperate your children (Colossians 3:18-21).

God works in our lives primarily through committed relationships. Your family is the primary laboratory for your character development. This is precisely the order of Scripture: Establish your identity in Christ, then focus on living out who you are at home. Notice the order in Colossians 3:10-25:

- God's great goal for His children is that we conform to His image: "Put on the new self" (verse 10).
- Our identity is no longer in racial, religious, cultural, or social ties: "There is no distinction...but Christ is all, and in all" (verse 11).
- Character is the focus of development once identity is established: "Put on a heart of compassion, kindness, humility, gentleness and patience" (verse 12).
- Character is developed in the context of relational living: "Bearing with one another, and forgiving each other" (verse 13).
- Love is the highest level of character development: "Beyond all these things put on love" (verse 14).
- The means by which all this is accomplished is Christ in you: "Let the peace of Christ rule in your hearts.... Let the word of Christ richly dwell within you" (verses 15,16).
- The primary setting for character development is the home: "Wives, be subject to your husbands....Husbands, love your wives....Children, be obedient to your parents....Fathers, do not exasperate your children" (verses 18-21).

As a parent, you are not just shaping your child's behavior, you are developing his character. Training a child means discipling him to be Christlike. Don't be a phony at home; your spouse and children will see right through it. You can't model perfection, but you can model growth.

Lord, help me be the spouse and parent You want me to be by remaining committed to be a growing child of God.

The Spirit explicitly says that in later times some will fall away from the faith, paying attention to deceitful spirits and doctrines of demons (1 Timothy 4:1).

A seminary student stopped by my office to tell me he was having difficulty getting to school on time. What should have been a five-minute drive lengthened to 45 minutes because a voice in his mind kept telling him to turn at intersections. Not wanting to disobey what he perceived to be the "still, small voice of God," he was treated to a tour of the city almost every morning.

A pastor's wife, desperately needing the comfort of the Holy Spirit and desiring His leading, passively believed that whatever entered her mind was from God. She soon found herself bound by fear and plagued by condemning thoughts.

These examples underscore the wisdom of John Wesley's words: "Do not hastily ascribe things to God. Do not easily suppose dreams, voices, impressions, visions, or revelations to be from God. They may be from Him. They may be from nature. They may be from the devil. Therefore, do not believe every spirit, but try the spirits, whether they be from God."[1]

In a survey of 1700 professing Christian teenagers, 70 percent admitted to hearing voices, like there was a subconscious self talking to them. I don't believe they are psychotic or paranoid schizophrenic. There is a battle going on for their minds. I have shared with many tormented people that they aren't going crazy but are under spiritual attack. They usually respond, "Praise the Lord, someone understands." It's freeing to know this truth, because if there is a battle going on for our minds, we can win that war.

Lord, today I choose to test the spirits and assume my responsibility to think upon that which is true.

Peace I leave with you; My peace I give to you; not as the world gives, do I give to you (John 14:27).

Peace on earth—that's what everybody wants. But nobody can guarantee external peace because nobody can control other people or circumstances. Nations sign and break peace treaties with frightening regularity. Couples lament that there would be peace in their home "if only he/she would shape up." No one can guarantee peace at home or on the job site. However, we should always strive to be peacemakers. Jesus said, "Blessed are the peacemakers, for they shall be called sons of God" (Matthew 5:9). Paul instructed, "If possible, so far as it depends on you, be at peace with all men" (Romans 12:18).

But let's face it: Peace with others isn't always possible, because peace doesn't just depend on us. Peace on earth is what we want; peace with God is what we have; the peace of God is what we need.

Peace *with* God is something you already have (Romans 5:1). It's not something you strive for; it's something you received when you were born again. The Prince of Peace reconciled you to God by shedding His own blood.

The peace *of* God is something you need to appropriate daily in your inner world in the midst of the storms which rage in the external world (John 14:27). There are a lot of things that can disrupt your external world because you can't control all your circumstances and relationships. But you *can* control the inner world of your thoughts by allowing the peace of Christ to rule in your heart on a daily basis (Colossians 3:15). There may be chaos all around you, but God is bigger than any storm. I keep a little plaque on my desk which reminds me: "Nothing will happen to me today that God and I cannot resolve."

The peace of Christ will rule in your heart when you "let the word of Christ richly dwell within you" (Colossians 3:16). And when you turn to Him in prayer, "the peace of God, which surpasses all comprehension, shall guard your hearts and your minds in Christ Jesus" (Philippians 4:7).

Prince of Peace, rule in my heart today. Give me Your peace and make me a peacemaker in all my relationships.

Do not turn to mediums or spiritists; do not seek them out to be defiled by them (Leviticus 19:31).

Where do mediums and spiritists get their "amazing" information and insights? Many of them are demonic channelers, but much of what is called "spiritism" and "psychic phenomena" is no more than clever illusion. These so-called spiritists give what is referred to as "cold readings." You go to them for advice or direction, and they ask you a few simple, leading questions. Based on the information you give they make general observations which are probably true of most people in your situation. But you're so impressed with the accuracy of their "revelations" that you start tipping them off to all kinds of details which they can fabricate into their "reading." This is not demonic; it's just mental and verbal sleight-of-hand.

But the mediums and spiritists that God warned against in Leviticus and Deuteronomy were not con artists, but people who possessed and passed on knowledge which didn't come through natural channels of perception. These people have opened themselves up to the spirit world and become channels of knowledge from Satan. The charlatan with his phony cold readings is only interested in bilking you of your money. But the false knowledge and direction which comes from Satan through a medium is intended to bilk you of your spiritual vitality and freedom.

There's big money in psychic/con artist operations, and a lot of magicians are raking it in. Many people crave to know something extra about their lives and their future, and they will pay handsomely if they think you can give them the inside information they desire.

When a psychic claims to have contacted the dead, don't believe it. When a psychologist claims to have regressed a client back to a former existence through hypnosis, don't believe it. When a New Age medium purports to channel a person from the past into the present, realize that it is nothing more than a familiar spirit or a fraudulent work of a con artist.

Lord Jesus, You are the way, the truth, and the life. I renounce any power or revelation from any other source than You.

October 20 THE EQUATION FOR WHOLENESS

Those who want to get rich fall into temptation and a snare and many foolish and harmful desires which plunge men into ruin and destruction (1 Timothy 6:9).

In his book *The Sensation of Being Somebody*, Maurice Wagner expresses a false belief in simple equations we tend to accept. He says we mistakenly think that good appearance plus the admiration it brings equals a whole person. Or we feel that star performance plus accomplishments equals a whole person. Or we believe that a certain amount of status plus the recognition we accumulate equals a whole person. Not so. These equations are no more correct than two plus two equals six. Wagner says: "Try as we might by our appearance, performance, or social status to find self-verification for a sense of being somebody, we always come short of satisfaction. Whatever pinnacle of self-identity we achieve soon crumbles under the pressure of hostile rejection or criticism, introspection or guilt, fear or anxiety. We cannot do anything to qualify for the by-product of being loved unconditionally and voluntarily."[1]

If these equations could work for anyone, they would have worked for King Solomon. He was the king of Israel during the greatest years in her history. If a meaningful life is the result of appearance, admiration, performance, accomplishments, status, or recognition, Solomon would have been the most together man who ever lived.

But God also gave the king an extra dose of wisdom to interpret his achievements. What was his commentary on it all? "Meaningless! Meaningless!...Utterly meaningless! Everything is meaningless" (Ecclesiastes 1:2 NIV). Take the advice of the wise king: All the stuff and status you can acquire don't add up to personal wholeness. Millions of people climb those ladders to success, only to discover when they reach the top that they are leaning against the wrong wall! The only identity equation that works in God's kingdom is you plus Christ equals wholeness and meaning.

Heavenly Father, I affirm that nothing in this world can make me more complete than I already am in Christ.

God's Ministry of Darkness

For we who live are constantly being delivered over to death for Jesus' sake, that the life of Jesus also may be manifested in our mortal flesh (2 Corinthians 4:11).

What is the point of troubled times in our lives? What is God trying to do? What is He trying to teach us? Peter wrote, "Beloved, do not be surprised at the fiery ordeal among you, which comes upon you for your testing, as though some strange thing were happening to you; but to the degree that you share the sufferings of Christ, keep on rejoicing; so that also at the revelation of His glory, you may rejoice with exultation" (1 Peter 4:12,13).

In God's ministry of testing, we learn a lot about ourselves. Whatever is left of simplistic advice such as "Read your Bible" or "Just work harder" or "Pray more" gets stripped away. Most people going through testing times would love to resolve the crisis, but they seemingly can't and don't know why.

In God's ministry of darkness we learn compassion. We learn to wait patiently with people. We learn to respond to the emotional needs of people who have lost hope. We weep with those who weep. We don't try to teach or instruct or advise. If God took away every external blessing and reduced our assets to nothing more than meaningful relationships, would that be enough to sustain us? Yes, I believe it would.

Perhaps God brings us to the end of our resources so we can discover the vastness of His. We don't hear many sermons about brokenness in our churches these days, yet in all four Gospels Jesus taught us to deny ourselves, pick up our cross daily, and follow Him. I don't know any painless way to die to ourselves, but I do know that it's necessary and that it's the best possible thing that could ever happen to us.

"No pain, no gain," says the body builder. Isn't that true in the spiritual realm as well (Hebrews 12:11)? Proven character comes from persevering through the tribulations of life (Romans 5:3-5). Every great period of personal growth in my life and ministry has been preceded by a major time of testing.

Lord, I submit to Your testing so I may come to the end of my resources and joyfully discover Yours.

Sing and Make Melody

Be filled with the Spirit, speaking to one another in psalms and hymns and spiritual songs, singing and making melody with your heart to the Lord (Ephesians 5:18,19).

How pathetically unaware we are of the biblical prominence of music in the spiritual realm. It is interesting to note that whenever the evil spirit came upon King Saul, David (the heir apparent to Israel's throne) would play his harp and the evil spirit would depart (1 Samuel 16:23). When Elisha was about to inquire of God, he said, " 'Now bring me a minstrel.' And it came about, when the minstrel played, that the hand of the LORD came upon him" (2 Kings 3:15). During the reign of David, more than 4000 musicians were assigned to sing in the temple night and day (1 Chronicles 9:33; 23:5). It is the mark of Spirit-filled Christians to sing and make melody in their hearts to the Lord and speak to each other in psalms, hymns, and spiritual songs (Ephesians 5:18,19).

On the other side of the truth lies the destructive power of secular music. A former satanic high priest showed me numerous symbols on popular record albums indicating commitment and bondage to Satanism. He told me that about 85 percent of today's heavy metal and punk music groups are "owned" by Satanists. They have unwittingly sold themselves to Satanism in exchange for fame and fortune. Few of these artists actually practice Satanism, but most are hopelessly lost and lead others astray through the godless message in their music.

God created sound and formed our bodies to respond to it. Our ears pick up the sound around us and send a signal to the brain. Some sounds irritate us; others soothe us. There is music that makes you want to march and music that puts you to sleep. Even without lyrics, music with harmony and order can affect the nervous system positively while discord produces a negative effect.

What role does music play in your life? Are you filling your mind and home with psalms, hymns, and spiritual songs? Or are you allowing destructive secular music to rob you of your joy and vitality in the Lord?

You are the God who sings over me, Lord. Thank You for the gift of music and for the songs You give me in the night.

The troubles of my heart are enlarged; bring me out of my distresses (Psalm 25:17).

Unlike our day-to-day emotions which are the product of our day-to-day thought life, emotional baggage from the past is always there. Years of exposure and experience in life have etched grooves in our memory banks which are triggered by current events.

For example, if your kind, loving grandfather was named Bill, you probably have a favorable emotional reaction to other people named Bill. But if the school bully was named Bill, your initial reaction to the Bills in your life is probably negative. If your spouse suggests, "Let's name our first child Bill," you might even react, "Over my dead body!"

I call these long-term emotions, which lurk beneath the surface, *primary emotions*. The intensity of your primary emotions is determined by your previous life history. The more traumatic your experience, the more intense will be your primary emotion. Many of these primary emotions will lie dormant and have very little effect on your life until something comes along to trigger them. Have you ever brought up a topic of conversation which upset someone and sent him storming out of the room? "What set him off?" you wondered. He was "set off" because a bad experience in his past was triggered by your topic. The trigger is any present event which he associates with the past conflict.

Most people try to control their primary emotions by avoiding the people or events which trigger them. But you can't isolate yourself completely from everything which may set off a response. You are bound to see something on TV or hear something in a conversation which will bring to mind your unpleasant experience. You must learn how to resolve previous conflicts or the emotional baggage will accumulate and the past will control your life.

During the next few days we will consider ways to resolve our emotional baggage from the past.

Lord, I don't want to be controlled by past events. Show me how I can resolve these issues so I can walk in freedom today.

Teach me your way, O LORD, and I will walk in your truth; give me an undivided heart (Psalm 86:11 NIV).

You have no control over a primary emotion, developed in the past, when it is triggered. It doesn't do any good to feel guilty about something you have no control over. But you can seek to resolve the past conflict, and you can immediately evaluate the present circumstance to bring it into perspective. For example, suppose you meet a man named Bill. He looks like the Bill who used to beat you up as a child. Even though he's not the same person, your primary emotion initially jumps to a 3 on a scale of 10. But you mentally tell yourself that this is not the same Bill, and you think yourself down to a 2.

You have not only used this process yourself thousands of times, but you have also helped others do it. Someone flies off the handle, so you grab him and tell him to get hold of himself. You are helping that person gain control of himself by making him think. Notice how this works the next time you're watching a football game and tempers explode on the field. One player grabs an enraged teammate and says, "Listen, Meathead, you're going to cost us a 15-yard penalty and perhaps the game if you don't simmer down." The player will see the conflict in perspective and will get himself under control by thinking clearly.

Some Christians assert that the past isn't important. If you're talking about truth, then I would agree. The truth is truth, past, present, and future. But if you are talking about what people are actually experiencing, I would have to disagree. Most of the people who argue that the past isn't important have major unresolved conflicts from the past which they are not allowing to surface. They are attempting to handle themselves by living in denial. Either that or they are extremely fortunate to have a conflict-free past. Those who have had major traumas and have learned to resolve them in Christ know how devastating the past can be to present reality.

Lord, I choose not to live in denial. Give me the grace to look at my past and the courage to face the truth.

Search me, O God, and know my heart; try me and know my anxious thoughts; and see if there be any hurtful way in me, and lead me in the everlasting way (Psalm 139:23,24).

Most people I deal with have had major traumas. Some have been ritualistically abused to such an extent that they have no conscious memory of their experiences. Others constantly avoid anything that will stimulate those memories. All of these people have had their emotions traumatized—and many are stuck there. Unable to process those experiences from the past, they have sought to survive and cope with life through a myriad of defense mechanisms. Some live in denial, others rationalize or try to suppress the pain with food, drugs, or sex.

This is not God's way, however. God does everything in the light. Knowing this, you can always count on God to bring your past conflicts to the surface at the right time so that everything can be brought into the light and dealt with. I have noticed that, when a person's conflict is deeply traumatic, God allows that person to mature to the point where he is able to face the reality of the past. I have prayed with many that God would reveal anything in the past which is keeping them in bondage—and God has answered those prayers. Why don't we pray this way more often in counseling? I'm disappointed at how often the "Wonderful Counselor" is left out of Christian ministry.

I am personally against drug-induced programs or hypnosis that attempt to restore a repressed memory by bypassing the mind of the person involved. Everything I read in Scripture about the mind challenges believers to be mentally active, not passive. Getting ahead of God in the healing process through drugs or hypnosis can throw some into a quagmire of despair they can't escape.

I believe the first step in God's answer for repressed trauma is found in Psalm 139:23,24. God knows about the hidden hurts within you which you may not be able to see. When you ask God to search your heart, He will expose those dark areas of your past and bring them to light at the right time.

Search my heart today, O God, and know my troubled thoughts. Lead me in the everlasting way.

It was for freedom that Christ set us free
(Galatians 5:1).

How does God intend for you to resolve hurtful, controlling past experiences? In two ways, which we shall consider today and tomorrow.

First, you have the privilege of evaluating your past experience in the light of who you are now, as opposed to who you were then. The intensity of the primary emotion was established by how you perceived the event at the time it happened. Remember: Your emotions are a product of how you perceived the event, not the event itself. As a Christian, you are not primarily a product of your past; you are primarily the product of the work of Christ on the cross. The flesh, which represents how you processed those events according to the world and without Christ, remains. But you are able to render it inoperative.

When a present event activates that primary emotion, many people believe what they feel instead of believing what is true. For example, people who have been verbally abused by their parents have a hard time believing they are unconditionally loved by Father God. Their primary emotions argue that they are unlovable to a parent figure. They believe what they feel and their walk is off course. Believing the truth and walking by faith is what sets us free.

Now that you are in Christ, you can look at those events from the perspective of who you are today. Christ is in your life right now desiring to set you free from your past. That is the gospel, the good news that Christ has come to set the captives free. Perceiving those events from the perspective of your new identity in Christ is what starts the process of healing those damaged emotions.

God's good news about our identity is revealed in 2 Corinthians 5:17: "Therefore if any man is in Christ, he is a new creature; the old things passed away; behold, new things have come." This is what you must believe first in order to be set free from your past.

Loving Lord, thank You for making me a new creation in Christ. Help me walk away from anything in my past that is restricting my freedom.

Be kind to one another, tender-hearted, forgiving each other, just as God in Christ also has forgiven you (Ephesians 4:32).

The second step in resolving past conflicts is to forgive those who have offended you. After encouraging Cindy, a rape victim, to deal with the emotional trauma of her rape, I said, "Cindy, you also need to forgive the man who raped you." Cindy's response was typical of many believers who have suffered physical, sexual, or emotional pain at the hands of others: "Why should I forgive him? You don't know how badly he hurt me!"

"He's *still* hurting you, Cindy," I responded. "Forgiveness is how you stop the pain. You don't forgive him for his sake; you do it for your sake."

Why should you forgive those who have hurt you in the past?

First, forgiveness is required by God. As soon as Jesus spoke the amen to His model prayer—which included a petition for God's forgiveness—He commented: "If you forgive men for their transgressions, your heavenly Father will also forgive you. But if you do not forgive men, then your Father will not forgive your transgressions" (Matthew 6:14,15). We must base our relationships with others on the same criteria on which God bases His relationship with us: love, acceptance, and forgiveness (Matthew 18:21-35).

Second, forgiveness is necessary to avoid entrapment by Satan. I have discovered from my counseling that unforgiveness is the number one avenue Satan uses to gain entrance to believers' lives. Paul encouraged mutual forgiveness "in order that no advantage be taken of us by Satan; for we are not ignorant of his schemes" (2 Corinthians 2:11). Unforgiveness is an open invitation to Satan's bondage in our lives.

Third, we are to forgive like Christ forgives in order to keep our hearts from bitterness. Paul wrote: "Let all bitterness and wrath and anger and clamor and slander be put away from you, along with all malice. And be kind to one another, tender-hearted, forgiving each other, just as God in Christ also has forgiven you" (Ephesians 4:31,32).

Your act of forgiveness will set the captive free, then you will realize that the captive was you!

Lord, teach me to forgive others from my heart as You have forgiven me.

Living with Sin's Consequences

Never take your own revenge, beloved, but leave room for the wrath of God, for it is written, "Vengeance is Mine, I will repay," says the Lord (Romans 12:19).

Forgiveness does not mean that you must tolerate sin. Isabel, a young wife and mother attending one of my conferences, told me of her decision to forgive her mother for continually manipulating her for attention. But Isabel tearfully continued, "She is no different. Am I supposed to let her keep ruining my life?"

No, forgiving someone doesn't mean that you must be a doormat to their continual sin. I encouraged Isabel to confront her mother lovingly but firmly, and tell her that she would no longer tolerate destructive manipulation. It's okay to forgive another's past sins and, at the same time, take a stand against future sins. Forgiving is not a co-dependent activity.

Forgiveness does not demand revenge or repayment for offenses suffered. "You mean I'm just supposed to let them off the hook?" you may argue. Yes, you let them off *your* hook realizing that they are not off God's hook. You may feel like exacting justice, but you are not an impartial judge. God is the just Judge who will make everything right (Romans 12:19). Your job is to extend the mercy of forgiveness and leave judgment up to God.

Forgiveness is agreeing to live with the consequences of another person's sin. Suppose that someone in your church says, "I have gossiped about you. Will you forgive me?" You can't retract gossip any easier than you can put toothpaste back into the tube. You're going to live with the gossip this person spread about you no matter how you respond to the gossiper.

We are all living with the consequences of another person's sin: Adam's. The only real choice we have in the matter is to live in the bondage of bitterness or in the freedom of forgiveness.

Heavenly Father, I give up my right to seek revenge or harbor resentment. I want to enjoy the freedom which comes from forgiving others.

THE PROCESS OF FORGIVENESS

Love your enemies, do good to those who hate you, bless those who curse you, pray for those who mistreat you (Luke 6:27,28).

Here are 12 simple steps you can use to walk through the process of forgiving someone who hurt you in the past.

1. Ask the Lord to reveal the names of the persons who offended you and the specific wrongs you suffered.
2. Face the hurt and the hate. If you are going to forgive from your heart, you must let God search the depths of your heart.
3. Acknowledge the significance of the cross. It is the cross of Christ that makes forgiveness legally and morally right.
4. Decide that you will not retaliate by using the information about the offender's sin against them (Luke 6:27-34).
5. Decide to forgive. Forgiveness is a conscious choice to let the other person off the hook and free yourself from the past.
6. Take your list of names to God and pray the following: "I forgive __(name)__ for __(specifically identify every remembered pain)__."
7. Destroy the list. You are now free. Do not tell the offenders what you have done. Your forgiveness is between you and God unless the offenders have asked you for forgiveness.
8. Do not expect that your decision to forgive will result in major changes in the other persons. Instead, pray for them (Matthew 5:44).
9. Try to understand the people you have forgiven. They are victims also.
10. Freedom is a result of forgiveness in you. In time you will be able to think about the people who offended you without feeling hurt or anger.
11. Thank God for the lessons you have learned and the maturity you have gained.
12. When appropriate, accept your part of the blame for the offenses you suffered. Confess your failure to God and to others (1 John 1:9) and realize that if someone has something against you, you must go to that person (Matthew 5:23-26).

Lord, teach me how to love unconditionally and forgive quickly those who hate me, curse me, or mistreat me.

We Are Butterflies

For it is God who is at work in you, both to will and to work for His good pleasure (Philippians 2:13).

We present Jesus as the Messiah who came to die for our sins. We tell people that if they accept Christ they will go to heaven when they die. What's wrong with that? First, it's only half the gospel. Second, it gives the impression that eternal life is something we get when we die. Jesus had to die for sins in order to cure the disease that caused us to die. Then He gave us life, making us new creations in Christ.

Suppose that you are a prostitute. One day you hear that the king has decreed that all prostitutes are forgiven. Since you're a prostitute, that's great news! But would it necessarily change your behavior or your self-perception? Probably not. You may dance in the streets for awhile, but chances are you would continue in your same vocation. You would see yourself as nothing more than a forgiven prostitute.

Now suppose the king not only forgave you, but he made you his bride as well. You're a queen. Would that change your behavior? Of course. Why would you want to live as a prostitute if you were a queen?

The church is the bride of Christ! You are far more likely to promote the kingdom if you are the queen rather than a forgiven prostitute. We are not redeemed caterpillars; we are butterflies. Why would you want to crawl in some false humility when you are called to mount up with wings as eagles?

"I would be filled with pride if I believed that," says the skeptic. You are defeated if you don't believe it! Humility is not putting yourself down when God is trying to build you up. Self-abasement has the appearance of wisdom, but it has no value against fleshly indulgence according to Colossians 2:23. Humility is confidence properly placed. We need to be like Paul and "put no confidence in the flesh" (Philippians 3:3). Let's put our confidence in God: "For it is God who is at work in you, both to will and to work for His good pleasure" (Philippians 2:13).

Lord, thank You for not only forgiving me but also for taking me as Your bride. May this realization shape my walk with You today.

A Very Real Devil

You formerly walked...according to the prince of the power of the air...the spirit that is now working in the sons of disobedience (Ephesians 2:2).

The devil is alive and functioning as the god of this world, and he often disguises his operation as intriguing, harmless fun. The fact that he is enjoying success in the entertainment industry is evident. Popular movies like *Ghostbusters*, *Poltergeist*, and *Field of Dreams* glorify experiences with spirits. Psychics and channelers are frequent guests on talk shows. New Age philosophy is being modeled in Saturday morning cartoons. And on Halloween we dress up our children as witches, goblins, slashers, and monsters. Meanwhile, behind the scenes, Satan is systematically destroying the fabric of our society because he has convinced us that he's just a harmless little man in a red suit carrying a pitchfork.

In 1990, a newspaper in Los Angeles reported that more women consulted mediums and spiritists than professional counselors for personal help and guidance. Isn't it amazing that a gullible public will accept such obvious expressions of the occult! Just change the name of a medium to a channeler and a demon to a spirit guide and suddenly it's acceptable, even sought after. The lure of knowledge and power is deceptive, sucking millions into the abyss and away from divine revelation and the ultimate power that is extended to those who believe (Ephesians 1:19).

The concept of Satan was not manufactured in the twentieth century. Orthodox Christianity has always held the belief in a personal devil (not just an impersonal force). C.S. Lewis wrote: "There is no neutral ground in the universe: every square inch, every split second, is claimed by God and counterclaimed by Satan."[1] A very real devil is intent on spoiling your life. But be assured that in Christ you have the authority to defeat Satan's schemes.

Father God, I will not accept any counterfeit power or knowledge. I determine to know Christ crucified, the power and wisdom of God.

A Change of Beliefs

God, being rich in mercy, because of His great love with which He loved us…made us alive together in Christ (Ephesians 2:4,5).

Twenty-three-year-old Jenny was a pretty Christian young woman with a seemingly pleasant personality. She had loving parents and came from a good church. But she was torn up inside, having never experienced anything but a depressive life. She had bombed out of college and was on the verge of being fired from her job. She had suffered from eating disorders for several years and medical treatment for her problems seemed futile.

I was in the midst of planning an intensive one-month spiritual retreat for some of our seminary students, and somehow I knew that Jenny needed to be there even though she wasn't a seminary student. I invited her and, to my surprise, she agreed to attend.

Shortly after we arrived I sat down with Jenny privately. "I didn't invite you here to change your behavior, Jenny," I said. "Your behavior isn't your problem."

"I've always been told that my behavior *is* my problem," she answered, looking a little surprised at my statement.

"I'm not worried about your behavior. It's your beliefs I'm interested in. I'm praying that you will change your beliefs about God and who you are in Christ. You're not a failure. You are a child of God, no better and no worse than any other person at this retreat. I want you to start believing it, because it's the truth."

For the first time in her life Jenny had been affirmed as the person of value to God that she was. And she began to believe it. During the next 30 days, a miraculous transformation took place in Jenny. Her circumstances didn't change, but she did.

Too often we try to change our behavior without changing our beliefs. It doesn't work that way. We must change our beliefs before we can make significant changes in our behavior. Nothing will change your behavior more than a true knowledge of God and who you are as His child.

Father in heaven, what a liberating privilege it is to call You my Father and realize that I am Your child.

TAKING EVERY THOUGHT CAPTIVE

We are destroying speculations and every lofty thing raised up against the knowledge of God, and we are taking every thought captive to the obedience of Christ (2 Corinthians 10:5).

Satan's perpetual aim is to infiltrate your thoughts with his thoughts and to promote his lie in the face of God's truth. If Satan can control your thoughts, he can control your behavior. He can introduce his thoughts, tempting you to act independently of God, as if they were your own thoughts or even God's thoughts, as he did with David (1 Chronicles 21:1), Judas (John 13:2), and Ananias (Acts 5:3).

One of my students exemplified how deceptive Satan's thoughts can be. Jay came into my office one day and said, "Dr. Anderson, I'm in trouble. When I sit down to study I get prickly sensations all over my body, my arms involuntarily raise, my vision gets blurry, and I can't concentrate."

"Tell me about your walk with God," I probed.

"I have a very close walk with God. When I leave school at noon each day, I ask God where He wants me to go for lunch. If I hear a thought that says Burger King, I go to Burger King. Then I ask Him what He wants me to eat. If the thought comes to order a Whopper, I order a Whopper."

"What about your church attendance?" I continued.

"I go every Sunday wherever God tells me to go." For the last three Sundays "God" told him to go to a Mormon church!

Jay sincerely wanted to do what God wanted him to do. But he was passively paying attention to a deceiving spirit (1 Timothy 4:1) instead of "taking every thought captive to the obedience of Christ" (2 Corinthians 10:5). In so doing he had opened himself up to Satan's activity in his life, resulting in the sabotage of his theological studies.

We must assume our responsibility for choosing the truth. We can't always tell whether the thought comes from the TV set, our memory bank, our imagination, or a deceiving spirit. Regardless of where a thought originates, examine it in the light of God's Word and choose the truth.

Lord, help me today as I assume my responsibility to take every thought captive to the obedience of Christ.

Our Only Valid Weapon

If you abide in My word, then you are truly disciples of Mine; and you shall know the truth, and the truth shall make you free (John 8:31,32).

We are more vulnerable to Satan's deception than to any of his other schemes. Why? Because when he tempts you or accuses you, you know it, but when he deceives you, you don't know it. If he can enter your church, your home, or your mind undetected and get you to believe a lie, he can control your life, home, and ministry. Sad to say, he is doing just that across our land by deceiving many people.

You cannot overcome Satan's deception by human reasoning; you can only do it by God's revelation. Jesus said, "If you abide in My word, then you are truly disciples of Mine; and you shall know the truth, and the truth shall make you free" (John 8:31,32). Jesus prayed, "Sanctify them in the truth; Thy word is truth" (John 17:17). It is critical that when you put on the armor of God you start with the belt of truth (Ephesians 6:14). The light of truth is the only valid weapon against the darkness of deception.

Here's an encouraging letter from a young woman who was trapped in deception until Jesus Christ set her free as we walked through the steps to freedom:

> Dear Dr. Anderson:
>
> I will always remember the day I came to you for counsel and prayer. Ever since that day I have felt such freedom. There are no more voices or feelings of heaviness in my brain. I'm even enjoying a physical sense of release. Satan has returned many times trying to clobber me with those old thoughts, but his hold on me has been broken.
>
> I'll never forget what you told me. You said that those negative thoughts about God and myself were lies from Satan. You said I have the power through Jesus Christ to rebuke Satan and get rid of the evil thoughts. It has taken me awhile to really believe that with all my heart, but lately I've decided to fight back—and it works!

Today, Lord, I purpose not to lean on my own understanding or put more confidence in my reasoning than in Your revelation.

The Lord's bond-servant must not be quarrelsome, but be kind to all, able to teach, patient when wronged, with gentleness correcting those who are in opposition, if perhaps God may grant them repentance leading to the knowledge of the truth, and they may come to their senses and escape from the snare of the devil, having been held captive by him to do his will (2 Timothy 2:24-26).

The main qualification for helping others find freedom is not an unusual giftedness or calling. It is godly character and the ability to teach. The instructions in the epistles for helping others find freedom in Christ are best summarized in 2 Timothy 2:24-26. It requires that the Lord's bond servant be mature in character as expressed by love for people and evidenced by the fruit of the Spirit. It is also important that we are able to communicate the truth so the captive can be set free.

The classic picture of deliverance is to bring in an expert who will call up the demon, determine its name and rank, then cast it out. This would make the deliverer the expert who gets his information from the demon. I believe there is a better way. I believe the deliverer is Christ. We don't have to send for Him; He already came.

As the Lord's bond servants, we shouldn't believe anything a demon says. We must seek to get our information from the Holy Spirit who will lead us into all truth.

We can't assume responsibility for someone else, but we can serve as the Lord's instrument to effect their freedom. It is every individual's responsibility to resist the devil, put on the armor of God, confess, forgive, renounce sin, and take every thought captive to the obedience of Christ. But according to 2 Timothy 2:24-26, by the grace of God we can help them.

Furthermore, this passage requires that we be absolutely dependent on God, because He alone can grant repentance and set the captive free. I always start any attempt at helping others by declaring my total dependence on God my Father.

Lord, make me Your bond servant that I may help others find their freedom in Christ.

I thank Christ Jesus our Lord, who has strengthened me, because He considered me faithful, putting me into service (1 Timothy 1:12).

When D.L. Moody found his life in Christ, he looked for some opportunities to teach at a church, but no one wanted to use the uneducated man. He started his own Bible study in a shoe store, and it wasn't long before kids were coming out of the woodwork. People couldn't help but notice him because he was bearing fruit, and few have left such an imprint as his upon the world.

Paul said, "I thank Christ Jesus our Lord, who has strengthened me, because He considered me faithful, putting me into service" (1 Timothy 1:12). Show yourself faithful by exploiting the opportunities around you. The needs of people are everywhere, so what are you waiting for?

A man in my church often expressed his frustration with his job. For 20 years he'd been working as a construction worker, and he hated it! Frustrated with his career, he wondered why God wouldn't call him out of there.

I asked him if he had ever expressed dissatisfaction about his job with his fellow employees who weren't Christians. He said, "Oh, sure. I complain right along with the rest of them."

I continued, "What do you suppose that does to your witness?" He was a little startled by my question. I added, "Do you realize that God has you exactly where He wants you? When you assume your responsibility to be the person God wants you to be as a construction worker, He may open a new door for you."

The Holy Spirit must have brought conviction because this man became a missionary at work. He displayed concern for the needs of his coworkers and their families and soon had a series of witnessing experiences to share. Within six months an opportunity arose and he left construction work. And all because he started to bloom where he was planted.

Heavenly Father, help me see the needs of my coworkers, friends, and family, and enable me to be Your ambassador to them.

By faith we understand that the worlds were prepared by the word of God, so that what is seen was not made out of the things which are visible (Hebrews 11:3).

Hope is not wishful thinking. Hope is the present assurance of some future good: "Now faith is the assurance of things hoped for, the conviction of things not seen" (Hebrews 11:1). Biblical faith is not a preference for what we would like to see, but a conviction that what is unseen is real. Biblical faith enables us to see the reality of the spiritual world we presently live in, with the assurance of heaven. Only with that kind of faith can we say with Paul, "For I consider that the sufferings of this present time are not worthy to be compared with the glory that is to be revealed to us" (Romans 8:18).

According to Scripture, the invisible world is more real than the visible world (Hebrews 11:3). The ultimate reality is spiritual, not physical. God is a spirit. Every physical thing we see is only temporal and passing away (2 Corinthians 4:18).

When Jesus appeared to the frightened band of disciples after His resurrection, He showed them both His hands and His side. Later the disciples informed Thomas of what they had seen, but he responded, "Unless I shall see in His hands the imprint of the nails, and put my finger into the place of the nails, and put my hand into His side, I will not believe" (John 20:25). Thomas was determined to walk by sight, not by faith. The only thing that was real to Thomas was what he could see.

Eight days later Jesus appeared again and said to Thomas, "Reach here your finger, and see My hands; and reach here your hand, and put it into My side; and be not unbelieving, but believing" (John 20:27). Thomas responded, "My Lord and my God!" (verse 28). Then Jesus blessed those of us who believe without seeing: "Blessed are they who did not see, and yet believed" (verse 29).

The object of our faith is not the tangible reality of this physical world. The object of our faith is the invisible God and His revealed Word.

Lord, You are the ultimate reality. I choose to evaluate everything in my life in the light of Your Word.

Be angry, and yet do not sin; do not let the sun go down on your anger, and do not give the devil an opportunity (Ephesians 4:26,27).

Suppose you possessed the means to give your child the best. What kind of parent would you be? What would be your role in determining what your child should be and do? Maybe you would be tempted to respond like the parents of a girl named Jill.

Jill's parents were high-tech professionals and nominal Christians. Jill had always been given every opportunity to be the best. Driven by her parents to perfection, her grades were tops. Her parents wanted her to attend their alma mater and join her mother's sorority, but she wanted to attend a Christian college.

When Jill came to my office she was anorexic, struggling with her thought life, and had been cutting herself. In making a list of the people she needed to forgive, her parents were right at the top. Her tears began slowly at first. "Lord, I forgive my father for never even considering what I would like to do with my life." Then the floodgates opened, and she was able to find her freedom in Christ. The voices stopped, the cutting stopped, and she was at peace in her mind. The spiritual component of her problem was resolved.

Soon the relational component was also resolved. Guided by her counselor, Jill reached a compromise with her parents. She attended their alma mater for one year, then transferred to a Christian school with their blessing.

I'm not saying that misguided, overcontrolling parents cause their children to have spiritual problems. But parents who don't learn how to speak the truth in love and express their anger without sinning may give the devil an opportunity in their family (Ephesians 4:25-27). And if you and your children don't learn how to bear with each other and forgive one another in the close confinement of a family relationship, you may give Satan an advantage (Colossians 3:13; 2 Corinthians 2:10,11). And if you don't humble yourself, cast your potential anxieties on the Lord, and adopt an alert and sober spirit, you may be devoured by your adversary, the devil (1 Peter 5:8).

Lord, help me be genuine and honest before my family, enabling them to be what You created them to be.

Owe nothing to anyone except to love one another; for he who loves his neighbor has fulfilled the law (Romans 13:8).

Many people demonstrate that their need to win when trying to resolve conflicts with others is greater than their regard for relationships. Why is winning so important to us? Why must we always be right? The person who is driven to win, to be right, or to be first is insecure. Insecure people are driven to perform.

Security comes from relationships, not achievements. A secure person is a person who is comfortable with himself and others. It is easy to communicate with a secure person, but you often end up clashing with a driven person. Would you rather be a lover or an achiever? Which would you prefer your spouse, children, coworkers, and friends to be?

Relationships are more important than achievements to God. Jesus declared that the two greatest commandments are to love God and love people (Matthew 22:36-40). The purpose of the Word of God is to govern our relationships with God and man. If our achievements in life don't enhance our relationships with God, our spouse and children, and others, then we are not fulfilling God's commandments.

Is there ever a time when we need to assert ourselves in conflicts? Yes, we need to stand our ground on moral issues. But we never have the right to violate the fruit of the Spirit in doing so. If what you do can't be done in love and self-control, then maybe it's better left undone. And remember: Your authority does not increase with the volume of your voice. When you resort to shouting in conflict you are reacting in the flesh. You have lost control of the only person you can control: yourself.

Anyone who accomplishes something at the expense of people or elevates tasks over relationships will sow the seeds of their own destruction and the destruction of those around them. Governments, institutions, and organizations exist for the cause and needs of people. The Sabbath was made for man, not man for the Sabbath. How easy it is to turn our priorities upside down.

Gracious Lord, help me today to love people and use things, and not to love things and use people.

But we all...are being transformed into the same image from glory to glory, just as from the Lord, the Spirit (2 Corinthians 3:18).

When you begin to align your goals with God's goals and your desires with God's desires, you will rid your life of a lot of anger, anxiety, and depression. The homemaker who wants a happy, harmonious family is expressing a godly desire, but she cannot guarantee that it will happen. So she'd better not base her identity and sense of worth on it or she will be a basket case of anger or resentment toward her sometimes less-than-harmonious family.

Instead she could decide, "I'm going to be the wife and mother God wants me to be." That's a great goal! Is it impossible or uncertain? No, because it's also God's goal for her, and nothing is impossible with God. Who can block her goal? She's the only one who can. As long as she cooperates with God's goal for her, her success is assured.

"But what if my husband has a mid-life crisis or my kids rebel?" she may object. Problems like that aren't blocking her goal of being the wife and mother God wants her to be, but they will put her goal to a serious test. If her husband ever needs a godly wife, and if her children ever need a godly mother, it's in times of trouble. Family difficulties are merely new opportunities for her to fulfill her goal of being the woman God wants her to be.

The pastor whose worth is based on his goal to win his community for Christ, have the best youth ministry in town, or increase giving to missions by 50 percent is headed for a fall. These are worthwhile desires, but they are poor goals by which to determine his worth because they can be blocked by people or circumstances. Rather he could say, "I'm going to be the pastor God wants me to be." That's a great goal because nothing can block him from achieving it.

God's basic goal for your life is character development: becoming the person God wants you to be. Because it's a godly goal, no one can block it except you.

Lord, I want to be the person You called me to be today. Thank You that by Your grace I can be that person.

The goal of our instruction is love from a pure heart and a good conscience and a sincere faith (1 Timothy 1:5).

Perhaps the greatest service performed by trials and tribulations in our lives is to reveal wrong goals. It's during these times of pressure that your emotions raise their warning flags signaling blocked goals, uncertain goals, and impossible goals which are based on our desires instead of God's goal of proven character.

People say, "My marriage is hopeless," then "solve" the problem by changing partners. But if you think your first marriage is hopeless, be aware that second marriages are failing at a far higher rate. Others feel their jobs are hopeless. So they change jobs, only to discover that the new job is just as hopeless. People tend to look for quick-fix solutions to difficult situations. But God's plan is for you to hang in there and grow up.

Is there an easier way to being God's person than through enduring tribulations? Believe me: I've been looking for one. But I must honestly say that it has been the dark, difficult times of testing in my life which have brought me to where I am today. I thank God for the occasional mountaintop experiences, but the fertile soil for growth is always down in the valleys of tribulation, not on the mountaintops. Paul says, "The goal of our instruction is love" (1 Timothy 1:5). Notice that if you make that your goal then the fruit of the Spirit is love, joy (instead of depression), peace (instead of anxiety), and patience (instead of anger) (Galatians 5:22,23).

How would you give hope to a woman whose husband just left? "Oh, we will win him back," you say. Great desire; wrong goal. Trying to manipulate that husband or the circumstance is probably why he left in the first place. It is better to say to the woman, "If you haven't committed yourself to be the wife and mother God has called you to be, would you now?" According to Romans 5:3-5, our hope lies in the proven character that comes through perseverance.

Father, enable me today to persevere through the trials of life and thereby develop strong character and hope.

The Way of Escape

No temptation has overtaken you but such as is common to man; and God is faithful, who will not allow you to be tempted beyond what you are able, but with the temptation will provide the way of escape also, that you may be able to endure it (1 Corinthians 10:13).

First Corinthians 10:13 is the shining good news in the midst of our fears and concerns about temptation. Where is the escape hatch that Paul is talking about here? In the same place temptation is introduced: in your mind. Every temptation is first a thought introduced to your mind by your own carnality or by the tempter himself. If you ruminate on that thought and consider it an option, you will eventually act on it, and that's sin. The first step for escaping temptation is to apprehend every thought as soon as it steps through the doorway of your mind.

Once you have halted a penetrating thought, the next step is to evaluate it on the basis of Paul's eightfold criterion for what we should think about in Philippians 4:8. Ask yourself, "Does this thought line up with God's truth? Is it suggesting that I do something honorable? Right? Pure? If this thought becomes action, will the outcome be lovely and contribute to excellence in my life? Will other believers approve of my actions? Is it something for which I can praise God?" If the answer to any of those questions is no, dismiss that thought immediately. Don't have anything more to do with it. If it keeps coming back, keep saying no. When you learn to respond to tempting thoughts by stopping them at the door of your mind, evaluating them on the basis of God's Word, and dismissing those which fail the test, you have found the way of escape that God's Word promises.

In contrast, if a thought enters your mind and it passes the Philippians 4:8 test of truth, honor, righteousness, etc., "let your mind dwell on these things" (verse 8) and "practice these things" (verse 9). "And the God of peace shall be with you" (verse 9), which is an infinitely better result than the pain and turmoil which follows when we yield to tempting thoughts and become involved in sinful behavior.

Thank You, Lord, for providing a way of escape from all my temptations. I am determined to win the battle for my mind.

One who looks intently at the perfect law...not having become a forgetful hearer but an effectual doer, this man shall be blessed in what he does (James 1:25).

While God has given us an infallible guide to life—His Word—the truth He wants us to follow for our freedom can be obscured by our bias and selfish indulgence. In the twentieth-century Western church I see at least five major hindrances which affect our understanding and application of the Word of God.

First, *there is a tendency to make doctrine an end in itself.* Christian maturity is not understanding the principles of the Bible; Christian maturity is character. If what we come to accept as truth doesn't affect our love for God and man, something is radically wrong (1 Timothy 1:5). "Knowledge makes arrogant, but love edifies" (1 Corinthians 8:1).

Second, *we can learn a lot about God from Scripture and not know Him at all.* Before his conversion, Paul knew the law, but he didn't recognize God in Christ when he saw Him. We're not asked to fall in love with doctrine. We're asked to fall in love with the Lord Jesus Christ.

Third, *we often encourage memorizing Scripture instead of thinking scripturally.* Our model should be, "The Word became flesh, and dwelt among us" (John 1:14). We are to incarnate the Word of God. We are to have our lives transformed by it, and our minds renewed by it.

Fourth, *we often hear the Word and then don't do it.* The will of God is thwarted by educating people beyond their obedience. Jesus taught: "If you know these things, you are blessed if you do them" (John 13:17).

Fifth, like the Pharisees, *we tend to neglect the commandment of God and hold to the traditions of men* (Mark 7:8). I believe this is one of the most serious problems affecting our churches today. Many seminary graduates are called as "new wine" (zealous to serve God according to the truth of His Word) to "old wineskin" churches (rooted in the traditions of men), and the results are disastrous for both.

Lord, renew me today by Your Word. I want to grow in my love for You, not just the truth about You.

In Him you have been made complete
(Colossians 2:10).

Colossians 2:6-10 reveals three levels in our relationship with Christ. If we are going to present every believer complete in Christ (Colossians 1:28), our discipleship must acknowledge the following order.

Level One ensures that our *identity* is firmly rooted *in Him*. This entails:

- Leading individuals to Christ and directing them to their scriptural assurance of salvation;
- Guiding them to a true knowledge of God and who they are in Christ;
- Helping them see the ways they are still playing God or rebelling against God's authority;
- Breaking down their defenses against rejection by accepting and affirming them.

Level Two deals with the issue of *maturity* in Christ, which Paul alluded to as "being built up in Him" (verse 7). The second level of discipleship is to accept God's goal of sanctification and grow in Christlikeness. This entails:

- Helping people learn to walk by the Spirit and by faith;
- Helping them get off the emotional roller coaster by focusing their thoughts on God instead of their circumstances;
- Encouraging them to develop self-control;
- Challenging them to resolve personal problems by forgiving others and seeking forgiveness.

Level Three reflects the issue of our daily *walk* in Christ, which is possible when our identity and maturity are in Christ. The third level of discipleship is to help believers live responsibly in Christ in their homes, on their jobs, and in society. The effective Christian walk involves the proper exercise of spiritual gifts, talents, and intellect in serving others and being a positive witness in the world.

Lord, I desire to be firmly rooted and built up in Christ today so I may walk in Him.

From Generation to Generation

I, the LORD your God, am a jealous God, visiting the iniquity of the fathers on the children, on the third and fourth generations of those who hate Me (Exodus 20:5).

The fact that demonic strongholds can be passed on from one generation to the next is well-attested by those who counsel the afflicted. This is not to deny that many problems are transmitted genetically or acquired from an immoral atmosphere. All three conditions can predispose an individual to a particular sin.

When you tear down a satanic stronghold which has been established in your family, expect resistance. One of my seminary students sat stunned after praying through this issue. "I can't believe it," he exclaimed. "I had to hang onto my chair to keep from running out of the room during that last prayer."

"What's your family heritage?" I asked.

"My mother is a psychic, totally into New Age!"

The devil doesn't want to give up his territory and will try to interrupt you when you take authority over him.

A very mature and responsible couple approached me at a couples' retreat and expressed their frustration for not being able to resolve their conflicts. I learned that the woman's mother was into Christian Science and had expressed at her birth, "This is not my child!" I led this dear woman in renouncing any familiar spirits passed on intergenerationally. The change in her life was remarkable as she claimed her position in Christ.

If you suspect that a satanic stronghold was established in your family, pray the following prayer:

Lord, I ask You to point out any satanic strongholds that may have been established in my family. Give me Your courage to stand up to the resistance I will encounter.

Discipline your son while there is hope (Proverbs 19:18).

An average child begins to struggle with his identity and seek his independence as he approaches the age of 12. The permissive parent starts to panic when the child assumes his own identity and starts pulling away. Fearing the worst, the parent becomes authoritarian by tightening the screws of discipline and restricting the child's activities. A power struggle ensues with predictable results. The child bolts, and the parent calls for advice.

The problem of the rebellious, stubborn, disobedient child was easily resolved in the Old Testament: The child was stoned by the men of the city (Deuteronomy 21:18-21). Sometimes we wish discipline were that simple! Yet this passage helps us understand that even decent parents who try to be good disciplinarians sometimes have stubborn and rebellious children. Why? Because you aren't the only influence in your child's life. And by the time he enters school you may no longer even be the predominant influence. During the formative years from birth to five, you have your greatest influence. Your most important task during that period (especially around ages two and three) is to break the child's will without breaking his spirit. It is then that you must establish boundaries of behavior that are progressively expanded until the child is on his own.

As parents, we must help our children establish their relationship with God so they know what it means to be a child of God. Once they go off to school, you can't go with them, but God can and does. If we don't help them establish their identity in Christ, they will establish their identity in the world. If we don't give them an eternal purpose and meaning in life, they will establish a temporal purpose and meaning.

Heavenly Father, guard my children from the conflicting messages and compromising values being thrown at them in the world today.

Let Us make man in Our image, according to Our likeness; and let them rule over the fish of the sea and over the birds of the sky and over the cattle and over all the earth, and over every creeping thing that creeps on the earth (Genesis 1:26).

In the original creation, Adam didn't search for significance; he was significant. He was given rule over all the other creatures God created (Genesis 1:26,27). God created Adam and gave him a divine purpose for being here: to rule over all His creatures. Was Satan on the scene at creation? Yes. Was he the god of this world at that time? Not at all. Who had the dominion in the garden? Under the authority of God, Adam did, that is until Satan usurped his dominion when Adam and Eve fell. That's when Satan became the god of this world.

Do you realize that the significant dominion Adam exercised before the Fall has been restored to you as a Christian? That's part of your inheritance in Christ. Satan has no authority over you, even though he will try to deceive you into believing that he has. Because of your position in Christ, you have authority over him. You are seated with Christ in the heavenlies (Ephesians 2:6).

First John 3:8 says, "The Son of God appeared for this purpose, that He might destroy the works of the devil." The whole plan of God is to restore fallen humanity and establish the kingdom of God where Satan now reigns. This work of God is not just for our personal victory but for all of creation. "For the anxious longing of the creation waits eagerly for the revealing of the sons of God. For the creation was subjected to futility, not of its own will, but because of Him who subjected it, in hope that the creation itself will also be set free from its slavery to corruption into the freedom of the glory of the children of God" (Romans 8:19-21).

Thank You, Lord, that I am part of Your redemptive plan. Show me my responsibility so I may live a life of purpose.

My God shall supply all your needs according to His riches in glory in Christ Jesus (Philippians 4:19).

Not only was Adam given a significant, authoritative role at creation, he also enjoyed a sense of safety and security. All his needs were provided for (Genesis 1:29). Adam was completely cared for in the garden. He had plenty to eat, and there was plenty for the animals. He could eat of the tree of life and live forever in God's presence. He lacked nothing.

When Adam sinned, he lost that sense of safety and security. Before, he was naked and unashamed. After, he wanted to hide from God and cover up. The first emotion expressed by fallen humanity was fear.

Safety and security is another facet of our inheritance in Christ. We have the riches of His kingdom at our disposal and His promise to supply all our needs.

Adam and Eve also experienced a sense of belonging in that perfect garden. Adam apparently enjoyed intimate, one-on-one communion with God before Eve was created. Then God said it was not good for man to be alone (Genesis 2:18). So He gave Eve to Adam—and Adam to Eve—to enrich his experience of belonging.

Before the Fall, Adam and Eve had a sense of belonging. But after the Fall they felt rejected, experiencing a need to belong. It is one of our greatest needs today. Notice that what were attributes before the Fall became needs after the Fall.

I believe that a true sense of belonging today comes not only from knowing that we belong to God, but also from belonging to each other. When God created Eve He established human community. It's not good for us to be alone. Aloneness can lead to loneliness. God's preventative for loneliness is intimacy—meaningful, open, sharing relationships with one another. In Christ we have the capacity for the fulfilling sense of belonging which comes from intimate fellowship with God and with other believers.

Lord, thank You that all my needs for safety, security, and belonging are fully met in You.

They sacrificed to demons who were not God, to gods whom they have not known, new gods who came lately, whom your fathers did not dread. You neglected the Rock who begot you, and forgot the God who gave you birth (Deuteronomy 32:17,18).

The New Age Movement cloaks the occult in the description of New Age enlightenment: "You don't need God; you *are* God. You don't need to repent of your sins and depend on God to save you. Sin isn't a problem; you just need to turn off your mind and tune in to the great cosmic oneness through harmonic convergence." The New Age pitch is the oldest lie of Satan: "You will be like God" (Genesis 3:5).

This thirst for knowledge and power has lured a fallen humanity to seek guidance from mediums and spiritists, and from such occultic practices as fortunetelling, tarot cards, palm-reading, Ouija boards, astrology, magic charming, and automatic writing. People all around us are ignoring the God who loves them and wants to guide their lives, and are instead seeking light and peace in the kingdom of darkness. Peace can only be found in the Prince of Peace, not in the prince of darkness.

Don't be carried away by the prospect of knowledge and power which is luring so many people in our culture today away from God. People such as the devotees of Simon in Acts 8:9,10 will continue to be astonished by those who practice New Age sorcery. Others, such as the customers of the demon-possessed slave girl in Acts 16:16-18, will contribute to the profit of those who exercise a spirit of divination. As in these examples from the early church, those who seek knowledge and power from the dark side will greatly interfere with the work of God, deceiving many by the counterfeit forces they employ. Other people will thirst after power to such an extent that they will sacrifice to the "goat demons" (Leviticus 17:7) and even sacrifice their own children to demons (Psalm 106:36-38).

Let the words of Deuteronomy 32:17,18 sober us to the reality that even believers are vulnerable to being lured away from the knowledge and power of God by our enemy.

Lord, I refuse to participate with the powers of darkness. You are my life and the light of my world.

For by grace you have been saved through faith; and that not of yourselves, it is the gift of God; not as a result of works, that no one should boast (Ephesians 2:8,9).

After Jesus claimed to be sent by God, some were seeking to seize Him, having come to the conclusion that He was not a good man. But others did believe in Him, "and they were saying, 'When the Christ shall come, He will not perform more signs than those which this man has, will He?' " (John 7:31). All the evidence was there. Some chose to believe; others chose not to. People do the same today. Faith is a choice. We choose to believe or not believe.

Faith is the operating principle of life. It is the means by which we relate to God and live our lives in freedom. Notice the variety of ways stated in Scripture by which faith affects our lives.

First, we are saved by faith (Ephesians 2:8,9).

Second, we "walk by faith, not by sight" (2 Corinthians 5:7).

Third, being found faithful is a prerequisite for ministry: "I thank Christ Jesus our Lord, who has strengthened me, because He considered me faithful, putting me into service" (1 Timothy 1:12). Paul then adds, "And the things which you have heard from me in the presence of many witnesses, these entrust to faithful men, who will be able to teach others also" (2 Timothy 2:2). This is more than being reliable, since a person could be counted on to follow through on an assignment and not be a believer. The added ingredient in faithful people is that they know the truth and can be counted on to be reliable.

Fourth, the quality of any relationship is determined by faith or trust: "Many a man proclaims his own loyalty, but who can find a trustworthy man?" (Proverbs 20:6). The words *faith*, *trust*, and *believe* are all the same word (*pistis*) in the original language. The man who has faith believes in something. The one who believes also trusts, or he doesn't truly believe. There is no concept that looms larger in life than faith, because what we believe determines how we live.

Lord, I affirm that I cannot please You without faith. I choose today to believe in You and trust in Your name.

By this all men will know that you are My disciples if you have love for one another (John 13:35).

Signs and wonders validated the ministry of Jesus and the apostles. After quoting from the prophet Joel and demonstrating that the outpouring of the Spirit at Pentecost was biblical, Peter preached about Jesus of Nazareth as "a man attested to you by God with miracles and wonders and signs which God performed through Him in your midst" (Acts 2:22). Of the apostles, Paul said, "The signs of a true apostle were performed among you with all perseverance, by signs and wonders and miracles" (2 Corinthians 12:12).

However, signs and wonders would also accompany false teachers and false prophets (Matthew 7:21-23; 2 Peter 2:1-22). In fact, biblical references to signs and wonders in the last days are nearly all credited to false teachers, false prophets, and false Christs (Matthew 24:11,24). The false prophet in the tribulation "deceives those who dwell on the earth because of the signs which it was given him to perform" (Revelation 13:14).

Jesus is no longer with us in the flesh, and there are no more apostles. Jesus identified the sign of a disciple as markedly different: "By this all men will know that you are My disciples, if you have love for one another" (John 13:35).

Does this mean that signs and wonders have ceased? I certainly don't want to be identified with an evil generation that seeks only after a sign, but I also don't want to be associated with the powerless, anti-supernaturalism evidenced in Western rationalism. Both the power of God and the wisdom of God are expressed in Christ. Paul said, "For indeed Jews ask for signs, and Greeks search for wisdom; but we preach Christ crucified, to Jews a stumbling block, and to Gentiles foolishness, but to those who are the called, both Jews and Greeks, Christ the power of God and the wisdom of God" (1 Corinthians 1:22-24).

Lord, reveal to me the true source of my spiritual experiences. If they are not from You, I renounce them and command Satan to leave my presence.

Then again He laid His hands upon his eyes; and he looked intently and was restored, and began to see everything clearly (Mark 8:25).

One of the greatest personal crises I have faced in the ministry revolved around the issue of forgiveness and a board member. I struggled relating to this man, and I knew that I couldn't continue on the way things were. So I decided to resign my pastorate.

The week before I was going to read my resignation to the congregation, I got sick. I was flat on my back with a temperature of 103.5 and I totally lost my voice. It was easy to recognize that God wasn't pleased with my decision. I began reading the Gospels and came upon Mark 8:22-26 where Jesus healed the blind man. I noticed that, after Jesus' first touch, the man said, "I see men...like trees" (verse 24). I suddenly realized that I saw this man like that: a big tree, an obstacle blocking my path.

Then Jesus touched the blind man again and he began to see people clearly, not as trees. I got the message. "Lord, I don't love this man. I know You do, and I want to. But You will have to touch me like You did that blind man. Lord, I need You to touch me so I can be the person You want me to be." And God did! I chose at that moment to forgive the man completely.

The next Sunday I went to church, not to resign, but to preach. My voice was still so husky that I almost couldn't speak. I confessed to the congregation my own independence and my desire for the Lord to touch me, to see people as people, not as obstacles to my goals. At the end of the sermon I invited anyone who desired a touch from the Lord to join me at the altar. Soon the altar area and the aisles in the front were packed with people. Eventually all but a few people had come forward. It was a revival!

Guess who was one of the few. To my knowledge he never changed, but I did. And I thank God to this day that He put me flat on my back to make me the pastor He wanted me to be. If I had had my way, I would probably be out of the ministry today.

Lord, touch me today that I may love the difficult people in my life as You do.

"Is not My word like fire?" declares the LORD,
"and like a hammer which shatters a rock?"
(Jeremiah 23:29).

If you attend a Christian fellowship where prophecies are part of public worship, I wonder if we should expect from God generic messages like, "I love you, My children" or "I'm coming soon." These statements are certainly true, but why would they need to be prophesied, since the Bible already clearly asserts God's love and Christ's imminent return? I have heard "prophecies" like these given in churches where many people were living in sin, lulling them into an unrighteous complacency.

The voice of a prophet is a consuming fire and a shattering hammer. A prophetic message should motivate people to righteousness, not placate them in their sin (1 Peter 4:17). God is more concerned about church purity than about church growth. Comfort only comes to those who are persecuted for righteousness' sake by allowing God's Word to purge their sin and shatter their self-centeredness.

Jeremiah relates two other evidences of false prophets: " 'Behold, I am against the prophets,' declares the LORD, 'who steal My words from each other' " (23:30). That's plagiarism: taking what God gave someone else and using it as if it were your own. " 'I am against the prophets,' declares the LORD, 'who use their tongues and declare, "The Lord declares" ' " (verse 31).

Declaring that what you are saying is directly from the Lord when it isn't, is an incredible offense to God. If God wants me to know something He will tell me directly. I believe in the priesthood of believers; however, God can and will encourage us and confirm His Word to us through others. "There is one God, and one mediator also between God and men, the man Christ Jesus" (1 Timothy 2:5). If someone says to you "God told me to tell you..." that person may be functioning as a medium. The gift of prophecy should reveal the secrets of the heart so people will fall on their faces and worship God (1 Corinthians 14:25). Then God will guide them by His Holy Spirit.

Lord, teach me not to quench Your Spirit nor to despise prophetic utterances but to examine everything and hold fast to what is good.

Therefore, take up the full armor of God, that you may be able to resist in the evil day, and having done everything, to stand firm (Ephesians 6:13).

A primary element in our protection from Satan and evil is the armor that God has provided for us and instructed us to put on in Ephesians 6:13-17. When we put on the armor of God we are really putting on Christ (Romans 13:12-14). And when we put on Christ we take ourselves out of the realm of the flesh, where we are vulnerable to attack, and we place ourselves within the dominion of Christ, where the evil one cannot touch us. Satan has nothing in Christ (John 14:30), and to the extent that we put on Christ, the evil one cannot touch us (1 John 5:18). He can only touch that which is on his own level. That's why we are commanded, "Make no provision for the flesh" (Romans 13:14), meaning, "Don't live on Satan's level."

It would appear from the verb tenses in Ephesians 6:14,15 that three of the pieces of armor—belt, breastplate, and shoes—are already on you: "having girded..."; "having put on..."; "having shod...." These pieces of armor represent the elements of your protection made possible when you receive Jesus Christ and in which you are commanded to stand firm. The Greek tense of "having" signifies that the action it refers to was completed before we were commanded to stand firm. That's the logical way a soldier would prepare for action: He would put on his belt, breastplate, and shoes before attempting to stand firm. Likewise, we are to put on the full armor of God after having already put on Christ.

When you read through Ephesians 6:10-20, you will notice the emphasis on the active part we must play on behalf of our own spiritual defense: "be strong" (verse 10); "put on" and "stand firm" (verse 11); "take up," "be able," "resist," and "stand firm" (verse 13); "stand firm" (verse 14); "taking up" (verse 16); "take" (verse 17); "pray at all times" and "be on the alert" (verse 18).

Over the next several days we will consider eacn of the six pieces of armor from Ephesians 6:13-17.

Teach me my responsibility in spiritual warfare, Lord, that I may be strong in You and in the strength of Your might.

November 24

Having girded your loins with truth (Ephesians 6:14).

The first piece of armor for the Christian warrior is the *belt of truth*. Jesus said, "I am...the truth" (John 14:6). And because Christ is in you, the truth is in you. However, continuing to choose truth is not always easy. Since Satan's primary weapon is the lie, your belt of truth (which holds the other pieces of body armor in place) is continually being attacked. If he can disable you in the area of truth, you become an easy target for his other attacks.

You stand firm in the truth by relating everything you do to the truth of God's Word. If a thought comes to mind which is not in harmony with God's truth, dismiss it. If an opportunity comes along to say or do something which compromises or conflicts with truth, avoid it. Adopt a simple rule of behavior: If it's the truth, I'm in; if it's not the truth, count me out.

When you learn to live in the truth on a daily basis, you will grow to love the truth because you have nothing to hide. You never have to cover up to God or anyone else; everything you do is in the light. Furthermore, when you live in the truth you dislodge the lies of Satan, the father of lies (John 8:44). Remember that if Satan can deceive you into believing a lie, he can control your life.

Jesus prayed, "I do not ask Thee to take them out of the world, but to keep them from the evil one" (John 17:15). How? "Sanctify them in the truth; Thy Word is truth" (verse 17). You will only dislodge Satan's lies in the light of God's revelation, and not by human reasoning or research.

The only thing a Christian ever has to admit to is the truth. Walking in the light and speaking the truth in love may seem threatening to some. But in reality truth is a liberating friend and the only path to fellowship with God.

Forgive me, Lord, for entertaining lies and walking in darkness. Give me courage to face the truth and to speak the truth in love.

THE BREASTPLATE OF RIGHTEOUSNESS

Having put on the breastplate of righteousness (Ephesians 6:14).

The second piece of armor God has provided for us is the *breastplate of righteousness*. When you put on Christ at salvation you are justified before our holy God. It's not *your* righteousness but Christ's (1 Corinthians 1:30; Philippians 3:8,9). So when Satan aims an arrow at you by saying, "You're not good enough to be a Christian," you can respond with Paul, "Who will bring a charge against God's elect? God is the one who justifies" (Romans 8:33). Your righteousness in Christ is your protection against Satan's accusations.

Even though we rejoice in our position of righteousness in Christ, we are well aware of our deeds of unrighteousness when we think, say, or do something apart from God. Standing firm in our righteousness requires us to live in continuous agreement with God according to 1 John 1:9: "If we confess our sins, He is faithful and righteous to forgive us our sins and to cleanse us from all unrighteousness." Confession is different from saying "I'm sorry" or asking forgiveness. To confess (*homologeo*) means to acknowledge or to agree. You confess your sin when you say what God says about it: "I entertained a lustful thought, and that's a sin"; "I treated my spouse unkindly this morning, and that was wrong"; "Pride motivated me to seek that board position, and pride doesn't belong in my life."

Satan will make confession as difficult for you as he can. He will try to convince you that it's too late for confession, that God has already erased your name out of the book of life. That's another one of his lies. You're in Christ; you're already forgiven. You are the righteousness of God in Christ (2 Corinthians 5:21), and He will never leave you. Your relationship with God and your eternal destiny are not at stake when you sin, but your daily victory is. Your confession of sin clears the way for the fruitful expression of righteousness in your daily life. We should be like Paul, who said, "I also do my best to maintain always a blameless conscience both before God and before men" (Acts 24:16).

Lord, I put on the breastplate of righteousness today and seek to maintain a blameless conscience before You and the people around me.

Having shod your feet with the preparation of the gospel of peace (Ephesians 6:15).

The next piece of armor is the *shoes of peace*. When you receive Christ you are united with the Prince of Peace. You have peace with God right now (Romans 5:1), but the peace of Christ must also rule in your heart if you are going to live victoriously, and that is possible only when you let the Word of Christ richly dwell in you (Colossians 3:15,16).

The shoes of peace become protection against the divisive schemes of the devil when you act as a peacemaker among believers (Romans 14:19). Peacemakers bring people together by promoting fellowship and reconciliation. "Blessed are the peacemakers, for they shall be called sons of God" (Matthew 5:9). Anyone can divide a fellowship, but it takes the grace of God to unite us in Him.

Too many Christians insist on common doctrine as the basis for fellowship. They reason that if we don't think the same and believe the same, there is no basis for peace. But common doctrine isn't the basis for fellowship; common heritage is. We're all children of God. If you wait to fellowship with someone until you agree perfectly on every point of doctrine, you'll be the loneliest Christian on earth. Instead of insisting on the unity of the mind, preserve the unity of the Spirit by taking the initiative to be the peacemaker in your relationships (Ephesians 4:3).

Some people like to play the devil's advocate in their relationships and churches. I ask, Why? He doesn't need any help! In His high priestly prayer, Jesus prayed, "I in them, and Thou in Me, that they may be perfected in unity, that the world may know that Thou didst send Me" (John 17:23). We have the promise that "the God of peace will soon crush Satan under your feet" (Romans 16:20). Ask God to use you to bring unity to your relationships by making you a peacemaker.

Heavenly Father, use me today to bring unity to Your family. Enable me to be a peacemaker.

Taking up the shield of faith with which you will be able to extinguish all the flaming missiles of the evil one (Ephesians 6:16).

Paul mentions three more pieces of armor that we must take up to protect ourselves from Satan's attack: the shield of faith, the helmet of salvation, and the sword of the Spirit, which is the Word of God. The first three (the belt of truth, the breastplate of righteousness, the shoes of peace) are established by our position in Christ; these last three help us continue to win the battle.

Contrary to popular perception, there is nothing mystical about faith. Biblical faith is simply what you believe about God and His Word. The more you know about God and His Word, the more faith you will have. The less you know, the smaller your shield will be and the easier it will be for one of Satan's fiery darts to reach its target. If you want your shield of faith to grow large and protective, your knowledge of God and His Word must increase (Romans 10:17).

These flaming missiles from Satan are nothing more than smoldering lies, burning accusations, and fiery temptations bombarding our minds. When a deceptive thought, accusation, or temptation enters your mind, meet it head-on with what you know to be true about God and His Word. How did Jesus deflect the missiles of Satan's temptation? By shielding Himself with statements from the Word of God. Every time you memorize a Bible verse, listen to a sermon, or participate in a Bible study, you increase your knowledge of God and enlarge your shield of faith.

We all struggle with tempting and accusing thoughts. If you are a healthy and mature Christian, they will bounce right off your shield of faith.

Lord, I raise up the shield of faith today and stand against tempting and accusing thoughts from the evil one.

And take the helmet of salvation (Ephesians 6:17).

The next necessary piece of spiritual armor is the *helmet of salvation.* Should your shield of faith be a little leaky and your daily victory elusive, be confident that the helmet of salvation guarantees your eternal victory. In the metaphor of armor, the helmet also secures coverage for the most critical part of your anatomy: your mind, where spiritual battles are either won or lost. As you struggle with the world, the flesh, and the devil on a daily basis, stand firm knowing that your salvation does not come and go with your success or failure in spiritual battle; your salvation is your eternal possession. You are a child of God, and nothing can separate you from the love of Christ (Romans 8:35).

People experiencing spiritual conflict tend to question their salvation or doubt their identity in Christ. Satan may disrupt your daily victory, but he can do nothing to disrupt your position in Christ. However, if he can get you to believe that you are not in Christ, you will live as though you are not, even though you are secure in Him.

The Christian warrior wears the helmet of salvation in the sense that he is the receiver and possessor of deliverance, clothed and armed in the victory of his Head, Jesus Christ. Satan is the ruler of this world, and the whole world is in his power (John 12:31; 1 John 5:19). Therefore we are still in his territory as long as we are present in our physical bodies. But since we are joined to the Lord Jesus Christ, the devil has no legitimate claim on us, for Christ has "delivered us from the domain of darkness, and transferred us to the kingdom of His beloved Son" (Colossians 1:13) The helmet of our position in Christ assures us of ultimate victory over Satan.

I love You, Father, and thank You that I am united with Christ and spiritually alive in Him.

And take...the sword of the Spirit, which is the word of God (Ephesians 6:17).

The Word of God is the only offensive weapon mentioned in the list of armor. Since Paul used *rhema* instead of *logos* for "word" in Ephesians 6:17, I believe Paul is referring to the spoken Word of God. We are to defend ourselves against the evil one by speaking aloud God's Word.

Why is it so important to speak God's Word in addition to believing it and thinking it? Because Satan is a created being, and he doesn't perfectly know what you're thinking. By observing you he can pretty well tell what you are thinking, just as any student of human behavior can. And it isn't difficult for him to know what you're thinking if he put the thought in. But he doesn't know what you're going to do before you do it. He can put thoughts into your mind, and he will know whether you buy his lie by how you behave.

Satan can try to influence you by planting thoughts in your head, but he can't read your thoughts. If you're going to resist Satan, you must do so verbally so he can understand you and be put to flight.

You can communicate with God in your mind and spirit because He knows the thoughts and intents of your heart (Hebrews 4:12). Your unspoken communion with God is your private sanctuary; Satan cannot eavesdrop on you. But by the same token, if you only tell Satan with your thoughts to leave, he won't leave because he is under no obligation to obey your thoughts. *You must defeat Satan by speaking out*. The good news is that most direct attacks occur at night or when you are alone.

One night I woke up absolutely terrified for no apparent reason, and I knew it was an attack from Satan. Without lifting my head from the pillow, I applied the two-step remedy suggested in James 4:7. In the sanctuary of my heart, I submitted to God. Then I was able to resist Satan with one spoken word—Jesus—and the fear was instantly and totally gone. I went back to sleep in complete peace.

Lord, give me courage to take my stand in this world and defeat Satan by speaking Your Word.

Responsibilities Over Rights

You were called to freedom, brethren; only do not turn your freedom into an opportunity for the flesh, but through love serve one another (Galatians 5:13).

Nothing will distort relationships faster than emphasizing our rights over our responsibilities. For example, a husband may chip at his wife because he feels he has a right to expect her to be submissive. A wife may nag her husband because she expects him to be the spiritual leader. Parents harass their children because they feel it's their right to demand obedience. Members are offended in the local church when they think their rights have been violated by pastors, boards, or other members.

Any time people insist on their rights at the expense of failing to assume their responsibilities, they are going down to defeat. For example, a pregnant woman may demand her right for an abortion. She says it is her body, and she can do whatever she wants with it. Then she proceeds to demonstrate her irresponsible use of her body to everyone! We don't have an abortion problem; we have an irresponsible sex problem.

In God's system, our focus is to be fulfilling our responsibilities, not insisting on our rights. Husband, having a submissive wife is not your right; but being a loving, caring husband is your responsibility. Headship is not a right to be demanded but an awesome responsibility to be fulfilled.

Similarly, wives, having a spiritual husband is not your right; but being a submissive, supportive wife is your responsibility. Parents, raising obedient children is not your right; but disciplining your children in the nurture and instruction of the Lord is your responsibility. Being a member of the Body of Christ and of a local church is an incredible privilege, not a right. This privilege comes with the awesome responsibility to behave as God's children and become a lover of people. When we stand before Christ, He will not ask us if we received everything we had coming to us. But He will reward us for how well we fulfilled our responsibilities.

Lord, help me relinquish my rights and focus on my responsibilities in all my relationships today.

Do not be wise in your own eyes; fear the LORD and turn away from evil (Proverbs 3:7).

Wisdom was certainly the way of the Old Testament as the book of Proverbs and other wisdom literature attest. However, in the Old Testament, wisdom was not understood as our ability to reason independently of God. Rather, it was an acceptance and knowledge of divine revelation. Biblical wisdom is seeing life from God's perspective. When wisdom degenerates to rationalism, our walk with God is reduced to an intellectual pursuit rather than a living relationship. Proverbs 3:5-7 pictures the relationship God desires with us: "Trust in the LORD with all your heart, and do not lean on your own understanding. In all your ways acknowledge Him, and He will make your paths straight. Do not be wise in your own eyes; fear the LORD and turn away from evil."

Turning away from evil signifies that there are moral boundaries. The will of God is to live inside those boundaries. We are free to live as the Lord leads as long as we stay morally pure and exercise biblical wisdom. Since all unbelievers are outside the moral boundaries of God, they can expect judgment. Christians living outside the moral boundaries can expect discipline. The writer of Hebrews would attest to the latter: "But if you are without discipline, of which all have become partakers, then you are illegitimate children and not sons" (Hebrews 12:8).

It's true that God does give us freedom to make choices on nonmoral issues, but He expects us to know His Word and make wise decisions. He has made His will known primarily in His Word, and He delights when we humbly submit to it and obey it. But we are not Old Testament saints. We are New Testament Christians. Christ has reconciled Jew and Gentile, and we possess both power and wisdom. What marks the church age is that we now have the presence of the Holy Spirit who will guide us into all truth. "For to us God revealed them through the Spirit; for the Spirit searches all things, even the depths of God" (1 Corinthians 2:10).

Thank You, Lord, for Your Word, which is a lamp to my feet, and for Your Holy Spirit, who will guide me into all truth.

To all who are beloved of God in Rome, called as saints: Grace to you and peace from God our Father and the Lord Jesus Christ (Romans 1:7).

Have you ever heard a Christian refer to himself as "just a sinner saved by grace"? Have you referred to yourself that way? What do sinners do? They sin! If you are no different from a non-Christian, or even if you perceive yourself as no different, what will happen? Your Christian life will be mediocre at best, with little to distinguish you from a non-Christian. Satan will seize that opportunity, pour on the guilt, and convince you that you are doomed to an up-and-down spiritual existence. As a defeated Christian you will confess your sin and strive to do better, but inwardly you will admit that you are just a sinner saved by grace, hanging on until the rapture.

In Scripture, believers are called "brethren," "sons of God," "sons of light," and "saints." You are not a sinner; you are a saint who sins. "For you were formerly darkness, but now you are light in the Lord; walk as children of light" (Ephesians 5:8). According to that passage, we don't have an identity problem; we have a walk problem.

We become saints at the moment of salvation and live as saints in our daily experience as we continue to believe what God has done and as we continue to affirm who we really are in Christ. If you fail to see yourself as a child of God, you will struggle vainly to live like one, and Satan will have little trouble convincing you that you are no different from who you were before Christ and that you have no value to God or anyone else. But appropriating by faith the radical transformation of your core identity from sinner to saint will have a powerful, positive effect on your daily resistance to sin and Satan.

Lord, open my eyes that I may see myself as You see me. Then enable me to walk as a child of light.

If they persecuted Me, they will also persecute you (John 15:20).

Everyone knows what it feels like to be criticized and rejected, often by the very people in our lives we desperately want to please. We were born and raised in a worldly environment which chooses favorites and rejects seconds. And since nobody can be the best at everything, we all were ignored, overlooked, or rejected at times by parents, teachers, and friends.

Furthermore, since we were born in sin, even God had no relationship with us until we were accepted by Him in Christ at salvation. Since then we have been the target of Satan, the accuser of the brethren (Revelation 12:10), who never ceases to lie to us about how worthless we are to God and others. In this life we all have to live with the pain of rejection.

The acceptance of God is not based on our performance but on His kindness and mercy. "But when the kindness of God our Savior and His love for mankind appeared, He saved us, not on the basis of deeds which we have done in righteousness, but according to His mercy" (Titus 3:4,5). "Wherefore, accept one another, just as Christ also accepted us to the glory of God" (Romans 15:7).

The thoughts and feelings of rejection which often plague us can be major deterrents to growth and maturity if we don't learn to handle them positively. Unfortunately, instead of taking a positive approach, we all learned early in life to respond to rejection by taking one of three defensive postures. Even Christians are influenced to react defensively to the rejection they experience in their family, their school, or society in general.

Over the next several days we will look at three ineffective and unnecessary ways to respond to rejection, and consider God's plan for helping us deal with rejection from others.

Thank You, Lord, for Your unconditional love and acceptance. Teach me to accept others as You have accepted me.

Everyone who exalts himself shall be humbled,
and he who humbles himself shall be exalted
(Luke 14:11).

A small percentage of people defend against rejection by buying into the dog-eat-dog system of the world and learning to compete and scheme to get ahead of the pack. These are the movers and shakers, people who earn acceptance and strive for significance through their performance. They feel driven to get on top of every situation because winning is their passport to acceptance. They are characterized by perfectionism and emotional insulation and they struggle with anxiety and stress.

Spiritually, the beat-the-system individual refuses to come under God's authority and has little fellowship with God. This person is committed to controlling and manipulating people and circumstances for his own ends, so it is difficult for him to yield control in his life to God. In our churches this person jockeys to be chairman of the ruling board or the most influential member on a committee. His motivation is not to serve God in this position, however, but to control his world because his self-worth is dependent on it. Beat-the-system controllers are some of the most insecure people you will meet.

Sadly, the controlling individual's defensive strategy only delays inevitable rejection. Eventually his ability to control his family, his employees, and his church diminishes, and he is replaced by a younger, stronger controller. Some survive this mid-life crisis, but many who make it to retirement don't enjoy much of it. Studies show that high-powered executives live an average of nine months after they retire. They base their lives in the world system they seek to conquer, but inevitably the world claims its own. "See to it that no one takes you captive through philosophy and empty deception, according to the tradition of men, according to the elementary principles of the world, rather than according to Christ" (Colossians 2:8).

Gracious Lord, teach me to be in this world but not of it. I choose Your kingdom to be my standard.

And coming to Him as to a living stone, rejected by men, but choice and precious in the sight of God (1 Peter 2:4).

"Pastor, I'm a loser," a high school boy told me dejectedly. He explained that he wanted to be a star football player, but had been cut from the team. Instead of being in the spotlight as an athlete, he had to settle for being a member of the pep band. And compared to star quarterbacks, clarinet players were losers at his school.

The largest group of people today respond to rejection like this boy did: by simply giving in to the system. They continue their efforts to try to earn approval, but the inevitable rejection by others prompts them to believe that they really are unlovable and rejectable. The system says that the best, the strongest, the most beautiful, and the most talented are "in." Those who don't fit those categories—which includes most of us—are "out," and we succumb to society's false judgment of our worth. As a result, a large segment of the population is plagued by feelings of worthlessness, inferiority, and self-condemnation.

This person may have trouble relating to God. If he blames God for his state, it will be difficult to trust Him. "You made me a lowly clarinet player instead of a star quarterback," he complains. "If I trust You with other areas of my life, how do I know You won't make me a loser there too?"

By giving in to the system's false judgment, this person can only look forward to more and more rejection. He has bought the lie and he even rejects himself. Therefore any success or acceptance which comes his way will be questioned or doubted on the basis of what he already believes about himself.

God has not equally distributed gifts, talents, or intelligence, but He has equally distributed Himself. Our sense of worth comes from knowing who we are as children of God. "See how great a love the Father has bestowed upon us, that we should be called children of God; and such we are" (1 John 3:1).

Heavenly Father, thank You for creating me the way You have and for making me Your child. I find my worth in You.

REBELLING AGAINST THE SYSTEM

If you consent and obey, you will eat the best of the land; but if you refuse and rebel, you will be devoured by the sword (Isaiah 1:19,20).

The third way people respond to rejection is to rebel against the system. They accurately sense the injustice of the world system.

Since the 1960s, this segment of society seems to be growing. These are the rebels and the dropouts who respond to rejection by saying, "I don't need you or your love." Deep inside they still crave acceptance, but they refuse to acknowledge their need. They will often underscore their defiance and rebellion by dressing and behaving in ways which are objectionable to the general population.

The rebel is marked by self-hatred and bitterness. He wishes he had never been born. He is irresponsible and undisciplined. He sees God as just another tyrant, someone else trying to squeeze him into a socially acceptable mold. He rebels against God just like he rebels against everyone else, because he sees God as a part of the establishment.

This person's rebellious attitude and behavior tend to alienate others and push them to defend the system he rejects. The establishment doesn't like to have the status quo questioned. So when the rebel criticizes the government or the schools, the establishment rises to defend them. But what is there to defend? When the rebel says the system is unfair, he's right. The world system is governed by the god of this world. It is hard, cold, and rejecting.

We are to submit to and pray for the governing authorities so that it may be well with us (1 Peter 2:18-21; 1 Timothy 2:1-4). But the means by which we evaluate ourselves and the standards by which we live are not of this world.

Lord, I pray for a submissive spirit and the wisdom to live my life according to the standards of Your kingdom.

December 7 — Why You Shouldn't Be Defensive

While being reviled, [Jesus] did not revile in return; while suffering, He uttered no threats, but kept entrusting Himself to Him who judges righteously (1 Peter 2:23).

There are two reasons why you should not be defensive when there is a critical, negative evaluation of you.

First, if you are in the wrong, you don't *have* a defense. If you are criticized for saying something which is out of order or doing something which is wrong, and the criticism is valid, any defensiveness on your part would be a rationalization at best and a lie at worst. You must simply respond, "You're right; I was wrong," then take steps to improve your character and behavior.

Second, if you are right, you don't *need* a defense. Peter encouraged us to follow in the footsteps of Jesus who "while being reviled, He did not revile in return; while suffering, He uttered no threats, but kept entrusting Himself to Him who judges righteously" (1 Peter 2:23). If you are in the right, you don't need to defend yourself. The Righteous Judge, who knows who you are and what you have done, will exonerate you.

A dear lady entered my office with a well thought-out list of "things for me" and "things against me." I suggested that she share the "things for me" first. That didn't take long! As she was going through the "things against me," the part of me that is made of earth wanted to respond to every allegation. But I didn't. When she was finished, there was an awkward pause before I said, "It must have taken a lot of courage to come in and share that with me. What do you suggest I do?" She started to cry.

Nobody tears another down from a position of strength or judges another without being judged. Judgmental people are people in pain. If you can learn not to be defensive when someone exposes your character defects or attacks your performance, you may have an opportunity to turn the situation around and minister to that person.

Lord, give me the courage not to react defensively. You are the only defense I need, and I entrust myself to You, who judges righteously.

My little children, I am writing these things to you that you may not sin. And if anyone sins, we have an Advocate with the Father, Jesus Christ the righteous (1 John 2:1).

People who are caught in the sin-confess-sin-confess-sin-confess cycle eventually begin to lose hope that they can experience any real victory over sin. Sheer willpower can't keep them from repeating the sin they just confessed, and Satan pours on the condemnation. Self-control seems like an illusion, and the Christian life is one of unending ups and downs.

Suppose there is a door you are commanded not to open. On the other side of the door is a dog that keeps insisting, "Come on, let me in. Everybody is doing it. You deserve to have a little fun. Who will know? You can get away with it." So you open the door and the dog roars in and bites you on the leg. Ironically, the dog instantly changes its story: "You opened the door. I have a right to be here. You'll never get away with this!" If such a thing happened, would you beat on the dog or on yourself?

Sin which is allowed to reign is like the dog that bites you on the leg and won't let go. Not realizing there is a dog, you beat on yourself for leaving the door open and cry out to God for forgiveness. He forgives you, but the dog is still there. Why not cry out to God and beat on the dog instead of yourself? James 4:7 tells us, "Submit therefore to God. Resist the devil and he will flee from you." We are correct in confessing our sin, but we have failed to follow the complete biblical formula which breaks the cycle: sin-confess-*resist*. We must first assume our responsibility for opening the door, then we must resist Satan and command him to leave if we are going to experience victory over sin.

We live as though God and a sick humanity are the only realities in the spiritual realm. We must turn to our righteous Advocate (1 John 2:1) and resist our perverted adversary if we are to experience victory and freedom over temptation and sin.

Lord, show me where I have opened the door of my life to sin that I may confess it to You and command Satan to leave in Your precious name.

You believe that God is one. You do well; the demons also believe, and shudder (James 2:19).

We all have some beliefs about the world we live in. Whatever we think will make us happy, satisfied, successful, etc. is what constitutes our belief system. We are walking right now by faith according to what we already believe. Be assured that the world system we were raised in didn't establish a biblical belief system in our minds. Because we came into this world separated from God, we learned to live our lives independently from Him. We were conformed to this world. Unless we were raised in a perfect Christian home, much of what we learned to believe didn't reflect biblical truth.

If you believe that you will only be satisfied by possessions, then you will probably never be satisfied. Jesus revealed that satisfaction does not come from material things: "Blessed are those who hunger and thirst for righteousness, for they shall be satisfied" (Matthew 5:6). If you believe you are successful because of status or the amount of toys you accumulate, you will certainly be at odds with Scripture.

God has a different standard by which we are to evaluate and achieve success. Joshua 1:8 states, "This book of the law shall not depart from your mouth, but you shall meditate on it day and night, so that you may be careful to do according to all that is written in it; for then you will make your way prosperous, and then you will have success." We can't make up our own definitions of satisfaction or success or determine what we want to believe. Faith must have an object, and for the Christian, that object is God and His Word.

The only difference between Christian faith and non-Christian faith is the object of our faith. To think that we will get what we want if we believe with all our hearts is a faith based on selfish desires. It originates within ourselves and depends on our own definition of faith. It's a form of religious self-hypnosis. It's like the Christian who says, "I don't know the Bible, but I have faith." For that person, faith is a substitute for knowledge and a compensation for ignorance.

Lord, I choose to believe today that You are the source of everything I need in life. I place my faith in You alone.

THE FEAR THAT EXPELS ALL OTHERS

In the fear of the LORD there is strong confidence, and his children will have refuge (Proverbs 14:26).

I was conducting a conference for the leadership of one of America's flagship churches. The pastor is one of the most gifted Bible teachers I know, and his staff is among the best. I asked the 165 leaders present if they had ever experienced a direct encounter with something they knew was demonic, such as a frightening presence in their room or an evil voice in their mind. Ninety-five percent answered yes. I went one step further to ask how many had been frightened by something pressing on them that they couldn't immediately respond to physically. At least a third raised their hand. Are these Christian leaders mentally ill? No, and neither are you or your children when you struggle against demonic influences in your life.

We warn our children about strangers in the streets. Don't you think we should warn them about "strangers" in their rooms? Our research suggests that 50 percent of Christian kids have encountered an evil presence in their rooms. Most of my students at seminary have had such an experience, and by the time they complete my class on resolving spiritual conflicts, several tell about having such an experience that semester. Would you know what to do if you or your child was terrorized by a presence alone at night? Do you fear such a possibility?

Most people fear demonic things they can't see, but have no fear of God. That's just the opposite of what Scripture commands. We are told to fear the Lord (Proverbs 1:7), but we are never told to fear Satan. Fear of the devil is an inappropriate response to the reality of the spiritual world. Knowing his schemes and learning to resist him and take authority over him is the biblical response.

Isaiah 8:13,14 reads, "It is the LORD of hosts whom you should regard as holy. And He shall be your fear, and He shall be your dread. Then He shall become a sanctuary." The fear of the Lord is the one fear that expels all other fears.

Lord, You are the only legitimate fear-object in my life. You are the omniscient, omnipotent, omnipresent God.

Greater is He who is in you than he who is in the world (1 John 4:4).

The Satanist organization is massive and extremely secretive. When you hear of satanic priests or rituals, you are hearing only about activities at the lowest level. You need not concern yourself too much with what you see or hear, since the Satanist activity which you read about in the newspapers or which is recorded in most police reports is usually the activity of mere dabblers. It's what you *don't* see that is pulling the strings and arranging events in Satanism. I have counseled enough victims of Satanism to know that there are infiltrators committed to infiltrating and disrupting Christian ministry.

To illustrate how human and spiritual forces of wickedness work together, ask any group of committed Christians this question: "How many of you have been awakened alertly or terrorized at 3:00 A.M.?" I ask that question regularly in my conferences, and about two-thirds of the participants raise their hands. Satanists meet from 12:00 to 3:00 A.M., and part of their ritual is to summon and send demons. The early morning hours are prime time for demon activity, and if you have awakened at that time it may be that you have been targeted.

I have been targeted numerous times. However, it's not a frightening experience for me, and it shouldn't be for you. John promised, "Greater is He who is in you than he who is in the world" (1 John 4:4). You have authority over Satan's activity and you have the armor of God to protect you. Whenever Satan attacks, you must "be strong in the Lord, and in the strength of His might" (Ephesians 6:10). Consciously place yourself in the Lord's hands, resist Satan with the spoken Word, and go back to sleep. You are only vulnerable when you are walking by sight instead of by faith or walking in the flesh instead of in the Spirit.

What should we do about Satan's hierarchy of demonic powers? Nothing! We are not to be demon-centered; we are to be God-centered and ministry-centered. We are to fix our eyes on Jesus, preach the gospel, love one another, and be God's ambassadors in our fallen world.

Father, keep me from losing my focus on the eternal. I choose to fix my eyes on Jesus, the author and finisher of my faith.

Pride goes before destruction, and a haughty spirit before stumbling (Proverbs 16:18).

Pride is a killer. Pride says, "I can do it alone. I can get myself out of this mess without God's help." Oh, no you can't! We absolutely need God, and we desperately need each other. Paul wrote, "We are the true circumcision, who worship in the Spirit of God and glory in Christ Jesus and put no confidence in the flesh" (Philippians 3:3). Humility is confidence properly placed. Examine the instructions on pride and humility in James 4:6-10 and 1 Peter 5:1-10. The context reveals that spiritual conflict follows the expression of pride. Pride is what caused Lucifer to be thrown out of heaven.

Jesus said, "Simon, Simon [Peter], behold, Satan has demanded permission to sift you like wheat" (Luke 22:31). On what basis could Satan make that demand? The context reveals the answer: "There arose also a dispute among them as to which one of them was regarded to be greatest" (Luke 22:24). Pride was Peter's downfall, and it opened the door to the devil's opposition.

The Lord says that pride goes before destruction and an arrogant spirit before stumbling (Proverbs 16:18). We must confess areas where we have not denied ourselves, picked up our cross daily, and followed Him (Matthew 16:24). In so doing we have given ground to the enemy in our lives.

Have we believed that we could be successful and live victoriously by our own strength and resources? We must confess that we have sinned against God by placing our will before His and by centering our lives around self instead of Him. We must renounce the self life and by so doing cancel all the ground that has been gained in our members by the enemies of the Lord Jesus Christ.

We must pray that God will guide us so that we will do nothing from selfishness or empty conceit, but that with humility of mind we will regard others as more important than ourselves (Philippians 2:3). We must ask God to enable us through love to serve others and in honor prefer others (Romans 12:10).

Loving Lord, I want my life to be marked by a humble spirit today. Forgive me for my proud, self-centered ways and independent spirit.

I have become all things to all men, that I may by all means save some (1 Corinthians 9:22).

The world at the end of the twentieth century is changing at an alarming rate. People are under tremendous stress to keep up with the rapid rate of change. The ecclesiastical challenge is to give anxious people the timeless message of Christ and present it in a contemporary way that relates to a changing culture.

Many of the older and mature saints who rightfully constitute the boards and committees in our traditional evangelical churches resist change. They are comfortable with the form of worship, style of music, and methods of teaching that brought them to Christ and helped them mature. They get uncomfortable when a young pastor comes in with new ideas.

Jesus said you can't put new wine into old wineskins (Luke 5:37). The wineskins don't represent the substance of our faith; they represent the package our faith comes in. Christian practices wear out their purposes and the next generation doesn't relate to them.

Jesus not only came to fulfill the law, but He also came to usher in a new age. The Jewish community was locked in tradition. Most of the opposition didn't come when He presented the truth, but when He confronted their traditions. When one doesn't conform to the customs and practices of the status quo, the establishment will be offended. The new wine often comes under the scrutiny, and sometimes the wrath, of the old wineskins.

I had the privilege of helping an established church through an organizational change. The pastor had been there for 30 years and had led the church from its beginnings to more than 1000 attenders. The organization had evolved with little planning or purpose, so we reorganized 26 committees into seven. Although the organizational change was significant, it took place without any dissension. The major key in this case was the vision and credibility of the pastor, who realized the need for new wineskins.

God is leading us into the twenty-first century, and we must learn how to adapt our ministry to a changing culture.

Lord, enable me to establish my life on the substance of faith, not the package of traditions and customs it comes in.

Now may the God of hope fill you with all joy and peace in believing, that you may abound in hope by the power of the Holy Spirit (Romans 15:13).

Lend me your hope for awhile, I seem to have mislaid mine.
Lost and hopeless feelings accompany me daily,
pain and confusion are my companions.
I know not where to turn; looking ahead to future times
does not bring forth images of renewed hope.
I see troubled times, pain-filled days, and more tragedy.
Lend me your hope for awhile, I seem to have mislaid mine.
Hold my hand and hug me; listen to all my ramblings,
recovery seems so far distant.
The road to healing seems like a long and lonely one.
Lend me your hope for awhile, I seem to have mislaid mine.
Stand by me, offer me your presence, your heart and your love.
Acknowledge my pain, it is so real and ever present.
I am overwhelmed with sad and conflicting thoughts.
Lend me your hope for awhile; a time will come when I will heal,
and I will share my renewal, hope, and love with others.[1]

The apostle Paul gives us the biblical basis for our comfort and hope: "Blessed be the God and Father of our Lord Jesus Christ, the Father of mercies and God of all comfort; who comforts us in all our affliction so that we may be able to comfort those who are in any affliction with the comfort with which we ourselves are comforted by God. For just as the sufferings of Christ are ours in abundance, so also our comfort is abundant through Christ" (2 Corinthians 1:3-5).

I praise You for hope, Lord. Help me be a source of hope in all my relationships and circumstances today.

The Spiritual Problem of Rebellion

Rebellion is as the sin of divination [witchcraft], and insubordination is as iniquity and idolatry (1 Samuel 15:23).

If you fail to bring your child under control during his early years, problems may not show up until he hits the age of identity, around 12. Most parents respond at this time by trying to control the child. But the authoritarian parent is most likely to produce a rebel. "But we have to reprove rebellious kids, don't we?" Actually, the Bible tells us *not* to reprove a scoffer (Proverbs 9:7-9). Why? Because rebellion is a spiritual problem, and it requires a spiritual solution.

Saul, the first king of Israel, rebelled against God by doing his own thing, making his own rules, and worshiping the way he wanted to. God sent a prophet to confront him. Part of the prophet's stinging rebuke was, "Rebellion is as the sin of divination [witchcraft], and insubordination is as iniquity and idolatry" (1 Samuel 15:23). As a result of Saul's disobedience, "an evil spirit from the LORD terrorized him" (1 Samuel 16:14).

God can use any means He chooses to discipline His children. Even Satan and his evil spirits can be an instrument in the hands of God (1 Corinthians 5:5). I'm not suggesting that you turn your child over to Satan. But willful disobedience usually cannot be dealt with by human reasoning. Have you ever tried to reason with a rebellious child? Prayer is our weapon for bringing down strongholds raised up against the knowledge of God (2 Corinthians 10:3-5).

Nor am I saying that you shouldn't discipline a rebellious child. On the contrary, you must uphold righteous standards, but you must do it in love and start early. God spoke to Samuel regarding Eli's failure to rebuke his sons: "I will carry out against Eli all that I have spoken concerning his house, from beginning to end. For I have told him that I am about to judge his house forever for the iniquity which he knew, because his sons brought a curse on themselves and he did not rebuke them" (1 Samuel 3:12,13). Eli was an effective priest but a defective parent.

God, give me the courage to hold up a behavior standard of righteousness before my children, and to do so in love.

I pray that in all respects you may prosper and be in good health, just as your soul prospers (3 John 2).

A few years ago a young woman flew out to Los Angeles from the East Coast with the understanding that I would spend some time with her. She professed to be a Christian, but her life was a mess. She was hearing demonic voices and was plagued with numerous problems. I'm surprised the airplane stayed in the air with her in it!

She told me that she had taken the first part of 3 John 2 as a personal promise: "Beloved, I pray that in all respects you may prosper and be in good health." "If God has promised prosperity, success, and health to me, why is my life all screwed up?" she complained.

"Finish the verse," I said.

" 'Just as your soul prospers,' " she continued.

I asked her pointedly, "How is your soul doing?" She told me she had submitted to three abortions as a result of illicit sexual affairs and she was presently living with another man outside of marriage. But she clung desperately to a misquoted promise.

I believe God wants us to prosper, but we must leave the definition of prosperity up to Him. In our sick Western world, we think prosperity is materialism. Try preaching that prosperity gospel in India, Somalia, or any Third World country. It's a cruel joke.

God is into soul prosperity. He wants our lives to be characterized by the fruit of the Spirit. And when our soul prospers, "He who raised Christ Jesus from the dead will also give life to your mortal bodies" (Romans 8:11).

Heavenly Father, may my soul prosper greatly in You today, and may my life be fruitful as a result.

False Christs and false prophets will arise, and will show signs and wonders, in order, if possible, to lead the elect astray (Mark 13:22).

You can identify a false prophet by the fact that not all his prophecies come true. Deuteronomy 18:22 instructs us not to believe the prophet whose prophecies fail. But Deuteronomy 13:1-3 also warns us about the false prophet whose signs and wonders *do* come true: "If a prophet or a dreamer of dreams arises among you and gives you a sign or a wonder, and the sign or wonder comes true, concerning which he spoke to you, saying, 'Let us go after other gods (whom you have not known) and let us serve them,' you shall not listen to the words of that prophet or that dreamer of dreams; for the LORD your God is testing you to find out if you love the LORD your God with all your heart and with all your soul." (See also Matthew 24:4-11,23-25; Revelation 13:11-14.)

Many Christians have become conditioned to think that anything relating to the miraculous automatically verifies that God is involved. God can still use signs and wonders to confirm the Word, but the Bible also warns that false Christs and prophets will arise seeking to lead believers astray with their "signs and wonders." Satan can also perform signs and wonders, but he only does so to direct our worship away from God to himself. Deuteronomy 13:5-11 reveals the seriousness of attributing to God the activity of Satan. Persons who were involved in it were to be executed, even if they were relatives. We are to love God, obey His Word, and test all signs, wonders, and dreams. Isaiah wrote, "When they say to you, 'Consult the mediums and the wizards who whisper and mutter,' should not a people consult their God? Should they consult the dead on behalf of the living? To the law and to the testimony! If they do not speak according to this word, it is because they have no dawn" (8:19,20).

Lord, I affirm my commitment to know Your Word and be led by Your Spirit. I ask for discernment and wisdom to test all things.

THE TRUE NATURE OF BONDAGE

Above all, keep fervent in your love for one another, because love covers a multitude of sins (1 Peter 4:8).

A missionary couple stopped by my office to talk about their misbehaving five-year-old daughter. The father lamented, "Neil, Sarah is so difficult to handle that we have to drop her off at my parents' home every other weekend so we can get away. We want to love Sarah, and we are going to choose to do that. But she is so difficult to be around that there are times we just hate her! She is ruining our home, and the pressure on our marriage is threatening to pull us apart."

I encouraged them to ask Sarah what was going on in her mind when she acted belligerently. They seemed a little skeptical, but they agreed to try. To their surprise Sarah admitted to receiving all kinds of bizarre thoughts as well as having frightening experiences in her room. The parents made an appointment with me and brought Sarah with them. Together we took a stand against the enemy. I heard from the parents six months later that Sarah was living a "normal" life.

Another father pulled me aside after a speaking engagement. "Neil, I have a problem with my 14-year-old daughter, Mindy," he began. "There's a barrier between us to the point that we can hardly talk. What should I do?" I suggested that he read my book *The Bondage Breaker* to become informed enough to help her.

While he was reading the book at home, Mindy asked him what he was reading. As he explained to her the material about the battle for the mind, she poured out her own story of mental assault. Finally knowing the true nature of her problem he was able to work with her toward resolving her conflict and their differences.

When an emotional barrier has been erected between parent and child, it will be difficult for the parent to resolve the spiritual conflict. If the problem persists for any period of time, the child will summarily reject all authority figures. Your child may be difficult to like at this point, but you must love your child enough to discern the true nature of his bondage.

Lord, open my eyes to the reality of the spiritual world today that I may be adequately equipped to love my family.

A Matter of Being Someone

If any man is in Christ, he is a new creature; the old things passed away; behold, new things have come (2 Corinthians 5:17).

Being a Christian is not just a matter of getting something; it's a matter of being someone. A Christian is not simply a person who gets forgiveness, who gets to go to heaven, who gets the Holy Spirit, who gets a new nature. A Christian, in terms of our deepest identity, is a saint, a spiritually born child of God, a divine masterpiece, a child of light, a citizen of heaven. Being born again transformed you into someone who didn't exist before. What you receive as a Christian isn't the point; it's who you are. It's not what you do as a Christian that determines who you are; it's who you are that determines what you do (2 Corinthians 5:17; Ephesians 2:10; 1 Peter 2:9,10; 1 John 3:1,2).

Understanding your identity in Christ is absolutely essential to your success at living the Christian life. No person can consistently behave in a way that's inconsistent with the way he perceives himself. If you think you're a no-good bum, you'll probably live like a no-good bum. But if you see yourself as a child of God who is spiritually alive in Christ, you'll begin to live in victory and freedom as He lived. Next to a knowledge of God, a knowledge of who you are is by far the most important truth you can possess.

After years of working with people who are in deep spiritual conflict, I found one common denominator: None of them knew who they were in Christ. None knew of their spiritual heritage. All questioned their salvation and the love of God. Are you aware that there is someone alive and active in the world today who is dead set against you seeing yourself as spiritually alive and complete in Christ? Satan can do nothing to damage your position in Christ. But if he can deceive you into believing his lie—that you are not acceptable to God and that you'll never amount to anything as a Christian—then you will live as if you have no position or identity in Christ.

Heavenly Father, I take my stand as a child of God in Christ. Thank You for giving me this gracious and unwarranted position.

He who practices the truth comes to the light, that his deeds may be manifested as having been wrought in God (John 3:21).

Satan's first and foremost strategy is deception. As long as Satan's influence in a person's life remains undetected, he is content to lie low and not show his hand. Like a snake in the grass, he quietly sneaks up on his prey and squeezes the life out of it.

But when you confront Satan's deception and expose his lies with the truth, his strategy changes from stealth to a pretense of power. He becomes the roaring lion that Peter warned about (1 Peter 5:8). The procedure that most Christian counselors follow in dealing with people in whom demonic strongholds have been exposed is to challenge the spirit to manifest itself, and then to cast it out. Inevitably there is a power struggle which can provoke the victim to either lapse into a catatonic state, become generally disoriented, or run out of the room. I've seen people get physically injured during such confrontations. This procedure can potentially create more harm than help, especially for the novice.

We must avoid buying into Satan's second strategy of power as much as we avoid swallowing his first strategy of deception. It isn't power per se that sets the captive free; it's *truth* (John 8:32). The power of the Christian is in the truth; the power of Satan is in the lie. To the Satanist, power is everything, but power is only effective in the darkness. The Christian is to pursue the truth because power and authority are already inherent in him. Truth is what makes an encounter with Satan effective. Satan's demonstration of power (which is also deceptive because his power has actually been broken by the cross) is intended to provoke a fear response. When fear is controlling a believer, the Spirit of God is not, and Satan has the upper hand. Fear of the enemy and faith in God are mutually exclusive.

Lord, I pray that Your presence will be manifested in my life today that Your name may be glorified in the world.

A Child's Best Defense

Let the little children come to me, and do not hinder them, for the kingdom of heaven belongs to such as these (Matthew 19:14 NIV).

I am often asked if little children can come under demonic attack. The answer is yes. Three of my seminary students have told me about strange behavior patterns in their respective children. At times each of these kids stepped out of character and misbehaved. No attempts at discipline seemed to work. I encouraged my students to ask their children if they were having thoughts which provoked them to misbehave. In all three cases they answered yes. When these parents dealt with the deception instead of the misbehavior, the discipline problems cleared up.

One young boy who was caught lying and stealing from his parents said, "Daddy, I had to do it. Satan said he would kill you if I didn't." The boy's father later told me that if he hadn't heard me speak about the battle for the mind he would have severely disciplined his son for trying to blame the devil for his actions. Instead, he confronted the enemy's lie and hugged his son for trying to save his life. The lying and stealing stopped immediately.

Proverbs 23:7 says, "For as he thinks within himself, so he is." Unfortunately, we see the behavior and try to change that. We need to find out what is going on inside. No one does anything without first thinking it; whatever controls the mind controls the behavior.

A child's best defense against demonic attack is his simple, trusting faith. Children are quick to believe, and they usually understand far more than we parents give them credit for. Furthermore, your children have the added protection of being under your authority. As you carefully and prayerfully guard and nurture your freedom in Christ, chances are that your children will walk in freedom also.

Loving Father, help me to establish in the minds of my children simple trusting faith that is based on Your eternal truth.

To each one is given the manifestation of the Spirit for the common good (1 Corinthians 12:7).

After I taught a class on spiritual gifts, a young man came to me and asked, "Is my gift prophecy or exhortation?"

Knowing him very well, I was careful as I responded, "I don't think either one is your gift. But if I have ever known someone who has the gift of helps, you're it. You're sensitive to the needs of other people and always ready to help."

A look of disappointment came over his face. "I knew it!" he responded. Struggling with a low self-image, he was pursuing what he wrongly perceived to be a greater gift. You will never be fulfilled trying to become something you are not.

God hasn't distributed gifts and talents equally, and for that reason alone we can be assured that our sense of self-worth isn't to be based on what we do. Our self-acceptance comes from our identity in Christ and our growth in character. Show me someone who understands who he is as a child of God and whose character exemplifies the fruit of the Spirit, and I will show you someone with a healthy self-image.

Every child of God has the same identity in Christ and opportunity to grow. When our identity is firmly established and we have matured to the point where the fruit of the Spirit is evident, we will feel fulfilled when we use our gifts and talents to edify others.

God has known us from the foundation of the world. He has entrusted us with certain life endowments. He will certainly lead us in a way that makes use of our gifts and talents. It is our responsibility to take advantage of every opportunity as it arrives. Tragically, many people go to the grave with their music still in them, never contributing to the symphony of God's work. They never realize their potential nor take the risks that faith requires. They hang onto the security of the tree trunk, but the fruit is always on the end of the limb.

Lord, I don't want to go to the grave without having accomplished my purpose. Use my gifts and talents to glorify You and edify others today.

Our Most Important Assignment

If anyone does not provide for his own, and especially for those of his household, he has denied the faith, and is worse than an unbeliever (1 Timothy 5:8).

When *love* is used as a verb in the Bible it requires the lover to meet the needs of the one being loved. Love must be given away. God so loved the world that He *gave* (John 3:16). The corollary to John 3:16 is 1 John 3:16-18: "We know love by this, that He laid down His life for us; and we ought to lay down our lives for the brethren....Let us not love with word or with tongue, but in deed and truth."

The essence of love is meeting needs, and our most important assignment from God is to meet the needs of those who are closest to us (1 Timothy 5:8). We tend to use the people closest to us instead of meeting their needs. So the busy homemaker is out resolving everybody else's child-rearing problems but her own. The pastor is available to everyone but his wife and children. And the executive will work overtime to solve company problems while ignoring needs at home.

Take an inventory of your family's needs. I'm not talking about the external needs like clothing, education, and food. I'm talking about gut-level needs that determine their sense of worth and belonging. When was the last time you hugged your child and told him you loved him? Have you noticed good character qualities in your spouse and pointed them out? If all you ever point out is physical qualities or achievements, your family members will base their worth on how well they perform and look instead of developing character. Do you regularly reinforce good behavior, or do you only notice the poor behavior? When your child does something nice, do you thank him? Does your child know that he is loved and valued from the way you talk to him?

Love can't be separated from action. Jesus said, "If you love Me, you will keep My commandments" (John 14:15). If you love your family members, follow through with loving words and deeds.

Lord, keep me from looking beyond the needs of those who are closest to me and from using my loved ones for my own purposes.

Now there are varieties of gifts, but the same Spirit. And there are varieties of ministries, and the same Lord (1 Corinthians 12:4,5).

Perspective is the value of distance. Step back from the details of 1 Corinthians 12–14, the classic passage on spiritual gifts. What is Paul trying to say? There are a variety of spiritual gifts and manifestations of the Spirit. In the midst of this diversity, there is unity, because there is only one Spirit and one Lord. God gives the gifts as He wills. Spirit gifts and manifestations come and go and come again for the purpose of accomplishing God's will. What remains is faith, hope, and love. These are the lasting and continuous standards by which we evaluate our ministry and our lives.

Paul says, "I write so that you may know how one ought to conduct himself in the household of God, which is the church of the living God, the pillar and support of the truth" (1 Timothy 3:15). Truth is the object of our faith. If we know the truth it will set us free to grow in love with the hope of eternity before us. The church is gifted to accomplish that objective. Gifts are a means to an end, never an end in themselves. When "gifts" become an end in themselves they fail to accomplish their purpose and become the basis for spiritual pride. Godly character is our goal, and it must take precedence over the gifts.

The overwhelming thrust of the rest of Scripture encourages us to seek God and trust Him to gift us as He sees fit for the edification of the church. "Seek not, forsake not" seems to be the balance we need. Our responsibility is to yield to the Holy Spirit. However He chooses to fill us is His responsibility.

On this Christmas Eve, let us consider the greatest gift of all: the gift of eternal life. And let us give thanks for the tremendous sacrifice ot love. Jesus came that we might have life, and then He laid down His own life for us. The Peace Child was sacrificed that we may have peace with God. What could possibly make Christmas merrier?

Thank You, Lord, for the gift of life. May the gifts You have entrusted to me be used to bring faith, hope, and love to others.

NOTHING IS IMPOSSIBLE WITH GOD

Behold, the bondslave of the Lord; be it done to me according to your word (Luke 1:38).

If God wants something done, can it be done? In other words, if God has a goal for your life, can it be blocked, or is its fulfillment uncertain or impossible?

I am personally convinced that no goal God has for my life is impossible or uncertain, nor can it be blocked. Imagine God saying, "I've called you into existence, I've made you My child, and I have something for you to do. I know you won't be able to do it, but give it your best shot." That's ludicrous! It's like saying to your child, "I want you to mow the lawn. Unfortunately, the lawn is full of rocks, the mower doesn't work, and there's no gas. But give it your best shot." Even secular scholars say that issuing a command that cannot be obeyed will undermine authority.

God had a staggering goal for a little maiden named Mary. An angel told her that she would bear a son while still a virgin, and that her son would be the Savior of the world. When she inquired about this seemingly impossible feat, the angel simply said, "Nothing will be impossible with God" (Luke 1:37).

You wouldn't give your child a task he couldn't complete, and God doesn't assign to you goals you can't achieve. His goals for you are possible, certain, and achievable. When God's will for us appears impossible, let's say with Mary: "Behold, the bondslave of the Lord; be it done to me according to your word" (Luke 1:38).

Imagine the overwhelming assignment that confronted Mary. She was to have a baby without being with a man. She was to raise the child who would save the world. The entire course of history would be altered, and the eternal destiny of believers would be changed. The fact that you are celebrating Christmas today is proof that Mary's child Jesus was indeed the world-changing Son of God.

Despite the staggering nature of the task announced by the angel, Mary gave herself to accomplish God's will. God is still looking for a few bondslaves who will dare to believe that nothing is impossible with God.

Lord, I yield to You as Your bondslave. I choose to believe that whatever You want me to do I can do.

Every branch that bears fruit, He prunes it, that it may bear more fruit (John 15:2).

Our goal is to abide in Christ, not to bear fruit. Jesus promised that if we abide in Him, we will bear much fruit (John 15:5).

In order that we may bear more fruit, God the Father prunes us. Sometimes well-meaning Christians have cut too much too soon, hindering growth. A dear but sadly abused child of God pictured her experience in the following poem:

A friend of mine whose grapevine died, had put it out for trash.
I said to her, "I'll take that vine and make something of that."
At home the bag of dead, dry vines looked nothing but a mess.
But as I gently bent one vine, entwining round and round,
A rustic wreath began to form, potential did abound.
One vine would not go where it should, and anxious as I was,
I forced it so to change its shape, it broke—and what the cause?
If I had taken precious time to slowly change its form,
It would have made a lovely wreath, not a dead vine, broken, torn.
As I finished bending, adding blooms, applying trim,
I realized how that rustic wreath is like my life within.
You see, so many in my life have tried to make me change.
They've forced my spirit anxiously, I tried to rearrange.
But when the pain was far too great, they forced my fragile form;
I plunged far deeper in despair, my spirit broken, torn.
Then God allowed a gentle one who knew of dying vines,
To kindly, patiently allow the Lord to take His time.
And though the vine has not yet formed a decorative wreath,
I know that with God's servant's help one day when Christ I meet
He'll see a finished circle, a perfect gift to Him.
It will be a final product, a wreath with all the trim.
So as you look upon this gift, the vine round and complete,
Remember God is using you to gently shape His wreath.

Father God, thank You for Your unconditional love and acceptance.

See how great a love the Father has bestowed upon us, that we should be called children of God (1 John 3:1).

Have you ever felt that God is ready to give up on you because, instead of walking confidently in faith, you sometimes stumble and fall? Do you ever fear that there is a limit to God's tolerance for your failure and that you are walking dangerously near that outer barrier or have already crossed it? I have met a lot of Christians like that. They think that God is upset with them, that He is ready to dump them, or that He has already given up on them because their daily performance is less than perfect.

It's true that the walk of faith can sometimes be interrupted by moments of personal unbelief or rebellion, or even satanic deception. It's during those moments when we think that God has surely lost His patience with us and is ready to give up on us. The temptation is to give up, stop walking by faith altogether, slump dejectedly by the side of the road, and wonder, "What's the use?" We feel defeated, God's work for us is suspended, and Satan is elated.

The primary truth you need to know about God in order for your faith to remain strong is that His love and acceptance is unconditional. When your walk of faith is strong, God loves you. When your walk of faith is weak, God loves you. When you're strong one moment and weak the next, strong one day and weak the next, God loves you. God's love for you is the great eternal constant in the midst of all the inconsistencies of your daily walk.

God wants us to do good, of course. The apostle John wrote: "I write this to you so that you will not sin" (1 John 2:1 NIV). But John continued by reminding us that God has already made provision for our failure so His love continues constant in spite of what we do: "But if anybody does sin, we have one who speaks to the Father in our defense—Jesus Christ, the Righteous One. He is the atoning sacrifice for our sins, and not only for ours but also for the sins of the whole world" (verses 1,2 NIV).

Lord, give me grace to correct my character defects and to help meet the needs of others.

Do nothing from selfishness or empty conceit, but with humility of mind let each of you regard one another as more important than himself (Philippians 2:3).

Once when I was pastoring I got a distress call: "Pastor, you better get over here or we're liable to kill each other." When I arrived at the house I persuaded them to sit down across the table from each other to talk through their problem. They whaled away at each other for several minutes, slamming each other with accusations and insults.

Finally I interrupted. "Time out! Each of you get your Bible." I asked the husband to read Romans 14:4: "Who are you to judge the servant of another? To his own master he stands or falls; and stand he will, for the Lord is able to make him stand." "That verse is talking about judging another person's character," I said. "Before God, each of you is responsible for your own character." They nodded their agreement.

Then I asked the wife to read Philippians 2:3: "Do nothing from selfishness or empty conceit, but with humility of mind let each of you regard one another as more important than himself." "That verse is talking about needs," I continued. "Before God, each of you is responsible for meeting each other's needs." Again the couple agreed with my statement.

"Do you realize what you have been doing the last two hours? Instead of assuming responsibility for your own character, you've been ripping apart your partner's character. Instead of looking out for your partner's needs, you've been selfishly absorbed with your own needs. No wonder your marriage isn't functioning." Before I left that day, they prayerfully committed to refocus their responsibilities according to the Word of God.

What kind of families and churches would we have if we all assumed responsibility for our own character and sought to meet the needs of those we live with?

Lord, I want to be able to say with Paul, "I have fought the good fight, I have finished the course, I have kept the faith."

Put on the Lord Jesus Christ, and make no provision for the flesh in regard to its lusts (Romans 13:14).

Paul instructs us to make no provision for the flesh. What if we *do*? We are told to take every thought captive to the obedience of Christ. What if we don't? James 4:7 admonishes us to "resist the devil and he will flee from you." What if we don't resist him? Is he required to flee from us if we don't take our stand against him? No, if we don't resist him, he doesn't have to go. We have the assurance of God's protection, but we must assume our responsibility to personally resist Satan.

Ephesians 6:10-17 outlines the armor of God which believers are instructed to put on in order to "stand firm against the schemes of the devil" (verse 11). But if we go into battle without some of our armor, are we impervious to getting wounded? No, if we fail to cover ourselves with the armor God has provided, we are vulnerable.

James 4:1 reveals that the source of our quarrels and conflicts is the pleasures that "wage war in your members." Paul instructed, "Do not let sin reign in your mortal body that you should obey its lusts" (Romans 6:12). The world, the flesh, and the devil are continually at war against the life of the Spirit within us. But what if we don't fight back? Will we still be victorious over the pleasures and lusts which strive to reign over us? No, they will control us if we remain passive.

Choosing truth, living a righteous life, and donning the armor of God is each believer's individual responsibility. I cannot be responsible for you, and you cannot be responsible for me. I can pray for you, encourage you in the faith, and support you, but if you go into the battle without your armor on, you may get hurt. As much as that may be a matter of concern for me, I still cannot make those decisions of responsibility for you. Those choices are yours alone.

Loving Father, thank You for investing Yourself in me. Equip me to graciously invest myself today in ministry to others.

I am the LORD your God....You shall have no other gods before Me (Exodus 20:2,3).

The doctrinal affirmations today and tomorrow will help you renew your mind and take your stand on the truth. I recommend that you read these Scriptural affirmations aloud at least once a week in the coming year.

I recognize that there is only one true and living God (Exodus 20:2,3), who exists as the Father, Son, and Holy Spirit, and that He is worthy of all honor, praise, and worship as the Creator, Sustainer, and Beginning and End of all things (Revelation 4:11; 5:9,10; Isaiah 43:1,7,21).

I recognize Jesus Christ as the Messiah, the Word who became flesh and dwelt among us (John 1:1,14). I believe that He came to destroy the works of Satan (1 John 3:8), that He disarmed the rulers and authorities, having triumphed over them (Colossians 2:15).

I believe that God has proven His love for me, because when I was still a sinner Christ died for me (Romans 5:8). I believe that He delivered me from the domain of darkness and transferred me to His kingdom, and in Him I have redemption, the forgiveness of sins (Colossians 1:13,14).

I believe that I am now a child of God (1 John 3:1-3). I believe that I was saved by the grace of God through faith, that it was a gift and not the result of any works on my part (Ephesians 2:8).

I choose to be strong in the Lord and in the strength of His might (Ephesians 6:10). I put no confidence in the flesh (Philippians 3:3), for the weapons of my warfare are not of the flesh (2 Corinthians 10:4). I put on the whole armor of God (Ephesians 6:10-17), and I resolve to stand firm in my faith and resist the evil one.

Lord, inscribe on my heart the truth of who You are and what You have done to secure my eternal salvation.

December 31 Apart from Christ I Can Do Nothing

I am the vine, you are the branches...apart from Me you can do nothing (John 15:5).

Add the following statements of doctrinal affirmation to those you began reading yesterday. Allow the truth of God's Word to saturate your heart and guide your steps in the coming year.

I believe that Jesus has all authority in heaven and on earth (Matthew 28:18), and that He is the head over all rule and authority (Colossians 2:10). I believe that Satan and his demons are subject to me in Christ because I am a member of Christ's body (Ephesians 1:19-23). I therefore obey the command to resist the devil (James 4:7), and I command him in the name of Christ to leave my presence.

I believe that apart from Christ I can do nothing (John 15:5), so I declare my dependence on Him. I choose to abide in Christ in order to bear much fruit and glorify the Lord (John 15:8). I announce to Satan that Jesus is my Lord (1 Corinthians 12:3), and I reject any counterfeit gifts or works of Satan in my life.

I believe that the truth will set me free (John 8:32), and that walking in the light is the only path of fellowship (1 John 1:7). Therefore, I stand against Satan's deception by taking every thought captive in obedience to Christ (2 Corinthians 10:5). I declare that the Bible is the only authoritative standard (2 Timothy 3:15-17). I choose to speak the truth in love (Ephesians 4:15).

I choose to present my body as an instrument of righteousness, a living and holy sacrifice, and I renew my mind by the living Word of God in order that I may prove that the will of God is good, acceptable, and perfect (Romans 6:13; 12:1,2).

Father God, I affirm that my life and sustenance come from You, and apart from You I can do nothing

Notes

February 10

1. Theodore Epp, *Praying with Authority* (Lincoln, NE: Back to the Bible Broadcast, 1965), p. 98.

April 15

1. Quoted from Martin Wells Knapp, *Impressions* (Wheaton, IL: Tyndale House Publishing, Inc., 1984), pp. 14-45.

May 31

1. "The Paradoxical Commandments" are reprinted with the permission of the author. © Copyright Kent M. Keith 1968, 2001. See Kent M. Keith, *Anyway: The Paradoxical Commandments* (New York: G.P. Putnam's Sons, 2002); and *Jesus Did It Anyway: The Paradoxical Commandments for Christians* (New York: G.P. Putnam's Sons, 2005).

August 8

1. *Los Angeles Times* (June 1989), part V, p. 1.

September 22

1. C.S. Lewis, *Screwtape Letters* (Old Tappan, NJ: Fleming H. Revell, 1978).

October 17

1. Martin Wells Knapp, *Impressions* (Wheaton, IL: Tyndale House Publishing, Inc., 1984), p. 32.

October 20

1. Maurice Wagner, *The Sensation of Being Somebody* (Grand Rapids, MI: Zondervan Publishing House, 1975), p. 163.

October 31

1. C.S. Lewis, *Christian Reflections* (Grand Rapids, MI: William B. Eerdman's Publishing Company, 1967), p. 33.

December 14

1. Adapted from the poem "Borrowed Hope," Eloise Cole.

FREEDOM IN CHRIST MINISTRIES
9051 Executive Park Drive, Suite 503
Knoxville, TN 37923
Phone: (865) 342-4000 • Fax: (865) 342-4001
E-mail: info@ficm.org • Web site: www.ficm.org